D1487797

Contributions to the Art of Music
in America by the Music
Industries of Boston
1640 to 1936

SERIES IN AMERICAN STUDIES

Editor-in-Chief: Joseph J. Kwiat

PROGRAM IN AMERICAN STUDIES
UNIVERSITY OF MINNESOTA

BENJAMIN CREHORE
of Milton, Pioneer musical in-
strument maker

From a daguerreotype
by courtesy of
Vose and Sons Piano Company

Contributions to the Art of Music in America by the Music Industries of Boston 1640 to 1936

By

CHRISTINE MERRICK AYARS

Master of Education in Music, Master of Science in Economic Research

NEW YORK
THE H. W. WILSON COMPANY
1937

JOHNSON REPRINT CORPORATION   JOHNSON REPRINT COMPANY LTD.
111 Fifth Avenue, New York, N.Y. 10003   Berkeley Square House, London, W1X6BA

87675

To My
Beloved Mother
My Ever Faithful Friend
and Helper

Preface

The original material obtained was written up in 1932 as a thesis for the degree of Master of Education in Music from Boston University School of Education and College of Music.

As the writer has been asked a number of times how this subject came to be selected, the following explanation may be of interest. The author was brought up in a home in which the history and progress of Boston had long been of interest. It was suggested to her that Boston, a musical centre from early times, had contributed greatly to the progress of music in the United States. That idea aroused her civic pride so that she looked into the subject and found that more or less had been written about Boston's performers of music, both vocal and instrumental, its conductors, and its composers. The field which seemed to have been covered only slightly and in a rather fragmentary way was the contribution to the advancement of the art of music made by Boston's music publishers, engravers and printers and instrument makers. There were some notable exceptions, such as the history of Jonas Chickering and of Chickering & Sons Company, and of Oliver Ditson Company, Inc. in William Arms Fisher's book *Notes on Music in Old Boston*. *One Hundred and Fifty Years of Music Publishing in the United States* had not yet appeared.

As the writer had had training in research and had been connected with business as well as with music, the subject of this study made a strong appeal and she decided to see what could be discovered and recorded for the benefit of future historians. It seems as if the collection of the information from those who knew the facts was undertaken none too soon, since several notable contributors have already passed on. The work has been most interesting as one "find" has led to another. Undoubtedly further intensive search would reveal still other contributions and fill in some remaining gaps, but how much the results would repay the effort is a question.

The material has now been revised to 1936 and the individual write-ups of all the present-day active concerns have been checked over by them for correct presentation of all the material about each and inclusion of the essential facts.

Other firms are listed from time to time in the Boston City Directories under the headings "Music Dealers and Publishers" and "Musical Instruments" or "Musical Instrument Manufacturing." They are not included in this volume, however, if the writer was unable to obtain information at least about the catalogs of the publishers or the type of instruments of the manufacturers. She felt that a mere statement of a firm's names, addresses, and length of time in business would add nothing of value to this study.

The reader may feel at times that the space devoted to the concerns is not in line with their relative importance. Such discrepancies are due partly to the amount of information available and partly to the consideration that where information about firms no longer extant is not generally available the write-up should be more full in order to have this information on record.

The author desires herewith to express her appreciation of the generous and hearty cooperation accorded her by all who have contributed to this volume, particularly the following:

Mr. William Arms Fisher, Oliver Ditson Company, Inc.; Mr. Henry R. Austin, The Arthur P. Schmidt Co.; Mr. Charles A. White, White-Smith Music Publishing Company; Mr. W. Deane Preston, Jr., The B. F. Wood Co.; Mr. Elbridge W. Newton and Miss Helen Leavitt, Ginn & Company; Mrs. Frances Settle, Silver, Burdett and Company; Mr. Oscar C. Henning, M. O. Henning & Son; Mr. William T. Small and Mr. Norton T. Mullen, The John Worley Company; Mr. William E. Merrill, Secretary, New England Music Trades Association; Mr. Henry I. Tinkham, formerly of Chickering & Sons; Mr. A. M. Hume, A. M. Hume Company; Miss Margaret Connell, Historian, Chickering & Sons; Mr. Henry L. Mason, formerly of Mason & Hamlin; Mr. James Cole, formerly of James Cole; Mr. Norman Jacobsen, Hook and Hastings Co.; Mr. Ernest M. Skinner, Aeolian-Skinner Organ Company, Inc.; Mr. Leslie H. Frazee and Mr. Harry U. Camp, Frazee Organ Company; Mr. William Gibbs; Mr. Erik Gould, John A. Gould & Sons; Mr. A. J. Oettinger, Musicians' Supply Company; Mr. Beal, Weeman, Beal & Holmberg; Dr. Dayton C. Miller, Case School of Applied Science; Mrs. William S. Haynes, William S. Haynes Company; Mr. William S. Haynes, Junior, Haynes-Schwelm Company; Mr. Harry

Bettoney, The Cundy-Bettoney Company; Mr. Thomas M. Carter, Carter's Band; Mr. Richard G. Appel, Music Department, Boston Public Library; Mr. William B. Goodwin, organ builder of Lowell, Massachusetts; Mr. Richard P. Law, Music Supervisor; Mr. A. C. Foster, Organ Blower Co.; Mr. Francis E. Appleton; Mr. Henry C. Lahee, Boston Musical Bureau; Mr. Edward Bailey Birge, Professor of Music, Indiana University; and *Catalogue* of the Stearns Collection of Musical Instruments, University of Michigan.

CONTENTS

INTRODUCTION   PAGE

Aim of This Study 1
Sources of Information 1

PART I. MUSIC PUBLISHING—VOCAL AND INSTRUMENTAL

A. The Pioneers and Early Publishers—Seventeenth and Eighteenth
Centuries 3

    The Bay Psalm Book - Rev. John Tufts - Rev. Thomas Walter -
    Josiah Flagg - William Billings - Early sheet music

B. Nineteenth and Early Twentieth Century Publishers Out of
Existence 7

    Peter Albrecht von Hagen, Sr. and Jr. - Francis Mallet - Johann
    Christian Gottlieb Graupner - H. Mann - Charles Bradlee - Col-
    onel Samuel H. Parker - The umbrella dealer publishers - Charles
    Edward Horn - Eben H. Wade - Elias Howe, Jr. - George P.
    Reed - Nathan Richardson - G. D. Russell - Joseph M. Russell -
    Jean White - Koppitz & Pruefer - L. A. Blanchard - George W.
    Stratton - White & Goullaud - John F. Perry - E. A. Samuels -
    Thompson & Odell - Damm & Gay - Whipple Music Co. - Louis
    H. Ross - H. B. Stevens & Co. - E. C. Ramsdell - Bates &
    Bendix - J. B. Millet Co. - Miles & Thompson and C. W. Thomp-
    son & Co. - William H. Gerrish - Herbert F. Odell - Ernest S.
    Williams - Wa Wan Press - Riker, Brown and Wellington, Inc.

C. Present Day Publishers

    1. General Music Publishers 28

        Oliver Ditson Company, Inc. - White-Smith Music Publishing
        Company - The Arthur P. Schmidt Co. - The Boston Music Com-
        pany and G. Schirmer, Inc. - The B. F. Wood Music Company -
        C. C. Birchard & Co. - Carl Fischer, Inc. - E. C. Schirmer Music
        Company

    2. Educational Music Publishers 54

        Start and early development of public school music - Ginn &
        Company - Silver, Burdett and Company - D. C. Heath & Com-
        pany - American Book Company

    3. Special Music Publishers

        a. Vocal and Pianoforte 69
           Charles W. Homeyer & Co., Inc.

b. Church Music 69
The Parish Choir - McLaughlin & Reilly Company

c. Instrumental—Chiefly Band and Orchestral 71
The Cundy-Bettoney Company - Walter Jacobs, Inc. - Geo.
B. Stone & Son, Inc.

d. Tracy Music Library, Inc. 76

D. Music Journals and House Organs

1. Music Journals 78
2. House Organs 85

PART II. MUSIC ENGRAVING AND PRINTING

A. Methods

1. Early Engraving and Printing 87
2. Present Music Engraving and Printing 88
3. Present Music Topography 90

B. Engravers

1. A Family of Earlier Engravers—The Schlimpers 91
2. Present Day Engraving Firms 91

White-Smith Music Publishing Company - M. O. Henning &
Son - Manicke & Dellmuth

C. Music Printers

1. Some Nineteenth Century Music Printers 94

Kidder & Wright - W. H. Oakes - Andrew B. Kidder - Edward
L. Balch - J. A. Cummings & Co. - Giles & Gould - Lenfest &
Anderson - Samuel W. Blair

2. Present Day Music Printers 96

White-Smith Music Publishing Company - John Worley Company - Stanhope Press (F. H. Gilson Company)

PART III. INSTRUMENT MAKING

A. Pianoforte Makers

1. Importance in the Pianoforte Industry of Massachusetts
Manufacturers as Shown by United States Census Figures
of 1860, 1927 and 1931 99
2. European Predecessors 102

3. Beginnings of the Pianoforte Industry in the United States. 104

John Harris - Samuel Blyth - Benjamin Crehore - William and
Adam Bent - Lewis Babcock - Hayts, Babcock & Appleton -
Alpheus Babcock - Francis Shaw - John Osborn - John Dwight -
Timothy and Lemuel Gilbert - Ebenezer R. Currier - Start of
pianoforte tuning by the blind

4. Present Day Manufacturers 111

Jonas Chickering and his early affiliations - Chickering & Sons -
Vose & Sons Piano Company - Henry F. Miller Piano Company -
Ivers & Pond Piano Company - Mason & Hamlin Company - Poole
Piano Company - M. Steinert & Sons Company, Inc.

B. Organ Manufacturers

1. Importance in the Industry of Massachusetts Organ Manufacturers as Shown by United States Census Figures of 1860,
1905, 1921, 1927 and 1931 131

2. Reed Organs

a. Early Development 135
b. Mason & Hamlin's Contribution 136

3. Early Organ Building

a. Beginnings 140

Early imported organs - Edward Bromfield - Thomas Johnston -
Adam and John Geib - William M. Goodrich - Ebenezer Goodrich - Thomas Appleton

b. The Advent of the Music Hall Organ, Boston 155

4. Some Important Organ Builders Out of Business 158

W. B. D. Simmons & Co. and affiliations - J. H. Willcox Co. -
Geo. S. Hutchings Company and affiliations - James Cole and
affiliations - Woodberry & Harris - Jesse Woodberry & Co.

5. Present Day Organ Builders 168

Hook & Hastings Co. - Aeolian-Skinner Organ Company, Inc. -
Frazee Organ Company

C. Bells and Bell Chimes Cast by Paul Revere and His Firm's
Successors 184

Paul Revere & Son - Revere & Blake - Paul Revere & Co. - Boston and Braintree Copper and Brass Company - Boston Copper
Co. - Henry N. Hooper & Co. -, Wm. Blake & Co. - C. T. Robinson - Blake Bell Co. - Bay State Brass Foundry & Blake Bell Co.

D. Band, Orchestral, Fretted and Miscellaneous Instruments

1. Standing of Massachusetts Makers 191

2. Violin and String Makers
   a. Some Important Former Makers 194

   Samuel Blyth - Benjamin Crehore - Green & Allen - Ira John-
   son White - Asa Warren White - Ire E. White - George
   Gemünder - J. Bonaparte Squier - Walter Solon Goss - Emile
   Berliner, inventor - Hugo Schindler

   b. Present Day Makers 202

   Weeman, Beal & Holmberg - Jacob Thoma & Son - John A.
   Gould & Sons - Henry F. Schultz - Edmund F. Bryant - J. H.
   Edler - Albert Lind - Musicians' Supply Company - O. H.
   Bryant & Son - P. Baltzerson - C. F. Stanley - F. Lincoln
   Johnson

3. Flute, Piccolo and Clarinet Makers

   a. Some Nineteenth Century Makers 212

   William Callender - Walter Crosby - August Damm - Eduard
   H. Wurlitzer

   b. Present Day Manufacturers 215

   Wm. S. Haynes Co. - The Haynes-Schwelm Co. - Verne Q.
   Powell Flutes, Inc. - The Cundy-Bettoney Co.

4. Brass, Percussion, Fretted and Miscellaneous Instrument
   Manufacturers

   a. Some Important Nineteenth Century Manufacturers... 222

   First brass band in the United States - European inventions
   preceding its formation
   Brass instruments - James A. Bazin's and Nathan Adams' rotary
   instruments - Elbridge G. Wright - J. Lathrop Allen - Allen
   & Hall - D. C. Hall & Co. - Quinby Bros. - Richardson &
   Lehnert - Graves & Co. - Patrick S. Gilmore's affiliations -
   Boston Musical Instrument Manufactory - Standard Band In-
   strument Company
   Percussion instruments - Elias Howe - Ira E. White - O. A.
   Whitmore - Blair & Baldwin
   Fretted instruments - Charles Stumcka - Pehr A. Anderberg -
   L. B. Gatcomb & Co.

   b. Present Day Manufacturers 229

   The Vega Co. - Geo. B. Stone & Son, Inc. - Charles A.
   Stromberg & Son - Charles W. Homeyer & Co., Inc. - The
   Cundy-Bettoney Co. - Ernest A. Anderberg - F. Porcella

APPENDICES

I.A. Firm Names and Addresses of Some Early Pianoforte Makers
      —Period 1810 to 1850 239
I.B. Other Boston Pianoforte Makers—Period 1840 to 1915.... 242

II. Other Boston Reed Organ Firms—Period 1850-1910 252

III. Other Boston Organ Builders—Period 1830-1910 254
     a. Organ Water Motors—Period 1870-1933 257

IV. Other Boston Makers of Band, Orchestral, Fretted and Miscellaneous Instruments
     A. Violin and Bow Makers—Period About 1845-1935 258
     B. Manufacturers of Musical Strings—Period 1885-1936 264
     C. Flute and Clarinet Makers—Period 1850-1900 265
     D. Brass Instrument Manufacturers—Period 1850-1915 266
     E. Drum Makers—Period 1850-1936 271
     F. Banjo, Guitar and Mandolin Makers—Period Around 1850-1915 274
     G. Makers of Miscellaneous Instruments and Accessories—Period 1885-1930 278

SOME INSTRUMENTS BY GREATER BOSTON MAKERS AND SOME OF HISTORICAL IMPORTANCE BY EUROPEAN MAKERS WITH THE PLACES WHERE THEY MAY BE SEEN OR HEARD

Spinets 281
Pianofortes 281
Lap Organs, Melodeons, Cabinet Organs 291
Organs 293
Illustrations of Organs 295
Bells 296
Chimes 298
Violin Family Instruments 300
Woodwind Instruments 301
Brass Instruments 302
Percussion 305
Fretted Instruments 306
Miscellaneous Instruments and Accessories 306

BIBLIOGRAPHY

General 307
Music Printing and Publishing 308
Pianofortes 308
Organs 310
Bells and Bell Chimes 312
Band, Orchestral, Fretted and Miscellaneous Instruments
     1. Violins 313
     2. Flutes and Clarinets 314
     3. Miscellaneous Instruments 314

GENERAL INDEX 315

INDEX OF PUBLICATIONS 325

Introduction

Aim of This Study

Music is largely dependent for its development on the preservation of its literature through printing and on progress in the making of the instruments by which it can be played. The aim of this study is to bring out what the music industries of Boston have done in these fields.

Their contributions are largely of five types:
Pioneering efforts.
Unique features of products, such as materials used.
Improvements in method and in construction of products, both
Unpatented improvements and
Patented inventions.
Quality of workmanship.
Special services to promote the art of music, such as:
Personal activities of the personnel.
Financial aid.
Erection of concert halls and library.
Collection of ancient instruments.

In the colonial days these contributions were due to the efforts of individuals. As the country developed, companies founded by men of vision and ability took the place of the single skilled artisan and all around musician and specialized in one field pertaining to music.

Some of the firms no longer in existence made contributions which have either served as steppingstones for successors or been generally adopted with only slight improvements since. Practically all the present day firms have made some contribution. These are described in whatever period of the company's history they occurred.

Sources of Information

The information for this study has been obtained from three sources, readings, correspondence and interviews. A bibliography of the readings is appended. Seventy-two different persons were interviewed, some several times. These were largely the heads of business houses or music departments. The industries represented are as follows—

Publishers	18
Music Loaning Library	1
Music Journal Editors	1
Engravers and printers	5
Music store salesmen	3
Pianoforte manufacturers and dealers	8
Pianoforte tuners	1
Organ builders and organ parts representatives	6
Violin makers	14
Flute, piccolo and clarinet makers	6
Band and fretted instrument makers	5
Band leader	1
Woodwind dealers	2
Music string makers	1

Addresses and dates of firms out of business have been taken largely from Boston City Business Directories. The year covered by some of these as far back as 1847 runs from July to July. Hence the years are approximate as a company may have been started or have ended in the second half of the previous year or the first half of the year in which the directory was published. Where addresses and dates have been taken from other sources, they are from books and publications as far as possible, but occasionally come from the memory of some person once connected with the firm concerned.

In general firms are discussed in chronological order by dates of founding, except in the Appendices, which are alphabetical.

The writer takes no personal responsibility for the statements in this volume, since they have all been based on the most reputable authorities accessible to her.

Part I. Music Publishing—Vocal and Instrumental

A. The Pioneers and Early Publishers—Seventeenth and Eighteenth Centuries

Boston's contribution to the development of music in the United States through the publishing field began just ten years after its settlement. Altho the Puritans of New England were opposed to music in general, the first book issued in the Colonies with the exception of an almanac, *The Freeman's Oath,* was a hymn book for church-singing, *The Bay Psalm Book* printed in 1640. Governor Leverrett wrote home in 1673, that there was "not a Musician in the Colony." Until the ninth edition in 1698, which contained thirteen tunes in two-part harmony, no music was included, however. "This crudely printed book, without bars except at the end of each line, is the oldest-existing music of American imprint," [1] though there is evidence that earlier did exist. The notes were cut on wood. The popularity of *The Bay Psalm Book* is shown by the surprising fact that it went through eighteen editions in England, the last in London, 1754. It also had in Scotland twenty-two editions, the last in 1756. [2]

"The first *American* book of sacred music published," [3] an instruction book on the art of singing by notes, was *A very plain and easy Introduction to the Art of Singing Psalm Tunes,* issued in 1712 or 1714. It was compiled by Rev. John Tufts [3] (1689-1750), a clergyman of Newburyport, Massachusetts, not far from Boston. This substituted letters for notes. A new edition of it was issued in 1726.

In 1721 Rev. Thomas Walter (1696-1725) of Roxbury, now a part of Boston, compiled *The Grounds and Rules of Music Examined or an introduction to the art of singing by note.* This was "the first practical American instruction book," and is said to be

[1] See Fisher, William Arms. *Notes on Music in Old Boston* p. 3.
[2] Information supplied by William B. Goodwin, organ builder.
[3] See Fisher, William Arms. *Notes on Music in Old Boston* p. 6.

the first music printed with bar lines.[4] It was issued from the press of J. Franklin when his brother, Benjamin, a lad of fifteen, was his apprentice in the printer's trade.

In Colonial times musicians and artists were not specialized in their skill as now. This is well illustrated by Josiah Flagg, who was a psalmodist, compiler and publisher of *A Collection of Best Psalm Tunes in Two, Three and Four Parts* issued in 1764, and a concert manager of vocal and instrumental music both sacred and secular. He included in his programs works of Bach and, as early as 1771, of Handel, who had been a dominating influence of English musical life since about 1717. His volume of about eighty pages was the largest collection printed in New England up to this time. "It is notable in that for the first time 'light music' was intermingled with Psalm Tunes and because the music was engraved by the noted silversmith Paul Revere, and further that it was printed on paper made in the Colonies." [5]

Josiah Flagg also introduced the London organist and composer, William Selby, who was largely responsible for the rapid progress of music in Boston after his arrival about 1771.[6]

The year of Beethoven's birth, 1770, saw the publication of a book of compositions by our first real American composer, William Billings (1746-1800), a tanner, who is said to have introduced into church choirs the use of the bass viol ['cello] and the pitch pipe to set the tune.[7] This work was *The New England Psalm Singer,* which contained "fuguing" pieces and primitive attempts at counterpoint. His music was on four staffs, treble, counter, tenor, bass. The title page bore the verse:

> O! Praise the Lord with one Consent
> and in this grand Design,
> Let Britain & the Colonies
> unanimously Join!

This book of 108 pages, 120 tunes, several anthems, 22 pages of elementary instruction and an essay on the nature and properties of musical sound was printed in Boston by Edes and Gill. [8] "Thus 140 years after the founding of Boston the first book of native

[4] Fisher, William Arms. *Notes on Music in Old Boston* p. 7.
[5] *Ibid* p. 10.
[6] Howard, John Tasker. *Our American Music* p. 64.
[7] Fisher, William Arms. *Notes on Music in Old Boston* pp. 12 & 13.
[8] Gilson, F. H. Company. *Music Book Printing* p. 5.

music was issued and with it the publication of American composition may be said to begin." [9]

Billings published also:

The Singing Master's Assistant in 1778, 104 p.
Music in Miniature in 1779, 32 p.
The Psalm Singer's Amusement in 1781, 103 p.
The Suffolk Harmony in 1786, 56 p.
The Continental Harmony in 1794, 199 p.

He more or less repeated his instructions in *Singing Master's Assistant.* They included various ideas of his own such as this quaint one—"Choristers must always remember to set flat Keyed Tunes to melancholy words and sharp Keyed Tunes to cheerful words." [10] He also gave directions for pendulum lengths for metronomic speeds and how to make one [11]—an early Maelzel!

That he had much common sense mingled with his aesthetic ignorance is indicated by the following statements which many modern singers might well consider. "N. B. Many ignorant singers take great license from these trills and without confining themselves to any rule, they shake all notes promiscuously and they are apt to tear a note in pieces, which should be struck fair and plump as any other. Let such persons be informed, that it is impossible to shake a note, without going off it, which occasions horrid discords." [12]

In 1774 Billings was director of a forty-eight member Singing Society at Stoughton. This was formally organized in 1786 as the Stoughton Musical Society and is still thriving. It is thus the oldest singing society in the United States. [13]

Another important compilation, *Laus Deo! The Worcester Collection of Sacred Harmony,* was printed from movable types at Worcester, Massachusetts, by Isaiah Thomas (1749-1831), the first edition in 1786. This printer advertised in the *Boston Independent Chronicle* of January 26, 1785, that specimens of his new types were to be seen in Battelle's Boston Book Store, State St. [14] In general the publications of music books were not common before the nineteenth century. [14-15]

---

[9] Fisher, William Arms. *Notes on Music in Old Boston* p. 11.
[10] Billings, William. *Singing Master's Assistant.* first edition Lesson X p. 13.
[11] *Ibid* Lesson VI p. 8.
[12] *Ibid* Lesson V p. 7.
[13] Howard, John T. *Our American Music* p. 53.
[14] Fisher, William Arms. *Notes on Music in Old Boston* p. 14.
[15] Only 66 tune books were listed in *Grove's Dictionary* American Supplement 1935 Edition for all the states during the period 1780-1800.

Publications of sheet music (in the United States) began as early as 1768 as an advertisement in the *Boston Chronicle* of October 17 shows "The New and Favourite *Liberty Song*" just published and to be sold at the London Book-store. [16]   The general publication of secular music started in Boston and Philadelphia in 1789, much being patriotic or echoing passing events.   Boston exceeded the rest of the country in sacred music, and Dedham, Newburyport, Salem, Northampton and Worcester added their share. English music which was reprinted consisted chiefly of songs of Hook, Dibdin, Shield, and Storace and representations of Haydn, Gluck, Pleyel, Mozart and Handel. [16]

[16] Fisher, William Arms. *Notes on Music in Old Boston* pp. 17 & 18.

B. Nineteenth and Early Twentieth Century Publishers Out of Existence

As has been shown, the contributions of Boston's earliest publishers were mostly in the field of church music, though some secular sheet music, chiefly patriotic songs, was brought out near the close of the eighteenth century. One of the latter was *Adams and Liberty,* widely known as the *Boston Patriotic Song.*

From the information available it appears that most of the publishers of the late eighteenth and the nineteenth centuries were musicians, who felt the lack of sufficient fine music to play on their various instruments. So they brought out reprints of standard European classical works or composed and published their own works or those of fellow Americans.

One of these was Elias Howe, Jr. who started in business for himself in 1840, just five years later than Oliver Ditson, with his own collection of jigs, reels, dances and airs arranged for the violin. The success of this first publication in the United States of a book of that type of popular music for the violin [1] led its author to bring out at a popular price different series of instruction books for strings, woodwinds, and accordeons. The basic idea was to present few instructions with many tunes for playing.

Good music for the pianoforte, which was constantly being improved and growing in popularity, was published by a number of firms no longer in existence, notably G. P. Reed & Co., Nathan Richardson, G. D. Russell & Co., Carl Pruefer, J. B. Millet Co.

Boston was early a centre for military and other bands and orchestras. Thus naturally it became probably the first city to publish band and orchestra music. The firm of Jean White was the first notable contributor in this field, starting in 1867, five years before Carl Fischer in New York City. E. A. Samuels starting about 1875 also specialized in band and orchestra music as did Thompson & Odell organized in 1878 and E. C. Ramsdell organized about 1886.

George W. Stratton made a unique contribution in the field of operettas, composing them expressly for children and publishing

---

[1] Statement of Edward F. Howe, son of Elias Howe, Jr.

them himself. In this he seems to have been a forerunner of today's school music publications of operettas.

As it is difficult to obtain information concerning publishers no longer in existence the material in this section is rather fragmentary. What has been gathered is presented in the following paragraphs.

Four distinguished musicians who came to Boston just before 1800 were active in the city's musical life and were the forerunners of music publishing as it is today. They were Peter Albrecht von Hagen, Sr. and Jr., Francis Mallet and Johann Christian Gottlieb Graupner.

Peter Albrecht von Hagen, Sr. [2-3] was born in Holland in 1750 and died in Boston October 3, 1803. He first came to Charleston, South Carolina in 1774. The revolution drove him back to Holland, but in 1789 he came with his wife, daughter and son to New York City. In 1796 father and son came to Boston, he as leader of the orchestra at Haymarket Theatre, and the son as a violin player. Mrs. von Hagen, a pianist and teacher, joined them later. The senior von Hagen was an organist, pianist, violinist, composer, conductor and a publisher as well. He opened a "Musical Academy" at 62 Newbury St. (later called Washington St.) where he had a music shop and became the first established music publisher in Boston, as P. A. von Hagen & Co. He issued the first copy of his *Musical Magazine* in December 1797 from 3 Cornhill, Boston. The company also had its "Warranted Imported Piano Forte Ware House" at the same location.

Peter Albrecht von Hagen, Jr. [3] was born in Holland in 1781 and died in Boston in 1837. He was a pianist, violinist, composer, teacher and publisher, at first with his father. In May 1798 Benjamin Crehore, maker of violoncellos, basses, harpsichords and pianofortes, joined the firm, which became P. A. von Hagen Jun. & Co. In 1799 the company moved to 55 Marlboro St. (another section of Washington St. then called Marlboro) and later that year to 3 Cornhill. Here the firm remained, maintaining till 1802 a separate "Piano Forte Ware House at 4 old Massachusetts Bank, head of the Mall."

[2] Spillane, Daniel. *History of the American Pianoforte* p. 49.
[3] For sources of information see
    Boston Music Directory 1929, Significant names in Boston's Musical History—A Roll of Honor p. 9.
    Fisher, William Arms. *One Hundred and Fifty Years of Music Publishing in the United States* p. 36-7.

Among this firm's "publications are *Adams and Liberty!*, *Adams and Washington, To Arms Columbia,* other patriotic songs, sentimental songs then in vogue and easy marches and dances." [4] "Of the many patriotic songs of this troubled period the most popular was *Hail! Columbia,* only rivaled by *Adams and Liberty.*" [4] Mr. Barrett, the actor manager, sang at the Haymarket Theatre, June 4, 1798, Robert Treat Paine's song *Adams and Liberty,* which had been published just three days before, [4] set to the tune *To Anacreon in Heaven.* [5] John Tasker Howard states that the author's first name was originally Thomas, but after this was advertised and became widely known as "The Boston Patriotic Song," and to avoid confusion with the freethinker of the same name he petitioned Congress to be allowed to assume the name of his father, one of the signers of the Declaration of Independence. [5]

Francis Mallet, [6] born in France 17-? came to the United States with Lafayette. He settled in Boston in 1793 and was a composer, singer, violinist, organist and pioneer publisher of music until his death in 1832. "He was for a time associated with Graupner in his 'Conservatorio' and in publishing as Graupner & Mallet. After withdrawing from this connection Mallet had his own music shop on Devonshire Street from 1805-07 where he did some publishing." [7]

Johann Christian Gottlieb Graupner settled in Boston in 1796 and died there in 1836. Like Josiah Flagg, the von Hagens and Mallet, he was a versatile musician. He was a player of all known instruments, oboe and double bass being his favorites, an eminent teacher of pianoforte. and all orchestral instruments, a conductor of the Federal Street Theatre Orchestra and co-organizer and organist of the Handel and Haydn Society. In 1810 he organized the Philharmonic Society (also given as Philharmonio and Philo Harmonic) made up of the "few instrumentalists of professional experience and a few amateurs. He had been oboist in Haydn's orchestra in London in 1791-92 and soon they practised Haydn's symphonies and gave concerts of which that on November 24, 1824 was the last." [8]

[4] Fisher, William Arms. *One Hundred and Fifty Years of Music Publishing in the United States* p. 37.
[5] Howard, John Tasker. *Our American Music* p. 30.
[6] *Boston Music Directory* 1929, Significant Names in Boston's Musical History—A Roll of Honor p. 9.
[7] Fisher, William Arms. *One Hundred and Fifty Years of Music Publishing in the United States* p. 115.
[8] *Ibid* p. 46.

In addition to all these activities, he composed, engraved and printed with his own hands his own and others' compositions at his Musical Academy, 6 Franklin St., Boston, from about 1800 to 1820. He was a pioneer in compiling educational works for the pianoforte, for in 1819 he wrote and published *Rudiments of the Art of Playing the Pianoforte, containing the elements of music* and "remarks on fingering with examples, thirty fingered lessons and a plain direction for tuning." "Judging from what has survived his output was more extended than that of his predecessor and contemporary von Hagen, and he ventured to publish some larger and more important works." [9]

Dedham, near Boston, was early a musical centre where in 1807 the firm of H. Mann printed and published *For the Gentlemen: A Favorite Selection of Instrumental Music for Schools and Musical Societies* by Oliver Shaw (1779-1848), blind singer, singing teacher and composer. Another work of his, *Columbian Sacred Harmony*, was published in Dedham in 1808 and *The Providence Selection of Psalm and Hymn Tunes* by Mann & Co. in 1815.

"Previous to this all books were printed from type, for the art of stereotyping which was invented about 1726 did not begin to come into general use until 1810, and was first introduced into America about 1813." [10]

Charles Bradlee began music publishing in 1827 at 164 Washington St. The place was burned out November 1, 1833 [11] and he continued at various addresses until 1846 after which his name disappears from the Boston Directory. He printed some songs of Oliver Shaw. His catalog was taken over by Oliver Ditson & Company.

At times Mr. Bradlee was in friendly association with Colonel Samuel H. Parker. [12] The latter took over William Blagrove's shop in 1811 and joined with others to form the firm of Munroe, Francis & Parker. In 1818 Parker moved to 12 Cornhill and in 1825 to 164 Washington St. where he stayed till driven out by fire as was Charles Bradlee on November 1, 1833. In January 1834 he went to 141 Washington St. and in December of the same year to 107 Washington St. There Parker's music store soon became a music centre.

---

[9] Fisher, William Arms. *One Hundred and Fifty Years of Music Publishing in the United States* p. 115.
[10] Gilson Company, F. H. *Music Book Printing* p. 6.
[11] From Fisher, William Arms. *One Hundred and Fifty Years of Music Publishing in the United States* p. 116.
[12] Fisher, William Arms. *Notes on Music in Old Boston* p. 33.

He with Johann Graupner was one of the organizers and first trustees of the Handel and Haydn Society. [12]

Among Parker's publications were, as announced in the *Columbian Sentinel* for October 18, 1817, "Three Sacred Songs by Moore delightfully set to music by Oliver Shaw of Providence and sung by him at late Oratorios." [13] What was "probably the earliest American folio collection of glees and catches for two, three and four or more voices was issued by Samuel H. Parker about 1823 when Oliver Ditson entered his employ." [14] "Its generous pages (10 x 14¼) contained such numbers as Danby's *Awake, Aeolian Lyre,* Mornington's *Here in cool grot,* Webbe's *When winds breathe soft* and Mazzinghi's *Ye Shepherds tell me,* together with others by Mozart, Shield, and Doctors Arne, Clarke, Calcott, and Stevenson." [15]

Oliver Ditson left him in 1826 to apprentice himself to Isaac R. Butts. Ditson started in business for himself in 1835 and as he was apparently getting ahead of Mr. Parker the latter took Ditson into partnership, as the copartnership notice in the *Transcript* of April 5, 1836 shows. [16]

Parker & Ditson
Dealers in Piano Fortes & Sheet Music.
107 Washington St.

From about 1825 to 1850 there was in Boston a peculiar business combination of umbrellas and music. John Ashton, Jr. followed by John Ashton & Co. [17] (E. H. Wade as partner) were umbrella makers 1820-1843 at 18 Marlboro St. and later 197 Washington St. They added music and instruments to their line in 1825.

Henry Prentiss, an umbrella maker at 33 Court St., added pianofortes and music in 1834 and published music as well until 1845. In 1847 the firm was Prentiss & Clark at the same address. This company had disappeared from the Boston Directory by 1850.

"Charles H. Keith, a Court St. umbrella maker from 1833, added music and instruments to his stock in 1835 and in 1840 took

---

[13] For a complete tracing of Samuel H. Parker and the firms leading up to the Oliver Ditson Company see Fisher, William Arms. *Notes on Music In Old Boston* pp. 22-9, 33-7 and *One Hundred and Fifty Years of Music Publishing in the United States* pp. 34-6, 39-44, 48-53.

[14] Fisher, William Arms. *One Hundred and Fifty Years of Music Publishing in the United States* p. 41.

[15] *Ibid* p. 56.

[16] Fisher, William Arms. *Notes on Music in Old Boston* p. 37.

[17] The firm appears in the *Boston Directory* of 1850 at 67-68 Court St.

in a partner for two years as Keith & Moore." As "a music dealer and publisher he continued under his own name until 1846 [18] when the catalog was purchased by Oliver Ditson & Co." [19]

The firm of W. H. Oakes was in business 1840-1851; at 197 Washington St. in 1847, and in 1850 at 383 Washington St.

Charles Edward Horn [20] was born in London, 1788, and died in Boston in 1849. He came to America in 1833 and to Boston in 1847 as conductor of the Handel and Haydn Society. He was a composer of English operas, an opera singer, conductor and publisher.

Eben H. Wade, John Ashton's former partner, did some publishing at 197 Washington St. between 1847 and 1856. In 1852 he advertised that his catalog comprised all of the music published by W. H. Oakes, C. Bradlee & Co. and A. & T. P. Ordway, making it the largest in the country. He stated he was also "publisher of Bertini's *Method for the Piano*." [21]

Elias Howe, Jr. (1820-1895) was a farm boy from Framingham who played the fiddle and made his own collection of jigs, reels, songs and popular tunes of the day, *The Musician's Companion*, when he was just twenty years old. He found a printer who had music type and was willing to print the volume even though he had to wait for his pay until Mr. Howe could obtain the money by selling the books. As this was the first collection published in the United States of this type of popular music arranged for violin, [22] the music dealers would not handle it for fear of ruining their sales of sheet music. So young Howe sold this volume through newspaper stands, book stores and anyone who would take it. As the price was reasonable the collection soon became popular, selling all over New England and gradually all over the country, so that the music dealers found it desirable to handle.

Encouraged by this success, Elias Howe, Jr. established his own publishing business, which is first listed in the Boston City Directory of 1843 at 7 Cornhill. He soon prepared and brought out instruction books also for violin, woodwind, accordeon, and

---

[18] It appears in the *Boston Directory* of 1850 at 67-68 Court St.
[19] From Fisher, William Arms. *One Hundred and Fifty Years of Music Publishing in the United States* p. 115.
[20] *Boston Music Directory* 1929, Significant Names in Boston's Musical History—A Roll of Honor p. 9.
[21] *Dwight's Journal of Music* 1852 Vol. 1, No. 1 p. 8.
[22] Statement of Edward F. Howe, son of Elias Howe.

concertina, the basic idea of which was to provide a few instructions with two or three hundred tunes at a popular price—around fifty cents. Among his earliest publications were—

> *School for the flageolet*—1843, containing over 150 pieces of music.
> *The complete preceptor for the accordeon* for both whole-toned and semi-toned accordeon—1843.
> *The accordeon without a master*—1846.

His "Without a Master" series was intended for self-instruction.

As a compiler he brought out *Howe's 100 Scotch Songs* with words and music in the 1840's. He was also the editor in 1848 of *The Ethiopian Glee Book,* in two volumes, containing the songs sung by the Christy Minstrels, with many other popular Negro melodies arranged for four part singing. Another edition appeared in 1849. For this work he used the pseudonym "Gumbo Chaff."

He continued publishing at different numbers on Cornhill, 9 in 1848 and 11 in 1850, until about 1850 when he sold out his catalog to Oliver Ditson with the agreement that he was not to resume music publishing for ten years.

Some of the other volumes of his catalog which Ditson reprinted are the following—

> *The violin complete: or the American system of teaching the art of playing the violin*—1850.
> *The Musician's companion, containing setts of cottillions arranged with figures and a large number of popular marches, quicksteps, etc. for flute, violin, clarionett, bass viol*—a compilation—1850.
> *Howe's School for the clarionett*—1851.
> *Howe's School for the fife*—1851.
> *Howe's seraphine and melodeon instructor*—1851.
> *The complete preceptor of the banjo* with music adapted to this instrument—1851 by Gumbo Chaff.
> *Howe's New clarionett instructor*—185-?.

In 1859 Russell & Tolman published *Young America's instructor for the flute* by Elias Howe, Jr., and Swett published *Howe's Drawingroom Dances*—music arranged for the pianoforte. In 1860 Ditson & Co. published *The Caledonia collection including all the famous national airs of Scotland, ancient & modern* compiled and arranged by Elias Howe, Jr. for violin.

In 1860 Elias Howe, Jr. again began publishing, starting once more from the bottom. He was then located at 33 Court St. but by 1870 had moved to 103 Court St.

Presently he brought out some other series, his *Musicians' Omnibus* in seven volumes in 1863 and his "Eclectic" series beginning about 1870. The former contained polkas, schottisches, waltzes, marches, etc. for violin, flute, cornet, clarionet with about a thousand tunes in each volume. The latter consisted of such works as—

> *Howe's eclectic school for the concertina* with instructions in German and English—1870.
> *Howe's eclectic school for the guitar without a master*—1872.

He published at least two other well known series, "The Diamond Series" [23] and "The Western Series." [23]

He also published more songs—*Howe's 500 sentimental, comic, Scotch and Irish songs*—1874, and *Howe's Duets for piano and violin or flute* in four volumes—187-?.

After his second start Elias Howe, Jr. published also band and orchestra music, and such small booklets as—

> *How to Choose a Violin* by Thos. Porter—for 25c.
> *The Violin How to Make It* by a Master of the Instrument.

To publishing was gradually added a general music store business, including importing of music, violins and trimmings, and repairing. An advertisement [24] in *The Apollo* in 1883 stated

"VIOLINS
New   Old

all prices from $1. to $100. More than three hundred different makers, American, German, French, Austrian, Italian, etc. Greatest assortment from the best makers to be found in the country."

About 1871 Elias Howe, Jr. began the collection of rare, old, stringed instruments for sale through his music store. Thus he was the first dealer to do this in a big way. [25] He specialized in

---

[23] Date of publication could not be ascertained from material available.

[24] *The Apollo*—February-March issue, Vol. 1. No. 4 & 5—1883 p. 73.

[25] Statements of Edward F. Howe, son of Elias Howe, and A. J. Oettinger, formerly connected with Elias Howe Co.

the violin family and later the plectrum instruments, the old time banjos and guitars. His last trip for this purpose was made in 1887. At that time he had the largest collection of any dealer in the country of ancient rare instruments [26]—violins, violas, 'cellos, violas d'amore, violas da gamba, and odd shaped instruments. [27]

Elias Howe died in 1895 and the corporation Elias Howe Co. was formed and incorporated in 1898 with his sons in charge of the business, William H. Howe being president. The firm, which was located at 88 Court St. from about 1880 to 1914, gradually stopped publishing, finally ceasing this phase of the business by about 1910, and specialized in materials for violin makers, repairing [28] and the sale of new instruments of the violin family and guitars, banjos, mandolins, ukeleles, strings and trimmings.

From about 1914 to 1924 while the store was located at 8 Bosworth St. the company manufactured patented devices and metal fittings. [29] This line was given up about the time they moved to 120 Boylston St., which was in 1924. In 1931 the company was sold out by assignment and the music catalog plates were destroyed as being too far out of date for reprints.

George P. Reed opened his music store in 1839 and published music under the name G. P. Reed at 17 Tremont Row. There P. J. Healy of Lyon & Healy got his start, rising from errand boy to bookkeeper and confidential clerk. [30] In 1850 Mr. Reed took his chief clerk, George D. Russell, into partnership as George P. Reed & Co. *Dwight's Journal of Music* in 1856 speaks of this firm as one of our three leading publishers . . . all of whom seem anxious to identify their names with the best list of works that have an enduring value. [31] The new publications sent for review to the magazine by this firm included works of Czerny, Baumbach, Cramer, Rossini, Meyerbeer, Mozart, Beethoven and American composers. [32] One spirited old pianoforte publication of theirs was *Agawam Quick Step*. In 1856 Mr. Russell left Mr. Reed to go into partnership with Nathan Richardson whose publications are discussed next.

[26] Statement of Edward F. Howe.
[27] For some of these instruments see Ernest A. Anderberg p. 234-5.
[28] For violin repairing and the "Colton Bridge" see Appendix IV p. 260-1.
[29] For a description of what the company manufactured see Appendix IV p. 272.
[30] *A Hundred Years of Music in America*—Chapter XV p. 340.
[31] *Dwight's Journal of Music*, March 22, 1856 pp. 198 & 199.
[32] They published a number of pianoforte arrangements of important operatic numbers and L. H. Southard's *New Course of Harmony*.

Nathan Richardson (1827-1859), who had been a pupil of Moscheles, Alexander Dreyschock and others, opened a "Musical Exchange" in 1854 at 282 Washington St. and remained there till 1856. In 1855 he published *Richardson's Collection of National and Operatic Melodies,* the *Minuet* of Mozart's E-flat Symphony arranged for pianoforte, songs of Robert Franz and Franz Schubert, and advertised his *Third Book of Concone's Vocal Exercises,* for the middle register of the voice,—price $2—as "The only complete edition in the country." [33]   In 1856 he brought out Stephen Heller's *Six Album Leaves* for pianoforte, *The Musical Drama, A Collection of Choruses, Quintettes, Quartettes, Trios and Concerted Pieces,* in three volumes, from standard operas arranged and translated by J. C. D. Parker, and other worth while publications.

The firm of Nathan Richardson was described in 1856 by *Dwight's Journal of Music* as "the youngest but not least enterprising" [34] of our (Boston's) three leading publishers.   The company's first mentioned publication was a new edition of the *Modern School for the Piano.* [35]   The editor commented that this "seems to have taken its place as a standard work." [34]   "This was published with the endorsement of William Mason, then in Weimar." [36]   It was "a technical work that included a series of large anatomical plates of the hand and forearm. . . It was the forerunner of the enormously popular work Richardson's *New Method for the Piano-Forte* published by Ditson in 1859 . . . a simplification of the earlier work discarding its complexities and adapting the book to the needs of beginners; but the feature which gave it such extraordinary vogue was the abundant use of so-called *Amusements,* tuneful recreative music that gave the pupil a happy relief from the 'studies' and purely technical work.   This was a new feature in instruction books for the piano." [37]

Other publications mentioned in the review [38] were a small instruction book, *First Book for the Pianoforte* by A. LeCarpentier, Professor of Music in the Conservatoire, which was stated to be "expressly for beginners and is extensively used in Europe"; [38]

[33] *Dwight's Journal of Music,* Vol. VI, March 3, 1855 p. 192.
[34] *Ibid* March 22, 1856 pp. 198 & 199.
[35] Third Edition already issued in 1855.
[36] Fisher, William Arms. *One Hundred and Fifty Years of Music Publishing in the United States* p. 57.
[37] *Ibid* p. 58.
[38] *Dwight's Journal of Music,* March 22, 1856 pp. 198 & 199.

Manual of Harmony by J. C. D. Parker; and *Twelve Sonatas for the Piano* by Muzio Clementi.

In 1856 G. D. Russell left Mr. Reed to form the partnership of Russell & Richardson, successors to the firms of G. P. Reed & Co. and Nathan Richardson, moving in March 1857 to 291 Washington St. This firm continued to publish high grade works. It advertised [39] itself as the only authorized publisher in America of the compositions of the noted pianist, S. Thalberg, in the only correct, personally revised edition. For a short time about 1858 the firm was known as Russell & Fuller. Richardson died in 1859 and that same year Henry Tolman, a publisher and a dealer in musical instruments and umbrellas who had been at 153 Washington St. in 1850, became a partner as Russell & Tolman. They were succeeded in 1862 by the firm of Henry Tolman & Co. which remained at the same address, 291 Washington St., until 1869.

Joseph M. Russell had conducted since 1850 a rival establishment at 61 Court St., at first with Patrick Gilmore the noted bandmaster as partner, and then as Russell & Pattee. This last named firm was located in 1861 at 66 Court St. and in 1862 at 108 Tremont St. In 1863 Joseph M. joined his brother George and the firm became G. D. Russell & Co. at 126 Tremont St. In 1877 the brothers separated, Joseph M. going to 59 Bromfield St. In 1884 they reunited as Russell Bros. at 126 Tremont St., but in two or three years they again separated, Joseph M. going to 10 Hamilton Place. After 1889 his name disappeared from the business directories. Meanwhile G. D. Russell continued at 126 Tremont St. until he died about 1888 and Oliver Ditson & Co. took over the business and the extensive catalogs of G. D. Russell & Co. and Russell Bros. These consisted mainly of classical European music, especially pianoforte music and studies, and "contained much of musical worth from forty-nine years of activity. In their best days in the seventies they employed in their retail department A. P. Schmidt." [40–41]

The firm of Jean White [42] was an important publishing house, founded in 1867, which specialized in band and orchestra music.

[39] *Dwight's Journal of Music* December 20, 1856 p. 93.
[40] Fisher, William Arms. *One Hundred and Fifty Years of Music Publishing in the United States* p. 117.
[41] See p. 38.
[42] Information largely supplied by Thomas King, formerly with Jean White.

It started at 80 Washington St. which became 226 when the street was renumbered some time previous to 1875. Mr. White died before 1886 [43] and by 1900 the Jean White Publishing Company, carried on by his wife, had moved to 521 Washington St. The business was bought over by Carl Fischer in 1908.

Mr. White served in the Civil War and played in one of the Union Army bands. After the war he was a trombone player at the Boston Museum until his death.

The company had a large mail order business for music and general music merchandise and sold some band and orchestral instruments.

The catalog included instruction books and studies for all the string, reed and brass instruments; instrumental music with the pianoforte; solos, duets, trios, and quartets; band and orchestra numbers. Mr. White reprinted many European works and published much that was original—compositions by Americans such as Arthur Harris, J. O. Casey, Ed. Christie, Ed. Byer, J. B. Klaus and C. W. Bennett, for many years bandmaster at the Charlestown Navy Yard.

The firm of Koppitz & Pruefer began in 1869 at 30 West St. Mr. Koppitz was the leader of the orchestra at the Globe Theatre. In 1873 after he died the firm became Carl Pruefer at the same address. Mr. Pruefer had a small music store in which he carried a general line of music and music merchandise and imported considerable sheet music. He also did some publishing, mostly reprints of European composers. One of his publications was *Those Tassels on the Boots.* [44] After his death his catalog was taken over by Oliver Ditson & Co. probably about 1887.

L. A. Blanchard opened a music store at 89 Court St. in 1870 and soon was listed as a publisher at the same address. In 1874 the business was located at 13 Tremont St. where it remained until the catalog was taken over by Oliver Ditson & Co. about 1887. For two years, 1875 and 1876, Blanchard probably manufactured some instruments as the firm was listed in the city directory under the heading "Musical Instruments" with other instrument manufacturers, as well as under "Music Dealers and Publishers."

[43] The firm was listed in the business directory of 1886 as "Jean White (estate)."
[44] Statement of John C. Miller, formerly with Carl Pruefer, and also Oliver Ditson & Co.

George W. Stratton[45] was born in West Swanzey, New Hampshire, August 1, 1830. He taught himself the clarinet and from the age of nine to twelve years played solos on his E-flat clarinet and led a concert band with the addition of one or two singers. After considerable study of music he established himself at the age of twenty in Manchester, New Hampshire, as a teacher of music, remaining there some sixteen years. For about three years he directed the orchestra of the Choral Society of Manchester and had to arrange music for it. After that he composed original numbers including four concert overtures and in 1857 a grand tragic opera *The Buccaneer,* given successfully twice. Ten selections from this were published.[46] That encouraged him to write little operas, on the plan of the large Italian operas, with a regular story which could be sung in the little towns and villages of America. The result was *The Fairy Grotto* which was such a success that it was soon followed by *Laila.* "The plan was entirely new, none similar having previously appeared, and the London (England) *Morning Post* said in a review of Mr. Stratton's operettas, as late as 1872, that no better works of the kind could be selected, because no others exist."[46] After *Laila* had also been performed with marked success the composer applied to a large Boston music publisher for terms of publication. The best offer he could get—five dollars upon every hundred copies—disgusted him so that he determined to keep it until he himself could publish it.

In 1867 Mr. Stratton moved to Boston and with his brother John W. established a wholesale house "in the general musical merchandise trade." John W. presently separated from his brother and established himself in New York City. At first the company was located at 375 Washington St., but by 1880 it had moved to 21 Hanover St., where it remained.

Presently the firm become wholesale agent for the Arlington Piano Co. Mr. Stratton also imported upright pianofortes from Berlin. In 1868 the firm advertised itself as "dealer in Brass & German Silver Rotary instruments of all kinds; importer of Violin Strings of every description; Publisher of Music, etc."[47] For a

---

[45] Account is taken from—*A Sketch of the Life of G. W. Stratton* printed in pp. 97-123. of the *Catalogue—Stratton Free Library and Art Gallery,* West Swanzey, New Hampshire. Second edition in 1900.

[46] *Ibid* p. 102.

[47] *Boston Directory,* 1868 p. 1055.

couple of years Mr. Stratton was also editor and proprietor of a music journal [48] which was discontinued when he went to Europe.

As soon as the business was well established *Laila* was published. The first edition of one thousand copies advertised only in music journals was exhausted in a few weeks. So other editions were published and by the time this sketch of his life was written 20,000 copies had been sold. One of the most interesting performances of this operetta was in the Academy of Music in Philadelphia by the pupils of the city schools numbering over 1,000 singers. [49] *Laila* was written for children from five to fifteen years of age and the heroine was intended to be about twelve years old. Because of requests for another operetta *Genevieve* was composed and written for more grown-up girls and intended for academies and seminaries. As Mr. Stratton's *Concert Overture No. 1* was used as the *Overture to Laila,* so *Concert Overture No. IV* was used as the *Overture to Genevieve.* Genevieve though more difficult was also a success, 15,000 copies having been sold "from Maine to California, Texas and Florida and some of the Territories." [50] The operetta circular issued by the company contained fourteen pages of notices and editorial reviews.

Because of requests for another operetta a larger more ambitious one was undertaken, with men and boys in it, handsomer stage scenery and costumes and an entirely new libretto, called *The Fairy Grotto.* This work was finished and published in Europe. Some 10,000 copies of this also were sold.

Mr. Stratton then lived in Europe for fourteen years traveling for his business, recovering from overwork and taking up the study of pianoforte.

In 1885 he gave to his native town of West Swanzey, New Hampshire, the "Stratton Free Public Library and Art Gallery" for which he provided some 2,000 of the best books in the English language, collected by persons experienced in handling books, and over 200 pictures which he had selected in Europe to be educational in the lines of art, history or architecture. The music volumes and sheet music were by the finest classical composers up to that date. The dedication, September 15, 1885, had as part of its exercises a

[48] For this Journal see p. 80.
[49] In *Catalogue—Stratton Free Library and Art Gallery,* West Swanzey, New Hampshire— Second edition—*A Sketch of the Life of G. W. Stratton* p. 106.
[50] *Ibid* pp. 107 & 108.

performance of *Genevieve* in the city hall of Keene, New Hampshire, with the Germania Orchestra and some soloists from Boston to take part.

In September 1886 Mr. Stratton gave some lectures on Europe and recitals of classical pianoforte music.

In 1892 Mr. Stratton again took up composing and published seven more operettas, namely—

> *The Sleeping Beauty*
> *The Minstrel of Capri*
> *Isadore*
> *The Mountain Nymphs*
> *Dobbs' Farm*
> *Lady Bountiful's Heiress*
> *Edelweiss*

In 1893 W. S. B. Mathews of Chicago in the monthly educational musical magazine *Music* commented favorably upon *Isadore* and *The Sleeping Beauty*. [52]

The popularity of Mr. Stratton's operettas is shown by the fact that *Laila* and *Genevieve* were issued in England by a London publisher in exactly the same form as the American edition. Later Curwen & Sons issued the operettas in a simplified, abridged and altered form with the substitution of what Mr. Stratton considered cheap music for some of his best pieces. As there was no international copyright treaty between America and England at that time the only way he could defend himself was to send circulars about his operettas to teachers, professors and conductors of music and to supply copies of his own edition, owned by the large French firm of J. Thibouville-Lamy Cie., to their London branch for sale for several years at a reduced price.

During Mr. Stratton's prolonged absences in Europe Howard Barnes was manager of the company which carried mostly the finest quality of new instruments, bows, strings and trimmings, as Mr. Stratton bought them direct from the makers. For example, he bought violins from Vuillame for around fifty dollars, which now would bring one thousand to fifteen hundred dollars. [52]

About 1890 Mr. Barnes apparently took over the business under his own name, as a dealer, continuing at 21 Hanover St. He moved about 1893 to 98 Hanover St., where he remained until

[51] Exact reference not given in *A Sketch of the Life of G. W. Stratton.*
[52] Statement of A. J. Oettinger, formerly with Geo. W. Stratton & Co.

the firm of Elias Howe Co. bought him out about 1898 and he went with the latter company as an official.

White Brothers were in business in the 1860's at 86 Tremont St. as music dealers, publishers and instrument makers. When Ira J. went to Malden about 1871, Asa Warren continued awhile in White & Goullaud. By about 1875 Louis P. Goullaud was in business alone at the same address. In 1880 he was at 108 Tremont St. and in 1885 at 6 Oliver St., but was out of business about 1886. He was the publisher of the score of *Evangeline,* an operetta extravaganza, by Rice. This was one of the most popular works of its kind and sells occasionally even today. [53]

The firm of John F. Perry & Co. was started about 1875 at 538 Washington St. He was the Perry formerly of White, Smith and Perry founded in 1867. [54] The new company had a music store, dealt in pianofortes, and published some music including minstrel songs. In 1880 the firm was located at 13 West St. and the catalog was taken over by Oliver Ditson & Co., probably about 1883 when the firm ceased to be listed in the city directory.

The firm of E. A. Samuels started about 1875 at 125 Tremont St. It was successively located at 126 Tremont St. in 1880, at 25 Congress St. in 1885, at 86 State St. in 1890 and at 179 Tremont St. in 1895. It was a small publishing house for band and orchestra music principally. Its catalog was taken over by Oliver Ditson & Co., probably some time about 1876, when the name disappeared from the Boston City Directory.

Thompson (C. W.) & Odell (Ira H.) started their music store and publishing business in 1874 at 121 Court St. as Woods, Odell & Thompson. [55] They also began manufacturing musical instruments around 1888 when located at 578 Washington St. They first made mandolins and guitars and repaired bow-stringed instruments. Mr. Odell was a flutist and Mr. Thompson a good cornet player. Probably because of these interests they also added the manufacture of good brass instruments. Their publishing gradually ceased and Carl Fischer purchased their catalogs of fretted instrument, band and orchestra music probably before 1900. About 1905 The Vega Company took over their manufacturing interests.

[53] Statement of John C. Miller formerly with Oliver Ditson & Co.
[54] See p. 35.
[55] See page 273.

In 1880-81 August Damm and Mace Gay were partners under the firm name of Damm & Gay, [56] publishing music most of which Mr. Damm composed. His works included cornet solos, many of which were played by A. Liberati, and flute, piccolo and band music and marches. His *Through the Air* piccolo solo has been played abroad as well as in the United States. This business ceased when Oliver Ditson & Co. purchased all the plates and music of the firm's catalog, and Mr. Gay settled in Brockton.

About 1881 L. E. Whipple opened a music store at 48 Winter St. for the sale of "Whipple's Specialties for Musicians" [57] of which he was manufacturer and sole proprietor. In addition he imported musical instruments and strings, was sole agent for Dustin Brass Band instruments and advertised himself as a "publisher of first class music for Military Band and Orchestra." [57]

About 1883 the Whipple Music Co. at 495 Washington St. advertised itself [58] as successor to L. E. Whipple and Quinby Bros., well known manufacturers of band instruments. The new company's business was described [58] as manufacturers and importers of band instruments and music of every description, publisher of military band, orchestra and sheet music and of *The Apollo,* [59] a new musical monthly.

The new monthly carried advertisements featuring "Whipple's Diamond Cornet," "Whipple's Specialties," and as a chief publication *Emerson's Solos for cornet and piano,* "nearly 1000 pieces arranged especially for and by the greatest living cornet virtuoso, Walter Emerson, complete in 2 volumes. Boards each $3., cloth, gilt $3.50." [60] There was also a premium list and an invitation to buy stock in the company, which may explain why it does not appear in the 1884 directory as still in business.

The firm of Louis H. Ross & Co. was started about 1885 at 3 West St. by Mr. Ross, a former clerk for White-Smith Music Publishing Co. By 1895 the company had moved to 32 West St. and in 1900 it was located at 178 Tremont St. In the *Boston Directory* for 1905 the name of this firm does not appear. But in 1906 Louis H. Ross is listed at 167 Tremont St. In 1908 he was at

[56] Information supplied by August Damm.
[57] *Boston Directory* 1881, Advertising Department p. 1523 and Appendix IV p. 269.
[58] *Boston Directory* 1883, Advertising Department p. 1550.
[59] For further description see section on Music Journals p. 82.
[60] *The Apollo,* Vol. 1, No. 4 & 5 February & March 1883 inside of front cover.

564 Washington St., in 1909 at 181 Tremont St.   In 1916 the firm name was given as Louis H. Ross Music Publishing Co. at 218 Tremont St. where it remained until 1922.

The business consisted of a music store and some publishing of songs and pianoforte music, principally marches.   White-Smith Music Publishing Company took over the numbers of the catalog which were reprinted, the rest being dropped.

H. B. Stevens & Co. [61] was started about 1887.   It was located at 169 Tremont St. in 1890, at 212 Boylston St. in 1900, at 211 Tremont St. in 1901-02, and in 1903 at 167 Tremont St.   Mr. Stevens died and George Abbott ran the business for a while before the catalog was purchased by Theodore Presser in 1903.   Mr. Stevens had a high class line of music publications, the bulk of them songs and pianoforte pieces.   Among his best selling numbers were the song *Celeste* by Edgar A. P. Newcomb, copyright 1890, and a song by Charles Dennée, *Sleep, Little Baby of Mine,* copyrighted 1891. This number was taken over by The Arthur P. Schmidt Co. in 1903 because that firm had so many of Mr. Dennée's works.   H. B. Stevens & Co. also published compositions by Homer Norris and had the agency of Laudy & Co. of London.

The firm of E. C. Ramsdell [62] was organized about 1886 starting at 15 Congress St.   By 1888 it was located in the old Music Hall Building where it remained until the company's catalog was bought out around 1907 by The Cundy-Bettoney Company.   This firm published band and orchestra music consisting largely of original compositions by Americans.   Among these is the well known *Boston Commandery March* by the bandmaster, Thomas Carter.

In 1894 the firm of Bates & Bendix [63] was listed at 98 Berkeley St.   It was located in 1900 at 282 Columbus Ave., and from 1904 to 1913 at 120 Dartmouth St.   Mr. Bendix went to New York state and the catalog was taken over by Walter Jacobs about 1913.

Mr. Bates played violin, was leader of different orchestras, among them that of the Boston Theatre, and supplied orchestras. Mr. Bendix also was a theatrical man.   They published mostly band and orchestra music for the theatre and some pianoforte

[61] Information about the publications supplied by Fred Schmidt of Oliver Ditson & Co.

[62] Information about the catalog supplied by Harry Bettoney of Cundy-Bettoney Company.

[63] General information about the personnel and publications of this company supplied by Thomas King.

music. One of their biggest selling numbers was *The Butterfly,* a pianoforte piece by Theodore Bendix. [64]

The J. B. Millet Co. was listed as a book publisher at 6 Hancock Ave. in 1893, at 221 Columbus Ave. in 1901, and at 120 Boylston St. in 1910. The name was changed about 1916 to J. B. Millet Publishing Co. The firm moved about 1917 to 8 Beacon St. where it remained until the name disappeared from the city directory of 1927.

In the latter part of the century the J. B. Millet Co. published the classical type of music, vocal, pianoforte, organ and orchestra. Their books, *Half Hours with the Best Composers* edited by Karl Klauser, were published in 1894. *The Universal Library of Music,* first copyrighted in 1894, had an introduction by George Proctor of the New England Conservatory. This contained *Graded Masterpieces in Composition* and copyright piano works of such American composers as Lowell Mason, Reginald DeKoven, Richard Hoffman, Edward MacDowell, Arthur Whiting, George Chadwick, Arthur Foote, Margaret Lang, Ethelbert Nevin, Horatio Parker, Edgar Kelley. The rights to both publications, which were examples of high grade printing and beautiful binding, were taken over in 1910 by the Musician's League of America.

They also published *Famous Composers and Their Music* edited by Theodore Thomas, John Knowles Paine and Karl Klauser. The 1891 and 1894 [65] editions were both in three volumes. The "1901 Extra Edition" consisted of sixteen volumes. Six of these contained biographies and discussion of the music of masters of the Netherland, Italian, German, French, Russian, Polish, Norwegian, English and American Schools. They were illustrated with pictures of the composers and beautiful colored plates of rare and valuable old instruments. The writeups were by such Americans as Mrs. Ole Bull, John S. Dwight, W. S. B. Mathews, H. M. Ticknor, Louis C. Elson, Henry E. Krehbiel, Arthur Foote and Philip Hale; by such English people as Mrs. Julian Marshall and Edward Dannreuthers; by such Frenchmen as Adolphe Jullien and Arthur Pougin; and such Germans as Wilhelm Langhaus and Philipp Spitta. The remaining volumes contained selected music of famous composers whose music had been discussed.

---

[64] Information supplied by Fred Schmidt.

[65] Though the firm name does not appear in the *Boston Directory* till 1893 a copy of the 1894 edition in the possession of the John Worley Company refers to the 1891 edition.

Miles (Jonas), a lawyer, and another C. W. Thompson (Charles W.), bought the retail store of Arthur P. Schmidt in 1889 and started a publishing business at the same location, 13 West St., about 1890. Mr. Thompson had begun as a boy with J. M. Russell and then had become chief clerk in Mr. Schmidt's retail store. Later the firm became C. W. Thompson & Co., which was located at A & B Park St. in 1910, at 2 Park St. in 1920 and finally at 77 Providence St. in 1925. This company had a general catalog of vocal, piano and instrumental compositions including standard teaching classics and popular songs of the day. As a whole it was more light than classical in type and mainly by local composers. This was taken over by the Boston Music Company in 1925.

The firm of William H. Gerrish was located at 43 West St. from about 1890, apparently after Mr. Gerrish gave up making reed organs,[66] till 1924. He died and his catalog was at 125 Purchase St. from 1925 to 1927 inclusive as "The Gerrish Collection" of Masonic music with Geo. R. Marvin as agent. It is still in the possession of some of his family. Mr. Gerrish was one of the best and finest publishers of the old school. His catalog of octavo music was church and Masonic choral music, in which order he was greatly interested. One of his best selling octavo numbers was his arrangement of *Still, Still with Thee When Purple Morning Breaketh.*

Herbert F. Odell, son of Ira H. Odell, began publishing music at 165 Tremont St. about 1905 as H. F. Odell & Company. He remained at this address as long as he was in this business. This firm's catalog[67] of music, largely for fretted instruments, and its trade journal, *Crescendo,* were taken over by The Vega Company about 1925.

Mr. Odell was a mandolin player, took charge of that playing when it was wanted at the Boston Opera House, and taught. He had the exclusive agency for Gibson of Kalamazoo, Michigan, fretted instruments, and an orchestra of sixty pieces, first called the Langham and later the Odell Orchestra. He also made many arrangements for Oliver Ditson Company, Inc. and for Carl Fischer. He died about six or seven years ago.

Ernest S. Williams, a cornetist, started publishing band and orchestra music about 1906 in Music Hall Building. He moved

[66] See p. 252.
[67] For further information about the Odell Edition see p. 230.

about 1910 to 40 Hanover St. and was out of that business by 1911. The firm of Walter Jacobs, Inc. bought his catalog [68] and he went to New York State where he teaches.

The Wa Wan Press [69] was founded in 1901 at Newton, Massachusetts, by Arthur Farwell who sold it in 1912 to G. Schirmer, Inc. of New York.

Mr. Farwell's avowed aim was "to issue unsalable works by American composers whatever their tendencies and artistic affiliations," especially "any music that developed in interesting fashion any folk music to be found on American soil." [70]

To finance and secure a regular distribution, subscribers were solicited to receive in periodical form the publications of the Press issued quarterly each year. This same plan has been followed by the Society for the Publication of American Music.

The contributions of this Press were twofold, they helped to awaken interest in our American folk songs, and they also helped to launch a number of Mr. Farwell's fellow composers, including Henry F. Gilbert, Edgar Stillman Kelley and Harvey Worthington Loomis.

Riker, Brown and Wellington, Inc. was established in 1929 at 739 Boylston St. by Mr. Riker with Mr. Brown, a New England Conservatory graduate and a composer, and Mr. Wellington with the aim of specializing in publication of meritorious works of American composers. The company was sold out in 1934 and is being reorganized under another name.

Their publications consisted of songs, small pianoforte compositions and octavo numbers, sacred or secular, for men's, women's and mixed voices. They made a specialty of finding and publishing manuscripts of old masters such as a group of five songs of Handel arranged for John McCormack by Samuel Endicott and four old Spanish piano selections from the repertoire of George Copeland and edited by him.

They introduced Samuel Endicott as a composer in the United States, Canada and abroad, and brought out songs and octavo works of Paul Allen of Brookline, Massachusetts, whose opera *Last of the Mohicans* published by Ricordi has been performed abroad many times.

[68] See Walter Jacobs, Inc. p. 74.
[69] For the following information see Howard, John Tasker. *Our American Music* pp. 439, 441, 442, & 621.
[70] *Ibid* p. 439.

C. Present Day Publishers

1. GENERAL MUSIC PUBLISHERS

In this group are included those firms which publish all types of music both vocal and instrumental.

OLIVER DITSON COMPANY, INC.

The pioneer and one of the foremost publishing houses of the present day in the United States is the Oliver Ditson Company. Through the Boston Book Store of Colonel Ebenezer Battelle, opened in 1783, and its successors, Colonel Parker and his music store connections, this Company has its roots as far back as 1783, [1] although it was not until 1835 that Oliver Ditson began to publish and copyright music at 107 Washington St.

The founder of this house, the fifth son of Joseph Ditson, was born in Boston at 74 Prince St. in 1811 and died in 1888. [2] When a lad of thirteen he entered the service of Colonel Samuel H. Parker, a publisher. In 1826 he left to apprentice himself first to Isaac R. Butts, the publisher of the *North American Review,* and then to Alfred Mudge.

This seven years' training as a printer, together with his fondness for music, and perhaps his friendship with the Graupner family, who were neighbors, led to his publishing for himself in 1835. His first two publications, announced in the newspapers of July 9, 1835, were compositions of Charles Zeuner, *The City Guards Quickstep* and the same arranged as a duet. The next year four more songs with music by Zeuner, organist at Park Street Church, were brought out. [3]

Soon after Mr. Ditson's establishment in his own business he published a folio collection of glees, and catches for two, three, four or more voices following the lead of his former employer. Seeing

[1] For complete tracing of this history see
Fisher, William Arms. *Notes on Music in Old Boston* pp. 22-9, 33-4; *One Hundred and Fifty Years of Music Publishing in the United States* pp. 34-6, 39-44, 48-53.
[2] Fisher, William Arms. *One Hundred and Fifty Years of Music Publishing in the United States* p. 47.
[3] For other early publications and catalogs purchased up to 1860 see Fisher, William Arms. *One Hundred and Fifty Years of Music Publishing in the United States* pp. 51-2, 56-62; for *Dwight's Journal of Music* p. 79.

the enterprise of Oliver Ditson, Colonel Parker took him into partnership in 1836. In 1842 Mr. Ditson acquired the interest of Colonel Parker, who withdrew all connection in 1856.

The company started early the reprinting of noteworthy European works. An outstanding example was the publication in 1845 of the first American edition of Haydn's *Creation*. [4] Folio pages were large in those days, as they were 10 x 15. Oliver Ditson while located at 115 Washington St. published from engraved plates, in two volumes, a complete edition of *The Piano Forte Sonatas* of Beethoven which was finished by March 1856, [5] possibly the earliest American edition of these works. The first American edition of J. Sebastian Bach's *Well-Tempered Clavichord Being the Celebrated 48 Preludes and Fugues* [6] was also brought out by Oliver Ditson in 1856, [7] in two quarto volumes for $5. This was edited by "Charles Czerny" and had a preface in which he stated that in marking the tempi and expression he had been guided by the character of each movement, his recollections of Beethoven's playing of some of them and his own ideas derived from thirty years study of this work. Other "choice" publications of the years 1856 and 1857 were *Mendelssohn's Songs Without Words, Mendelssohn's Four Part Songs* with the English text by J. C. D. Parker, *Ditson's Standard Operas, Garcia's Complete School of Singing* and *Kreutzer's Forty Studies for the Violin*.

John C. Haynes entered Mr. Ditson's employ in 1845 as an office boy. When he was admitted to the firm in 1857 it assumed the name of Oliver Ditson & Co. After Oliver Ditson's death in 1888 Mr. Haynes became president in 1889, retaining this position until 1907.

As the business grew [8] Mr. Ditson's friend, John Henry Howard Graupner, who had been taught music engraving by his father, Gottlieb Graupner, was in charge of the music printing and engraving department from 1850 or earlier to 1888.

[4] Fisher, William Arms. *One Hundred and Fifty Years of Music Publishing in the United States* p. 57.
[5] This work was several years in preparation as a review in the first volume of *Dwight's Journal of Music* April 10, 1852 p. 3 states "About half the Sonatas are already issued."
[6] This fact was called to Mr. Fisher's attention by Albert Riemenschneider of Baldwin-Wallace College after the publication of his book *One Hundred and Fifty Years of Music Publishing in the United States*.
[7] This work was advertised in *Dwight's Journal of Music* Nov. 1, 1856 p. 40 as nearly ready. The publisher's name appears in the books as Oliver Ditson, which was changed early in 1857 to Oliver Ditson & Co. upon Mr. Haynes' admission to partnership.
[8] For more details about the growth of the business see Fisher, William Arms. *One Hundred and Fifty Years of Music Publishing in the United States:* Chronology of Oliver Ditson Company, Inc. pp. 84 & 85 and Seventy Years More pp. 71-82 covering the years from 1860 on.

In 1860 Mr. Ditson established John Church, a young man with him from boyhood, in Cincinnati and sold his interest to him in 1871. This is the now well-known John Church Company, "preeminent for high grade classical and standard music," [9] with four branches located in New York, Chicago, Leipzig and London. It is now owned by Theodore Presser Company of Philadelphia and has no branches.

In 1864 the firm of Lyon & Healy was established in Chicago by Mr. Ditson. This company has been the Chicago agent of the Ditson Company ever since.

The New York branch of Oliver Ditson & Co., Chas. H. Ditson & Co., [10] with Charles H. Ditson as its head was established in 1867 after the purchase of the music plates, stock and goodwill of Firth, Son and Company. By purchase two other catalogs and businesses were added, namely those of William Hall & Son of New York in 1875 and of J. L. Peters of New York in 1877. This branch was closed at the same time that the Oliver Ditson Company retail store on Tremont Street, Boston was given up.

The Philadelphia branch was started in 1875 with the purchase of the catalog of Lee & Walker. The stock of music and plates of G. André & Company were purchased in 1879 and the entire catalog, stock and music plates of F. A. North and Company in 1890. This branch, J. E. Ditson & Co., of which James Edward Ditson was in charge until his death in 1881, was discontinued in 1910.

The Ditson store soon became the centre of Boston's musical life and Mecca of music lovers and professionals, especially before Mr. Ditson moved to an office upstairs. To music publishing and selling an instrumental department was added for the sale of pianofortes and all kinds of orchestral instruments. This began as the John C. Haynes Company, a separate business at a different address, [11] and was amalgamated with Oliver Ditson & Co. around 1900. Generally speaking the instruments carried were made by other manufacturers.

In 1930 the retail store of the Oliver Ditson Company at 178-9 Tremont St. was closed out, while the catalog and publishing business was purchased by Theodore Presser Company of Philadelphia. This was in line with the trend toward consolidation of

---

[9] *American History and Encyclopedia of Music*—The Music Trades p. 342.
[10] For locations see Fisher, William Arms. *One Hundred and Fifty Years of Music Publishing in the United States* p. 72.
[11] For addresses see p. 265. Name at start John C. Haynes & Company.

large business everywhere. At the present time the publishing
business of each company is run autonomously with William Arms
Fisher in charge of the policies of the Oliver Ditson Company, as
Vice-President and Publication Manager, at 359 Boylston St.

In the period 1860-90 there were many reprints of standard
and classical works. The first American edition of Bach's *Passion
Music According to St. Matthew* with a translation by John S.
Dwight was published in 1869. Besides this many important new
works were issued, such as [12]—

> *Praise to God*—George F. Bristow—1860
> *Festival Cantata*—Eugene Thayer—1872
> *St. Peter*—John K. Paine's oratorio—1874
> *Ruth and Naomi*—Dr. Leopold Damrosch—1875
> *46th Psalm*—Dudley Buck—1877
> *Redemption Hymn*—J. C. D. Parker—1877
> *The Blind King*—J. C. D. Parker's choral ballad—1883

This same period was the time of great expansion. The company took over the catalogs of 50 other firms. [13] In Boston these
included L. A. Blanchard, Charles Bradlee, [14] Charles H. Keith,
A. & J. P. Ordway, [14] J. F. Perry & Co., Carl Pruefer, G. D. Russell
& Co., Russell Bros. and E. H. Wade.

Printed catalogs of 1890 list 100,000 titles classified as follows [15]—vocal music, 45,000; octavo music, 4,000; instrumental
music, 48,000; books, 3,000. These figures included both inactive
numbers and others entirely out of print.

Some idea of the present volume of publications of this large
publishing house can be gained from the following figures for
1932 supplied by Mr. Fisher. The total catalog of the company
was 20,295 active numbers, distributed as follows—

Text books, musical literature, operas, operettas and collections—vocal, choral and instrumental .	2600
Piano music	5121
Organ music	370
Violin and other stringed instruments . . .	587
Orchestra	767
Band	451
Vocal music	3461
Octavo music	6916

---

[12] Fisher, William Arms. *One Hundred and Fifty Years of Music Publishing in the United States* p. 57.
[13] For partial list see Fisher, William Arms. *One Hundred and Fifty Years of Music Publishing in the United States* pp. 74 & 75.
[14] Through taking over the catalog of E. H. Wade, see p. 12.
[15] Fisher, William Arms. *One Hundred and Fifty Years of Music Publishing in the United States* p. 75.

Since 1932 new numbers have been added and others discontinued, as is always the case with any active music publisher.

The octavo catalog of sacred and secular songs for men's, women's and mixed voices is the largest in the United States. [16] Much school music and many publications for children are also included in the catalog.

With such a tremendous list of publications it is impossible to estimate the influence of this company for the advancement of music not only in the United States but also in the whole world. The following publications were selected and described by Mr. Fisher as being unique and outstanding.

The Music Students Library was started over thirty years ago with one volume in 1897. Since then other volumes have been added, making a total of forty-two to date. This series of educational text books includes every essential branch of musical instruction, as pianoforte, organ, violin, voice, ear training, harmony, counterpoint, form, instrumentation, acoustics, conducting, history, appreciation and definitions. These works have been prepared by experts in these different fields of music, such as Professor Clarence G. Hamilton of Wellesley College, Mary Venable, Arthur Heacox, Sir John Stainer, Gustav Strube, Heinrich Wohlfahrt translated by John S. Dwight, Ernst Pauer, Percy Goetschius, Karl W. Gehrkens.

The Musicians Library, begun in 1903, is a series of anthologies without parallel in America or Europe. [16] These hundred volumes were planned to embrace all the masterpieces of song and pianoforte literature. They were edited by the best authorities to be had, as the following illustrations will show—

Composer	Editor
Bach	Ebenezer Prout
Beethoven	Eugen d'Albert
Mozart	Carl Reinecke
Mendelssohn	Percy Goetschius
Schumann (piano works)	Xaver Scharwenka
Anthology of French piano music	Isidore Philipp
Anthology of German piano music	Moritz Moszkowski
Franck	Vincent D'Indy
Brahms (songs)	James Huneker

[16] Statement of William Arms Fisher.

Composer	Editor
Franz	William Foster Apthorp
Negro Melodies	S. Coleridge Taylor
English Folk Songs	Cecil J. Sharp
English Songs	Granville Bantock
French Folk Songs	Julien Tiersot
Modern French Songs	Philip Hale
Opera Songs	Henry Krehbiel

The first publication of a method of class instruction was *Mitchell's Class Methods for the Violin* issued in 1912. This was based on the pioneer experiences of Dr. Albert G. Mitchell in teaching violin classes in the Boston Public Schools. In 1838 Boston had been the leader in introducing music into the public schools under the guidance of Lowell Mason. Again under Dr. Mitchell's leadership it was the pioneer in initiating the now generally accepted class instruction movement. Later the company published Dr. Mitchell's books of class instruction methods for viola, clarinet, cornet and slide trombone, Bornschein's methods for violoncello and T. P. Giddings' pioneer methods for pianoforte.

In 1915 the first volume of the *Famous Singers Series,* another unique publication, appeared. These were song antholo- gies, books of favorite selections of famous singers like Julia Culp, Geraldine Farrar, Alma Gluck, Marcella Sembrich and Emma Calvé and edited by them.

The Music Students Piano Course, of 20 books, the first of its kind on a large scale, was issued in 1918. Experts in this field of music, Clarence G. Hamilton, Dr. John P. Marshall, Will Earhart, Dr. Percy Goetschius and William Arms Fisher, comprised the board of editors. This was designed as a series of text books for a five-year course of music study for the average intelligent person at the time when the granting of school credit for private pianoforte study made a standard necessary as a basis for granting it. This was the first course of this type issued by a publisher "with- out any strings attached." It has been adopted by the National Federation of Music Clubs as the standard course of study for pianoforte.

Another unique publication is the *Philharmonic Orchestra Series,* one of the first series of orchestral compositions issued in the United States with full orchestral score for the conductor. It was started in 1921 because of the development of instrumental school music, and now contains over 45 numbers.

The Course of Study in Music Understanding, which appeared in 1924, is unique in being the first and only series of correlated books on music appreciation. It planned to cover five years of study as follows—

Year	Subject	Author
First year	The Fundamentals of Music	Karl W. Gehrkens
Second year	From Song to Symphony	Daniel Gregory Mason
Third year	Musical Instruments	Edgar Stillman Kelley
Fourth year	Epochs in Musical Progress	Clarence G. Hamilton
Fifth year	Masters of the Symphony	Percy Goetschius

The Symphonic Band Series, edited by Clifford Page, Mayhew L. Lake and Richard L. Halle, was started in 1926 and now consists of fourteen volumes for school use.

The Analytic Symphony Series, edited by Dr. Percy Goetschius, was begun in 1927. This series of about forty volumes has no duplicate in Europe or America. [17] Its object is to provide playable two-hand piano scores of the great symphonies, symphonic poems and overtures with analytical notes on the structure and orchestration, notes on the significance of the composition and its salient points, and a brief biography of the composer. Some works are published for two hands for the first time in this series, for example D'Indy's *B Flat Symphony,* Saint Saens' *C Minor Symphony* and Sibelius' *E Minor Symphony.*

The Pocket Music Student Series, started in 1927, was aimed to give music students and lovers needed information on such points as musical terms, noted names in music, listening, pianoforte technic, sight singing, conducting, etc. So far eighteen of these books have been issued.

Among other publications are operettas, cantatas and the *Oliver Ditson Series* containing many works of master composers, and songs which are general favorites, planned for the moderately filled purse, and the *New Fifty Cent Series* planned to serve a similar purpose.

"The Ditson Edition" contains upwards of three hundred standard educational works for the pianoforte, organ, violin, violoncello, and voice.

[17] Statement of William Arms Fisher.

These publications with their authors and editors bespeak the great contribution made by the Oliver Ditson Company to the advancement of music throughout the musical world.

WHITE-SMITH MUSIC PUBLISHING COMPANY

Charles A. White, as a composer, had found that it was difficult for Americans to get their works published. Hence in 1867 he with W. Frank Smith, previously a retail clerk at Oliver Ditson's, and John F. Perry of New Bedford organized the company, White, Smith and Perry, located at 298 & 300 Washington St.

"Charles White, born in Dighton, Massachusetts, played the violin at an early age and, starting out as a dancing master, was at one time professor of dancing and fencing at the United States Naval Academy when it was located at Newport, Rhode Island. It was at this time that he wrote a number of successful songs which were published by Oliver Ditson & Co." [18] After he had gone into the publishing business his songs, *Put Me in My Little Bed, I'm Goin' Back to Dixie, When the Leaves Begin to Turn,* and best known of all *Marguerite* attained a nationwide sale. The last named was so popular in its day that over one million copies of it have been sold. Altogether Mr. White wrote and published over one thousand compositions, many of them under various pen names.

In 1874 the firm became White, Smith & Co. at 300 Washington St. as Mr. Perry withdrew and carried on as a separate publisher and dealer in music and pianofortes until about 1883. About 1890 the company was first listed in the directory as White-Smith Music Publishing Co. Upon the death of Mr. Smith in June 1891 his interests were bought by Mr. White, who took his son Daniel L. into partnership. After the death of Charles A. White the company was incorporated in 1897 with Daniel L. White as President. Upon his death in August 1919 his only son Charles A. White, grandson of the founder, became and still is president of the company.

This firm was one of the earliest to specialize in engraving, printing and binding of music, starting this phase of the business within a few years after its establishment. The firm's contribution in this field will be discussed under the heading "Music Engraving and Printing."

[18] Fisher, William Arms. *One Hundred and Fifty Years of Music Publishing in the United States* pp. 120-21.

For a while after its establishment this company had a retail store also, in which pianofortes and other instruments were sold.

From about 1880 to 1890 the office and music printing establishment were located at 516 Washington St., in 1890 they were at 32 West St., and from 1891 at 62-64 Stanhope St. until they were moved in October 1919 to the company's own building, which has large fireproof vaults, at 40-44 Winchester St., Boston, Massachusetts.

The White-Smith Music Publishing Company has a large, varied catalog of publications of the better grade, such as reprints of standard works of master composers, original works of some well-known American composers, methods and vocal school music. The kinds of music published include—

> Pianoforte Music Catalog.
> *Graded Teaching Pieces for Piano* by such modern composers as Charles Wakefield Cadman, H. N. Redman, G. Marschal-Loepke.
> Organ Catalog, considered good. [19]
> Violin Catalog.
> Vocal sacred and secular music:
>> Song Catalog.
>> Sacred Songs with various accompaniments.
>> A Catalog for the Catholic Service.
>> *The Church Choir Year*—anthems, operettas, cantatas, etc. mostly by American composers.
>> Patriotic and Memorial Occasions Catalog.
>> Secular Octavo Music Catalog, which is well-known. [19]
> "Universal Series"—first popular priced (originally fifty cents a volume) folio collections of standard works, [19] now some two hundred volumes.

Their special features are their "Teacher's Library," "Edition White-Smith" and the "Stanhope Edition of School Music."

The "Teacher's Library" is a collection of original exclusive copyrighted educational and recreational works chiefly for pianoforte, organ, violin, voice, and flute method.

"Edition White-Smith" consists of over three hundred reprints of standard instruction works—methods, studies, exercises and recreations for pianoforte, organ, violin, violoncello, double bass, mandolin, guitar, clarinet, cornet, flute and voice. In the pianoforte group appear such names as Bach, Beethoven, Brahms, Cle-

[19] Statement of Charles A. White.

menti, Cramer, Czerny, Grieg, Heller, Moszowski, Wolff; in the violin group de Beriot, Kayser, Kreutzer, Mazas, Wohlfahrt; in voice Concone, Sieber, and Vaccai.

The "Stanhope Edition" of nearly three hundred numbers contains a graded series of supplementary school music books by Frederick H. Ripley, formerly headmaster of a Boston School, and Harry L. Harts. These books contain exercises as well as songs and are specially arranged to suit the range of children's voices. Much of the music is original.

The books were issued as follows:

1907 *Song Development for Little Children,* kindergarten and elementary grades.

1917 *Song Development I* for the same grades, accompanied and unaccompanied.

1928 *Song Development II* for grade three, unaccompanied.

1929 *Song Development III* for grade four, unaccompanied. *Unison Choruses* for intermediate and high schools. *Songs and Choruses* for high schools.

The Edition also includes unisons, two, three, and four part songs for unchanged voices, male quartets, choruses; music for special occasions; and violin music for schools arranged, bowed, cued and fingered by Dr. Albert G. Mitchell.

Starting as it did, the fostering of American composers and promotion of their works has always been an aim of this Company. Its contribution in this line has been the publishing of the principal works of Charles Wakefield Cadman, the band fundamentals of Carl Webber, and some works of Geoffrey O'Hara, Bruno Huhn, Gertrude Ross, a western composer, Charles Huerter, and H. N. Redman. A popular number of Mr. Cadman's is his *Land of the Sky Blue Water.* Adam Geibel's *Kentucky Babe* is also one of their publications.

Among the recent publications by this company are the following—

Junior Choir Yearbook by Harry L. Harts, arranged to cover the different seasons of the church year—1933.

The *Junior Choir Anthem Book,* composed and arranged by Carl F. and Lenore A. Mueller for unison voices with optional alto. Described in *The American Organist* as "a splendid collection for every junior choir."

Thompson's Harmony by John Winter Thompson.

Key to Thompson's Harmony—for teachers using the harmony book.

Class or Individual Lessons for Beginners by Mrs. Allene K. Bixby—1935.

Drums and Bugles for Private and Class Instruction by Carl Webber—a rudimentary method book.

The Rose and the Ring, an operetta extravaganza—text by Mary W. Kingsley and music by Carrie Ballard. Susan T. Canfield reviewing this in the *Music Educators Journal* [20] described it as follows: "The lines are merry chatter, the synchronization of words and melody so well accomplished that the musical dialogue is expressive and musically interesting. The parts whether for the small or mixed voice combination are beautifully written, vital, well scored."

THE ARTHUR P. SCHMIDT CO. [21]

This publishing house, which has won an international reputation, was founded by Arthur P. Schmidt, a German of Prussian stock, born in Hamburg, April 1, 1846. He came to the United States when he was twenty years old and worked first in J. M. Russell's music store on West St., Boston, in 1866. When he established his own business in October 1876 by opening a retail music store at 40 Winter St., he made a specialty of importing works of foreign composers. He gradually began publishing the works of American composers, the first in 1877, so that he has been called "Pioneer Publisher of American Music." In 1889 Mr. Schmidt sold out his retail business at 13-15 West St. to Miles and Thompson and then moved to 146 Boylston St. He moved in April 1903 to 120 Boylston St. where the firm is now located. It has had a New York branch almost from its start, and one in Leipzig since before 1908.

"Mr. Schmidt withdrew in great measure from active participation in the business in 1916 and formed The Arthur P. Schmidt Co. of his coworkers and helpers—Mr. Harry B. Crosby, Mr. Henry P. Austin and Miss Florence J. Emery. He died May 5, 1921." [22]

The general varied catalog of this firm now comprises vocal, choral (including cantatas and operettas), pianoforte, organ, violin, and orchestra music; and theory, harmony, history and appreciation books by Stephen A. Emery, Arthur Foote, Arthur E. Heacox, Cuthbert Harris, Walter R. Spalding, Thomas Tapper and Edward MacDowell. The catalog of songs and pianoforte pieces is exten-

[20] *Music Educators Journal* May-June 1935 p. 55.
[21] See also Charles W. Homeyer & Company p. 69.
[22] From Fisher, William Arms. *One Hundred and Fifty Years of Music Publishing in the United States* p. 120.

sive and representative. Mr. Schmidt was one of the first to devote attention to these types of compositions and his concern has maintained its prominence in these lines.

One of their major features of the present day, "Schmidt's Educational Series," was started about 1910 to gather together a representative set of educational works all copyrighted as original material or editions. The pianoforte and violin collections are its strongest features, and it also includes organ, violoncello and vocal compositions, the latter containing Colonial and Early American music by pioneer song composers. "Schmidt's Educational Series" was appraised by *Musical America* as follows—"No series of educational music published in America deserves warmer commendation than 'Schmidt's Educational Series.'"

The Boston group is especially indebted to Mr. Schmidt for his early recognition of their abilities. He published the symphony of John K. Paine, which was probably the first appearance in print of the score of a large orchestral work by an American composer. [23] He was the first to recognize the gifts of Arthur Foote, George Chadwick, Henry Hadley, Mrs. H. H. A. Beach and many other leading American composers. "He also appreciated the genius of Edward MacDowell when he returned in 1889 from Europe with his reputation entirely European and could find no New York publisher for his manuscripts." [24]

The firm has made a specialty of the works of American composers in both large and small forms.

The list of important publications of this firm is a long one and includes the following—

Composer	Compositions
Mrs. H. H. A. Beach	Most of her works, including the *Gaelic Symphony, Piano Quintet, Piano Concerto, Violin Sonata, Mass in E Flat*, many songs, pianoforte pieces, choruses, etc.
George W. Chadwick	Many works, including orchestral scores, such as his second and third symphonies, *Piano Quintet*, etc.

[23] Foote, Arthur. Tribute in *Musical America*, May 28, 1921.
[24] "Mrs. MacDowell Laments Passing of Mr. Schmidt." Chicago, May 7—*Musical America* May 28, 1921.

Composer	Compositions
Arthur Foote	All his works, including orchestral compositions and chamber music—notably his *Francesca da Rimini, Suite in D Minor* and *Suite in E.*
Edward A. MacDowell	Many works, including *Lamia, Suite in A,* and orchestral scores.
John K. Paine	All his important works except his oratorio of *St. Peter.*
Henry Hadley	Whom it introduced, and his notable *Four Seasons Symphony.*
Marion Bauer	Most of her compositions.
Gena Branscombe	Most of her compositions.
Mabel Daniels	Most of her compositions.
Margaret Lang	All of her compositions.
Frank Lynes	All of his compositions.
John W. Metcalf	Vocal and instrumental works.
G. A. Grant-Schaefer	Pianoforte, vocal and choral works.

Later American and Foreign Resident Composers

Ernest Harry Adams	Pianoforte works and songs.
Edward Ballantine	Pianoforte music and songs.
Florence Newell Barbour	Pianoforte works and songs, choruses, etc.
Felix Borowski	Violin and organ works.
George A. Burdett	Organ works.
Rossetter G. Cole	Compositions in various forms.
Ralph Cox	Songs and choruses.
Charles Dennée	Pianoforte works, songs, etc.
Henry M. Dunham	Organ works.
Carl and Reinhold Faelten	All original material and other works included in the "Faelten System."
Rudolf Friml	Pianoforte works.
Rudolf Ganz	Pianoforte works and songs.
Walter Howe	Choral music.
Bruno Huhn	*Invictus* and other songs and choruses.
Harold Vincent Milligan	Songs, organ and choral music, and modern editions of early American music.
T. Tertius Noble	Choral preludes for organ, and other church music.
F. Addison Porter	Pianoforte compositions.
Sigismond Stojowski	Pianoforte works and *Violin Concerto.*

This house has also published original works of such foreign composers as M. Moszkowski of Poland, pianoforte studies; George Woodhouse, of London, technical works for pianoforte; Franz Drdla of Vienna, violin music, and the modernists—

Roy Agnew, of Australia	Pianoforte compositions and songs.
Ellen Coleman, of England	Pianoforte compositions.
Sigfrid Karg-Elert, of Germany	Organ compositions.
Florent Schmitt, of France	Pianoforte compositions.
D. Sequeira, of Nicaragua	Pianoforte compositions.
Trygve Torjussen, of Norway	Pianoforte compositions.

THE BOSTON MUSIC COMPANY AND G. SCHIRMER, INC.

This business started in the Fall of 1885 with the opening of a small shop at Number Two Beacon St. by Gustave Schirmer, Jr. (1864-1907), the second son of the founder of G. Schirmer Company, the New York publishing house. In preparation for this he had been sent abroad five years before at the age of seventeen for a thorough apprenticeship in music publishing and for the study of music itself. [25] He issued in 1886 his first publication, *Concert Etude,* by Arthur Whiting. [25] In the latter part of this year he moved to 28 West St. where the business became well known as the Boston Music Company. As the business expanded 26 West St. was also occupied.

Owing to the serious illness of his father, Gustave Schirmer, Jr. returned to New York in 1890 and shared with his brother, Rudolph, the management of G. Schirmer, Inc. until his death in 1907. William Arms Fisher wrote of him as follows—"The sudden taking off of G. Schirmer, Jr. on July 15, 1907, robbed American publishing of a man of high ideals and catholic taste who looked upon music publishing not as a mere business for profit, but as a profession and a service to the art he himself loved so deeply and genuinely." [26]

Upon the death of Gustave Schirmer, Jr. control of the Boston Music Company passed to his son Gustave. The latter moved the publication headquarters December 1, 1922 to 11 E. 44th St., New York City. It was moved in 1935 to 3 E. 43rd St. The business itself was retained at West St. until it was moved March 1, 1926 to

[25] Fisher, William Arms. *One Hundred and Fifty Years of Music Publishing in the United States* 1783-1933 p. 122.
[26] *Ibid* p. 124.

116 Boylston St. There it now consists of retail, wholesale and mail order selling, with customers located as far away as the Orient, South America and Australia.

The New York house, G. Schirmer, Inc., published largely classical and standard works such as "Schirmer's Library of Musical Classics," containing many of the most popular numbers of "Peter's Edition," for which it had been exclusive agent, and a "Collection of Operas and Operettas in Vocal Score" consisting of standard works new and old. Consequently the Boston Music Company has featured music of the better type of modern composers in its own publishing. At the present time its catalog comprises vocal music, including octavo choruses, and pianoforte, organ and orchestra music, consisting of more copyright numbers than many catalogs.

In addition it took over in 1919 the Hatch Music Company catalog of easy pianoforte compositions and in 1925 the catalog of C. W. Thompson. Since 1922 it has had the exclusive agency of Carrie Jacobs-Bond's compositions. It is also the American Agency for publications of the English firm Winthrop Rogers, Ltd., and is the eastern representative of and closely affiliated with the Willis Music Company of Cincinnati, noted for its educational school music. Through its connections the Boston Music Company carries operettas, cantatas and orchestral music, particularly for schools.

Gustave Schirmer, Jr. was the first publisher to recognize Ethelbert Nevin's talent as he published in 1888 his three songs Opus 3—*Deep in a Rose's Glowing Heart, One Spring Morning* and *Doris*. Nevin's widely popular *Sketch Book* was issued this same year and followed in 1891 with *Water Scenes* containing the enormously popular *Narcissus.* [27]

In his book *One Hundred and Fifty Years of Music Publishing in the United States* Mr. Fisher has the following interesting account of how *The Rosary* by Nevin came to be one of the Boston Music Company's copyright numbers. "When Nevin wrote *The Rosary* he happened to be in New York and so submitted it to Rudolph Schirmer. The latter saw his brother Gustave the next day and handing him the manuscript said to him 'Here's a charming little song which I think you should be permitted to publish in the Boston Music Company catalog for you have most of Mr. Nevin's other compositions.' With these words he turned over to G. Schirmer

[27] Fisher, William Arms. *One Hundred and Fifty Years of Music Publishing in the United States* p. 123.

the song which has sold the greatest number of copies recorded in modern times. Thus upon a generous impulse one brother gave a fortune to the other." [28]

New works by modern composers, especially Daniel Protheroe, Leo Sowerby, and Rudolf Friml, whose *Arabian Suite* is one of the company's publications, are constantly being brought out. Matilde Bilbro of the South is a composer introduced by this firm.

This company's major publications are the *Boston Music Company's Popular Concert Library*, "Boston Music Company Edition," and the "John M. Williams' Piano Books and Educational Series Music."

The first is a collection of compositions which are orchestrated for small, full and grand orchestra. The composers are mainly the more modern ones and include such well known names as Albeniz, Cadman, Debussy, De Koven, Friml, MacDowell, Nevin, Palmgren, Stoessel and Toselli.

The "Boston Music Company Edition" of nearly four hundred copyrighted numbers consists of both church and recital compositions for voice, pianoforte, violin, organ and brass instruments, albums for voice, violin and chamber music trios, and combinations of instruments such as violin and pianoforte, violoncello and pianoforte, and mandolin and pianoforte. The song albums are of American, Finnish, French, Italian and Russian composers especially. The list of pianoforte works contains such names as Heller, Marschal-Loepke and Schytté, and repertory albums for pianoforte by American, Finnish, French, German, Italian and Russian composers.

The "John M. Williams' Piano Books" is a graded course of study which they have had for ten years. In that time considerably over one million copies of these books have been sold and conservatories, schools and colleges all over the United States are using them.

THE B. F. WOOD MUSIC COMPANY

This company was founded by Benjamin Frank Wood of Lewiston, Maine, a graduate of the New England Conservatory of Music, a teacher of pianoforte and organ, and an organist and choir director in Maine. He was also associated with A. P. Schmidt

[28] *Ibid* pp. 122 & 123.

as general manager for about three years. The company was incorporated in Maine in November 1893, but since 1917 has been a Massachusetts corporation. John Aiken Preston, also an experienced teacher of pianoforte, and Chester W. Greene were prominent during the early years of the company in the development of editorial policies.

This "company was among the first to establish its business upon the policy of 'Protection of the Retail Dealer'—a policy to which may be attributed much of its phenomenal success—and in this respect its lead was followed by many other publishing houses." [29]

Because of the growth of business, branch offices were opened in New York, London, and Leipzig, Germany. The London branch was under the management of D'Auvergne Barnard, the well known English composer, from its opening in September 1905, until his recent death. Edward Barnard, for some years manager of the New York office of Bosworth and Company, has succeeded him. In October 1920 the company moved into its own building at 88 St. Stephen St., Boston, and discontinued the New York office which was then no longer needed.

Mr. Preston died July 22, 1914 and Mr. Wood July 19, 1922. Since the latter's death the business has been carried on with his nephew, Harold W. Robinson, as president of the company and John A. Preston's nephew, W. Deane Preston, Jr. as vice president.

From its start the company has devoted itself to the publication of easy educational music for the pianoforte, voice and violin. It also handled for some years the Bosworth and Cranz Editions of the classics.

Mr. Wood concentrated his efforts in supplementing his copyrights with classic teaching material in "Edition Wood," which was started soon after the company's founding. It now numbers over 1000 volumes and has thus become the second largest Edition in the United States and one of the largest in the world.

"Edition Wood" consists of studies, recreations and classical works. Such composers' names appear as Bach, Otto Barth, Beethoven, Bertini, Chopin, Clementi, Czerny, Jules Devaux, Mozart, Louis Plaidy, Sartorio, Schubert, Schumann, Tschaikowsky, and for violin F. Mazas, I. Pleyel and O. T. Sevick.

[29] *Music Trade News.* September 1930 p. 11.

"Wood Octavo Series," an edition of choral works, begun in September 1931, now consists of some two hundred numbers.

Early in 1932 was inaugurated a new feature—the publication of band music, with the issuance of the *Criterion Band Book* containing fourteen compositions. Its specialties are a full conductor's score, melody books for all instruments, parts or provision for less common band instruments and parts for a string choir.

Margaret Anderton's copyright arrangement of excerpts from famous classical works as used in her classes was also issued in 1932.

"Important composers whose works have been introduced to the public through this company are: Otto Barth, Arthur L. Brown, H. L. Cramm, Caroline H. Crawford, Jules Devaux, Paul Ducelle, Rudolf Eckhardt, Robert B. Eilenberg, Mae Aileen Erb, C. W. Krogmann, Edwin Vaile McIntyre, L. E. Orth, L. J. Quigley, Arnoldo Sartorio, A. Tellier, Max Werner and many others." [30]

C. C. BIRCHARD & CO.

This company, now located at 221 Columbus Ave., was founded by Clarence C. Birchard in 1901 with the publication of *The Laurel Song Book,* edited by William L. Tomlins.

The aim of this song book was to furnish school music with texts of definite literary value and subjects that would interest and inspire American youth, emphasizing joy, hope, brotherhood and courage as the dominant emotions of American life. This volume was the pioneer in the use of the art songs of the great composers, as distinct from the purely folk song type of material, drawn largely from central European sources, which at one time predominated in music readers used in the schools.

This book brought out for the first time in a school song book works of many American composers. Texts were selected from the great poets and writers of the English-speaking world.

The same principles were followed in the next book in the Birchard catalog, *The Laurel Music Reader,* also edited by William L. Tomlins and published in 1906, and in later books, all of a supplementary nature rather than a graded series.

The School Song Book edited by Osbourne McConathy, first published in 1910, revised and enlarged in 1930, was adopted in over five thousand cities and towns.

[30] *Music Trade News.* September 1930 p. 11.

Under the editorship of M. Teresa Armitage the "Laurel Series" was expanded by addition of:

Junior Laurel Songs for upper grades, containing good texts and beautiful music of moderate difficulty in diversified arrangements.

Laurel Unison Books for unison singing of great operatic and classic masterpieces.

Folk and Art Songs consisting of fresh folk songs and material from great masters, for intermediate grades, and correlating with other subjects.

Senior Laurel Songs for high school, with compositions from every representative period of music history to and including the present.

The Laurel S. A. B. Book for junior high school.

Singing Youth for junior high school.

Books have also been published for glee clubs and choral groups, such as *Laurel Songs for Treble Voice, The Laurel Glee Book* for male voices, *The Check Book* of part songs for high school boys, edited by Peter W. Dykema, and *Concert Songs for Girls* by M. Teresa Armitage for girls of high school age.

In the series of "Laurel Music Text Books" American composers were represented for the first time in vocal school music, especially Harvey Worthington Loomis and Arthur Farwell, and also Arthur Edward Johnstone, Edgar Stillman Kelley, Horatio Parker, Clayton Johns, George W. Chadwick, Arthur Foote, Henry Holden Huss, and others.

The "Twice 55 Series" started in 1913 with the publication of *Eighteen Songs and Choruses for Community Singing,* prepared at the request of the Music Supervisors' National Conference and edited by Peter W. Dykema, Hollis Dann, Will Earhart and Osbourne McConathy. This book was planned to contain the cherished songs of the country. Although this collection is now one of the largest of its kind, containing as it does 176 favorite melodies arranged for choral performance, one of its principal features is the low price of fifteen cents per copy. The series has been expanded till it now includes six different books for various vocal groups. Altogether several million copies of this series have been sold.

Octavo music for part singing was started early. The "Laurel Octavo Choruses" catalog of over a thousand pieces includes works of both foreign and American composers, among the latter Joseph W. Clokey and Samuel Richards Gaines particularly. This led to what has now developed into two more catalogs with numbers in each for both mixed and treble voices.

"The Birchard Cantatas and Choral Specialties" catalog contains works by leading choral composers of the day, some for average high school and college groups, some for children in the grades, some combining both adults' and children's choruses and others for choral societies. Several of these works have been given by symphony orchestras in conjunction with prominent choral organizations.

"The Birchard Operettas and Operas" catalog includes works by contemporary composers, abridged editions of standard operas for stage or concert use in which the difficult recitatives are replaced by spoken dialogue but the famous choruses and arias are preserved, chorus parts only of standard operas and Gilbert and Sullivan operettas, and operettas and operas for treble voices only. In the case of the simplified and abridged editions of the Gilbert and Sullivan operettas the choruses are in unison and two parts, and difficult songs, recitatives and choruses are omitted. Special stage guides based on authentic editions are available for them. The English translations of the standard operas have led the way to more adequate and dignified translations of foreign operas and have been used by outstanding choral and operatic societies throughout the country. [31]

"Birchard Novelties for Children" offers juvenile operettas and singing games with folk lore and folk music in historic, patriotic and fanciful subjects.

The "Laurel Library Books" catalog comprises music textbooks on such subjects as theory, appreciation, singing, creative music and on the teaching of music in public schools from pre-school age into high school. The latest addition to the teaching books is *Music Integration in the Junior High School* by Lilla Belle Pitts published in 1935.

The publishing of orchestral works with the new feature of complete conductors' scores for school use was begun about 1920. Previous to this the conductors of school orchestras had had to rely on the pianoforte part or violin cued parts for a score.

Publications for toy symphony orchestras were begun about seven years ago when the rhythmic orchestra or band developed from a playtime kindergarten activity into an educational project.

[31] Statement of C. C. Birchard & Co. in "The Birchard Operettas and Operas" p. 40.

The "Birchard Catalog of Instrumental Music" now includes *The Church-Dykema Modern Orchestra Training Series* and "The Gordon Orchestra and Band Training Series," separate pieces for bands and school orchestras, collections for junior and senior high school and community orchestras, music for ensembles, compositions for solo instruments, miniature scores of contemporary symphonic works for conductors, and symphonic works. The last named constitutes this company's latest development in the instrumental field. During the last several years they have published large orchestral works, all new and original, with the definite aim of helping modern American composers. The first of these works to be published were *Aladdin Suite* by Edgar Stillman Kelley, *The Ocean* by Henry Hadley and *Overture to a Drama* by Arthur Shepherd. The other composers whose works are included are—

Nicolai Berczowsky
Ernest Bloch
George Whitefield Chadwick
Frederick S. Converse—*California, Flivver Ten Million* and *Scarecrow Sketches*
Herbert Elwell
Louis Gruenberg
Howard Hanson—*Nordic Symphony* and two other works
Sandor Harmati
Charles E. Ives
Frederick Jacobi
Philip James
Werner Josten
Charles Martin Loeffler
Daniel Gregory Mason
Douglas Moore
Harold Morris
Bernard Rogers
Edward Royce
Leo Sowerby
William Grant Still
Albert Stoessel
Randall Thompson
Edgar Varèse
Bernard Wagenaar
Paul White
Emerson Whithorne
T. Carl Whitmer

One symphonic suite by a foreign composer, G. Francesco Malipiero, is also included.

CARL FISCHER, INC.

This New York company, [32] founded by Carl Fischer in 1872, opened its Boston branch in 1908. This is a retail store located at 252 Tremont St. It is also the Boston representative of the Buescher Band Instrument Company of Elkhart, Indiana.

This firm is best known for its orchestra and band publications as it has the largest violin, orchestra and band catalogs in the United States. What is not so well known is that it has good pianoforte and vocal catalogs. In 1930 its *Manual of School Music* of four sections—I. Orchestra Music, II. Band Music, III. Choral Music, IV. General, Miscellaneous, Instruments and Music Literature— appeared in response to the growth of school music throughout the country.

A great contribution of this house has been its seven volume publication, *The Master School of Modern Pianoforte Players and Virtuosi,* by Alberto Jonas in collaboration with many of the best experts as editors. It took eight years to prepare the first volume of this work of pianoforte study which came out in 1922. The last appeared in 1929.

This company publishes all the works of Fritz Kreisler and Mischa Elman, and original songs by Rachmaninoff, Leo Ornstein and Clarence White, the colored composer and violinist. It was also the first company under Olin Downes' leadership to publish Russian songs with both Russian and English texts by such composers as Arensky and Rimsky-Korsakoff.

The publications of this firm are treated in some 200 catalogs, thematic lists and leaflets covering every class of vocal and instrumental music.

Since October 1930 this house has been the American representative of the Oxford University Press.

This concern, although a New York house, is included in this book because it has been publishing more works of New England composers since the establishment of its Boston Branch. [35]

---

[32] For further information about its founder and early beginnings see Fisher, William Arms. *One Hundred and Fifty Years of Music Publishing in the United States* 1783-1933 pp. 105-7.
[83] Statement of Mr. Burgstaller, manager of the Boston branch.

New England composers who have been introduced or many of whose works have been published, include—

Julius Chaloff	Songs and pianoforte pieces.
Bainbridge Crist	Majority of his songs.
Richard Czervonky formerly of the Boston Symphony Orchestra	Songs and violin selections.
Henry Hadley	Songs and pianoforte, violin and orchestra works.
Maude Cuney Hare	Creole songs in creole patois.
Werner Josten	Songs.
Edmund Severn	Songs and pianoforte pieces.

Some of Max Heinrich's own songs and his revision of the pioneer master editions of the songs of Brahms, Schubert and Schumann were also brought out by this company. In addition this firm has purchased the catalogs of two of the more important earlier Boston publishers, Thompson and Odell and Jean White. [34]

E. C. SCHIRMER MUSIC COMPANY

Edward Schirmer, a younger brother of Gustave Schirmer, came to the United States in August 1840. In 1878 his thirteen year old son, Ernest C., became an apprentice in his Uncle's music store at 701 Broadway, New York. In October 1891 he became business manager of the Boston Music Company and was admitted to partnership in January 1902. In 1917 he withdrew and established E. C. Schirmer with the publication of "The Concord Series," a graded series of school textbooks edited by Thomas Whitney Surette and Archibald T. Davison. [35] The name for the series came from Mr. Surette's Summer School held in Concord, Massachusetts, in 1915. From the company's inception it has been associated with the Summer School, opening a store in Concord for the period of the session. Its Boston address is 221 Columbus Avenue.

As its catalog shows, the company's aim has always been the publication of only the finest quality music.

Although this firm has specialized in choral music for the educational field it was not included in the group of "Educational Publishers" because it has expanded the scope of its publications to

[34] For further information about these concerns see p. 22 for Thompson and Odell and pp. 17-18 for Jean White.
[35] Fisher, William Arms. *One Hundred and Fifty Years of Music Publishing in the United States* p. 124.

include much vocal music not intended primarily for school use, some music for pianoforte and some for instruments.

"The Concord Series" consists of music and books on the teaching of music. The graded series was based on the song plan, which is shown by the fact that the first books for grades one to six contain only songs. Some exercises of solfeggi were added later in pupils' books.

The series covers nine grades and comprises a book of folk songs for rote song use in the first three grades; unison and part songs for grades four to six, consisting of either folk songs or songs by classical composers, the fourth grade songs starting in unison and gradually becoming part songs; *The Concord Junior Song and Chorus Book* for grades seven to nine; and three corresponding teachers' books with accompaniments; a manual, *The Concord Teacher's Guide*; and junior and senior books for treble voices, *The Concord Song Book for Women's Voices.*

Other books in "The Concord Series" are—

Kindergarten Book of Folk Songs by Lorraine D. O. Warner.
Home and Community Song Book by Mr. Surette and Dr. Davison.
Harvard University Glee Club Collection of Part Songs for Men's Voices by Dr. Davison, four volumes of songs, tried out by the Glee Club. This consists mainly of the best choral works of the Italian, English Madrigal and Spanish schools of the sixteenth century.
Radcliffe Choral Music for Women's Voices edited by G. Wallace Woodworth.
Vassar Choral Music for Women's Voices edited by Dr. D. E. Harold Geer.
Two volumes of chorales by J. Sebastian Bach—the first edited by Elsmith & Surette and the second by T. W. Surette alone.
Concord Hymnal and *Anthem* books.
The Concord Piano Books—a series of four volumes progressing from the early forms of music to the classics, by Katherine K. Davis.
Concord Duet Books for First Sight Playing in two volumes by Katherine K. Davis. Other solo pieces and duet books for pianoforte.
Operetta plays.

"The Commonwealth Series" also started in 1921 is a general series for voice and pianoforte.

In 1929 the "A Cappella" series of unaccompanied music for all voices was started. A large part of the music is from the sixteenth century. It is edited by Henry Clough-Leighter.

The "St. Dunstan Edition of Sacred Music" edited by the Rev. Walter Williams, Director of St. Dunstan's College of Sacred Music, was begun in 1931. It consists of vocal music for Episcopal and Catholic choirs all of which has been tried out in the college. Father Williams has collected old and rare music, mostly unpublished previously, and also includes much by the modern Spanish and Belgian schools.

The catalog also includes a new edition of chorus parts only, of ten Bach cantatas in both German and English texts, with the idea of saving considerable expense for choruses through the omission of the solo parts. These cantatas have been printed in the form used by the Bach Cantata Club of Cambridge or by the Bethlehem, Pennsylvania, Club. Chorus parts for cantatas of Handel, Mozart, Schubert, Beethoven, Brahms and a few modern works are in preparation.

The instrumental music of this firm is for violin, violoncello and string quartets. The violin quartets are unique in being an intermediary step between easy material and that for regular quartets.

Among their more recent instrumental publications are—

Gradus Ad Symphoniam—A Treasury of Ensemble Music for School and Home. This consists of nine books for strings and pianoforte—books 1-5, 8 and 9 compositions of classical composers and books 6 and 7 containing only folk songs.

The Jankel Book of Folk Tunes—by Rudolf Jankel arranged for violin and pianoforte.

A Suite for Oboe and Pianoforte by Gilson.

Music appreciation is represented by the *Wellesley College Appreciation Album* in two volumes, edited by Edwin Greene. It consists of the materials used in the Wellesley College appreciation course.

The theory of music is represented by—

Principles of Musical Theory by Renée Longy-Miquelle, one of "The Concord Series."

Principles of Harmonic Analysis by Walter Piston of Harvard University.

The company is also bringing out *Violin Harmony* by Hugo Norden.

The new vocal music offers an interesting variation from love, sentimental and religious songs. Some of the compositions are—

The City—Choral Suite of Five Poems set to music for a six part chorus of mixed voices.

A cappella—Opus 14 of H. Leroy Baumgartner.

Four Odes of Horace for mixed voices with pianoforte, set to music by Randall Thompson. An inquiry from Switzerland received recently by E. C. Schirmer Music Co. seemed to indicate that there are no foreign settings of Odes of Horace.

O Night by Robert Delaney for mixed voices with pianoforte or pianoforte and string quartet.

Americana—A Sequence of Five Transcripts for Mixed Voices by Randall Thompson. The words are bits taken from *The American Mercury* and include such piquant sounding titles as *The Staff Necromancer, God's Bottles* and *Sublime Process of Law Enforcement.*

New American composers introduced by this company are—

Aaron Copland—choruses.

Robert Delaney, a Guggenheim fellowship holder—choral music.

Randall Thompson, a Prix de Rome and Guggenheim fellowship holder—vocal music.

Other Americans whose works they have published are—

Heinrich Gebhardt—piano and instrumental compositions.

George Newell of Texas and Mexico—piano selections.

This company is also sole American agent for—

Compositions of Paul Juon.

Honegger—*King David.*

"Chester Polyphonic Library"—English Catholic music, specially the ancient edition for liturgical correctness.

2. Educational Music Publishers

Most of the present day publishers are issuing more or less music which can be considered educational in the sense that it is of a type tending to create a taste for finer music, although it may be more recreational than strictly intellectual. Hence the term educational music publishers is used here to connote publishers of music designed for school and college use.

Since the publications of music for school use have kept pace closely with the development of school music, the progress of music in the schools is sketched briefly here.

The teaching of vocal music in the public schools of the United States was first undertaken in the grammar grades of Boston Public Schools by Lowell Mason in 1837 [1] and continued by him until 1841, when he was succeeded by Benjamin F. Baker. Music was not taught in the primary grades of Boston until 1864 when Luther Whiting Mason was appointed to supervise its introduction because he had been successful in introducing it in those grades in Cincinnati in 1857. Under Julius Eichberg's supervision music was first put into some of the Boston high schools in 1869. Its extension in 1872 into all the high schools of the city formed a complete public school system.

Originally music was taught as a special subject by a special teacher. Gradually this teacher became a supervisor of the grade teachers who were made responsible for its teaching.

"The development of music in the high school as a serious study has taken place almost wholly within the present century and mostly within the last fifteen years," [2] especially instrumental music.

"The aims of school music teaching have shifted considerably from epoch to epoch, but always in the direction of values more and more clearly musical. In the introductory period the aim was to have every child learn to sing and the values most thought of were those of recreation following mental fatigue from other studies. In the next generation the aim was to have every child learn to read music as a key to understanding its treasures, a value which

---

[1] The authorities made no appropriation so he had to serve this year without salary and supply his own books and materials.
[2] Birge, Edward Bailey. *History of Public School Music in the United States,* published 1928, p. 161.

was mainly concerned with the child's future. The child-study movement was largely responsible for making clear the present aim of school music—for every child to appreciate and take pleasure in music not in a vague and indefinite future but here and now." [3]

The various graded book series reflect clearly the changing aims and their authors' views on methods, namely whether singing can best be taught by rote or scale and sight reading. The earliest books seem primitive and almost ludicrous in comparison with the modern ones and show what progress has been made. The present day series are far ahead of European publications for a similar purpose, although Vienna in particular has attractive books for children. Yet it is to be hoped that there will be further progress in the matter of suitability of the songs for children's voices and in the quality of the music and texts of many selections.

Mr. Birge comments on high school music books published during the period of sight reading emphasis as follows—"The High School Music books of the period (1885-1905) edited by such men as Eichberg, Veazie and Tufts were of a high order of excellence, containing standard part songs and selections from operas and oratorios, and school music publishers had already begun to issue well edited choruses in pamphlet form for both grammar and high schools." [4]

GINN & COMPANY

This firm was established in 1867 by Edwin Ginn for the publication of educational textbooks of all kinds. The offices were located for many years at 29 Beacon St. and are now at 15 Ashburton Place. The publishing plant, called the Athenaeum Press, is at 215 First St., Cambridge, in a building owned by the company.

The first graded series of school music books issued in the United States was the "National Music Course" compiled by Luther Whiting Mason and published by Ginn & Company in 1870. The sale of these books contributed largely to the business success of this company, but three years old at that time.

The need for graded material and a well organized method was so well met by this course that its use in the United States became practically universal. "It was also the prototype of all the many methods which followed it. Moreover its influence was

[3] Birge, Edward Bailey. *History of Public School Music in the United States* p. 159.
[4] *Ibid* p. 138.

international as a translation of this course was published in Leipzig and used in German schools, and the method was adopted by the Japanese Government for use in the schools of that country following a three years' sojourn there by Mr. Mason as a governmental supervisor." [5]

The course consisted of four pupils' books, a teacher's manual and charts. Mr. Newton, head of the Music Department, thinks that Mr. Mason was assisted by Julius Eichberg in the compilation of his fourth book. The song material was largely German and harmonic with its prevailing use of thirds and sixths in two-part songs. Mr. Mason used the tonic sol-fa modulator and Galin-Paris-Chevé notation, a modification of the tonic sol-fa, using numbers instead of syllables as a temporary step preceding study of the staff. Its basic principle is the revival of the movable "do." The second book, which was for intermediate use, developed music reading through a study, first in the key of C, of the scale, common intervals, simple rhythms and two-part singing. Then other keys were studied. In basing the start of music reading on rote songs Mr. Mason was the first advocate of the song method of teaching.

In 1885 Ginn & Company published the "New National Music Course," a revision by L. W. Mason of the "National Music Course."

In 1896 this firm published, as the result of its Turner Centre, Maine, Summer School, "The Mason Music Course," designed especially for rural schools. According to Osbourne McConathy "this course was distinctive in that it had two textbooks and a manual for teachers which gave instructions and directions and included accompaniments to the songs of the textbooks." [6]

The next series of Ginn & Company, the "New Educational Music Course," by James McLaughlin, George A. Veazie and W. W. Gilchrist was issued from 1903-1906. It consisted of two primers, five readers, introductory and primary sight singing melodies, covering the first nine grades, and two teachers' manuals, one for the elementary and the other for higher grades. Later two more books were added, the *Intermediate Song Reader* for fifth and sixth grades and the *Junior Song and Chorus Book* for junior high schools.

[5] Birge, Edward Bailey. *History of Public School Music in the United States* p. 99.
[6] *Ibid* p. 133.

In line with the advance in school music objectives the underlying principles of these books were to develop the child in the four essentials of music education—good musical conceptions through the songs, voice training, sight singing and musical interpretation. This series has been extensively sold.

The next series of this company is "The Music Education Series" prepared by Thaddeus P. Giddings, Will Earhart, Ralph L. Baldwin, and Elbridge W. Newton, as managing editor, and published in 1923.

"This is the first course divorced from 'method,' that is, material is furnished consisting entirely of songs sufficiently beautiful and easy to be used by adherents of any method. And to other essentials of music education is added an organized course in music appreciation with phonographic records made expressly for the purpose. The course in listening grows out of the vocal material of the series and consists largely of instrumental classics. This course has served more than any other." [7]

This series follows the Standard Course of Study adopted by the Music Supervisors' National Conference and is arranged in four-book, five-book and eight-book courses to meet the needs of various sizes of school systems, differing only in the number of songs. The eight-book course is one book to a grade. There are two teachers' manuals, one for the shorter book course and the other for the eight-book course, a home edition of four volumes with accompaniments, *Adventures in Music* for rural schools with a pamphlet teachers' guide and weekly outlines for teachers. In 1935 the book *Magic of Song* for intermediate assemblies (fifth and sixth grades) was added to this series. In addition there are five cases, containing fifty-four music appreciation records to be used with a music appreciation textbook.

A basic high school series "The Musical Art Series" was brought out about the same time as "The Music Education Series." This consists of a chorus book and smaller books of hymns, patriotic songs, Christmas carols, folk songs and college songs. In 1932 *Assembly Songs and Choruses* for high school use came out.

Ginn & Company is the only music publishing house which has made its own music appreciation records. This was done in 1926 with members of the New York Philharmonic Orchestra led

[7] Copyright letter of January 1932 of Elbridge W. Newton of Ginn & Company p. 8.

by Henry Hadley, whom Mr. Newton considers the best recording conductor. Great care was taken to make the records clear cut and the usual number of woodwind instruments was doubled to bring out their tone color distinctly.

When the "National Music Course" was published there were few teachers prepared to use a graded series like this to advantage. So the company started a school, called the National Summer School of Music, which was organized October 1, 1886, in Boston. Daily sessions were held through the entire first year and diplomas were granted September 2, 1887. The first summer sessions were instituted in 1888 and the first diplomas for summer school work were granted in 1891.

The first faculty consisted of

High School Department

George A. Veazie	Chelsea
O. B. Brown	Malden
Samuel H. Hadley	Somerville

Grammar School Department

J. B. Sharland	Boston
J. M. Mason	Boston
Henry G. Carey	Boston
W. S. Tilden	Framingham
L. B. Marshall	Arlington

Primary School Department

Luther W. Mason	Boston
George A. Veazie	Chelsea
W. S. Tilden	Framingham

Eastern sessions of the summer school, which was a three-year course, have been held in Boston, Plymouth in 1896, Glens Falls 1898, and Asbury Park, New Jersey. At the twelfth session, held at Asbury Park, the subjects taught were music, drawing, physical culture and vertical penmanship. Western sessions were held at Chicago and Detroit. The eastern sessions were discontinued first. [8] The advance in the subjects taught is shown by the list of courses of the last sessions held at Lake Forest, Illinois, namely child voice, chorus, ear training, elements and notation, harmony, history, interpretation, melodic construction, methods for grades and high schools, practice teaching, sight singing and orchestra.

[8] Exact date is not obtainable.

SILVER, BURDETT AND COMPANY

This company was founded in Boston by Edgar O. Silver at 50 Bromfield St. in 1885. Branches were opened soon afterwards in New York, Chicago and San Francisco. In July 1922 the home office was transferred from Boston to Newark, New Jersey, as a more central location. The Boston office, for many years at 221 Columbus Ave., is now located at 581 Boylston St. and is a centre for the company's business in New England.

The second series of graded song books issued in the United States was "The Normal Music Course" compiled by John W. Tufts and H. E. Holt. This was originally published by D. Appleton and Company in 1883. The publishing rights for this course were secured in 1885 by Silver, Burdett and Company who started their business with this and the "Ward Rational Method of Reading." Mr. Holt was a pupil of Mr. Mason and assisted him as one of the music supervisors in Boston from 1869-1898. Mr. Tufts edited and composed the music for the various books "in which he was the first to use pictures illustrative of the text and drawn by himself." [9]

"The National Music Course" had demonstrated that all children could sing. So "The Normal Music Course" was designed to serve the double purpose (1) of providing plenty of exercises and songs graded so that the grade teacher could conduct the music lesson, and (2) of covering every problem so thoroughly that the children would be compelled to read music. [9]

The basis of the method was the teaching of the major scale as a melody from which all the intervals were developed. Both tonal and rhythmic dictation were emphasized and in dictation much use was made of the modulator, charts and five fingers to represent the staff. Ta te ti note names were used to designate the length of the notes, as rhythm was taught by the watching of a swinging pendulum instead of by beating time. The double process involved for the children, of thinking of pitch and ta te ti note names at the same time, was probably the reason why children could not read music easily after mastering the tonal and rhythmic problems. [9]

The series consisted of first, second and introductory third reader for soprano and alto voices, and two third readers, one for

[9] Birge, Edward B. *History of Public School Music in the United States* p. 114.

changed and the other for unchanged voices, drill charts of exercises and songs for elementary grades in nine keys, a high school book and a teacher's manual. The harmony of the two and three part music was contrapuntal, being the result of different melodies written one below another.

The "Cecilian Series of Study and Song" by John W. Tufts was published in 1892 as supplementary school music. There were four books in the complete series for the eight grades, each divided into exercises and songs, a one-book *Common School Course* and the *Euterpean, Polyhymnia* and *Avedean* collections for high schools and choral societies.

In 1898 the "Modern Music Series" was published by Scott, Foresman and Company, and the publishing rights for this were acquired by Silver, Burdett & Company in 1901. This graded series was the joint product of Robert Foresman, who planned the books and determined the governing psychology, and Eleanor Smith, who as editor passed on all the material, translated many of the verses and wrote many of the songs. [10]

This series consisted of a primer with rote songs, a first book introductory to two-part singing, a second reader of graded unison and two-part songs, a third book in two parts—one for changed and the other for unchanged voices—of songs by notable composers with three-part singing prominent, and a fourth book for high schools. In addition there were a complete one-book course, five supplementary books of songs, and teachers' manuals. The arrangements were varied and special attention was paid to boys' voices.

This course was another step forward in music education because it pioneered in sponsoring the idea of teaching music reading through singing only songs of the highest quality.

The material included folk songs, typical songs of the important music epochs and selections from the classical masters and good modern writers. The rote songs were of two types, those directly related to the studies and the sight reading exercises given below them in rhythmic and tonal form, and those not directly related but to be studied for these two points.

Because these songs accorded with the new ideas of the child study movement and were joyous and buoyant this series soon became very popular, especially in the middle section of the country.

[10] Birge, Edward B. *History of Public School Music in the United States* p. 154 & 155.

In 1910 appeared *The New Normal Music Course* by Tufts and Holt, a revision of their earlier series.

In the same year were published *The Child's First Studies in Music* and two books of graded songs by Samuel W. Cole, Supervisor of Music in Brookline and teacher at the New England Conservatory. Cole & Lewis' *Harmonia* for part choruses of mixed voices also appeared in 1910.

The Progressive Music Series published in 1914 with Horatio William Parker, Osbourne McConathy, W. Otto Miessner and Edward Bailey Birge as editors was this company's next important set of graded textbooks.

The basic idea of this series was the song method and in general it followed the principles of the "Modern Music Course." It contained a suggested weekly program for the aid of the grade teachers. It was the first course to use many selections of modern composers, some being composed especially for the series.

It consists of four books for the eight grades, three teachers' manuals with accompaniments and additional rote songs and a primary song book for sight reading. There is also a Catholic edition with a Gregorian chant supplement, and a one-book course for rural schools. It was used quite extensively before the publication of the company's latest series.

The "Music Appreciation Course" by Mabelle Glenn, Margaret Lowry and Margaret De Forest was published in 1926. It is a complete course from the first grade through senior high school, correlated with vocal lessons and can be used with any series of textbooks. There are two teachers' manuals and three pupils' music note-books for the grades, two pupils' music note-books for junior high school, a manual for these note-books, a supplementary book of *Listening Lessons* by Agnes Moore Fryberger and *Music Appreciation for Junior High School.* The course leaves detailed analysis of form for more advanced study.

The latest vocal graded series is *The Music Hour* edited by Osbourne McConathy, W. Otto Miessner, Edward B. Birge and Mabel E. Bray. The first numbers in this were published in 1927 and others have been added gradually to date.

The song is the basic method of approach in this series also. The song material was selected from standard sources, folk song literature and original works of contemporary composers. It is graded to correlate with the history and geography studied in the respective grades. Many illustrations are used—great art pictures for the mood of the song and art correlation, composers' portraits for music history, and instruments of the orchestra for orchestral correlation. The many beautiful three-color illustrations are the first appearance of this feature in a textbook series. There is detailed rhythmic work for each grade. Two-part songs begin in the fifth grade and three-part in the sixth.

The series consists of six pupils' books for six grades; two teachers' manuals covering elementary grades two and three, two more teachers' manuals for intermediate grades four and five, a teacher's guide for the fifth book (grade six); *Music of Many Lands and Peoples* ("the silver book") for junior high school; *Highways and Byways of Music* ("the bronze book") for the seventh grade just out; and one-book and two-book courses for rural schools, and a manual for rural schools.

There is also a Catholic edition for six grades with Gregorian chants mingled with the other songs, and a Gregorian Manual.

The "silver" and "bronze" books, so called from the color of their covers, are washable and the paper used inside has no shine to bother the eyes. These new features were introduced in 1932.

More than two hundred and fifty Victor records are also correlated into six units with teachers' guides for their use in the music appreciation work of *The Music Hour* series.

In addition to these main series Silver, Burdett & Company has collections of supplementary school music, notably the "Silver Song Series" for all the grades and high school, and collections of special types of songs.

They also have supplementary sheet music, the "Beacon" series of octavo music, and operettas. Especially noteworthy among the latter are *Rosamunde* with music by Schubert and *The Frantic Physician* with music by Gounod, both librettos adapted and arranged by Alexander Dean. The music of the latter has been arranged for high school and professional production in both piano-vocal score and complete orchestration by Marshall Bartholomew. Its overture is published separately.

A review of *Le Médecin Malgré Lui* speaks of it as being of the Gilbert and Sullivan range and describes it thus, as filling a real lack, "Few works as interesting as this one come to the reviewer's desk. For situations including larger units, and therefore more established techniques, there have been few works by standard composers and dramatists available, works suitable to young voices." [11]

In 1924 Silver, Burdett & Company started publishing their *Symphony Series of Programs for School and Community Orchestras* edited by Frederick A. Stock, George Dasch and Osbourne McConathy for junior and senior high schools. One noteworthy feature of this series is that it was the first collection in which the second violins always play a melody. This is a graded course beginning with simple music for each instrument and gradually increasing in difficulty. There are five programs out now and a sixth is in preparation. Every number has a conductor's score.

In addition to their "Symphony Series" the company's orchestra publications include two sinfoniettas, *From the Western World* by Anton Dvořák arranged by Rudolph Kopp, and *Sinfonietta* adapted by George Dasch from Franz Schubert's *Sonatina Opus 137*. Both sinfoniettas are arranged for both small and large orchestras and have a conductor's score.

Their theory and reference books include such varied subjects as harmony, psychology with reference to music, *Music in the Junior High School* by John W. Beattie, Osbourne McConathy and Russell V. Morgan, and *Human Values in Music Education* [12] by James Mursell.

This company started the first summer school in 1884 at Mr. Holt's home in Lexington, Massachusetts. This was the pioneer school established exclusively for the training of music supervisors. In 1889 this school for drawing and music was called the American Institute of Normal Methods and in 1891 it was incorporated in Boston with Henry E. Holt, J. W. Tufts, Leonard B. Marshall and Samuel W. Cole as members of the faculty. Fred A. Lyman of Syracuse, New York, was also a teacher during the early years. A diploma is granted for a three-year course consisting of a three-week session each summer with ten recitation hours a day. Eastern sessions have been held in Boston; on the Hudson, and Staten Island, New York; and for some years at Lasell Junior College at Auburndale, Massachusetts. Western sessions have been

---

[11] Canfield, Susan T. *Music Educators Journal*—May-June 1935 p. 55.
[12] Selected by the National Education Association as among the 60 Best Educational Books for 1934.

held at Northwestern University, the last at Lake Forest in 1929. Now they are combined at Lasell.

Following Mr. Holt's example the publishers of the other leading music courses held summer schools for training teachers of music before the normal schools were equipped to give this. Later, teachers' colleges and universities established summer courses for the training of classroom music teachers. The leading music supervisors taught the methods and principles of each textbook series and also gave valuable instruction in the art of song leading and the treatment of children's voices. Many teachers received real inspiration for their work from participating in the chorus singing under an able director. Naturally the meeting and contacts with other supervisors constituted one of the most valuable features of these schools.

"Though these schools were each devoted to teaching the pedagogy of a particular method, their general atmosphere was by no means commercial. Their educational level was high and one may wonder how thousands of music teachers would have received adequate training without them." [13]

The advance in the program of this house's summer school is shown by the prospectus of the 52d year of The American Institute of Normal Methods in 1935.

At this session the school had three divisions—a demonstration school of elementary grade pupils in cooperation with a Newton public school, a new junior division of high school age and a senior division for teachers and supervisors. The first three grades had purely vocal work. Beginning with the fourth grade through the eighth orchestral and piano class work and folk dancing were given, and private instruction as desired by the pupils. The Junior group which had been tried experimentally the previous year was run like a summer camp with sports as well as music study. This last included ensemble instruction, chamber music groups and private instrumental instruction. The Senior division had methods of teaching, chorus and conducting, harmony and ear training, sight reading, orchestration, instrumental class teaching, a supervisors' symposium and art supervision.

The other special new features were four clinics—Conducting, A Cappella, Orchestral and Folk Festival. There was also an

[13] Birge, Edward Bailey. *History of Public School Music in the United States* p. 129.

opportunity to study instruments privately with Boston Symphony artists who had had experience in teaching.

For the last four years the school has also had exhibits of works of the different schoolbook publishers helpful to supervisors.

D. C. HEATH & COMPANY

Mr. D. C. Heath, who had opened the New York office of Ginn & Company and later was a partner of Ginn & Heath, established his own business of D. C. Heath in 1885, the year the partnership was dissolved. The Boston office is now located at 285 Columbus Ave.

In 1889 this company published a graded school series known as "The Public School Music Course" by Charles E. Whiting. This was based on the scale method as it was intended for sight reading. It used ta ta te te for time names of notes, and numbers and letters with sharps and flats beside them were printed below the different scales.

The songs were illustrated and they and the exercises were graded. Two-part songs were put in the first book. The series consisted of six books, a supplementary third book with accompaniments, an additional girls' edition of the sixth book, an *Institute Reader* for books one through six and a *Young People's Song Book* for part singing.

A revised edition by Charles E. Whiting was issued in 1908 called the "New Public School Music Course" which is still sold somewhat. In this the folk song, with its motif and theme, is stated to be the keynote. The technical material is grouped as exercises. There are five readers, the fifth having two editions, one for girls only, the other for mixed voices, and teachers' manuals. The *Young People's Song Book* with from one to four part exercises and songs is an elementary course for ungraded schools. There is also a *High School Choralist* by the same author.

This company has made it a policy not to publish graded series of music books and is confining its music publications to occasional volumes which they believe have special merit, as for example *A Gateway to Music* by Wilton W. Blanké and Jay Speck. This has been adopted in Philadelphia as a basal textbook in elementary music theory.

AMERICAN BOOK COMPANY [14]

The American Book Company was incorporated in New Jersey in 1890. This company was succeeded by American Book Company, incorporated in New York in December, 1907. Its headquarters are in New York. It has maintained an office in Boston from the beginning of the original Company.

When the company was organized it purchased from another school book publisher, among many important school books, "Loomis's Progressive Music Lessons," which contributed to musical progress. This series of five books which for many years were generally used in schools throughout the United States did much to create the demand for new methods and new books in school music.

In 1895 American Book Company brought out the "Natural Music Course" by Ripley and Tapper. Its editors were Frederic Ripley, headmaster of the Prince School of Boston, and Thomas Tapper, the well-known authority on music pedagogy. The basic principle was the scale drill sight reading method for which it contained many exercises. It was prepared at the request in 1877 of Julius Eichberg, then Director of Public School Music Instruction in Boston, to consider the presentation of music from the standpoint of the grade teacher. [15]

This course omitted much earlier technic such as hand signs, ladders and intervals as a study, with the aim of having the notes mean something definite to the pupils. The rhythm was joined to melody and the rhythm building scheme common in France was hit upon. This meant adopting a certain note as a standard and tying it with other notes to produce all the higher note values used. [16] This course made an important contribution to music education and was long and widely used in many parts of the United States. [17]

In 1908 the "Eleanor Smith Progressive Music Course" was published. The idea of this course was to teach music reading and the principles were similar to those of an earlier course which she published under the name "Modern Music Series."

[14] Parts of the copy of this write-up were prepared by George W. Benton, a Director of the Company.
[15] Birge, Edward Bailey. *History of Public School Music in the United States* p. 117.
[16] *Ibid* p. 120.
[17] *Ibid* p. 121.

Franklin Square Song Collection—a series of five volumes of the best songs and choruses brought together for school use up to that time, [18] was acquired from Harper and Brothers in 1900.

The "Hollis Dann Music Course" was published during the years 1914-1917. "Mr. Dann was fortunate in having in the preparation of this series the able assistance of Mr. Harvey Worthington Loomis and Mr. Arthur Edward Johnstone in the adaptation of the material necessary for the elaboration of his plan for the series. Mr. Loomis was particularly valuable for his contributions to the lyrics and Mr. Johnstone for the music of certain selections required to elaborate the method of the series." [19]

The Hollis Dann series combined songs with a solfeggio system. The books of the series contain many tuneful exercises, some of which were "made to order" for the purpose of illustrating a particular musical principle or a technical point for the mechanics of the study of music. In addition to this there are many songs of fine quality in the series.

The Hollis Dann series proved to be one of the most widely used and popular series ever published. It is still popular where its method is preferred. In addition to the series for the grades, Mr. Dann prepared a separate book of *Junior Songs* for use in junior high schools.

The first three books of a new series of song material has just appeared in 1935 under the title, "Hollis Dann Song Series." This new material is destined to add to the popularity of the music course bearing the name of Hollis Dann.

In 1925 and 1926 Foresman's "Books of Songs" by Robert Foresman were published. These books were developed on the new ideas of sense training, the development of feeling. Hence the basic theory is music reading and self-expression through song. There are nine volumes of these Books of Songs, not including manuals and workbooks, but including a *Higher Book of Songs* for high schools.

From the standpoint of musical quality and gradation the Foresman "Books of Songs" rank very high and the series as a whole is rated as one of the best. Practically all the selections are either folk songs or by classical composers. A few of the selections are by contemporary composers.

[18] Statement of American Book Company.
[19] Information supplied by George W. Benton.

The American Book Company early recognized the importance of summer music schools, and started one in 1895 at Cataumet, Cape Cod, Mr. Ripley's summer home. In 1896 the school was held at Hingham, Massachusetts, under the direction of Clarence C. Birchard. Mr. Birchard had an exceptional faculty including, among others, William L. Tomlins, Julia Ettie Crane, Frances E. Howard, and Hollis Dann. In 1897 the session was held in Symphony Chambers, Boston.

The three-year certificate course thus inaugurated was continued in New England only into the early 1900's. After that one or more summer schools were carried on in New York, Chicago, and elsewhere until the colleges and normal schools of the country recognized the success of the summer schools of the music textbook publishers and took up the problem of training music teachers to take care of the growing demands of the schools. Feeling that the summer schools had achieved their object, the American Book Company gave up its teaching and left that work to those institutions which had incorporated in their curricula courses specially designed to carry on the training of music teachers.

3. SPECIAL MUSIC PUBLISHERS

Under this heading are included the firms which so far have specialized in only a few types of music.

a. *Vocal and Pianoforte*

CHARLES W. HOMEYER & CO., INC.

Mr. Homeyer, who had been selling for other Boston retail music stores, started his own business about 1900. The firm consisted of Arthur P. Schmidt and Charles W. Homeyer. About 1918 Mr. Homeyer bought out Mr. Schmidt's interest. When the business was incorporated in 1932, two fellow workers became members of the firm, the name of which was changed to Charles W. Homeyer & Co., Inc. It is now located at 498 Boylston St.

While this firm is known mostly for music and instrument jobbing and retailing, it has done some publishing, practically from its inception, of pianoforte pieces, vocal songs and choruses, mostly of the art type, and some teaching material. Most of the publications are of foreign works for which this firm has the American rights, though some are by Americans.

The pianoforte music includes works of modern French, Spanish and Russian composers for which this company has the American rights, arranged and edited by George Copeland, and a pianoforte solo edition of eleven standard symphonies edited by John P. Marshall. These last have been used for study and analysis by a number of colleges and universities.

The songs include compositions by Carrie Bullard, Samuel Endicott and John Adams Loud, and the choruses are for all combinations of voices including some school music for three parts.

b. *Church Music*

THE PARISH CHOIR

This publishing business was started by Reverend Charles L. Hutchins in 1873 or 1874 in Buffalo, New York, and devoted solely to Episcopal Church music.

The first publication was a musical edition of a church hymnal. This was followed by a Sunday School hymnal.

In 1874 Rev. Mr. Hutchins started in his church what was probably one of the first vested boy choirs at a period when that was considered next cousin to papacy. He began with a quartet, then a double quartet and finally had a full choir. To supply the need for music he brought over some numbers by local English organists and reprinted them in 1874 under the name, "The Parish Choir." At first the publications were only occasional, not more than fifteen or twenty numbers a year. Gradually within a year or two they became more regular until fifty a year were published.

When Rev. Mr. Hutchins moved to Medford, Massachusetts, in 1877, he established his own publishing business and organized a boy choir at Grace Church, Medford. Through his weekly publications, which were intended for organists and clergymen, he brought out a total of eighteen hundred vocal octavos of carols, anthems, hymn tunes, Te Deums and communion services until his death in 1919, when regular publication ceased. Occasional numbers have been brought out to the present time. The office is now located at 355 Boylston St.

Aside from fifty to sixty Americans, the numbers were by English organists and other English composers of sacred music, notably A. H. Brown, C. Simper, J. Stainer and Arthur Sullivan.

The Parish Choir has also published some of the most widely used musical settings of Episcopal Church hymnals, one in the year 1880, "which left a place hardly filled by its successor given to plain song," [1] another in 1892, extensively used, and one in 1916.

MCLAUGHLIN & REILLY COMPANY

"The promulgation of the 'Motu Proprio' of Pope Pius X in 1903 inaugurated a reformation in Catholic music and banned many of the masses of the florid type," [2] which made the publishing of liturgical music for the Catholic service a specialty. The following year (1904) this firm was established as the Liturgical Music Co. at 171 Tremont St. by James M. McLaughlin, Director of School Music in Boston and Dr. James A. Reilly, singer and choirmaster, with the aim of publishing music of the Catholic service and school

[1] Statement of William B. Goodwin.
[2] Fisher, William Arms. *One Hundred and Fifty Years of Music Publishing in the United States* p. 126.

music. Mr. McLaughlin presently withdrew and about 1905 established the Catholic Music Publishing Co. at 167 Tremont St. In 1909 the Liturgical Music Co. took over the Catholic Music Publishing Co. At that time the firm name was changed to McLaughlin & Reilly Company and the business was incorporated. Since Mr. McLaughlin's death, the business is being carried on by Dr. Reilly and his son, William Arthur Reilly.

The company's business has been expanded to include anthems, sacred songs and communion services for both Catholic and Protestant use while continuing Catholic ritualistic music, hymn books, masses and motets. Its school octavo choruses are by such educators among others as George Veazie, James M. McLaughlin, F. J. McDonough and J. Lewis Browne.

Upon the death of William E. Ashmall in 1927 this firm bought his business, started in New York City in 1887 and continued in Arlington, New Jersey, until his death there. He had published *The Organist Journal,* a monthly, for twenty-five consecutive years beginning in 1889. This contained pieces selected from the works of both classical and modern masters arranged for the organ. McLaughlin & Reilly Company have not continued this journal but have his organ and anthem music.

For the company's publication, *The Caecelia,* see page 81 in the section on Music Journals.

In addition to being music publishers, importers and dealers the firm added in September 1934 the carrying of band and orchestral instruments and music for parochial schools, Legion bands, and junior fife and drum corps. They are sole distributors for Crusader and Colonial music instruments and agents for York musical instruments, Ludwig drums and rhythm instruments, and Rexcraft bugles.

c. Instrumental—Chiefly Band and Orchestral

THE CUNDY-BETTONEY COMPANY [3]

W. H. Cundy is first listed in the Boston City Directory of 1868 as having a music store at 1195 Washington St. For a short time the firm was Cundy & Whitcomb. Mr. Cundy seems to have moved frequently since he was given at various addresses in successive years, such as Continental Building 1869, 1135 Washing-

[3] See pp. 219-21 for instrument manufacturing of The Cundy-Bettoney Company.

ton St. in 1870, the same with 717 Tremont St. added in 1873, 1317 Washington St. in 1875, 55 Court St. and 717 Tremont St. in 1878, 186 Washington St. in 1890 and 93 Court St. from about 1900 until the business was bought and taken over by Mr. Bettoney.

Mr. Cundy was a fine clarinet player and a good, all around musician. He had studied clarinet in the English Military Band Conservatory at Kneller Hall, England,[4] and became a member of Patrick Gilmore's band. In his retail store he dealt largely in imported instruments, string, woodwind and brass. He was agent for Higham Band Instruments made in England and was largely instrumental in making well known in the United States the Buffet Clarinet made in Paris by Buffet-Crampon.[5]

Mr. Cundy also started an engraving and publishing business, probably soon after he opened his store, as some of his music bears addresses of early locations like 1123, 1135 and 1195 Washington St. He described his business as follows—"Dealer and importer of Sheet Music Domestic & Foreign; Italian, German & French strings of best quality; Pianos, Melodeons, Cottage Organs, and Musical Merchandise of every description. Sheet Music and Music Books sent by mail to any part of the U. S. on receipt of retail price."[6]

A noteworthy series published by Mr. Cundy was his "Cundy's Five Cent Series of Popular Music for Voice and Piano for the People." The publisher stated that the series was presented "for the public patronage believing it will fill a vacancy that has long been needed, viz: that of SUPPLYING CHOICE MUSIC at a price that all may be permitted to purchase. Our object is to enable every one to add to their home enjoyments, the choice music productions of the day, in a neat form, on two open pages (which dispenses with the annoyance of turning leaves while playing) and is printed on paper manufactured expressly for this purpose and which can be folded." On the back of one of the 6½ x 10 pages 112 selections were listed. They included such numbers as *Those Tassels on the Boots* by Frank Cooper, *Paddle Your Own Canoe* by Harry Clifton, *Flying Trapeze* by Alfred Lee and such favorites as *Then You'll Remember Me, Heart Bowed Down, Harp that once thro' Tara's*

[4] Statement of A. J. Oettinger, at one time an employee of Mr. Cundy.
[5] Statement of Harry Bettoney, who adds that Boris, Woods & Co. of 608 Washington St. in business only a few years imported the first of these clarinets just two weeks ahead of Mr. Cundy.
[6] On back of Cundy's "Five Cent Series of Popular Music."

Halls, Robin Adair, Annie Laurie, I Dreamt I Dwelt in Marble Halls, and Verdi's *Anvil Chorus.*

This seems to have been a copyrighted edition which was entered according to Act of Congress of 1869.

Apparently this series sold well for the publisher printed on the back page of some numbers—"Of Cundy's 'Five Cent Series of Music' with which the public is so well acquainted, we have only to say that since its introduction to the musical class it has been fully appreciated. It is now distributed over every part of the U. S. and has found its way into nearly every household in our country." He then added "The great success of the above has induced the publisher to put in book form, neatly bound, some of their finest selections of music, entitled 'Cundy's Edition of Popular Music.' Each book contains $8.00 worth of sheet music comprising 25 pieces—vocal and instrumental and may be obtained for the small sum of thirty-five cents."

In 1907 Mr. Harry Bettoney, who had started in 1900 the publication of educational works of music for all kinds of wind instruments, bought out the Cundy Music Publishing Co. The music department is now located in Jamaica Plain.

The Cundy-Bettoney Company has specialized in music for clarinet, flute and saxophone for all of which they have extensive catalogs and a European as well as American clientele. They also have some music for cornet, trombone, and orchestra, and methods for clarinet, flute, saxophone, cornet and trombone. The publications consist of music popular at home and in school, about 75 per cent being reprints of classical European works.

WALTER JACOBS, INC. [7]

Walter Jacobs was born at Oberlin, Ohio. As a boy of ten he became interested in the guitar through hearing a group of Negro street guitarists. By diligent practising he taught himself and did much playing. At the age of twenty-one he came to Boston and began teaching. He soon learned to play banjo and mandolin and taught them also. Along with this he composed and published his own compositions, until he was one day persuaded by "Tommy" Allen, the violinist, to purchase, for five dollars, about ten numbers of his, including the now widely known galop, *Whip and Spur.*

[7] For information about the various music journals published by this firm see the next section on Music Journals.

This incident led to the organization in 1894 at 167 Tremont St. of the Walter Jacobs' publishing house, which has specialized in band and orchestra music. It was located later successively at 169 Tremont St., 165 Tremont St. and 8 Bosworth St. The firm was incorporated in 1921 and moved about twelve years ago to its present address, 120 Boylston St.

This concern started as a guitar, banjo and mandolin music publishing house and consequently has a considerable catalog for "Fretted Instruments and Mandolin Orchestra." It consists of methods, studies, such as "Weidt's Elementary Studies" for class and private instruction—five graded volumes for each instrument; collections, like *Jacobs' Easy Guitar Collection of Solos and Duets* and *Jacobs' Banjo Collection*; and sheet music for mandolin, standard and tenor banjo, guitar, mandola, and mando-cello.

This company has purchased a number of other catalogs, several of them containing noted publications. These are given below.

> L. B. Gatcomb, fretted instrument catalog taken over in 1904. This contained *The Darkey's Dream* by George L. Lansing and *On the Mill Dam* by Babb.
>
> Theodore Bendix, as a New York publisher. This was a general catalog, which included clarinet and 'cello methods, purchased in 1909. The most noted number in this was his suite *A Love Episode in Birdland*.
>
> Ernest S. Williams' catalog of band and orchestra, vocal and instrumental music, original numbers and reprints, purchased in 1911. The copyright numbers included *The National Emblem* march by Bagley, *The Commander* march by Hall and *The Columbia Collection of Patriotic and Favorite Home Songs,* a big seller.
>
> Jean Missud, Bandmaster of the Salem Cadets, entire orchestra catalog acquired in 1914. The company obtained all the rights to *Our Director* march by Bigelow through this purchase.
>
> Bates & Bendix, entire general catalog (chiefly band and orchestra) purchased in 1919. This contained Theodore Bendix' popular composition *The Butterfly.*
>
> "Virtuoso Music School" of Buffalo, New York, music publications purchased in 1933. This includes the noted *Eby Scientific Method for Cornet and Trumpet*, for Clarinet, Saxophone, French Horn, BB-flat Bass, Sousaphone, etc. and *Arban's Method for Trombone, Baritone and Other Instruments in the Bass Clef.*
>
> Mace Gay of Brockton, Massachusetts, entire band, orchestra and pianoforte catalog acquired in 1934. This included many of the earlier marches of R. B. Hall, notably *De Molay Commandery*, and *Bay State Commandery* march by Burrell.

The Walter Jacobs firm published more or less motion picture type of pianoforte, organ and orchestra music for twenty-five years, being particularly active in this field from 1908-1929. Then the invention of the vitaphone caused the discontinuance of organ and orchestral playing in motion picture houses. Their catalog, "Jacobs' Piano Folios" of over 100 volumes in four series of loose leaf collections, with photoplay usage indicated by Del Castillo, which is primarily designed for the use of photoplay pianists and organists, is widely used. It includes American copyright compositions of every type required for the musical interpretation of motion pictures. Practically all these numbers are orchestrated.

The earliest successful songs published by the house were *By the Watermelon Vine* (*Lindy Lou*), the ballad *Some Day When Dreams Come True* and *My Dusky Rose* by Thomas S. Allen. The *Jacobs' Evergreen Collection of Fifty Famous Old Songs* is one of their best known collections.

The company has a comprehensive general band and orchestra catalog. This includes many marches—"The Walter Jacobs Standard Marches and Galops" for orchestra and for band, *R. B. Hall's Band Book of His Most Famous Marches,* for band and orchestra and *10 World Famous Band Marches,* such as *Our Director, De Molay Commandery, Bay State Commandery, Up the Street* and *National Emblem* arranged for orchestra and pianoforte. For the Bicentennial of George Washington's birth in 1932 *The Father of His Country* march by E. E. Bagley was published. In addition the company has a catalog of "Overtures, Suites and Selections" for orchestra and for band, many of the standard numbers being arranged by R. E. Hildreth, "Program Pep Novelties of Various Types" for small and large orchestra, and two concert compositions for band by R. E. Hildreth. Many numbers in the various publications of the company are by Norman Leigh, the pen name of Arthur Cleveland Morse, the present editor of *Jacobs' Band Monthly* and *Jacobs' Orchestra Monthly.*

In 1929 the company began publishing for school bands and orchestras and now has a number of collections and series for this field. It is partly classical music with some popular, but not much modern material.

The collections for both band and orchestra are:

Jacobs' Evergreen Collection of Fifty Famous Old Songs.

Jacobs' Album of Master Classics.
Jacobs' Ensemble—original compositions.
Jacobs' Concert Album—standard concert numbers.
American Composers' Series of Light Program Numbers—mostly arranged by R. E. Hildreth.

The publications for band alone are:

Walter Jacobs' Select Repertoire for Young Bands.
Jacobs' School and Community Band Book—original compositions mostly by A. J. Weidt.
Jacobs' Band Book of Classics—concert numbers.
Jacobs' Band Book of Military Marches—two volumes of standard marches.

The publications for orchestra alone are:

Jacobs' Loose Leaf Collection of Standard Marches—three volumes.
Jacobs' Folio of Classics—three volumes of light classical numbers.
Jacobs' Folio for School Orchestras—three volumes of original compositions.

Within the last few years they have begun publishing the "Walter Jacobs' School Choruses and Octavo Miscellany" and the "Delta Series" to be used in conjunction with bands and orchestras, since they are adding to their specialties music in which these activities can be combined.

GEO. W. STONE & SON, INC.

Since the founder of this company, George B. Stone, devoted considerable time to writing on and teaching drum subjects, the company publishes instruction books for percussion instruments. These include:

Methods for drumming—rudiments and exhibition beats—such books as the *Dodge Drum Instructor for Drums and Bells* and *Military Street Beats* by George B. Stone.

Methods for bells, xylophone, chimes and tympani.

Technical studies and solos for these same instruments.

d.   Tracy Music Library, Inc.

This unique service deserves some description because there is nothing just like it in the whole country. It was started by George Lowell Tracy who studied with Sir Arthur Sullivan in England and was his agent afterward in the United States. After some years P. B. Metcalf became associated with Mr. Tracy and bought out Mr. Tracy's interest in the Tracy Music Library in 1900, retaining the name. For a few months the business was located at 131 Tremont St., but presently it was moved to 165 Tremont St. After about eight or nine years at this location Mr. Metcalf moved to 1 Beacon St., where the business was incorporated in 1925.

The company carries standard music—operas, operettas, musical comedies, oratorios, cantatas, excerpts and orchestral accompaniments for rent. It makes arrangements of music as ordered for individuals, publishers, schools and musical organizations. Music has been sent on a rental basis to all parts of the United States and to Canada, Alaska, Honolulu, Cuba, Porto Rico, Isle of Pines, the Philippines, and the Republic of Argentina.

For graduation exercises the firm also furnishes whole school departments with octavo and vocal scores and orchestral parts on the same basis.

The library has unique editions of Gilbert and Sullivan operettas and specializes in these and other light operas. The company does this because its heads believe that the Gilbert and Sullivan operas "have an educational value far above any of the modern works. Each of the collaborators was preëminent in his line so that their combined efforts have given the world a set of classics which has never been surpassed."

The service of the library, which is conducted on the basis of consideration of the problems of the musical director or supervisor from an educational point of view, is adapted to all kinds of amateur organizations, educational, religious, and charitable institutions. It is a complete service which includes music—vocal scores for principals, chorus parts, librettos, orchestration, and music directors' guides, added in 1934; stage—costumes and property plots, stage directors' guides including diagrams, chorus positions, etc., wardrobes for the entire cast, and scenery. They even furnish printing—programs, throw-aways, cuts, and synopses. The furnishing of wardrobes and stage settings was done to reduce the total cost of productions in order that organizations could at least make ends meet and thus enable them to give more productions with their attendant educational benefits.

D. Music Journals and House Organs

1. Music Journals

Boston has also had a number of music journals and house organs of publishers and instrument makers. Those mentioned below include all the writer could discover, but the list is doubtless quite incomplete.

MUSIC JOURNALS

April 1, 1820-22. Euterpeiad or Musical Intelligencer.
> A four-page weekly "Devoted to the diffusion of musical information and belles lettres." Edited by John P. Parker of Milk Street and published by Thomas Badger, Jr. Contained music history, biography, criticism, editorials, and some separate music numbers.

1835-1836. The Musical Library.
> Co-editors Lowell Mason and George James Webb, the founders of the earliest school for music, the Boston Academy of Music, 1833-47, which laid the foundations for the development of public school music.

1837-1840. The Music Cabinet.
> Co-editors George James Webb and W. Haywood. This reproduced music and contained articles and news about music.

May 2, 1838-1839. Boston Musical Gazette.
> Semi-monthly journal devoted to the Science of Music, published by Otis Broaders & Co., 120 Washington St. Editor, B. Brown; occasional contributors, Lowell Mason, G. J. Webb, T. Comer, N. Mitchell, J. S. Dwight, T. Powers and J. R. Parker. Price $3. per annum, Kidder & Wright, printers & proprietors.
>
> Contained articles on musical history, biographical sketches of composers and performers, reviews of compositions, accounts of concerts, musical societies, academies and schools, observations on the kindred arts and some sacred or secular music.

August 1838 to ?. The Seraph.
> "A monthly publication of Church Music, consisting of Psalm and Hymn Tunes, Chants, Anthems, etc.; Original and Selected. By Lowell Mason." [1] This contained eight pages of music and was

---

[1] *Boston Musical Gazette* Vol. 1, No. 8, August 8, 1838, Advertisement p. 64.

intended to "be similar in its character to 'Occasional Psalm and Hymn Tunes' recently published by the Editor, (Bartholomew Brown) and is designed as a continuation of that work." No's 1-8 were published by G. W. Palmer & Co., 131 Washington St. and No. 9 by Jenks & Palmer. Price $1. per year. An advertisement of issue 8 (Apr. 1839) stated "choirs supplied with the work for $9. per dozen copies of each number for the year." [2]

April 10, 1852-Sept. 3, 1881. Dwight's Journal of Music.

Edited and published by John S. Dwight [3] and owned by him for six years. Price $2. per annum. Then it was sold to Oliver Ditson & Co. and published by them with him as editor till Dec. 12, 1878. Its publication was then continued by other publishers.

This journal contained critical reviews of concerts, oratorios and operas; notices of new music at home and abroad; summaries of significant musical news from foreign and American papers; correspondence from musical persons and places; essays on musical styles, schools, periods, authors, compositions, instruments, theories, education, and on music in its various bearings and places of performance; translations from the best German and French writers upon music and art; occasional notices of associated arts; and poems, stories, anecdotes, and advertisements.

"This had a longer career than any journal of its kind in the country. It was recognized here and abroad as generally true to the highest standards in art and had the credit of having contributed to the musical culture, taste and character of Boston." [4]

Sept. 1, 1853-1855. Boston Musical Journal.

A semi-monthly issued at A. N. Johnson's music store, 90 Tremont St., with B. F. Baker and A. N. Johnson as editors. The latter apparently published also *The Handel Collection of Church Music.*

May 1, 1855-Feb. 15, 1857. Massachusetts Musical Journal. Title varies—Vol. I No's 1-4, 6-12, 1855 headed as above. Massachusetts Musical Journal No. 5 had the words "and Keynote" added. Vol. 2 No's 1-3 read Boston Musical Journal and Literary Gazette.

A semi-monthly edited first by Eben Tourjée at Fall River with J. R. Miller, A. N. Johnson's partner, as Boston editor, but beginning Aug. 1, 1855 at 282 Tremont St., Boston, with B. F. Baker and Eben Tourjée editors and Almy & Milne of 20 Main St., Fall River, still the printers. Price $1. per annum, 6 cents a single copy. From May 1, 1856 until the magazine's discontinuance Feb. 15, 1857

[2] *Ibid.* Vol. 1, No. 23, March 6, 1839, p. 184.
[3] For an estimate of him see *Music,* Vol. XV March 1899—"John S. Dwight, Editor, Critic, and Man" by W. S. B. Mathews pp. 525-40.
[4] Dwight, John Sullivan. *Memorial History of Boston.* Editor, Justin Winsor, 1881, Vol. 4. p. 436.

B. F. Baker was both editor and proprietor, and it was printed by Stacey and Richardson, 11 Milk St., with the words "and Literary Gazette" added.

This publication aimed at the diffusion of general musical information to promote and cultivate music and the improvement of church music. It contained editorials, news, correspondence about music, advertising and some pages of music.

Feb. 25, 1860-August 1871. Boston Musical Times.

The first and second volumes were issued fortnightly, then it became a monthly review of music, art and literature, published first by Russell and Tolman, and printed by Edward L. Balch. Price $1. From Vol. III No. 1, March 1, 1862 to August 1868 it was published by Henry Tolman and still printed by Balch. From then on it was issued by G. W. Stratton with D. Clapp & Sons, printers, except for Feb.-Dec. 1869, when S. T. Gordon of 706 Broadway, New York, shared in the publication and the subheading was "Boston and New York." It contained articles, bulletins of publications, correspondence, some original compositions and advertising.

Around 1869. Blanchard's Brass Band Journal. [5]

Price $1. Arranged for brass bands of ten or twenty performers.

September 1869-October 1895. Vols. 1-41. The Folio.

Published on the 15th of each month by White, Smith and Perry. This was "a monthly journal devoted to music, art and literature," edited at first by Dexter Smith. It stated "musical, artistic and literary events transpiring in Boston, New York, London, Paris and other centres will be duly chronicled, while choice sketches, biographies, poetry, etc. together with a complete bulletin of publications will be found in every number in addition to two beautiful pieces of music," [6] one vocal and one instrumental. It also contained technical discussions, portraits, illustrations, and some advertising, and circulated among music lovers and teachers. Terms $1. per annum.

1872-1878, copyrighted 1877. Vols. 1-14. Dexter Smith's Musical, Literary, Dramatic, and Art Paper.

A monthly magazine devoted to music, drama, art and literature. It contained some vocal and pianoforte music in addition to articles, news and advertising, and was edited, published and owned by Dexter Smith. Price $1.75 per annum.

A Hundred Years of Music in America described Dexter Smith as a musical journalist as follows—"as Writer of words for music this may be called his specialty and as a writer of song poems of a

---

[5] Information from *Dwight's Journal of Music*, October 1869 p. 35 and see L. A. Blanchard for publisher p. 18.
[6] *The Folio* "Salutatory," September 1869—Vol. 1, p. 4.

simple and popular character he has scarcely an equal." [7]   He was also connected with Oliver Ditson Company's *Musical Record.*

April 1874-January 1877. The Organist's Quarterly Journal and Review. Devoted to Organ Music for Church Services with occasional pieces for the concert room.

This was a high grade specialized journal edited by Eugene Thayer and published by White, Smith & Co. at 298 & 300 Washington St. Price for single numbers $1.00, annual subscription $3. Each number contained twelve pages of music and articles relating to organs, organists and organ playing. The editor's aims, which seem to have been followed, were to provide organists with a paper devoted to their interests, to help supply organ music suitable for church services, to present essays and articles about organs, organists and organ playing, to give a concise, reliable history of the organ, full descriptions of great and celebrated organs, biographies of noted composers and players, analyses of great organ compositions, discussions of matters pertaining to the organ and organ playing, and to provide original music from the best representative organists of both continents and for reprints of choice music not previously available to American organists. [8]

1874 to date. The Caecilia.

Published by Johannes B. Singenberger, composer of twenty masses and other ritual music, at St. Francis, a suburb of Milwaukee, Wisconsin, until 1927. Then his son, Otto A., carried it on until September 1929 when it was taken over by McLaughlin & Reilly with Otto A. Singenberger as editor. This is a monthly review of "Catholic Church and School Music." Till the World War it was published in German as well as in English. It discusses music fundamentals, the liturgy, chants, transcriptions of Gregorian music; and contains articles by priests, items of interest by organists, choir masters and school music supervisors, and twelve to sixteen pages of music.

1878-1898. Monthly Musical Record.

Established by Oliver Ditson & Co. in place of *Dwight's Journal of Music.*

1898. Musical Record (Successor to previous).

A high class magazine edited by Philip Hale and published by Oliver Ditson Company, Inc. This was combined in January 1901 with the *Music Review,* a pocket-size monthly magazine, started by Oliver Ditson Company, Inc. in October 1898 to bulletin publications of the house. It was entitled *Musical Record & Review.*

---

[7] *Hundred Years of Music in America*—Chapter XVI, "Literary Factors in Musical Progress" p. 406.
[8] From the "Prospectus" of No. 1, April 1874.

January 1901.   Musical Record & Review.

> This was edited by Thomas Tapper for two years.   Then *The Musician* was purchased from the Hatch Music Company of Philadelphia and combined with *Musical Record* while the *Review* was dropped.

November 1903.   Musical Record combined with The Musician.

> This was edited by Mr. Tapper till August 1907 when he was succeeded by Mr. W. J. Baltzell who conducted the magazine till Dec. 31, 1918.   In 1919 the Henderson Publications of New York took over this monthly and in May 1922 it passed into the hands of Paul Kempf.   In 1935 it was sold and the present publisher is Eugene Belier.   The editor is Nicholas de Vore.

Around 1883.   Vol. 1—No. 4 & 5 was February & March 1883. The Apollo. [9]

> Supposedly a musical monthly, it was called a journal of music, literature and art edited by T. D. Tooker, A.M.   Price $1. per year, single copy 10c.   The double number 4 & 5 states the aims of the new Whipple Music Co., its publisher—to publish in this journal copyright music for pianoforte in combination with cornet, violin, or voice, and the articles were to be prepared with special reference to usefulness for bands, orchestras, musical societies, teachers and scholars.

January 1880-1891.   The Musical Herald.   Vol. 1-13.   Vol. 14 to November 1898 published in Chicago.   The Musical Herald starting with Vol. 10 entitled Boston Musical Herald.   Beginning with Vol. 14 entitled The Musical Herald of the United States.

> A monthly music review which "appeals to the public purely on its merits as an educational journal."   The first editors were William Apthorp, Louis C. Elson, Luther L. Holden, Francis H. Jenks, S. Brenton Whitney, and managing editor Eben Tourjée.   This was published by the Musical Herald Company, Music Hall.   Price $1.50 per annum. In Chicago it was edited by George H. Wilson, but the publisher is not stated.   Price $1.00 per year, single copies 10 cents.   It contained articles on music, correspondence, criticism of new publications, reviews of concerts, etc., advertising and some vocal and pianoforte music.

January (?) 1887-?.   Trifet's Monthly Galaxy of Music.

> "A magazine of vocal and instrumental music for the masses" copyrighted and published by F. Trifet, 408 Washington St., Boston.

---

[9] This journal is not listed in the *Union List of Serials* so exact beginning and closing dates and numbers of issues are not obtainable.

It cost $1.00 per year, "one month, one dime" and was sold by news-dealers in the United States and Canada. It contained vocal music such as *I Stood on the Bridge at Midnight,* and pianoforte music and advertising, but no articles. Judging by press comments in the magazine it had a wide distribution.

Vol. I No. 1, September 1, 1887—February and March 1899. Gatcomb's Banjo and Guitar Gazette. In November 1887 (Vol. 1 No. 2) The Banjo Herald edited and owned by W. C. Bryant of Brockton was consolidated with it and owned by Mr. Gatcomb. By September 1894 (Vol. VIII No. 1) called Gatcomb's Musical Gazette.

This was an interesting and inspiring 9¼ x 12 eight page magazine intended for banjo, mandolin and guitar players, published by L. B. Gatcomb & Co., originally a bimonthly, single copies 10c, fifty cents a year. Edited from September 1887 to July-August 1889 by B. E. Shattuck, then by L. H. Galencia, guitarist and business manager of the Boston Ideal Banjo, Mandolin and Guitar Club. It contained about three pages of music. Under the head "Banjo Pickings" were interesting items concerning prominent teachers and players of the day.

By 1894 it was monthly with a $1. per year subscription price. It was then edited by E. C. Burbank and contained 6 pages of music. The September 1894 issue stated among other items that "Walter Jacobs, as guitar soloist, and well known performer on mandolin, guitar and banjo is with the Thurston Concert Co. of Boston for the coming season."

In 1899 the Gazette in a new yellow cover had again become 50c a year, foreign subscription 62c.

1894-February 1924. Cadenza.

Published by the firm of Partee in the interest of mandolin, guitar and banjo playing. It was taken over in 1908 by Walter Jacobs, Inc. and published by this firm until 1924. It contained articles of interest to individual players and fretted instrument organizations, and musical numbers, the majority of which were original, but some were arrangements of standard works. Price 10c a copy early, but 15c at discontinuance.

February 1901-1904. The Musical World, consolidated in February 1904 with The Musician.

Philip Hale, Editor in Chief, Henry T. Finck, Louis C. Elson and others were the editors. [10] This was published monthly for the Musical World Publishing Company by the J. B. Millet Company except

---

[10] "Philip Hale and Louis C. Elson were the musical critics of this era most noted for fair but severe comments." Statement of William B. Goodwin, organ builder.

the music. This was published by A. P. Schmidt and consisted of a dozen or more pages of their copyrighted numbers, mostly original.

It was a high grade magazine carrying general articles about music, biographical notes about composers and artists, and full-page illustrations of them. Special features were "The World of Music," which contained reviews, obituaries, etc.; "Notes and Queries" about the history and esthetics of music; and a "Record of Current Events," and advertisements of musicians. Price $1. per year.

About 1905-1930. Crescendo.

A publication for teachers of stringed instruments. Edited and published by H. F. Odell Company until 1925 when it was taken over by The Vega Company and carried on until 1930.

January 1910 to date. Jacobs' Orchestra Monthly.

Jacobs' Orchestra Monthly was founded as a general orchestra magazine for amateurs and professionals, and the band monthly as a general band magazine.

1916 to date. Jacobs' Band Monthly.

Under the leadership, first of Myron Freese and then of C. V. Buttleman, they were the first magazines to support unreservedly the school band and orchestra movement. [11] The latter editor was a local and national aid to this movement and one of the prime movers in organizing the New England Festival Association. [12] Each of these magazines had gradually become "An Educational Magazine for School and Community Musicians," at the price of $1. the year. They contain instructional articles of historical value, recreational articles about music, articles to aid school music supervisors, and "The Students Round Table," a technical department of questions and answers conducted by leading teachers and soloists.

The music consists of original copyrights and copyrighted arrangements of standard works and gives the parts for the different band and orchestra instruments.

The editors of *Jacobs' Orchestra Monthly* to 1935 are [13] (dates inclusive)

Managing Editor
  Walter Jacobs Jan. 1910-Feb. 1924
  C. V. Buttleman March 1924-June 1930
  Arthur C. Morse July 1930 to present

Associate Editor
  Erastus Osgood Jan.-March 1910
  Willard E. Ingalls April-Oct. 1910
  Arthur C. Morse Jan. to June 1928
  Myron Freese Jan.-June 1929

[11] Statement of Walter Jacobs.
[12] Statement of Arthur C. Morse.
[12] Information supplied by Arthur C. Morse.

Literary Editor
Myron Freese Nov. 1910-June 1929
Editor
C. V. Buttleman Jan.-July 1918
Norman Leigh (name of Arthur C. Morse as a composer) July
1929 to June 1930
The editorial tenures of *Jacobs' Band Monthly* are synchronous with
the *Orchestra Monthly*.

January 1917-July 1930. Melody, originally The Tuneful Yankee.
Founded as *The Tuneful Yankee,* the name was changed to *Melody*
January 1918. It was published by Walter Jacobs, Inc., for motion
picture organists and pianists. The editors of this were: [14]
Editors
Munroe H. Rosenfeld, Founding to Dec. 1917
Lloyd Loar Feb. 1925-Dec. 1927
Norman Leigh Jan. 1928 to end
Managing Editor
C. V. Buttleman Jan. to July 1918 and March 1924 to June 1930.

This magazine contained articles of general interest to its public,
news and technical articles on interpretative scoring and playing for
motion pictures. The music consisted of practically all copyright
compositions by Americans. Original price $1. per year, 10c a copy.
Discontinuance price $2. per year, 25c a copy.

2. HOUSE ORGANS

1898. Music Review.
For this magazine of the Oliver Ditson Company, Inc. see page 81.

About 1914-1922. Scherzo.
This was a medium for dealers, featuring new publications of the
White-Smith Music Publishing Company.

September 1928. Vol. I No. 1 to date. The Birchard Broadsheet
News of School Music.
This publication of C. C. Birchard & Company is "A Journal for
Supervisors, Published to Record the Progress of Birchard Music
in the Schools." [15]

[14] Information supplied by Arthur C. Morse.
[15] Subheading of this house organ.

Part II.   Music Engraving and Printing

A.   Methods

1.   Early Engraving and Printing

The notes of the first music printed in the United States were cut on wood as we have seen, [1] and the printing was done directly from the wood on the paper.

Music engraving in Europe dates as far back as 1700 and the music plates of that period were made of copper.   So the plates engraved by Paul Revere for Josiah Flagg's book, *Collections of Best Psalm Tunes,* in 1764 were made of copper.   He also engraved the music and words of *The New-England Psalm-Singer: or, American Chorister* published in 1770.   He taught himself to engrave on copper.   Another early engraver was Thomas Johnston who did this from 1746 until his death in 1767.   He "engraved music on copper and printed the tunes then in most frequent use in the form and size of the psalm book to be bound up with it.   In 1755, he engraved psalm tunes with rules to sing them for the Brattle Street Church revision of the Psalms of David. . . These were sold separately . . . and may be found with any Psalm Book of that period." [2]   He was a versatile person as he was also a japanner, heraldic painter, decorator of clocks and furniture, and a pioneer organ builder.

When music types of engraving tools were not available the printing was sometimes done by the use of special ink and paper and a process similar to the modern hectograph or mimeograph.

The proofs from the copper plates, the pewter plates used later, and from the modern block tin, a soft composition of lead, tin and some zinc backed with iron, were pulled with either green or black ink.   The latter requires more time and is more expensive as the engraving must be filled in with softened beeswax which holds the ink for printing.   The proofs were printed on a copper plate hand press.   This method of printing directly on the sheets

---

[1] See p. 3.
[2] Williams, Cornelia B. compiler. *Ancestry of Lawrence Williams,* Part II, pp. 178-9.

from the plates was generally used until the invention of the lithographic process by Aloysius Senefelder in 1796, and for small editions until not long ago.

In 1753 Christopher Sower of Germantown, Pennsylvania, printed what was probably the first book in the United States to be printed by the typographic method from music type. In 1770 Edes and Gill of Boston printed *The New England Psalm-Singer* by this method.

The early sacred sheet music may have been printed from either engraved plates or music type, for William M'Alpine on page 406 of *The Boston Chronicle* of October 17, 1788, advertised as follows:

"William M'Alpine

Informs his customers and others that, being obliged to raise a sum of money in a few months—He intends to dispose of his stock under the common wholesale price if applied for soon. Most of the BOOKS are of his printing and binding, and will be warranted good.

Among which are

Watts Psalms and Hymns, bound as one volume or separately, with or without tunes; New England Psalms, with or without tunes. . . "

Music publications both engraved and typographical were comparatively rare in America until the beginning of the nineteenth century.

2. PRESENT MUSIC ENGRAVING AND PRINTING

The hardened steel die stamps used in modern engraving for music notation and text letters are generally imported from Germany and are much better cut than formerly. [3] Special hammers and iron plates are used to punch these stamps.

Engraving is done by hand with the aid of cutters for the staff lines, slurs, leger lines, balkens, bar lines, etc., and steel stamps to imprint the clefs, accidentals, rests, notes and other music notations, and text letters on the composition plates. T squares and dividers are used in spacing the alignment of bar lines and rests according to their values. The chippers and scrapers made of softer steel

[3] Statement of Oscar C. Henning of M. O. Henning & Son.

are employed to finish off the engraved plates. The latter are made today of block tin—a composition of lead, tin, and some zinc—which is softer and permits easier working than the earlier copper or pewter plates.

Up to about 20 years ago, or before the offset press was invented, most of the music printing was done from stone by the lithographic process on what are termed "flat-bed" presses. The majority of these were manufactured by R. Hoe & Co. The method is to pull an impression of the work on the engraved plate on a sheet of transfer paper, which is imported from China and so called a rice paper. This transfer is then pressed upon the lithographic stone. These stones are imported from Solenhofen, Bavaria, a province in Germany. The impression on the stone is then rolled up with ink and powdered rosin is spread over it. Then it is etched with an acid in order to hold it on the stone. The printing is done directly from the stone in the press. After the edition is run off, the work is polished off the stone with sand and water, and the stones are used over again, until they are worn too thin for use, when occasionally they are backed-up with slate for their preservation. The plates are kept for future transfers as they are so soft that they would quickly be destroyed by printing from the plates.

Present printing, however, is now largely done by photolithography, or from zinc, on an offset press, which is a much faster method of printing. The copy of music, either the original manuscript copy or a sharp pulloff from the engraved plate, is photographed, a negative is made, and then printed on a sensitized or a zinc plate. The plate is then etched and placed in the rotary offset, and the edition is run directly from the plate, which is freshly inked for each sheet printed. The offset process means that the work is offset from the zinc to the rubber blanket, and the rubber blanket coming in contact with the paper prints the work.

Engraved music, instead of music set in type, is now largely used for making line plates for text books. This process consists of taking from the engraved plate a black and white proof from which a photo line plate is made. An electro is then made for printing from type presses.

Engraved plates, lithographic stones, zinc press plates, and electrotype plates can be kept as long as desired, for future editions, but where the camera is employed, the films are all that it is necessary to retain.

3.   PRESENT MUSIC TYPOGRAPHY

A font of music type consists of about four hundred different characters.   So it takes a skilled worker to combine the type representing clefs, lines, note heads and stems, etc. to form a correct representation.

The compositor first estimates the amount of music which will go into one line and the number of lines to a page.   He then sets five lines for the staff, places the various characters for the music notation, and adds the words like ordinary reading matter except that they are spaced for each syllable to come beneath the note to which it is to be sung.

When all the type is set and the spaces are filled in with blank "quads," it is "locked up" in an iron frame or "chase" for a page of music.   A rough print or proof is pulled and any necessary corrections are made.

The first improvement after printing directly from type was the art of stereotyping, invented about 1725, not generally used until 1810, and first introduced into America about 1813. [4]   In this a metal composition, largely lead, is poured into the mould or impression made in the papier-maché and gives an exact counterpart of the type.   This gave a great impetus to music book printing of all kinds because it saved the expense of resetting a book for a later edition and it was no longer necessary to keep the type standing or wear it out.

Electrotyping, introduced about 1840, has now superseded stereotyping.   Through electrolysis a wax mould of the type is coated with copper.   When this "shell" is sufficiently thick it is removed, backed up with type metal for thickness and strength, beaten to correct any unevenness on the face and shaved to standard thickness.

The typographic method permits the use of many different sizes of characters and styles of text type, and is useful where there is much printing interspersed with music as in text books.   The printing is done on ordinary presses.

[4] F. H. Gilson Company. *Music Book Printing* p. 6.

B. Engravers

1. A FAMILY OF EARLIER ENGRAVERS

In the nineteenth and early twentieth centuries the Schlimper family was noted in Boston for fine work in music engraving. [1] The first of them to do engraving was Frederick W., listed in 1870 at 5 Boylston Place, and from around 1885 till his death before 1900 at Belle Ave., West Roxbury. He was a flute player, taught flute many years at the New England Conservatory of Music, and an engraver. He did much engraving for the firm of Carl Prüfer. His son, Charles F. W., was listed as a music engraver at 5 Boylston Place in 1878 and 1879, but went into manufacturing from then till about 1900 when, at 57 Belle Ave., he again took up music engraving until his death in 1919. His brother Henry was in various types of work till about 1885 when he took up music engraving for firms like Oliver Ditson until his death before 1915.

2. PRESENT DAY ENGRAVING FIRMS

WHITE-SMITH MUSIC PUBLISHING COMPANY

The White-Smith Music Publishing Company has an engraving department with a complete equipment of music dies for any class of work.

M. O. HENNING & SON

The founder, M. O. Henning, served his time learning the engraving trade in Leipzig, Germany, with Breitkopf and Härtel. He came to the United States in August 1880. He finally secured work in one of the few music engraving shops in New York City. First he worked for Max Houschkel, then for Christian Huber. Both these shops employed German engravers and had but three of them including Mr. Henning.

In 1882 Mr. Henning established his own business in Dedham, Massachusetts, starting with about four or five men. He retired

[1] Statements of John C. Miller, formerly of Oliver Ditson Company, Inc. and A. J. Oettinger.

about 1930 from active participation in the business, but still keeps his interest in the firm which is carried on by the family.

The first publishers for whom Mr. Henning did engraving were the Boston firms Jean White, W. H. Cundy and J. B. Millet Company. The firm now engraves for Boston and New York publishers, and has also done the engraving for some important music volumes for the University of Michigan.

The works engraved by this firm are vocal and instrumental, classic and the better type of modern music. Illustrations of the kind of works engraved by them are as follows:

Oliver Ditson Company, Inc.
> *The Musicians Library.*
> *The Music Students Piano Course.*
> *The Philharmonic Orchestra Series* scores and parts.
> *The Analytic Symphony Series.*

C. C. Birchard & Company
> "Laurel Song Books."
> *The Church-Dykema Modern Orchestra Training Series.*

E. C. Schirmer Music Company
> "Concord Series of Books" and octavo music.
> "Commonwealth Library of Music."

B. F. Wood Music Company
> "Edition Wood" of pianoforte music and studies.

Ginn & Company
> *Assembly Songs and Choruses.*
> *Home Edition* Volume II.

Silver, Burdett & Company
> *Symphony Series of Programs for School and Community Orchestras,* the orchestral scores and parts.
> School and college textbooks.

Juilliard Music Foundation
> Orchestral Scores and Parts of compositions by American composers.

Oxford University Press
> "Oxford University Piano Course."

Simon and Schuster, Inc.
> Songs and pianoforte transcriptions by Gershwin.

Orchestral Works of American Composers
    Ernest Bloch—*Concerto Grosso.*
                  America.
    Frederick Converse—Some orchestral works.
    Henry Hadley—Some orchestral works.
    Edgar Stillman Kelley—*Pilgrim's Progress.*
    Charles Martin Loeffler—*Evocation.*
    Daniel Gregory Mason—*Chanticleer.*
                  *Three Pieces for Flute, Harp and String
                  Quartette*, published by the Society for
                  the Publication of American Music.

MANICKE AND DELLMUTH

This firm was established at Dedham, Massachusetts, in 1887 by Ernst Manicke and William Dellmuth. Mr. Manicke died in 1918 and the business is still carried on under the same name by William Dellmuth at 252 Bussey St.

They have engraved for publishers in Cincinnati and New York, but mostly for Boston firms. Of recent years the music engraved has been classical or better class modern compositions.

Among the works engraved by this firm are publications of The Arthur P. Schmidt Co. such as many of the important compositions by the "Boston group of composers"—Arthur Foote, George W. Chadwick, John K. Paine, Mrs. H. H. A. Beach, and also works of Charles Dennée, Mrs. M. H. Gulesian and Carl and Reinhold Faelten.

C. Music Printers

1. SOME NINETEENTH CENTURY MUSIC PRINTERS

A partial list of music printers of the latter half of the nineteenth century follows:

KIDDER & WRIGHT'S
Music
Stereotyping & Printing
Establishment
No. 32 Congress St., Boston

They advertised that they were prepared to execute orders for stereotyping or printing music in any style desired by publishers, as they had "Music Types of SIX different PATTERNS, and FIVE SIZES, . . . which no establishment can present." [1] They also did book and job printing and were the printers and proprietors of the *Boston Musical Gazette*. Their advertisement gave six samples of music notes, etc.

W. H. OAKES, 383 Washington St., 1840-50
This firm also did some publishing.

ANDREW B. KIDDER possibly earlier a partner in Kidder & Wright
7 Cornhill in 1850
23 Water St. in 1870
Changed to A. B. Kidder & Son and located at 22 Milk St. in 1880.

EDWARD L. BALCH
21 School St. around 1853
34 School St. around 1856 till he moved to 14 Kilby St. in 1868

He printed the first twelve volumes of *Dwight's Journal of Music,* then Oliver Ditson & Co. took over the publishing from John S. Dwight with the April 1868 issue. He also printed *Boston Musical Times* when it was published by Russell & Tolman and Henry Tolman through the August 1, 1868 number.

---

[1] *Boston Musical Gazette,* September 5, 1838, page 80.

J. A. Cummings & Co.

> 13 School St. started in 1867
> 15 School St. 1868 till about 1875
> While at this address they printed "Cundy's Five Cent Series of Popular Music." They advertised themselves as "Steam job printers."
> 248 Washington St. in 1875
> 252 Washington St. in 1895
> By this date they advertised themselves as printers, publishers and electrotypers and the name had been changed to J. A. Cummings Printing Co.
> 172 Oliver St. in 1905 till the name disappeared from the directory in 1909.

Giles & Gould

> This started as John F. Giles at 37½ Cornhill about 1869. In 1870 J. Frank Giles advertised himself as "Electrotyper & Stereotyper." [2] Sometime in 1870 the firm became Giles & Gould at 89 Washington St.
> This firm printed *The Organist's Quarterly Journal and Review.* Both men had a reputation for doing good work.
> About 1874 they moved to 3 Court Ave. By 1875 they had apparently separated, for J. F. Giles was listed alone that year at their last address.
> Later addresses were:

J. Frank Giles

> 2 Jackson Place in 1880
> 26 Hawley St. in 1890. His name disappeared from the directory by 1900.

Geo. Gould was at 221 Washington St. in 1875 and 18 Post Office Square in 1880. His name disappeared from the the directory by 1890.

Lenfest & Anderson

> 21 School St. in 1870. Anderson apparently left or died as T. H. Lenfest's name appeared alone at the same address in 1880.

Samuel W. Blair, 298 Washington St. about 1890

> This firm advertised in the business directory [3] "Publisher, printer and engraver, sheet music and music books—Banjo Music a specialty."

[2] *The Folio* Vol. 2 No. 3 March 1870 p. 67.
[3] *Boston Directory* 1890 Advertising Dept. p. 1945.

2. PRESENT DAY MUSIC PRINTERS

It may be interesting to compare conditions in the music printing industry and the relative importance of Massachusetts firms in this industry both before and after the onset of the depression. The United States Census of Manufactures gives the total number of establishments for the whole country as 119 in 1927 and 103 in 1931. The total value of the product (sheet music and music books combined) was $17,146,715. in 1927 and $12,203,657. in 1931, a decrease of 28.8 per cent. In 1927 there were four states doing a volume of business of over one million dollars each, namely New York, the largest, Massachusetts next, Illinois and Pennsylvania. In 1931 there were only three doing that volume of business—New York first with $7,677,757., Massachusetts second with $1,112,415. and Illinois third with $1,008,181.

WHITE-SMITH MUSIC PUBLISHING COMPANY

This firm started engraving, printing and binding a few years after its founding in 1867.

It was one of the first firms to use the lithographic process in its printing which is largely sheet music. The founder of the company also experimented some forty to fifty years ago with the photographic process but gave it up as the method was not then perfected.

Besides its own publications this company has done printing of all types of music for large and small publishers located all over the United States, and individuals as far away as Cuba, Hawaii, South America and South Africa. English and Spanish guitar and mandolin instruction books have been the principal works printed for the Spanish-speaking countries, and English and French instruction books for Canada. It also helped to establish a music printing plant in Canada.

JOHN WORLEY COMPANY

This firm originated in Philadelphia about sixty years ago under the name of the Zabel-Worley Company. John Worley, a partner in this concern, withdrew from the Zabel Brothers, who then represented the Zabel interests, came to Boston in 1904 and established an up-to-date music printing and binding establishment. When Mr. Worley died in 1920, Wm. T. Small, who had been with The B. F. Wood Music Company, took over the Worley interests and has been carrying them on ever since at the present address of 166 Terrace St., Roxbury, Massachusetts.

This concern has a small engraving and a complete bookbinding department.

The John Worley Company uses all methods of music printing, principally lithographic, also photo-lithographic (from zinc), and some typographic or from the electrotype plates. It was one of the first concerns in the country to use photo-lithography in the printing of music, and executes, at the present time, a considerable amount of work by this process. It also photographs and prints from manuscript and reproduces books of every kind, and makes titles by every process in one or more colors.

The company prints all forms of vocal and instrumental music, mostly for Boston publishers, but also has customers throughout the country and even in Hawaii and Australia. Many of the standard editions are printed by the Worley Company, notably the works of the Ditson catalog, The B. F. Wood Music Co., E. C. Schirmer Music Co., C. C. Birchard & Co., Arthur P. Schmidt Co., and Walter Jacobs, Inc.

STANHOPE PRESS (F. H. GILSON COMPANY)

This company was established in 1878 by F. H. Gilson and is now carried on by his son, A. P. Gilson. It is one of the oldest of the six to eight concerns in the United States using the typographic method. This firm was located first at 75 Milk St. By 1890 it was at 15 Stanhope St. and in 1900 at 54-60 Stanhope St. It now shares the White-Smith Music Publishing Company building at 40-44 Winchester St.

This firm specializes in music book printing and has printed for publishers located all over the United States.

It has made improvements in the designs of various music type characters, such as the bars on eighth note stems, for a better balanced and more harmonious page. Any regular foundry type faces desired are used for the words.

More high grade hymn books have been printed by this company than by any other music printer in the country. [4] These include hymn books for many different denominations.

This firm has also printed many school music books as it makes a specialty of school and college textbooks.

[4] Statement of A. P. Gilson.

Part III. Instrument Making

A. Pianoforte Makers

1. Importance in the Pianoforte Industry of Massachusetts Manufacturers as Shown by United States Census Figures of 1860, 1927 and 1931

The first census giving separate figures for musical instrument manufacturing was in 1860. This showed 223 establishments in the United States with a total invested capital of $4,431,900. Of these, 110 with an invested capital of $3,644,250 produced annually pianofortes worth $5,260,907. Massachusetts had 22 or one-fifth of the pianoforte establishments, with a capital of $923,000. These produced instruments worth $1,583,500 or 30 per cent of the annual total of pianofortes.

The Biennial Census of Manufactures for 1927 shows the conditions in the pianoforte manufacturing industry in normal times. The latest census available, that of 1931, shows the situation in one of the industries hit hard by the depression. The figures from these censuses for the entire country and individually for the three largest pianoforte producing states are compared in the following table.

TABLE NO. 1

NUMBER OF ESTABLISHMENTS MANUFACTURING ALL STYLES OF PIANOFORTES AND TOTAL ANNUAL VALUE PRODUCED IN 1931 AS COMPARED WITH 1927

Regions Compared	Number of Establishments		Total Annual Value Produced		% of Decrease
	1931	1927	1931	1927	
United States	50	124	$15,293,048	$75,490,661	79.7
New York	19	53	5,312,235	28,431,507	81.3
Illinois	13	22	4,456,059	17,668,781	74.8
Massachusetts ...	5	10	1,502,812	6,614,451	77.3

Massachusetts has been important in the manufacture of pianofortes from early times to the present. In 1860 it produced
30 per cent of the annual total. By 1927 its proportion of the
total product had dropped to 8.8 per cent, but in 1931 it had slightly
increased to 9.8 per cent of the entire volume.

Massachusetts was the third state in production of grands and
the sixth largest producer of uprights in both years. The number
and value of instruments manufactured in the entire country and
in Massachusetts alone is shown in table No. 2 which follows.

TABLE NO. 2

Type of Instruments	United States			Massachusetts		
	1931	1927	% of De-crease	1931	1927	% of De-crease
Number of Instruments [1]						
Uprights	20,167	150,407	86.6	790	4940	84.0
Grands	31,203	61,759	49.4	3162	7689	58.9
Value Produced [1]						
Uprights	$2,888,316	$33,709,334	91.4	$130,851	$1,356,113	90.3
Grands	9,892,430	30,732,850	67.8	1,136,819	4,766,367	76.1

In 1927 the production of electric pianofortes was given separately only for Illinois, which made over $2,000,000 worth, and
New York. All other states made only 133 electrical instruments.
In 1931 the production of electric pianofortes was not given separately for any state.

From these sets of census figures certain facts appear. The
trend toward consolidation and large scale production is outstanding. In 1860 one hundred and ten establishments produced
pianofortes worth $5,260,907, while in 1931 only fifty, less than
half the number of factories, manufactured pianofortes worth
$15,293,048, an increase of 190.7 per cent. That year's product
probably represented only a fraction of what these same plants
would produce in normal times. It may be open to question whether
the present large scale production permits the quality of workmanship of the more custom built pianofortes of earlier times. How-

[1] Includes player and reproducing type of pianofortes.

ever, the need for sufficient capital and necessity of economizing in the overhead and purchase of materials for manufacture to help meet the inroads of the phonograph and the radio on pianoforte sales have been no inconsiderable factors in this result. Another interesting point is the change in the relative importance of grands as shown by the larger volume of grands manufactured in the entire country and particularly in Massachusetts between 1927 and 1931 in comparison with the number of uprights. This was undoubtedly due to the increasing popularity of baby grands which constituted in 1931 the largest number of pianofortes made.

2. European Predecessors

What has been accomplished can be appreciated better if we realize the status of the pianoforte in England, France and Germany, the centres of pianoforte making in the early nineteenth century.

Square pianofortes were first made in England by some Germans, Johann Zumpe and his fellows, who arrived there in 1760.

The Dutchman, Americus Backers, in 1772 made important improvements in the action substituting direct lever action for Cristofori's intermediary under-hammer. His invention is known as "English action." There were also three strings to each note. [1]

In 1780 John Broadwood remodeled Zumpe's action, moved the wrest plank to the back of the case opposite the keyboard, brought the compass to five octaves—F to F, substituted pedals for hand controlled levers to lift the dampers, and used crankshaped under-dampers in place of the "mopstick" arrangement. This improved and reconstructed instrument was patented in 1783. By 1794 the compass had been extended to six octaves—C to C. [2]

In 1786 John Geib, a craftsman of Longman and Broderip, incorporated the "hopper" into the action.

The term "grand" was first used for a pianoforte in 1777, and the first entry of a grand on Broadwood's books was in 1781.

Uprights in the last of the decade 1770-80 were constructed to resemble a bookcase and were called cabinet pianos. They were horizontal instruments turned up on the broad end, upon a stand. Not until 1800 was the idea of extending the strings below the level of the keyboard, with the bottom of the instrument upon the floor, put into practical effect by John Isaac Hawkins of Philadelphia, who patented his upright in America, and in England in his father's name. [3] The strings were perpendicular, had the same length as in a grand of that day, and had three in unison fixed to the same screw. It had "a complete iron frame within which the belly is suspended independent of the case; resistance to the drawing power of the strings is also met by metal rods at the back of the case; there is an upper bridge of metal and a system of tuning by mechan-

---

[1] James, Philip. *Early Keyboard Instruments* p. 54.
[2] *Ibid* p. 55.
[3] Hipkins, A. J. *A Description and History of the Pianoforte* p. 111.

ical screws; an equal length of string throughout; a hopper action anticipating Wornum's and metal supports for it. So many new ideas were surely never grouped before in one musical instrument. It is remarkable as containing the original essays for many improvements since made use of or re-invented. . . . It will now be seen why I give the rare distinction of originality in invention to Hawkins." [3] The instrument stood about five and a half feet high, and the frame containing the keyboard was pivoted in the manner of the falling front of a bureau to economize space. [4]

Not until 1820 was the great increase of tension and the use of thicker and heavier strings, made possible by this change, given real recognition. It is interesting to note that Mr. Stodard, the English employer of William Allen and James Thom who patented a metal frame for grand pianos, bought their patent and refused to enforce observance in order not to hinder further improvements.

In France Sebastien Erard made the first French square piano in 1777, and his first grand in 1796. One of the most important inventions which has made possible the modern pianoforte was an action which contained the germ of the double escapement. This "provided for a quick repetition of the stroke by releasing the key only a very short distance." [5] Though this improvement was made in 1808, it was not patented until 1821 by Erard's nephew, Pierre.

There was also a South German action, improved in Vienna, which was called the German or Viennese action. "This differed from the English action in that the axis of the hammer was not fixed but rose with the key lever at the end of which was a short strip of wood having a slot wherein the hammer butt was centered." [4]

These were the instruments which served as models for our early American makers. The importance of American achievements in this kind of instrument making is well illustrated by the fact that the best American pianofortes "serve as ideals for followers of Cristofori's art in every country of the globe. And the principal improvements which have placed the piano of today beyond comparison with its progenitors of half a century ago have emanated from the brain of our own instrument makers." [6]

[4] James, Philip. *Early Keyboard Instruments* p. 57 footnote 3.
[5] *Ibid* pp. 56 & 57.
[6] *American History and Encyclopedia of Music* p. 313.

3. Beginnings of the Pianoforte Industry in the United States

A few spinets were made in this country before the pianoforte. *The Boston Gazette* of September 18, 1769, stated "That a few days since was shipped for Newport a very curious spinnet being the first [1] ever made in America, the performance of the ingenious Mr. John Harris of Boston (son of the late Mr. Joseph Harris of London, Harpsichord and Spinnet Maker)." [2] His advertisement in *The Boston Chronicle,* November 14, 1788, showed him a newcomer then.

Another maker of spinets was Samuel Blyth of Salem. A fine specimen made by him in 1789 is described and pictured in *Early Keyboard Instruments* by Philip James. [3]

It has been thought by many that Benjamin Crehore of Milton built the first pianoforte in this country. Daniel Spillane stated, however, that John Behrent produced the first pianoforte on this continent in Philadelphia in 1775. Benjamin Crehore he credited with having exhibited in 1792 a harpsichord with improvements suggested by the pianoforte. From this date forward he became known as a repairer of these instruments mechanically. He "was a very ingenious man, accounted one of the best mechanics of the time, and was always consulted about anything difficult in that line." Thomas Appleton for whom Benjamin Crehore worked later, was told by Isaac Crehore, an aged relative of Benjamin, that the latter in making his first pianoforte (sometime before 1800) copied an English instrument, probably a Broadwood. The pianofortes imported from England had short sounding-boards. Benjamin Crehore introduced into his the long sounding-board, such as was used in 1887 when Mr. Appleton wrote his statement about "The Early Boston Piano Makers," and made only about ten to twelve a year. One of his pianofortes, a square, is on exhibition in the Music Division of the Boston Public Library and another in the Essex Institute,

---

[1] Daniel Spillane states in his history that it is proven that the first spinets made in the colonies were the product of Gustavus Hesselius of Philadelphia 1742.

[2] James, Philip. *Early Keyboard Instruments* p. 111.

[3] *Ibid* p. 112 and Plate XXXII.

Salem, Massachusetts. "His shop was the training school of the brothers Lewis and Alpheus Babcock [of Milton] who served their apprenticeship there." [4] He also made some uprights but they failed to stay in tune. As Peter von Hagen Jr. was in actual partnership with Crehore from 1801-07 Mr. Spillane thinks that the former was connected with the production of Crehore's first pianoforte. At least he tuned the pianofortes. These were sold first in a warehouse on Common St. and after 1805 on Essex St. The business failed because of the competition of Mallet & Shaw.

Other instrument makers prominent in the early nineteenth century were William and Adam Bent. "A press notice of 1799 speaks of William Bent as an expert mechanic whose grand piano attracted much attention." [5] This business apparently started in 1798 as Bent & Green [6] at 90 Newbury St. From 1800 to 1807 William and Adam Bent were musical instrument makers at 26 Orange St. Then William Bent alone made pianofortes first at 24 Orange St. and then at 49 Newbury St. about 1809. When Mr. Appleton visited the Bents' shop in 1803 he found them finishing off two pianoforte cases, veneered with bird's-eye maple, which was about that time first introduced as an ornamental wood. He took particular notice of this because he was then an apprentice in cabinet-making. According to Mr. Appleton, "William Bent invented the first leather splitting machine, got a patent on it, . . . and went to Philadelphia, where he carried on a leather business. Adam also retired from business and became a land speculator." [7]

When William Bent moved to Philadelphia, Lewis Babcock and his younger brother Alpheus had a shop on Winter St. In 1810 [7] they joined with Thomas Appleton, then a pipe organ manufacturer, and the Hayts brothers, Charles and Elna, importers of music and musical instruments, in putting up a large building on Milk Street, on the site of the birthplace of Benjamin Franklin, for the manufacture of pianofortes and organs under the name of Hayts, Babcock & Appleton. Crehore, then rather an old man, worked for them for a time. "James Cogwell, at that time accounted the best Cabinet-maker in Boston, was persuaded by Mr. Babcock to give up that business and take charge of making the cases for the instru-

---

[4] *American History and Encyclopedia of Music* p. 317.
[5] *Ibid* p. 318.
[6] See section on Band, Orchestral, Fretted and Miscellaneous Instruments p. 195.
[7] *American Musician.* "The Early Boston Piano Makers," July 2, 1887, Mr. Appleton's Statement.

ments. John Osborn was his apprentice and, after learning the cabinet business, then learned in our factory the interior work of Pianos and afterwards set up for himself in Pantheon Hall . . . probably about 1814." [8] In 1812 the firm had troubles arising from the war and the Hayts went to Buffalo. [8] Captain John Mackay of Weston took their place supplying the capital. Lewis Babcock died in January 1814. When the firm failed in the panic of 1819 the shop on Milk Street was sold to settle the affairs of the firm and the partners all separated.

Alpheus was in business again in 1821 at 11 Marlboro St., and in 1822 at Parkman's Market, Cambridge St., with Captain Mackay and the latter's brother, G. D. Mackay. Alpheus Babcock's iron plate was invented about this time and patented December 17, 1825. An instrument containing this invention was shown at the Fourth Annual Exhibition of the Franklin Institute in October 1827 and was referred to thus, "Especial mention is made of a horizontal pianoforte by A. Babcock of Boston, of an improved construction, the frame which supports the strings being of solid cast iron and strong enough to resist their enormous tension. This instrument was finished in the highest manner possible." [9] "In 1830 he took out a patent for 'cross-stringing pianofortes,' together with an iron ring intended for string hitching purposes, which no doubt gave rise to the expression 'Babcock's iron ring.' " John Mackay while connected with Babcock took out a patent August 14, 1828 for a new method of covering (and boring the shankholes of) hammer heads.

An excellent example of A. Babcock's fine work can be seen in a small square pianoforte of his now in the Denver Art Museum, City and County Building, Denver, Colo., still in playable condition. Its name plate reads—"A. Babcock for G. D. Mackay, Boston, Mass." This instrument has an action more akin to that in present use than that contained in some pianofortes of other later makers, and has a sweet tone. The beautiful case shows his fine craftsmanship as a woodworker. One of his instruments made for G. D. Mackay was owned and used by Lowell Mason for fifty years, from

---

[8] *American Musician.* "The Early Boston Piano Makers," July 2, 1887, Mr. Appleton's Statement.

[9] For a diagram and discussion of A. Babcock's iron plate compared with Conrad Meyer's unpatented iron plate see Daniel Spillane's *History of the American Pianoforte* pp. 120-4.

1820-1870, and another of these is now in the parlor of the House of the Seven Gables, Salem, Massachusetts. [10]

Babcock's pianofortes ranked very high as far back as 1822. In 1824 he won a prize at the First Mechanical Arts Exhibition of the Franklin Institute, Philadelphia, as follows—"Premium no. 47 to the maker of the best horizontal piano is adjudged to A. Babcock of Boston for specimen no. 327 which is a horizontal pianoforte made for J. Mackay, Boston. It has received the high approbation of the judges. Every part of the interior mechanism has the highest finish and its tone and touch are excellent. Strings of the lower octaves are covered with flattened wire. It entitles its maker to the silver medal having been considered the best of the four square pianofortes exhibited." [11] In 1825 he again won a silver medal at a similar exhibit. When A. Babcock went to Philadelphia in 1829 and joined J. G. Klemm, who had been an agent for Babcock pianofortes, Captain Mackay consulted Thomas Appleton about someone to take his place and Mr. Appleton recommended his joining Jonas Chickering. [12]

According to the *Columbia Sentinel,* Mr. Mallet had a repository on Devonshire Street in 1805 in which he had for sale an assortment of English and American pianofortes including those of Francis Shaw. The latter had been an expert pianoforte and musical instrument maker in London. He came from there via New York to Boston about 1804. "Shaw holds a significant place in the early Boston Records for he took out the first patent relative to an improvement in the pianoforte or to any musical instrument ever granted by the National Government to a resident of Massachusetts." [13]

John Osborn was one of the foremost pianoforte merchants of the country from 1815 to 1835. In 1815 he was at "back of 3 Newbury St." and immediately became noted for the superiority of his pianofortes, coming into general notice for his instruments in New York and Philadelphia in 1819. [14] In 1819 he moved to Orange Street where he had as apprentices or journeymen Jonas Chickering, Lemanuel and Timothy Gilbert, John Dwight, William

[10] For exact dates, names and addresses of the various affiliations of the Babcocks, Ebenezer Currier, Lemuel Gilbert (Daniel Spillane always speaks of him as Lemanuel), and Timothy Gilbert see Appendix I pp. 239-41.
[11] Spillane, Daniel. *History of the American Pianoforte* pp. 85 & 86.
[12] *American Musician.* "The Early Boston Piano Makers," Mr. Appleton's Statement.
[13] Spillane, Daniel. *History of the American Pianoforte* p. 54.
[14] *Ibid* p. 57.

Danforth, and Elijah Bullard. "Stray allusions to Osborn, about 1820-24, in occasional items in the Boston and New York papers, indicate that he was ranked as the very best piano-maker in the country." [14]   One of his square pianofortes with six legs and two drawers for music was in the exhibit held by Chickering & Sons in 1902. On business trips to Baltimore he had become acquainted with James Stewart, a Scotchman, who learned pianoforte making of the Harpers in Baltimore. In 1820 Mr. Osborn persuaded Mr. Stewart to enter into partnership with himself. Stewart was a pianoforte maker of ability with a brain fertile in improvements, among which was a better arrangement of the sounding board. The second patent issued to a Boston resident was given to him for this in 1822. [15]   He was probably the first manufacturer to export pianofortes out of the United States, for in 1817 from his Baltimore shop, 96 Hanover corner of Conway St., he had shipped to Havana and the West Indies. When Osborn and Stewart disagreed, both being quick-tempered men, James Stewart induced Jonas Chickering, whom he had met in Osborn's establishment, to become his partner in a shop on Tremont Street in 1823. This was the start of Chickering & Sons, whose presiding genius became the "Father" of the modern pianoforte.

Osborn was at 12 Orange St. in 1820-21, at 1 Boylston Square in 1823, later at 471 Washington St. where he remained until he moved to Albany in 1829 and died in New York in 1835.

John Dwight, who subsequently became a partner of Newhall, [16] applied for a patent in 1824, about sixteen months ahead of A. Babcock, for a "longitudinal iron bar," thus anticipating a minor feature of Babcock's iron plate.

Timothy and Lemanuel Gilbert began business separately. Lemanuel was out of business a while, but started again in 1839 on Washington Street. "In 1841 he [Lemanuel] was granted a patent which was a modification of the square English fly action.". . . No hammers or hoppers were used, the jack setting in the hammer-heel after the style of the square action [17] of the period of 1890. He patented a variety of improvements. The most significant was an upright action for which a patent was taken out as early as June 18, 1850. This had "a method of projecting the whole hammer

[14] Spillane, Daniel. *History of the American Pianoforte* p. 57.
[15] *Ibid* p. 85.
[16] See Appendix I p. 250.
[17] Spillane, Daniel. *History of the American Pianoforte* p. 90.

in close proximity to the strings—after the manner of the upright action soft-pedal" [17] of 1890. Some other ingenious principles were also included in this patent. Lemanuel became quite noted in his time among pianoforte makers as an expert, but his instruments were surpassed all along by those of his brother. [18] He went out of business in 1863 and died some time later.

About 1826 Timothy Gilbert went into partnership with Ebenezer R. Currier, who had also been apprenticed to John Osborn. He (Currier) had obtained a patent in 1831 for a pianoforte "with a shifting action like the grand for horizontal instruments, also placing the keyboard midway so as to give a compass of seven octaves, according to the stringing diagram and other models." [19] He also patented a down-striking grand action.

George Vose has in his possession a beautiful instrument over one hundred years old made by Currier & Co. It has a perfect harp scale, a half-iron plate, six octaves and one pedal. The case is finely finished crotch mahogany.

Some time about 1840 the firm Timothy Gilbert & Company became very important in the trade and had many agencies scattered over the country. In New York they had in 1848 a direct agency at 339 Broadway with Berry & Waters first and then Horace Waters as agent. Timothy Gilbert in 1841 patented ideas and inventions relative to uprights and squares, and outlined a modification of the English "flying action" (tape-check action), ideas afterward claimed by Wornum in England. [18]

"Timothy Gilbert anticipated the present upright action in use in the United States and bequeathed to the trade many very potent technical ideas in connection with the improvement and development of the upright." [20]

A great stir was caused by their Aeolian-pianos in 1847. [21] They were made after the designs of Obed Coleman whose patent of April 17, 1844 they had bought in 1846. The pianoforte part had a beautiful tone quality but it did not stay in tune with the organ section, whose free reeds remained in tune. They also took over several other patents for minor details between 1850 and 1860.

[18] Spillane, Daniel. *History of the American Pianoforte* p. 91.
[19] *Ibid* p. 96.
[20] *Ibid* p. 46.
[21] *Ibid* pp. 91 & 92.

T. Gilbert & Company went out of business nominally in 1868 but the name was used later.

It appears from the frequent forming and changing of partnerships in the early 1800's that a skilled mechanic who had been trained in some good shop or factory started out for himself alone or with another such mechanic and presently dissolved that partnership to form another.   Such makers were often spoken of as "seceders."   Small capital was required to start, but as businesses grew more funds became necessary and many changes of ownership were due to this lack.

What information about other former firms the writer has been able to gather from pianoforte manufacturers, dealers and tuners is given in Appendix I B.

Along with the growth of pianoforte manufacturing in Boston an occupation has developed which has been taught to the blind all over the country with great success, namely, pianoforte tuning. This movement was started at the Perkins Institute and Massachusetts School for the Blind, founded in 1832 by Dr. S. G. Howe, with Lowell Mason as the first teacher.   Mr. J. W. Smith was the teacher who instructed the blind to take a pianoforte apart, repair, put together and tune it.   For many years now graduates of this school have cared for the tuning and repairing of the pianofortes in Boston city schools. [22]

Aside from a few outstanding inventions like Erard's repetition action and Steinway and Sons' combination of the full metal plate and the overstrung scale, it is difficult to assign the improvements to any one manufacturer as the changes have been by gradual steps.   Many experiments were tried for one that was really successful.

Furthermore, competition in this line has always been so keen that as soon as one manufacturer made a real improvement, others bought one of his instruments, took it apart, studied it and copied the idea.   If the invention was patented, some way was generally found to produce the same effect by a construction sufficiently dissimilar to avoid infringement.   Improvements and inventions by American firms, whose source is generally acknowledged, are discussed under the respective manufacturers.

[22] Dwight, John S. *Memorial History of Boston.* Justin Winsor Editor p. 460.

4. Present Day Manufacturers

CHICKERING & SONS

History [1]

As "The Oldest in America. The Best in the World," for many years a slogan of this company, Chickering & Sons has a long and honorable history.

The founder of this company was Jonas Chickering, son of a blacksmith, born in Mason Village, now Greenville, New Hampshire, April 5, 1798. He grew up in New Ipswich, New Hampshire, where he spent three years learning the trade of cabinet-making with John Gould. His interest in the pianoforte was aroused when he was sent for to repair the only one in New Ipswich, belonging to Miss Mary Montgomery, daughter of General John Montgomery. This pianoforte once owned by Princess Amelia, daughter of King George III of England, had been made in London in 1782 by Christopher Ganer. It is now [1] in the New England Conservatory, to which it was bequeathed by a descendant of Miss Montgomery.

This experience led Jonas Chickering to come to Boston in 1818 and in 1819 to work for John Osborn, with whom he mastered the details of pianoforte construction. In the latter's place he met James Stewart, whose partner he became in Stewart & Chickering in 1823. Their two-room shop was on Tremont Street in a building next to King's Chapel. There the first Chickering was made. This square pianoforte, "Number One" (1823), though thin and without the resonance of the larger instruments, still retains its sweet and singing quality. It together with the first upright and first grand made by this firm have been given to Mr. Henry Ford for safekeeping in his Edison Institute Museum at Dearborn, Michigan.

They moved in 1824 to 20 Common St., where they remained until Mr. Stewart resigned in 1827 and returned to London to become associated with Messrs. Collard and Collard. Jonas Chickering, needing more capital for his growing business, formed

---

[1] Dates are taken from the letter written January 29, 1930, for the Massachusetts Tercentenary Celebration by Miss Margaret E. Connell, Historian of Chickering & Sons.

a partnership in 1830 with Captain John Mackay, a prosperous sea captain and a former partner of Alpheus Babcock.[2]   It was in this year that Mr. Chickering presented an elaborate upright pianoforte.

The firm then became Chickering & Mackay with a good-sized factory on Washington Street.   Captain Mackay made frequent voyages to South America, where he sold the sweet-toned six-octave pianofortes in different parts and returned with rosewood and mahogany for cases.   Even today, these six-octave pianofortes can still be found in Buenos Aires and other places in South America. It is said that this firm was supplying pianofortes, then ranking high in price and character,[3] to every available commercial point in the East, South, and as far West as civilization had advanced.   By its establishment of the first agencies known all through the parts of the country open to commerce, this company became the pioneer developer of the pianoforte trade of America.[3]

In 1841 Captain Mackay was lost at sea with his ship on what was intended to be his last trip.   Mr. Chickering then purchased Captain Mackay's interest in the business from his heirs and conducted it alone under the name "J. Chickering, Piano Maker," employing three hundred men and turning out thirteen hundred pianofortes yearly.

In 1848 Jonas Chickering's three sons were admitted into the firm as partners, and the name was changed to "Chickering & Sons."

The first World's Fair held in London in 1851 in the specially constructed Crystal Palace was the first time when American pianoforte manufacturers were represented in a foreign exhibition. Chickering & Sons had an exhibit superintended in person by Jonas and Charles Francis Chickering, who returned with many awards and the First Prize Medal.   Contacts were also established with influential people and prominent European artists.

A great misfortune befell the company when the factory and its entire contents, including beautiful paintings, autographed portraits and mementoes, given by great artists and prominent men to Jonas Chickering, were burned December 1, 1852, with a loss totaling more than one quarter million of dollars.

[2] See also page 107.
[3] Spillane, Daniel. *History of the American Pianoforte* p. 88.

Mr. Chickering at once purchased land in what was then called "The Neck," an undeveloped strip of land on the outskirts of the city leading to Roxbury, and began building a new factory. The premises comprised an entire square of about five acres situated on the westerly side of Tremont Street between Camden and North-hampton Streets. When completed in 1855 this was said to be the largest building in the United States under one roof with the sole exception of the Capitol in Washington, D. C. Dubbed "Chickering's Folly" at one time, it had a capacity for making five thousand pianofortes a year. The rough stock was taken in at the lower door in one wing, passed up that through the main building and down the other wing, and delivered in the warerooms finished. Thus almost literally forests entered at one end of the building and came out the other perfect pianofortes. Unfortunately, Jonas Chickering did not live to see it completed, as he died December 8, 1853.

The sons continued the business, Colonel Thomas E. Chickering having charge of the manufacturing aided by his younger brother, George H. Chickering. C. Francis Chickering, "who was one of the most accomplished scale draughtsmen of his time," [4] settled in New York City in charge of the wholesale department which outgrew two locations, first at Broadway and Reade Streets and then at 11 East 14th St. So Chickering Hall was built to provide suitable warerooms for demonstration and sale of the pianofortes, with offices connected and a large auditorium for recitals. This was located at Fifth Avenue and 18th St., and from its dedication in 1875 it became the musical centre of New York for twenty-five years. In 1901 the trend of business was away from its location, hence the hall was given up, and the wholesale and retail departments were moved to the Boston factory so that the entire business was under one roof.

New scales and other improvements were made from time to time by C. Francis Chickering, and the pianofortes were displayed at all exhibitions, both local and international, obtaining many first medals and awards which helped the company's prestige.

The business grew amazingly so that the most important cities in the United States had a representative selling Chickering pianofortes, "and many foreign countries had representatives regularly

[4] *American History and Encyclopedia of Music* p. 320.

sending in orders." [5]   Over 200,000 Chickering pianofortes had been built up to 1932. These consisted of squares, discontinued some years ago, uprights, grands, players with the pianola player reproducing mechanism and Ampico pianofortes. In the last ten years practically only grands and reproducing instruments have been made. The pianofortes have been shipped to all parts of the world from Finland to India.

One of the most signal awards showing the company's world-wide standing was made at the Exposition Universelle, Paris, France, in 1867. A "First Gold Medal" for excellence had been awarded the Chickering pianoforte by the four juries of six hundred men whose duty it was to make decisions about awards. The Emperor, Napoleon III, in conjunction with the "Superior Council," decided that in addition to the excellence of its instruments, the contribution of the company to the advancement of music called for further recognition. So he issued a "Decree" naming "Mr. Chickering of Boston, Manufacturer and Exhibitor of Pianos, Chevalier of the Legion of Honor," and personally conferred the decoration on Charles Francis Chickering.

This is the highest award ever made to any pianoforte manufacturer and is still in the possession of the company.

Incidentally, it may be of interest to note that Mr. Chickering took one of these pianofortes, which had been carefully chosen, as a gift to Liszt in Rome. After playing on it some time before Mr. Chickering and his friend, Mr. Poznanski, Liszt gave Mr. Chickering what he had never before given any pianoforte manufacturer, a testimonial letter setting forth his supreme satisfaction with the Chickering pianoforte. This instrument was Liszt's favorite in Weimar, and it, with another Chickering, is now preserved in the Imperial Conservatory at Budapest, Hungary, by the Government in the room in which the composer left them. [6]

In all, the company has received one hundred and thirty-one medals for its pianofortes shown at exhibitions in America and foreign countries. Those awarded at world fairs are as follows:

Great International Exposition, London, England, 1851.
Exposition Universelle, Paris, France, 1867.
Exposition International de Chile, Santiago, 1875.
International Exhibition, Philadelphia, Pennsylvania, 1876.

[5] Tercentenary Letter by Miss M. E. Connell p. 7.
[6] *Ibid* p. 6.

International Exhibition, Sydney, New South Wales, 1879.
Cork International Exhibition, Cork, Ireland, 1883.
Crystal Palace Exposition, London, England, 1884.
World's Fair, Chicago, Illinois, 1893.
Panama-Pacific Exposition, San Francisco, California, 1915.

A unique contribution of this company was a revival of the making of early keyboard stringed instruments and viols as an aid to providing the best in music. Arnold Dolmetsch, the greatest living authority on musical instruments and music of the 16th, 17th, and 18th centuries, was brought over for this purpose in 1906. This Swiss-French expert had a department in the factory at 791 Tremont St., Boston. There, with the assistance of a few Chickering craftsmen, he made in four years a total of about 100 instruments, 33 clavichords, 13 harpsichords, a few virginals and spinets, several lutes, octavinas and psalteries, and the balance "Chests of Viols." Each of these last consisted of six instruments of the violin family, 2 treble viols—the viola d'amore—2 tenor viols, and 2 bass viols— the viola da gamba and the violone tuned an octave lower. The harpsichords had two banks and strings of 16 foot pitch.

Mr. Dolmetsch purchased all the necessary supplies, which included materials difficult to obtain, such as pearwood and quills from crows for plucking the harpsichord wires, and tested each instrument personally.

As most instruments of these types still in existence were in poor condition, the making of these fine replicas brought about a renaissance of playing on the instruments for which the music of Bach, Scarlatti, Purcell, Rameau, and other early composers was written.

Mr. Dolmetsch gave concerts and lectures demonstrating the instruments, both locally and in many other cities and various colleges. He played all these instruments well, but usually played the viola d'amore or harpsichord, and Mrs. Dolmetsch played the viola da gamba or harpsichord. Four series of concerts were given in Chickering Hall, Boston, in the years 1906, 1907, 1908, and 1909, Mr. Dolmetsch conducting,[7] assisted by many members of the Boston Symphony Orchestra and other talent such as C. W. Adams, G. Longy, C. Lenom, A. Maquarre, A. Brooke, A. Sautet,

[7] From 1911-1914 Mr. Dolmetsch had a department in the Gaveau Factory, Paris. Since then he and his family have had a workshop and school at Haselmere, England, and conduct an annual "Festival of Chamber Music."

F. Mueller, P. Sadony, M. Kunze, A. Gietzen, A. Bak, F. Mahn, Arthur Hadley, and the Misses Alice and Laura Kelsey.

Purchasers of these Dolmetsch harpsichords and clavichords include Arthur Whitney, who wrote *The Lesson of the Clavichord*; E. B. Dane, Chestnut Hill, Massachusetts; Henry Gideon, New York City, who gave many concerts and lectures using his harpsichord; Frank Taft, Montclair, New Jersey; the late E. F. Searles, Methuen, Massachusetts; O. G. Sonneck, Washington, D. C.; John Wanamaker, Philadelphia, Pennsylvania; E. P. Warren, Liverpool, England; Ferruccio Busoni; and Smith, Wellesley, and Vassar Colleges.

There have been two noteworthy celebrations of the company's long period of service. The first was the Eightieth Anniversary held in Chickering Hall, Boston, April 14, 1903, with only employees of Chickering & Sons and their immediate families present. The program consisted of five songs sung by Miss Mary Ogilvie, accompanied by Mrs. S. B. Field, a short historical address by Dr. Edward Everett Hale, and pianoforte selections played by B. J. Lang.

The second was a three day celebration of the Hundredth Anniversary held in April, 1923. The series of events began with a "Family Gathering" of officials and employees of the company in the great factory. This consisted of commemoratory exercises, a fine concert and the presentation of a gold watch to each of the thirty-one employees who had been with the company twenty-five years or more. It closed with a banquet and dancing.

The next day a bronze tablet commemorating the work of Jonas Chickering, the gift of Chickering representatives from all over the world, was presented at the factory before invited guests and the factory organization. The same afternoon a Centennial Concert was given in Symphony Hall. The program was opened appropriately by the Handel and Haydn Society and other numbers were given by the Boston Symphony Orchestra, Mmes. Elly Ney and Germaine Schnitzer, Messrs. Guy Maier, Lee Pattison and Erno von Dohnanyi.

The closing event was a dinner at the Copley Plaza Hotel. Mr. Courtenay Guild was chairman of the National Committee and introduced the speakers. Mr. Calvin Coolidge, then Vice-President of the United States, was the principal speaker. Others were Mayor James M. Curley and Mr. Richard Lawrence. A concert program was given by Mr. von Dohnanyi and Messrs. Maier and Pattison.

The Chickering Brothers died one after another, Thomas E. on February 14, 1871; Charles Francis on March 23, 1891; and George H. on November 17, 1893. The men who had been associated with Jonas Chickering and later with George Chickering continued the business until 1908, when Chickering & Sons became one of the subsidiaries of the American Piano Company, a large holding company, along with William Knabe and Company, and Foster Armstrong Company. It retained its own organization, officers and name. The manufacturing was moved out to Rochester, New York, about 1929. Haines Brothers, Marshall and Wendell and other companies have also become part of this larger organization. This had an output of eighteen thousand pianofortes a year in 1909, making it one of the largest industries of its kind in the world. August 1, 1932 the Aeolian American Corporation was formed by merging certain assets of the Aeolian Company with those of the American Piano Company and all the manufacturing was concentrated in separate plants in Rochester.

The present Boston offices and warerooms of the company are located in the Ampico Hall Building at 146 Boylston St.

Inventions

Mechanical improvements and inventions constitute the real reason why the Chickering pianoforte attained its world-wide eminence. "The two most prominent features in the recent wonderful development of the piano manufacture in America are the invention and gradual perfection of the iron frame and the introduction of the overstrung scale." [8] Alpheus Babcock had been the first to introduce the iron plate into the pianoforte, patenting it in 1825, but his plate extended across only one-half of the instrument. [9] Jonas Chickering made the first grand pianoforte with a full iron frame cast with the parallel bars in one piece. This invention, [8] patented in 1837 [10] and applied to the construction of his first grand pianoforte in 1840, was one of the epoch-making inventions which helped to revolutionize the pianoforte manufacturing industry.

[8] *American Cyclopaedia.* Vol. XIII p. 492.
[9] Parker, Richard C. *A Tribune to the Life and Character of Jonas Chickering.* Footnote p. 45.
[10] This date is given by the company's Historian, Miss Margaret Connell. Daniel Spillane in his *History of the American Pianoforte* p. 92 stated that Chickering's square metal plate together with an improved damper arrangement was patented October 8, 1840.

The American climate necessitated an iron frame to sustain the tension of the strings in order that the instrument could stand for some time without constant tuning. "For the successful introduction of the iron frame Jonas Chickering has been called the 'Father of the piano as we know it today.' " [11] Because the iron frame made a sharp thin tone, it was not generally adopted outside of Boston until after 1855. [12] Then the extension of the compass to seven octaves made the resistance of the wood frame unequal to the tension of the strings.

In 1843 the house patented a new "deflection of the strings" by which strength was added to the frame. [13] In 1845 Mr. Chickering invented the first practical method for over-stringing grand and square pianofortes. This principle was applied to Chickering uprights in 1849, giving them a great advantage over those of foreign make in resonance and in their ability to stay in tune. The invention of the circular scale for square pianofortes was another improvement of this company.

Patents were granted in 1868 and 1869 for a combination truss frame and other improvements in the construction of uprights. In 1872 the double bearing agraffe was patented. Other inventions have been along the lines of new scales and improvement of the action.

In 1901 the first "quarter grand" model, the smallest grand piano of modern construction, was introduced. It was perfected in 1904.

M. Welte and Son of Freiburg, Germany, and Ludwig Hupfeld of Leipsic were the pioneers about 1904 in developing and marketing the modern reproducing pianoforte. The first American reproducing pianoforte, the invention of Charles Fuller Stoddard of the American Piano Company, was arrived at independently. [14] The instrument he perfected was introduced by this company under the trade name "Ampico." Chickering & Sons brought out the first Chickering with the Ampico in 1911. Any possible difficulty was avoided by an agreement with the Welte Company admitting the validity of their patent, and royalties were paid in exchange for

[11] *American History and Encyclopedia of Music* p. 320.
[12] *American Cyclopaedia.* Vol. XIII p. 492.
[13] *Jonas Chickering and His Work* p. 37, in Richard C. Parker's book.
[14] *Encyclopaedia Britannica.* Supplement to Edition XIII Vol. 2, Musical Instruments, Mechanical p. 1007.

rights in the use of master recordings. [15]   These recordings had to be entirely re-edited for use on the Ampico.

A second American invention producing the same effect by different mechanical means is the Duo-Art of the Aeolian Company.

These reproducing pianofortes were all alike in general arrangement of pneumatics, in the division of the keyboard into halves for expression in playing, in possessing devices for automatic rerolling, recording and repeating, in elimination of the recorded expression and substitution of human control.   The Ampico has the following special features:

"Both a crescendo pneumatic system and an instantaneous accent pneumatic system, which it can use in combination, to control the air-tension behind the hammers.   These systems may be operated independently for separate effects or concurrently for combined; thus producing an unusual smoothness in crescendo and diminuendo as well as a delicate shading.   There is also an 'amplifier' for special effects of volume and the extended perforations in the music-sheet produce the greatly desired 'singing' quality of tone." [16]

Mr. Stoddard maintains a fine laboratory where the minutest details of musical expression are studied so that the mechanical playing of the Ampico used in the various makes of the American Piano Company possesses a beauty formerly undreamt of. [16]

Chickering pianofortes with the Ampico have been adopted by Harvard, Wellesley, Smith, Teachers' College Columbia University, Exeter Academy, New England Conservatory, and many other schools and colleges for teaching music appreciation.   An extensive library of Artists' Record Music Rolls of classical, American and popular dance compositions has been developed.   Recordings have been made by about fifty artists and include such names as Harold Bauer, Teresa Carreño, Ossip Gabrilowitsch, Leopold Godowsky, Edvard Grieg, Josef Hofmann.

Other Contributions of Jonas Chickering [17]

Jonas Chickering entered heartily into the musical life of Boston, influencing the whole course of music in the United States. He had a fine tenor voice so he joined the Park Street Church choir and the Handel and Haydn Society almost as soon as he came to

[15] Statement of Mr. Spain of Chickering & Sons.
[16] *Encyclopaedia Britannica.* Supplement to Edition XIII Vol. 2, Musical Instruments, Mechanical p. 1008.
[17] Tercentenary Letter by Miss M. E. Connell pp. 3 & 4.

Boston. He was Vice-President of that Society three years, President from 1843-49 and Trustee from 1831 till his death. While President, he acted as conductor for a while, leading the chorus and sometimes singing himself. He was chairman of the Music Committee of Trinity Church and sang in its choir until he died.

He was a true representative of American hospitality, entertaining and giving many struggling musicians the means for an education. His pianofortes and warerooms were freely opened for rehearsals and concerts of all concert-giving societies, amateur clubs and individuals. He was also one of the heaviest contributors to the Boston Music Hall enterprise.

It was through the united efforts of Mr. Chickering and Lowell Mason, then a professor in the Boston Academy of Music, that music was introduced into the Boston public schools, the former contributing the pianoforte and the latter giving his services gratis for a year (1837) in the Hawes School in South Boston for the experiment.

"It is small wonder, then, that this citizen who took his part also as juryman, justice of the peace, vestryman and President of the Massachusetts Charitable Mechanic Association was once described by a friend as 'like his pianofortes, Upright, Grand and Square.' "

The Chickering Halls

In Boston there have been four Chickering Halls, the last being erected on Huntington Avenue near Massachusetts Avenue and opened February 8, 1901, with a concert by Mme. Antoinette Szumowska, M. Pol Plançon and the Kneisel Quartet. These Halls have been used for many recitals.

Chickering Hall in New York, however, is the one which is noted because it was such an important factor in the musical life of that city.[18] It was dedicated November 15, 1875, when it was opened for the first appearance of Hans von Bülow in America, with an orchestra under the direction of Dr. Leopold Damrosch and a Beethoven program. A remarkable series of concerts by von Bülow and chamber music soirées with Dr. Damrosch, George Matzka and Frederick Bergner followed. No pianist who has come to America since has ever given so many concerts in so short a period

---

[18] For source of information in the following paragraphs see *The Commemoration of the Founding of the House of Chickering & Sons*, 1823-1903 Chickering Hall, N. Y. pp. 79-90.

in one hall as von Bülow.   Mme. Carreño-Sauret and M. Sauret
with others gave concerts that first season.

In January 1876 the new organ built by Roosevelt was played
by noted New York organists.   It was used by many local organists
for recitals, and Frederic Archer of England gave his first American
performance on it.

The Hall was used by many choral societies, the Mendelssohn
Glee Club, English Glee Club, New York Vocal Society, Harlem
Mendelssohn Union, The Manhattan Choral Union, the Choral
Club, the Musurgia, St. George's Glee Club, Orpheus Glee Club,
Banks Glee Club, Lenox Hill Vocal Society, Metropolitan Musical
Society, Palestrina Choir and the Rubinstein Club.

String quartets appeared here, too; New York Quartet with
William Mason as assisting artist on April 15, 1876; the quartet
composed of Theodore Thomas, Joseph Mosenthal, George Matzka
and Frederick Bergner; the Philharmonic Club led by Richard
Arnold; and the Beethoven String Quartet led by Gustav Dann-
reuter.   After the disbandment of Theodore Thomas' New York
orchestra, Chickering & Sons tried to establish in 1878 a permanent
orchestra with G. Carlberg as conductor.   Remenyi and Wilhelmj
were soloists.

In 1882-83 popular orchestral concerts were conducted by
Philip Herfort and the "Historical Cyclus" of vocal concerts was
projected by Maurice Strakosch.   The next season Georg and Lillian
Bailey Henschel gave there the first of their joint song recitals.

In 1886-87 the conductor, Frank Van der Stücken, started
a series of symphonic concerts in which he brought forward novelties, among them MacDowell's *Ophelia,* part of J. K. Paine's
Nativity and Berlioz' *Trojans in Carthage.*   The next year he gave
five concerts devoted solely to works of American composers.

In 1887-88 Anton Seidl disclosed original and advanced ideas
in conducting, and brought forward such novelties as Wagner's
Symphony in C and Brückner's *Fourth Symphony* in a series of three
concerts.

In 1888-89 orchestral series were given by Theodore Thomas
and Mr. Van der Stücken who gave concerts the following season
also.   Illustrated lectures on music were given by Dr. F. L. Ritter
the latter season.

In 1890-91 the Boston Symphony Orchestra held their New York concerts in Chickering Hall. These were among the most influential concerts given in New York. The Manuscript Society, founded to encourage American musicians by performances of their compositions, made its bow December tenth.

In 1898 an important series of orchestral concerts was given under the management of Chickering & Sons with Anton Seidl as conductor, and Franz Rummel made his appearance as a soloist. Other soloists were Xaver Scharwenka and Richard Hoffman.

Artists who made their American debut in this Hall were Rafael Joseffy, October 13, 1879, who played Chopin's *Concerto in E Minor* and Liszt's *Concerto in E Flat* with an orchestra under Dr. Damrosch; Edmund Neupert, the Norwegian pianist, who played Grieg's concerto dedicated to himself; and Mme. Emma Nevada November 5, 1885. The Italian violinist, Teresina Tua, was heard there in the 1887-88 season, and Signor Campanini and Mme. Ilma di Murska on return visits. Vladimir de Pachmann and Mme. de Pachmann appeared there in April 1890.

The Madrigal Singers and Richard Hoffman, who had been playing the Chickering pianoforte for fifty-two years, gave concerts there shortly before the close of the Hall in 1901. Among novelties introduced to New York in Chickering Hall were Theodore Thomas' *Festival March,* Brahms' *Double Concerto,* part of Saint-Saens' *Samson and Delilah,* Beethoven's *Ritter-Ballet,* Grieg's *Autumn Overture* and *Peer Gynt Suite,* Rubinstein's *Don Quixote,* a suite of Arthur Foote's and Tschaikowsky's *Fifth Symphony.*

At various times since 1901 wholesale and retail departments have been established in New York. Once was in connection with Ampico Hall, which was used for several years in the same way as Chickering Hall. At present the building is used by the Knabe Company.

Artists Endorsing and Using the Chickering Pianofortes

Endorsers of these instruments were Franz Liszt, Saint Saëns, Gottschalk, Wehle, Gounod, Thalberg, De Pachmann, Carreño, Georg Henschel and von Bülow. Jenny Lind was probably the greatest singer ever heard in the United States when she made her tour in 1850. She was accompanied on the Chickering at her concerts.

A list of seventy-six eminent performers, teachers and composers for the pianoforte, all users of the Chickering, appears as "The Roll of Honor of the Chickering Piano" on pages 77 and 78 in the book issued in 1903 in commemoration of the eightieth anniversary of the company's founding. This included more European than American names, showing the instrument's standing in the musical world of that time.

Great artists of later days using the pianoforte on their tours include Busoni, Chemet, D'Alvarez, von Dohnanyi, Dumesnil, Lhevinne, Maier, Mirovitch, Elly Ney, Pattison, Germaine Schnitzer, Telmanyi, and many others.

VOSE & SONS PIANO COMPANY

This company, incorporated in 1889, was founded in 1851 by James Whiting Vose, who served an old fashioned apprenticeship in expert cabinet making in Milton and Boston. He then began to study pianoforte construction, especially action and key making. After experience in cabinet work, organ and pianoforte key making and action building in various Boston shops, he began to make pianofortes at the age of twenty, first putting his name on them in 1851. The first appearance of his name in the Boston Business Directory was in 1852 [19] at 328 Washington St., as "Vose, Jas. (Keys alone)."

Pianoforte No. 1, made in the first factory at 328 Washington St., Boston, is a square with a highly ornamental full iron plate, a beautiful rosewood case and fine set of ivory keys. It still has a good tone and is in the possession of the company at their factory, 791 Tremont Street, Boston.

This company has always aimed to make a "pianoforte of exceptional musical value and durability." An illustration of how early it became noted for the quality of its instruments is found in the following statement taken from an advertisement in *Dwight's Journal of Music* in 1857. James W. Vose's premium piano-fortes made in 335 Washington St. "won a silver prize medal for fine musical tone and perfect action, and a bronze medal for superiority of exterior at the last previous Massachusetts Charitable Mechanic Association Exhibition." [20] The company has not gone in for the

[19] The Directory year ran from July 1851-July 1852.
[20] *Dwight's Journal of Music*, Vol. X, Feb. 28, 1857 p. 176.

concert business, however. Its policies have been continued and developed for eighty odd years by Willard Atherton Vose and its present president, George Atherton Vose, son and grandson respectively of the founder, along the lines started by him.

During these years more than 102,000 square, upright and grand Vose pianofortes have been sold to churches, educational institutions, professional musicians, and music lovers in all parts of the country, and a few have been exported. Both upright and grand player pianofortes and Welte-Mignon electric reproducing pianofortes have also been made.

At the present time three-quarter grands and very small uprights are their most popular models.

Vose pianofortes are used and endorsed by such educational institutions as Chicago Musical College; Horner Institute of Fine Arts, Kansas City; University of Wyoming; University School of Music, Lincoln, Nebraska. A square Vose pianoforte has long been in use in the late Ex-President Coolidge's home at Plymouth, Vermont.

HENRY F. MILLER PIANO COMPANY

This company was established by Henry F. Miller (1825-1884), who was a noted improvisateur. He first intended to become a pianist and organist, then worked in his father's jewelry store, and later studied pianoforte making with the firm of Brown & Allen. Then he worked five years with the Emerson Piano Company. He started his own business in 1862, being associated with N. M. Lowe and J. H. Gibson. After a comparatively short time, he became sole proprietor. After his death his five sons continued the business. [21]

During three generations of manufacture at Wakefield, Massachusetts, some 55,000 instruments were made, some uprights, but mostly grands. Little mechanical change has been made in the last twenty-five years from the master instrument which had proven satisfactory. Player pianofortes, called "Playerfortes," were made for about twenty years and quite a business was done in these from 1920-1928. Pianofortes were also made with the Welte-Mignon reproducing mechanism for about twelve years until four years ago.

In 1931 the factory was moved to New York City to cut overhead costs and to obtain the advantages of large purchases by manu-

[21] From Pauer, Ernst. *The Pianist's Dictionary* p. 148.

facturing in the same building as the Winter Company. It is entirely separate in organization, however. [22] The Boston wholesale and retail office is located at 234 Boylston St.

Mr. Miller aimed for beauty of design and tonal supremacy. His instruments have been called "the sweetest toned piano in the world," and the concert grands have been used by artists abroad as well as in the United States. Their standing was described as follows—"among art products of national manufacture, this company represents the highest attainments." [23]

Dr. Maas used the Miller pianoforte, for *The Boston Post* of April 14, 1882 commented—"The grand piano used by Dr. Maas possessed a rare and beautiful quality of tone as well as great volume and carrying power." Dr. William H. Sherwood—pupil of Kullak, E. F. Richter and Liszt—who established the Sherwood Music School of Chicago, Illinois, used the "Henry F. Miller Artist's Grand Piano" for his concert tour of the United States during the season of 1881-82. *The Cleveland Voice* of February 26, 1882 said this of the instrument used in Dr. Sherwood's Cleveland concert—"The Henry F. Miller Concert Grand Piano used by Mr. Sherwood was admired. Its great power and breadth of tone, combined with remarkable purity and sweetness, readily account for the increasing popularity of the piano."

George Copeland was brought up on and used Miller pianofortes, and the company sponsored his recitals in Jordan Hall. At the present time many teachers of pianoforte use this instrument.

The company has had two halls for concerts and recitals, the first on Washington or Tremont Street, and the second at 396 Boylston St. from 1903-1926. This was intended for recitals by users of Miller Pianofortes.

IVERS & POND PIANO COMPANY

About 1870 William H. Ivers, who had had a thorough mechanical training in pianoforte building, began building pianofortes under his own name in Dedham, Massachusetts. Later it became Ivers & Son. Handel Pond, an accomplished young musician who had made his mark in a parallel line, felt that if his ideals of tone

[22] Statement of Mr. Carter, Salesroom Manager, of the Henry F. Miller Piano Company, Boston.
[23] *American History and Encyclopedia of Music* p. 324.

and musical quality could be incorporated into the Ivers pianoforte, a new standard would be set. So, in 1880, the Ivers & Pond Piano Company was founded. In 1897 Mr. Ivers resigned as President, relinquished his interest and retired. Mr. Pond succeeded him in office until his death in 1908. The present heads of the company are his sons, Clarence H. Pond, President, and Shepard Pond, Treasurer. This is one of the two [24] greater Boston firms whose traditions are still carried on by the family of the founder. Its office is at 258 Boylston St., and its factory in Cambridgeport, Massachusetts.

This company makes a first quality pianoforte for home and school use. In place of artist exploitation it has done consistent national advertising for fifty years. From the start, it made squares, now obsolete, uprights and grands. In 1903 it added to its line grand pianofortes with player and the Welte-Mignon reproducing mechanisms. The company has made and sold between 79,000 and 80,000 instruments, distributed all over the United States, and a few outside. Because of their reasonable price and durability as well as quality "over 600 leading musical and educational institutions have endorsed this instrument by buying it for their own use, a record we believe unequalled in the annals of American piano building." [25] At one time it received from the New England Conservatory the large order of one hundred pianofortes.

This was the first company to import into the United States in 1904 the electric driven reproducing instruments of M. Welte and Sons of Freiburg, Germany, and also the first recordings. The earliest style was an upright without keys which looked like a sideboard or ice chest.

This company has many patents for refinements of the mechanism of its instruments.

MASON & HAMLIN COMPANY

Since this company was organized in 1854 for the manufacture of reed organs, its earliest history is sketched in the section on Reed Organs. The manufacture of pianofortes was begun in 1880, and the first were brought out in 1882. These were uprights. Then followed baby parlor and finally concert grands.

[24] The other such firm is Vose & Sons Piano Company.
[25] From *Ivers & Pond Policy—Past and Present* 1880-1926.

By 1904 the fine quality of these pianofortes was recognized in the United States and abroad, as was attested by the artists using them. When the company required more capital to develop its business, the need was supplied by the Cable Company of Chicago, owned by the Haverfingers of Minneapolis, since this firm made no high-priced quality instrument and desired one. The management continued as before. By the time the Haverfingers sold their interest in 1924 to the American Piano Company, the Mason & Hamlin pianoforte had won a reputation second to none, both in the United States and abroad. The American Piano Company introduced the Ampico into all styles of Mason & Hamlin grands and the Welte-Mignon reproducing mechanism into their uprights.

Up to the time the American Piano Company reorganized and the Aeolian Company bought the Mason & Hamlin Company, about 35,000 pianofortes had been manufactured. They were made for a long time in Cambridge, Massachusetts, later in the former factory of Hallet, Davis & Company in Neponset, and since 1932 in a separate plant of the Aeolian American Corporation at Rochester, New York.

The Mason & Hamlin Company contributed in 1900 a major invention, the tension resonator. Various attempts had been made previously to overcome the loss in tone quality due to the inability of the slightly-arched wood sounding board of the pianoforte to retain its tension under varying climatic conditions which often caused the wood to contract and flatten. In this invention the underside of the arch or crown of the sounding board was re-enforced by bars at right angles to the grain of the board, which was parallel to the bridge in order to help resist the downward pressure of the strings due to their 40,000 pound tension. There were also two cases, and continuous outer and lower inner rims to hold the iron plate and sounding board. This construction gave greater strength, preserved the elasticity of the sounding board and also unified the various contributory tonal factors.

The result of this invention has been to give Mason & Hamlin pianofortes a remarkable singing tone. While it is still somewhat of a question how permanently effective the tension resonator is in fulfilling its mission, this invention has spurred on other pianoforte manufacturers to make efforts to attain the same end.

This company has also developed the finest sustaining tone pedal used in a pianoforte. [26]

The seventieth anniversary of the founding of the company was celebrated in 1925 by a gathering of the company's employees in Jordan Hall. The program consisted of music by Harold Bauer and the Mason & Hamlin Employees' Orchestra, and an address by the President, Henry L. Mason. A silver bowl was presented by the company to Harold Bauer, who had played their pianoforte ever since he came to the United States, twenty-five years before.

A roster of prominent artists who have used this pianoforte is significant. William H. Sherwood played the first concert grand of Mason & Hamlin used with the Boston Symphony Orchestra, in 1895. Rachmaninoff played it in 1909 in the United States. Harold Bauer has used it in Europe and Australia, as well as in the United States from 1900-1925. Other users have been Ossip Gabrilowitsch, Ben Moisewitsch in Europe, Alexander Brailowsky, Maurice Ravel, Frank Sheridan, George Copeland, Martinus Sieveking. Dame Melba was accompanied by one on a transcontinental tour of fifty concerts in the United States. She also bought two small grands and took them to her home in Australia.

The English pianists, Herbert Fryer and Katherine Goodson, were introduced to the United States and their tours were managed by the company.

POOLE PIANO COMPANY

This company was founded in 1893 by William H. Poole, who had made pianoforte parts earlier. It was incorporated in 1917.

It has made to date approximately 25,000 upright, grand, and some player pianofortes sold only at wholesale all over the United States. While the Poole pianoforte is less expensively built than some makes, it is rated as a good instrument.

Shepard Pond, the treasurer of this company, has a controlling interest in it. The Poole Piano Company now occupies space in a part of the Ivers & Pond Piano Company factory in Cambridgeport.

[26] Statement of Henry L. Mason.

M. STEINERT & SONS COMPANY, INC.

Morris Steinert, the founder of this company, was born at Scheinfeld, Germany, in 1831. As a boy he had lessons on the harpsichord and guitar and incidentally learned to play the violoncello. He came to the United States in 1854 and joined Maretzek's opera-orchestra as a 'cellist, then traveled with a minstrel troupe, and for a time worked in Savannah, Georgia, as an organist and clerk in a music store.

This firm was founded at Athens, Georgia, in 1860. [27] The outbreak of the Civil War led Mr. Steinert to move north to New Haven, Connecticut, where he opened a music store, taught, organized an orchestra and as the first dealer established by Steinway & Sons, [27] built up a prosperous business which gradually spread out through New England and the Middle West. The exclusive Steinway franchise has remained continuously with the company.

The company also represented the Aeolian Company early, handling pianofortes, reed organs, the Aeolian Orchestrelle and pipe organs. "During the last quarter of the nineteenth century Steinert was the largest music house in the world, dealing in all sorts of instruments and printed music as well as pianos." [27] In this period the company became established in Boston under Alexander Steinert, son of the founder, and the headquarters of the business has remained in Boston.

Morris Steinert died in 1912 and his son Alexander became the head of the firm. His brother Rudolph, Alexander's son Robert S. who entered in 1916, and Rudolph's son Alan, also actively engaged in the business. Another son, Alexander Steinert, Jr., is one of the well known young American composers. Alexander Steinert died in November 1933 and Robert S. Steinert became President of the Company, while Jerome F. Murphy, who became associated with the founder in 1898, succeeded in 1934 to the general management and control of the business. The offices and warerooms are now located at 162 Boylston St.

In 1903 the company began the manufacture of its own pianofortes while still holding its dealer franchises for other makes. Several grades of pianofortes were made in the former Jewett Factory at Leominster, under a fine supervisor trained in Denmark, and were finished in Boston. Steinert was the finest. The others

---

[27] Statement of Jerome F. Murphy, of M. Steinert & Sons Company, Inc.

were the Jewett, Woodbury, Curtis and Berkshire. In all 60,000 were made of which 45,000 were Jewetts, and more of these pianofortes than of any other make have been sold in New England. [27] Players have been put only in the Jewett uprights. No reproducing pianofortes have been made by this company. The Steinert pianoforte was originally called Hume after one of the company's salesmen. But in 1916 when only between 300 and 400 of them had been sold the name was changed to Steinert and it became a widely concertized pianoforte, which achieved a world-wide distribution.

In 1932 the company ceased manufacture but retained exclusive distribution of Jewett and Curtis pianofortes made to their own specifications.

The company is now one of the largest pianoforte houses in the world, with exclusive agencies for Steinway, Hardman, Krakauer, Mathushek, Jewett, Weber, Harrington, Steck, Stroud, Wheelock, Cable, Lindeman, Schubert, Brambach, Knabe, and Curtis pianofortes; the Estey and Aeolian organs; and the Hammond Electronic Organ.

Steinert stores, serving the greater part of New England, are located in Boston, Worcester and Springfield, Massachusetts, and Providence, Rhode Island. The extent of the company's business is shown by the fact that it makes regular shipments almost monthly to every continent.

Steinert Hall at 162 Boylston St., which many consider the most perfect concert hall in Boston acoustically, was opened for general concert use on December 16, 1896, with a concert by the Kneisel Quartet. This organization gave most of its Boston recitals there. This hall has been the scene of some famous debuts, notably Harold Bauer's about 1900, Fritz Kreisler's upon his return to the United States as a young man, and Paderewski's first Boston recital. De Pachmann and other famous concert artists have played here to crowded houses.

Up to 1920 when the radio began to take business away from concert halls the company operated New England's leading concert management bureau, with concert series in all large cities under direction of the brothers Rudolph and Albert Steinert.

Morris Steinert was one of the founders of the New Haven Symphony Orchestra and his home was a musical centre. He

[27] Statement of Jerome F. Murphy, Jr. of M. Steinert & Sons Company, Inc.

endowed a prize in the Yale University School of Music in 1906 besides three scholarships.

During extended travels in Europe he collected, as a hobby, a variety of stringed and keyed musical instruments, obtaining a specimen of every style from early 18th century to modern piano-fortes. When he exhibited these instruments in the International Exhibition for Music in Vienna in 1892, it was found that they surpassed similar collections in European Museums. They were loaned to the World's Columbian Exposition in Chicago in 1893 and to the Pan-American Exposition in Buffalo in 1901. They were used by Mr. Steinert on his lecture tours in the United States, which included lectures at Yale, Harvard, Columbia and other universities.

Upon his death [28] many instruments were donated to Yale University, where they are on display in Woolsey Hall. "The remainder of the collection was stored in a Boston warehouse cellar and was brought to light again in 1934. These instruments are now in process of restoration, among them the pianoforte on which Beethoven scored the 'Eroica', and the famous Astor pipe organ-piano, reputedly the only one of its kind in the world." [29]

[28] Statement of Jerome F. Murphy, Jr., but see Grove's Dictionary, American Supplement p. 373 for another date.
[29] Statement of Jerome F. Murphy, Jr.

B.   Organ Manufacturers

1.   Importance in the Industry of Massachusetts Organ Manufacturers as Shown by United States Census Figures of 1860, 1905, 1921, 1927 and 1931

In 1860 when the first census of musical instrument manufacturing was taken, there were in the United States forty melodeon establishments with an invested capital of $418,400 and an annual product worth $646,975 and twenty pipe organ building establishments with an invested capital of $184,000 and an annual product worth $324,750.   Massachusetts had at that time ten melodeon establishments with a capital of $57,900 and an annual product worth $114,670 and seven pipe organ building establishments with a capital of $81,500 and an annual production value of $161,000. Thus it made 17 per cent of the melodeons and almost 50 per cent of the pipe organs.

In 1888 the pipe organ builders south and west of Greater Boston were located as follows—one in Springfield, Massachusetts, (Steere & Turner), five in New York, three in Philadelphia, several in Chicago, a few in the middle west [1] and one or two in the south. [2]

By 1905 the reed organ trade was centralized in the middle west, especially Illinois, but was carried on also in Michigan, Indiana and Ohio on a large scale.   The pipe organs were not centralized, although more high grade instruments were probably made in Boston than anywhere else.   Ohio and Illinois also were large contributors. [3]

In 1927 there were altogether sixty-three reed and pipe organ manufacturing establishments in the entire United States.   This number had shrunk by 1931 to forty-two.   Of this number Massachusetts had four, or almost 10 per cent of the total.   These were all pipe organ establishments as reed organs have not been made in Massachusetts, at least since 1921.

The total number of instruments of each type and their value is shown in the Table below for the United States for the years 1905, 1921, 1927 and 1931.

[1] Statement of James Cole.
[2] Statement of William B. Goodwin.
[3] See *American History and Encyclopedia of Music*, The Music Trades p. 328.

NUMBER AND VALUE OF REED AND PIPE ORGANS MANUFACTURED [4]

Number and Value of Instruments Produced	1931	1927	1921	1905
Number of Instruments				
Reed Organs	1,279	3,091	7,879	113,065
Pipe Organs	917	2,471	2,187	901
Total	2,196	5,562	10,066	113,966
Value of Product				
Reed Organs	$ 167,944	$ 385,280	$ 748,314	$4,162,319
Pipe Organs	5,283,331	16,782,128	8,963,011	1,989,979
Total	$5,451,275	$17,167,408	$9,711,325	$6,152,298

From this Table the decline in popularity of reed organs is quite apparent. On the other hand the pipe organs show a decrease in number of 62.8 per cent and in value of 68.6 per cent from 1927 to 1931 after the onset of the depression; but a gain in value of 165.4 per cent over the year 1905 for almost the same number of instruments. This occurred despite the fact that prices for materials and the value of the products were not at a peak in 1931.

Complete figures by states are not given in either the 1927 or 1931 censuses in cases where the production value would represent the product of just one manufacturer, thus showing his business. Consequently the exact rank of Massachusetts among the states is not available. However, the proportion which the value of pipe organs produced by Massachusetts builders bears to the total annual value of pipe organs produced in the United States has increased from 1921 to 1931 as shown by the table given below.

Year	Total Value Produced— Dollars	Value Produced by Mass. Organ Builders	
		Dollars	% of Total Value
1921	$ 8,963,011	$ 789,227	8.8
1927	$16,782,128	$1,538,123	9.2
1931	$ 5,283,331	$ 797,777	15.1

[4] Figures taken from Biennial Census of Manufactures Summary Table I p. 1123.

In 1931 the census states that the value of the pipe organ annual products not given for Connecticut, Maryland and New Jersey were larger than those of some states which were given and the same is probably true for some states not listed separately in 1927. Among those given individually in the more normal year of 1927 the five Massachusetts manufacturers made larger, more expensive instruments on the average than the rest, the figures being as follows:

Massachusetts	$16,718	Average value per organ			
California	6,895	"	"	"	"
New York	6,097	"	"	"	"
Illinois	3,927	"	"	"	"

2. REED ORGANS

a. Early Development

The reed organ, seraphine, harmonium, or melodeon is a keyboard instrument deriving its tone from a free reed which vibrates upon the passage of forced air.

"Known from an early time in China" through the mouth blown Cheng, free reeds were greatly developed in 1810 by a Frenchman named Grenié. [1] Around the time that Sebastien Erard made his experiments Eschenbach of Bavaria, Greeks, Anton Häckel of Vienna, and other Germans developed various instruments using the free reed. Kratzenstein of Russia may have been the first European inventor to make practical "speaking reeds." [2] The first instrument of real importance embodying the free reed with metal tongues was the Harmonium invented and patented, including the name, August 9, 1840, by Alexander Debaine in Paris. The French Harmoniums were generally constructed on the "force system" in which the wind apparatus forces air upwards through the reeds producing a somewhat harsh, strident tone.

According to Henry A. Goodrich in *Church Organs: Some Early Builders in New England* Ebenezer Goodrich's greatest invention was the musical reed of the reed organ, which he used as a stop in his parlor organs fourteen years before any other reed was known.[3] His friend, Lowell Mason, urged him to make an entire reed organ. Apparently he followed his advice and gave his first such instrument to the eminent portrait painter, Gilbert Stuart. Henry L. Mason stated that reed keyboard instruments were first made in the United States in 1818. Unfortunately Henry A. Goodrich neglected to state when Ebenezer Goodrich made this gift and thus permit making sure whether his was the first referred to above.

The early instrument of about this date and later generally had exhaust bellows. In this a vacuum is created in the so-called air chamber below the reeds by the exhausting power of the pedals, and an air current rushing down from above to fill it naturally

[1] Mason, H. L. *The History and Development of the American Cabinet Organ.*
[2] Statement of William B. Goodwin.
[3] For further information about this see pp. 151-2.

passes through the reeds, causing them to "Speak" into the chest, thus giving a more refined tone.

James Carhart, who took out a patent in 1846 for a single suction or exhaust bellows, was the first to apply this system to the melodeon. James A. Bazin, a French Hugenot who came to the United States from the Island of Jersey in 1778 first to Boston and later settled in Canton, Massachusetts, was an early instrument maker who developed his "Patent Organ Pianoforte" probably from the lap organ, as he also made these instruments. As an elderly man he was Town Clerk of Canton, 1840-49. He also invented some of the first thread winding machines.

Generally there were two pedals, the right for the single bellows and the left for a swell, which started so suddenly as to give an explosive forte effect. The cases resembled a square pianoforte. One of the best instruments was the new organ-melodeon made by the George A. Prince Company of Buffalo, one of the pioneer and largest melodeon manufacturers. This had two banks of keys, four sets of reeds and one independent pedal set of one and one-half octaves.

Charles E. Austin, presumably son of Charles Austin, Concord, New Hampshire, reed organ maker, was in Lowell from 1876 till his death about 1915. He made there pianofortes and springs, as he devised the curious "grasshopper-spring," giving a more equal pressure on the bellows which was used later in pipe organs by all makers, [4] probably after Hamlin's discovery.

This was the general situation of reed organ manufacture before Emmons Hamlin, a gifted mechanic of the Prince Company, discovered in 1849 the art of voicing reeds by slightly bending or twisting the tongue. The revolutionizing results of this discovery are discussed in the contribution of the Mason & Hamlin Company. What information was available about other Boston reed organ manufacturers none of whom are now active is given in Appendix II.

b.   Mason & Hamlin's Contribution

The two partners of this company became acquainted through the Mecca of Boston's musical life in 1854, the Oliver Ditson store. Lowell Mason had met there Emmons Hamlin from Buffalo and suggested to his son Henry, just returned from his study of music

[4] Statement of William B. Goodwin, Lowell, Massachusetts, organ builder.

in Europe, that they start business together making reed organs. Oliver Ditson and Lowell Mason each loaned them five thousand dollars with which to begin.

Their first product, the Organ-Harmonium, appeared in 1855 and won a gold medal at the Massachusetts Charitable Mechanic Association Exhibition in 1856. Their melodeons won a silver medal at the same exhibition. [5] The first named had double bellows operated by two foot blow-pedals in alternation, five octaves and a variety of tonal color through its unique feature, voiced reeds. It became so popular that other manufacturers adopted that name for instruments of entirely different construction. Hence in 1861 the name Cabinet Organ was introduced and copyrighted by Mason & Hamlin for their practically new instrument, the case of which enclosed all the space occupied and allowed enlargement of the action. Another improvement was the automatic bellows swell which was later changed to the universally used "Knee-swell."

A reed organ labelled "Mason & Hamlin Organ Co." the second organ used in the Mormon Tabernacle before the installation in 1867 of the famous pipe organ is now on exhibition in the Mormon Museum in Salt Lake City, Utah. The first organ used in the Salt Lake City Theatre, a "Mason & Hamlin Cabinet Organ," is also on display there.

The company's largest reed organ made up to 1867 was described in *Dwight's Journal of Music* [6] as "truly a magnificent instrument, whether we consider its tone power, or the completeness of the entire work." It consisted of 16 complete sets of reeds or vibrators, 22 stops, 2 manuals and a complete pedal keyboard (27 note compass) the lowest tone of the 32 ft. being CCCC. The stops were arranged as follows:

Upper Manual; Viol d'Amour, Hautboy, Flute, Fifteenth, Vox Humana

Lower Manual; Diapason 16 ft., Diapason 8 ft., Bourdon, Gamba, Cornet Anglais, Bassoon, Euphone, Principal

Pedals; 8 feet, 16 feet, 32 feet

Mechanical; Full Organ, Tremulant, Manual Coupler, Pedal Coupler, Forte Coupler, Forte Upper Manual, Forte Lower Manual.

The compass of each manual was five octaves, every stop in each comprising 61 vibrators and having its own peculiar tone.

[5] *Dwight's Journal of Music*, Vol. 10, Oct. 25, 1856 p. 31.
[6] *Ibid* Vol. 27, No. 6, June 8, 1867 p. 48. "Great Reed Organ by Mason & Hamlin" from the N. Y. *Musical Gazette*.

"Many of the stops closely resembled those of the same name in pipe organs." The Euphone "was a remarkable stop its tone being very peculiar, entirely different from that produced heretofore by any free reed." It was an 8 foot tone.

"The 'Full-Organ' mechanical stop draws the complete power of the two manuals independent of the various stops. The 'Tremulant' acts on the Cornet Anglais alone. The 'Forte Upper Manual' and 'Forte Lower Manual' are separate swells, one for each manual, while the two combined can be operated by the foot. Each stop works on the pneumatic principle, a new feature in reed instruments.

"The case is an elaborate affair, richly ornamented with walnut carvings and gilt pipes in front. It stands 12 ft. 3 in. high, is 6 ft. 9 in. wide, and 3 ft. 3 in. deep. An elegant carving representing the various instruments from which the stops are named surmounts the top, the whole presenting a very beautiful appearance." [7]

The reed organ was brought to its greatest perfection in the Liszt organ. This had 16, 8, 4 and 2 foot sets of reeds, an "aeolian harp" set, subbass, octave-couplers and a new invention—a pedal point operated by pressing a projection with the knee to retain a note, like sostenuto. Mason & Hamlin introduced in their "Pedal-Organs" a 32' reed, a great and effective novelty in such instruments. All this made it possible to produce tone like the woodwind, brass, string, contra basso and corno of 16' pipe organs. A large library of pieces to be played on it was established and concerts to exploit the instrument were given at 154 Tremont St. where a portion of the second floor had been turned into a concert hall. For a number of years over 1000 Liszt organs were shipped annually to England alone.

The business continued to grow and prosper so that, with one possible exception, it was the largest in the United States up to about 1880 when it was making Cabinet, Chapel, Liszt, drawing room models and portable reed organs. Then, however, western manufacturers, who were able to buy materials for less and so to make instruments more cheaply, cut into the volume of business considerably. So the company devoted attention for a time to small pipe organs and then in 1882 the first Mason & Hamlin pianofortes were built. The reed organ gradually became a less and less im-

[7] *Dwight's Journal of Music* Vol. 27, No. 6, June 8, 1867 p. 48. "Great Reed Organ by Mason & Hamlin" from the *N. Y. Musical Gazette.*

portant part of the business as the public taste for these instruments declined, until finally about 1918 or 1919 the manufacture of cabinet organs ceased and any orders received were sent to a highly respected competitor, the Estey Organ Company of Brattleboro, Vermont.

Addresses for this company while it manufactured reed organs with approximate years are as follows:

1855—Cambridge cor. Charles St.
1864—274 Washington St.
1867—164 Tremont St.
1869—154 Tremont St.

3. Early Organ Building

a. Beginnings

The first real impetus to instrumental music in America came through the introduction of organs into the churches. How reluctantly this was done is shown by the fact that the organ willed in 1713 by Thomas Brattle to Brattle Square Church, Cambridge, Massachusetts, was declined. The construction of an organ seems to have been so little understood then that the church refused "a pair of organs" in declining this instrument. Provision was made in case of refusal for the organ to go to King's Chapel on the same terms, namely—it was "given and devoted to the praise and glory of God in said church if they shall accept thereof and within a year after my decease procure a sober person that can play skilfully thereon with a loud noise." [1] By tradition the organ sat in the porch of King's Chapel for seven months before it was unpacked.

This instrument, set up in 1714, has long been considered the first pipe organ used in a church in the Colonies. It was probably the first pipe organ in New England and the second in the Colonies, since Mr. Lahee in his *Annals of Music in America* states that the first pipe organ to reach America from Europe was placed in the Episcopal Church at Port Royal, Virginia, in 1700. [2] Apparently it was difficult to find a good sober organist here as Edward Enstone was persuaded to come from England soon after 1714 to be the Brattle organ's second organist. In 1756 it was sold to St. Paul's Church, Newburyport, Massachusetts, where it was used until it was resold for $450 to St. John's Church, Portsmouth, New Hampshire. [3] Until sometime after 1903 the organ was in the Chapel in active use. It is still playable.

When William B. Goodwin repaired the Brattle organ he made the following notes of the probable original specifications of this instrument, built as a parlor organ and used as such in William Brattle's home at least as early as 1711. The one manual had a DD to e[3] compass. The only proved original stops were Stopped

---

[1] Lahee, Henry C. "Organs and Organ Building in New England." *New England Magazine,* December 1897 p. 487.
[2] Lahee, Henry C. *Annals of Music in America* p. 3.
[3] Goodrich, Henry A. *Church Organs: Some of the Early Builders of New England* p. 5.

ELIAS HOOK

*of E & G. G. Hook, organ
builders, from a steel engraving*

WILLIAM MARCELLUS
GOODRICH

*early organ builder, probably
from a miniature by his sister,
Sarah Goodrich*

SARAH GOODRICH was sister-in-law and sister respectively of Thomas Appleton and Ebenezer Goodrich. She was a pupil of the noted portrait painter Gilbert Stuart, and painted a miniature of him which is in the Boston Museum of Fine Arts.

EBENEZER GOODRICH

pipe and reed organ and pianoforte maker, from a miniature painted by Sarah Goodrich. Courtesy of Miss Caroline E. Locke

THOMAS APPLETON

organ builder, from a miniature painted by Sarah Goodrich. Courtesy of Mrs. Arthur N. Mansfield

Diapason 8 ft., and Fifteenth 2 ft. The Principal 4 ft., Sesquialtera III R. (3 rows of pipes) and Dulciana 8 ft. (Ten. G.) may have been added later. The wooden pipes were of oak and the organ had brass pallet springs (under the valves). The organ was built by Smith, Harris and Jordan of England and was 4 ft. 5 in. wide, 2 ft. 7 in. deep and 8 ft. 9 in. high. The case was mahogany.

According to the description by Charles Shaw, member of the American Antiquarian Society, of the Old Brick edifice of the First Church, Boston, reared in 1712 near the market place, "In this Church was introduced the first organ ever admitted into a Congregational Church in this town." [4] He omitted the exact date, unfortunately.

In 1728 after Dean Berkeley's return to England, he sent an organ to the town here bearing his name. When this church declined the gift it went to Trinity Church, Newport, Rhode Island. This instrument had 13 stops and 498 pipes [5] as compared with the small Brattle organ. It was in use for 111 years and was reconstructed then by Henry Erben of New York, the case and 2 stops being retained. The other stops, action and keyboard in a pine case went to Kay Chapel, Newport, and Hook & Hastings built a new organ within the original case. [6] This has again been rebuilt.

The next organ put into a church in New England was in Christ Church, Boston. This organ was purchased for £320 from William Claggett, an expert engraver of Newport, Rhode Island, who came to Boston and set it up. Its gilded pipes must have been striking against the vermilion choir loft wall back of it. Whether Mr. Claggett imported or made it is as yet undetermined. William Price, who carried on the dickerings with Mr. Claggett, was its organist for five years, the first of which was without pay. Thomas Johnston repaired this instrument as early as 1750 and rebuilt it in 1752, being required to retain what parts of it he could. By agreement with the church he was to build a new organ of his own "with an echo equal to that of Trinity Church [7] (an organ imported in 1736)." In 1759 he completed and was paid for his organ which

[4] Shaw, Charles. *A Topographical and Historical Description of Boston*, 1817, Boston, printed and published by Oliver Spear, p. 238.

[5] Lahee, Henry C. "Organs and Organ Building in New England." *New England Magazine*, December 1897, p. 489.

[6] *Ibid* p. 490.

[7] Williams, Cornelia Bartow. *Ancestry of Lawrence Williams*—Part II Ancestry of His Mother Cornelia Johnston Descendant of Thomas Johnston of Boston, p. 177.

was described by Charles Shaw as "remarkable for the sweetness of its tones." [8]

This in turn was partly or wholly replaced by William Goodrich in 1821. It is considered that he retained the Johnston case as the middle part of the organ front, adding to it on both sides to provide room for his larger organ of 2 manuals and 16 stops. According to the church records his pay was $1200 and the old organ. The Goodrich organ was repaired in 1834, possibly by Stevens & Gayetty who acquired Mr. Goodrich's business after his death. In 1884 Hutchings, Plaisted & Co. rebuilt this and placed the Stevens organ from Trinity, Lawrence, behind the old case. [9] This organ still has a tracker-action.

Another early organ was one belonging to a mysterious Richard Halliburton, who received permission from Christ Church, Boston, May 10, 1738, to place and fix up his organ in the church belfry for his use, and safekeeping in case of fire, together with the right to remove it when he desired.

In 1743 St. Peter's Church (Episcopal) of Salem, purchased by subscription an imported organ. A footnote in Foote's *Annals of King's Chapel* states that John Clark had leave to put up his organ in St. Peter's, [10] while Henry K. Oliver states that this was built by John Clarke of London. According to the latter, "In 1754 the parish procured another made by Thomas Johnston of Boston, and presented its old one to the Episcopal Parish of St. Michael's in Marblehead; . . . This organ of 1754 was, in 1770, exchanged for another, and the latter for another in 1819" [11] "imported from England by Dr. B. L. Oliver who had it in his private residence, and who almost neglected his profession, so fond was he of playing upon this instrument." [12] The Hooks placed a two manual organ here in 1844 and Hutchings has replaced one which has also been rebuilt.

Who built the first organ in this country seems to be in dispute, for Mr. Lahee states that the first pipe organ completed in this country was built by John Clemm and placed in Trinity Church,

[8] Shaw, Charles. *A Topographical and Historical Description of Boston*, 1817. Boston, Oliver Spear, p. 258.
[9] Statement by a member of the Hutchings company to William B. Goodwin, organ builder, Lowell, Mass.
[10] Foote, Henry Wilder. *Annals of King's Chapel from the Puritan Age of New England to the Present Day*, 1882. Boston, footnote p. 210.
[11] This information disagrees with the account in *Ancestry of Lawrence Williams* p. 177. Since Mr. Oliver stated that he played on the Oliver organ in 1823 it would seem likely that he knew about the previous organs.
[12] *Visitor's Guide to Salem*. Published by the Essex Institute 1927, St. Peter's Church, p. 156.

New York City, in 1737, while Mr. Spillane who had access to the Philadelphia Historical Society records claims that Mathias Zimmerman built an organ in Philadelphia before 1737.

Unless it is found that William Claggett built the organ he put up in Christ Church in 1736, the first attempt at organ construction in New England was a large organ erected by Edward Bromfield, Jr., who later essayed harpsichords about which no information is available. This organ, built in 1745, "had two rows of keys and many hundred pipes, his intention being 1200, but he died before he completed it." [13] This organ was moved during the siege of Boston from the Old South Church to a store belonging to William Phillips for safekeeping. It was unfortunately burned there so we cannot see the instrument of which was written "the workmanship of the pipes and keys surprisingly nice and curious, exceeding anything of the kind that ever came out here from England." [14]

The Johnston organ built for St. Peter's, Salem, somehow came into the possession of Hook & Hastings around 1889. [15] It had but one manual and six stops. "On the name board was an inscription in German text, in ivory as follows—'Thomas Johnston, fecit, Boston, Nov., Anglorum, 1754.' . . . He died in 1768 and was succeeded by Dr. Josiah Leavitt, previously a practising physician, [at Sterling, Mass. 1774-1787] who for a number of years engaged in the business." [16] The latter built the organ which the First Universalist Society, Boston, was using in 1817. [17]

"The Brattle organ was replaced at King's Chapel in 1756 by a new instrument imported from London. Tradition has it that it was sent as a gift from the King to the Church of England in Boston and that it was selected or approved and played upon by no less a musician than George Frederic Handel. But a list of eighty names, preserved in the church files, shows that 623 pounds was raised by subscription to pay the original cost of 500 pounds and the transportation charges.[18] A letter from the shippers, Thomlinson, Trecothick & Co., dated June 15, 1756, stated that the organ had been thoroughly tried by Mr. Stanley and several other of the lead-

[13] *A Hundred Years of Music in America* p. 325.
[14] Hood, George. *A History of Music in New England* p. 152.
[15] When, how or what became of this instrument the company is now unable to tell.
[16] *A Hundred Years of Music in America* p. 326.
[17] Shaw, Charles. *A Topographical and Historical Description of Boston, 1817.* Oliver Spear, p. 260.
[18] For this history and many more interesting details see Frederick N. Shackley's article "Organ's History Covers 170 Years—Sketch of the Instrument Formerly in King's Chapel, Boston, and now in the First Baptist Church, Brockton, Mass." *The Diapason* April 1926 p. 36.

ing organists, and *The Boston Gazette and County Journal* of August 30, 1756 informed its readers that the organ "is esteemed by the most eminent masters in England to be equal, if not superior to any of the same size in Europe." In view of these statements it has been assumed that the tradition is correct, since the King presumably would take an interest in an organ for his Boston Chapel and so his favorite musician would naturally have some share in its selection.

This organ was repaired in December 1782 and in September 1788 before William Goodrich by an agreement of May 6, 1824 repaired it, inserted sub-bass pipes to give it a pedal, and put in a double bellows for $300, to be paid for partly by a deed of pew No. 56 valued at $175. Again in 1844 the organ was repaired. In 1860 Simmons & Willcox enlarged the organ to a notable instrument for the time. The shippers' letter spoke of directions from Mr. Bridges and that he had found it so hard a bargain to carry through that they had had to advance some money to him and to pay him the entire remainder on delivery, which suggests that he was the builder. But a specification of the Simmons & Willcox organ prepared by C. F. Loring, Esq., and given in *Dwight's Journal of Music* states that the case and original pipes retained were made in 1755 in London by Adam Smith. In 1883 this organ was remodelled by Hook & Hastings. The original front case and pipes were retained and the Pedal then contained 30 keys. The same company added an echo organ in 1892. The present organ was put in by the Ernest M. Skinner Company inside a new case made like the old one, but somewhat larger and containing pieces of wood of the original case and the original crown and mitres restored.[19] They installed the old organ in 1910 in the First Baptist Church, Brockton, Mass., where it has been replaced since 1925 by a modern electric organ.

Christ Church, Cambridge, celebrated in 1764 the inauguration of an organ made in 1761 by Snetzler of London, the best maker of the day. This was procured through the efforts of Barlow Trecothick, Esq., later Lord Mayor of London, who was a brother-in-law of the rector, Rev. Mr. Apthorp. "Although like other English organs of the day it had no pedals, and a compass of less than five octaves, it was considered on all sides a very fine instrument, and was apparently rather too much for the simple skill of colonial

---

[19] Information supplied by Rev. Dr. John Carroll Perkins, Minister Emeritus.

workmen for there are constant entries of expenses for 'fixing' it." [20]
This organ figured in the American Revolution in 1775, when the
company of Captain John Chester from Wethersfield, Conn., was
quartered in the church, and the colleges and other buildings in
Cambridge were occupied as barracks by the provincial troops after
the Battle of Lexington. The men undoubtedly removed the metal
organ pipes and probably the window weights "to be molded into
bullets which on June 17 were a part of the ammunition used at
Bunker Hill." [21] "On the last Sunday [at the instance of Mrs. Wash-
ington] services were held in the church by Col. William Palfry,
and were attended by General Washington and his wife, Mrs. Custis
and others. Whether there were enough pipes left in the organ to
allow of its use on that day, we are not informed." [21] When a
funeral service was held in June 1778 for a British Lieutenant, who
had been killed through a misunderstanding, the Americans came
into this Tory Church, which had been closed, and "plundered, and
ransacked and defaced everything they could lay hands on . . . and
ascending the organ loft, destroyed the bellows and broke all the
pipes of a very handsome instrument. Pieces of the organ were
strewn about Cambridge for a long time after this desecration;
they were picked up even in the roads." [22]

When the Church was reopened "the organ wholly torn to
pieces" was repaired. "The efforts to restore the organ to a service-
able condition were numerous, but only a portion of the destroyed
stops were ever replaced. In the correspondence with Christ
Church, Boston, it transpired that a number of the pipes had been
'loaned' to the old North." [23] The organ was put in some sort of
order and served until 1844 when it was at last removed and replaced. This history was related by John Bachelder when he presented the relics to the New England Conservatory of Music in
1884. [24] One pipe of that organ, Tenor C, 4 ft., bottom pipe of the
octave, is still in use in the Blossom Street Baptist Church, Lowell,
Massachusetts. [25] It has a good tone. The organ which replaced
this was a new one presented by the senior warden, possibly the

---

[20] *Christ Church, Cambridge—Some Account of Its History and Present Condition—Especially Prepared for Visitors.* Cambridge, 1893, p. 17.
[21] *A Hundred Years of Music in America* pp. 325 & 326.
[22] *Christ Church, Cambridge—Some Account of Its History and Present Condition—Especially Prepared for Visitors.* Cambridge, 1893, p. 46.
[23] *Ibid* p. 51.
[24] *A Hundred Years of Music in America* p. 325.
[25] Information supplied by William B. Goodwin, organ builder, Lowell, Mass.

work of George Stevens. [25]   It continued in use only until 1860 when another was purchased by the parish.

William Selby, a prominent Boston organist from 1772-1789, helped in obtaining better concerts and choruses. The first recorded concerts in the United States had been held December 1731 in Boston, 1736 in New York and the first song recital was given in America in Charleston, South Carolina, in 1733. [26]

The Brattle Square Church, Cambridge, apparently repented its earlier decision and in 1790 ordered an organ built in London. Even then there was opposition to its use by some church members.

Other early New England organ builders were John Rowe (1795-1812) and Adam and John Geib. The Geibs were supposed to have built the organ used in North Church, Salem, Massachusetts. [27]   John Geib & Son, organ builders, were in business in New York from 1802-1806. In 1806 Adam and another John Geib from England started the later well known pianoforte business of this family.

One of the first important organ builders of America was William Goodridge, born at Templeton, Massachusetts, July 21, 1777. He altered his last name to Goodrich and took a middle name of Marcellus. "His first knowledge of the Organ was gathered by his visiting a Mr. Bruce who had been assisting a Dr. Josiah Leavitt of Sterling, to construct a small Organ of wooden pipes, and on his return to Templeton [he] made one for himself.

"About 1798 Mr. Goodrich was a while employed in the shop of Mr. [Henry] Pratt of Winchester, N. H., in making a small Organ of wooden pipes. Here he obtained a further knowledge of Organ building and learned to make and voice wooden pipes. [Mr. Pratt's first organ built about 1790 can be seen in the Public Library of Winchester, N. H. It has 1 manual and 6 stops and the metal pipes were made out of old tea leaf tin foil.] The relations of Mr. Goodrich say that he first came to Boston in 1799. Here he got acquainted with a Captain Joshua Withole (?) who had an Organ, a 'Chamber Organ,' which was built by Jenney's, an engraver of Boston, for his own use. Mr. Goodrich became acquainted with Mr. Withole and, their tastes running in the same

[25] Information supplied by William B. Goodwin, organ builder, Lowell, Mass.
[26] Lahee, Henry C. *Annals of Music in America* p. 4.
[27] Lahee, Henry C. "Organs and Organ Building in New England." *New England Magazine,* December 1897 p. 492.

line, he accepted an invitation to reside with him. Here he learned to make metal pipes. He was for a number of weeks with Mr. John Mycall at Newburyport, repairing and tuning his Organ.

"Residing in Boston he became acquainted with Mr. Mallet of Charlestown, Organist [of the] Catholic Church there at that time, who taking an interest in him, took him inside the Organ and showed him the mysteries of the interior. Mr. Goodrich then tuned a number of Pianofortes and also tuned Mr. Mallet's Organ. In 1804 he formed a connection with a Mr. Benjamin Crehore of Milton in the Manufacture of Pianos, but this subsisted only a few months.

"In November 1804 Mr. Goodrich and his brother opened a little shop near the Junction of Cambridge and Chambers Sts. and there constructed a small chamber Organ. About this time Bishop Chevereux wanted an Organ for the Catholic Church [in] Boston. Mr. Goodrich's friend 'Mallet' being a Catholic and an Organist, was consulted, and proposed Mr. Goodrich as the builder. The Bishop and Mr. Goodrich met and it was decided that he should build it. This was his first 'Church Organ.' It was begun early in 1805 and was finished and put up in 1806. In 1822 he supplied the same church with a larger Organ, taking the other one in part payment. In 1806 Mr. Goodrich repaired and tuned the English built Organ in Brattle St. Church. This was the first time that he ever entered a 'Church Organ' other than his own for the purpose of making repairs. It was presumed that at this time the old fashioned single bellows was taken out and a new one of the double kind substituted. [The first organ went to Sommersworth, Vermont, in 1834.]

"This year also Mr. Goodrich built an Organ for Dr. Gannett's Church at Cambridgeport, which was finished and put up in January 1807. This Organ was divided into two parts, half on each side of the Pulpit window. This Organ in 1828 was received in part payment for a new one built by him and was afterwards destroyed. It was a poor instrument. In 1807 he built an Organ for Mr. Saml. Cabot Jun. and another for a church in Walpole, N. H. He also repaired the English Organ in 'King's Chapel' and put up an English Organ in an Episcopal Church, Portsmouth, N. H.

"In 1806 Mr. Goodrich accidentally got acquainted with Mr. Thomas Appleton, . . . of Boston. From 1807 Mr. Appleton and Mr. Goodrich worked together until 1811.   In the meantime Mr. Appleton married Mr. Goodrich's sister [Beulah].   In 1808 or 1807 Mr. Goodrich repaired an Organ in Christ Church.   This Organ was originally built by Mr. Thomas Johnston, Boston, in 1752.   Also this year Mr. Goodrich repaired the English Organ in Trinity Church.   In 1809 he removed his place of business from [Parkman's Market] Cambridge St., [where Hutchings & Plaisted made a great reputation later] to a shop in Somerset Place.   In 1810 he built an Organ for Dr. Channing's Church in Federal St.   In June 1811 he was employed in putting up and exhibiting Maelzel's Pan Harmonicon, [a combination of wind instruments played by machinery], which was brought from Europe to Boston.

"On leaving Boston in 1811 he left Mr. Appleton in possession of his tools and shop.   On his return in 1812 he found that Mr. Appleton had formed a connection with partners under the firm name of Hayts, Babcock & Appleton.   This Establishment situated in Milk St. nearly opposite the Old South Church manufactured Pianofortes and Organs.   Mr. Goodrich entered into the employment of this firm and attended to the finishing, voicing and tuning a Church Organ and several Chamber Organs which were in progress.   In 1813 and 1814 [he] had a small shop in Boston and built two or three Organs.

"In June 1815 Mr. Goodrich went again into the above firm, but in October they failed, and the concern was transferred to the firm of MacKay & Co., in which Mr. Goodrich became a Partner. In 1820 this concern was entirely broken up and a separation of all the partners took place.   During the 5 years that he was with this concern they built 12 Church Organs and six Chamber Organs.

"Mr. Goodrich remained in the old building after the rest had gone and built an Organ for the Christ Church, Boston.   This was finished in 1821.   After finishing this Organ Mr. Goodrich went to Montreal to tune and put in order a large Organ made by Elliot, London and put in the Episcopal Church a year or two before.   On this excursion he tuned and repaired Organs in the Catholic churches and had the promise to build the great Organ in the Great Catholic Cathedral Montreal but he did not live to do it.   In June 1821 after his return from Canada Mr. Goodrich removed into a building in Harlaem Place erected for his use by Mr. J. Child, in which he continued until May 1828.   He built an Organ here for Dr. Channing's

Church, Federal St. [He] began this in 1821 [and] finished [in] 1822. In 1822 he built an Organ for St. Paul's Church to be used until he should complete their large one contracted for in 1821. In 1824 he built a large Chamber Organ for Dr. G. K. Jackson, Organist [of] Brattle St. Church, but was finished after his death for Mr. John Snowdon. In 1824 Mr. Goodrich voiced and tuned an Organ built by Mr. Appleton for Mr. Parkman's Church.

"In 1825 he repaired and tuned an English Organ in King's Chapel and added a Sub Bass. [The] same year he repaired and added [a] Sub Bass to the Organ in Grace Church, N. Y. From Aug. to Dec. this year he built one for the Universalist Church, Providence. He also built one for the Unitarian Church in Portsmouth, which was finished and put up in March 1826. In 1826 Mr. Goodrich built an Organ for the St. Paul's Church comprising 3 Manuals and a Pedal with a Double Diap. Bass, a stop which until then had never been introduced here. This Organ was 28 feet high, 16 ft. wide [had] 1700 pipes [and cost] $4500. In 1827 he built one for [the] Old Congregational Society, Cambridge, and one for Dr. Gannet's Church, Cambridgeport, the old Organ built in 1806 being received in part payment.

"After moving to Cambridge in 1828 as before mentioned, he built the first Organ for the Episcopal Church, Lowell. He commenced the same year the Park St. Church Organ, which was completed and put up in [the] winter [of] 1829-30 [for] $2000. In 1829 he built two Organs, one for Charlestown, N. H., and the other for Dover, N. H. [for] $1000 & $1100. In 1830 [he] built one for Salem which was finished and put up in 1831, Feby. Also one for Nantucket which was put up in June 1831 [for] $1400. Also in 1830 [he] built one for [the] Unitarian Church, E. Cambridge.

"In the Summer of 1831 he began a small Church Organ with one row of keys and Pine Case, purchased by [the] Episcopal Church, Pittsfield. The Treble was enclosed in a Swell case, but he disliked this plan as he found it impossible to voice the pipes so as to give them a good tone and sufficient power. He never before or afterwards constructed one of this kind. In 1832 Mr. Goodrich built 4 Organs of the same size, 2 rows [of] keys, each $1000. [The] 1st went to Congregational Society, Jamaica Plain, 2nd [to] First Baptist Church Lowell, 3rd [to] Unitarian Society Templeton,

Mass., and the 4th was taken by the Unitarian Society in Sudbury, Mass.

"In 1833 Mr. Goodrich built a church O[rgan] for the Unitarian Society Charlestown, Mass., which was finished and put up in Aug. 1833. This was the last Organ that he ever wholly finished. He was building one for a Society just forming when he died, Sunday, Sept. 15, 1833." [28]

When the original PanHarmonicon was lost at sea William Goodrich built another like it. After exhibition at a museum in Boston for a time this also was sent to foreign parts. [29]

"He was a self-taught and exceedingly ingenious mechanic, a student of general knowledge, a diligent investigator, with a correct musical ear and considerable proficiency in music. He united these faculties in his devotion to organ building with such success that during the time he continued in business, from 1805-1833, but three foreign organs were introduced into Boston, while his instruments became known throughout the whole of the United States." [30] He was a man of strong character and "made a study of foreign manufactures and domestic failures." [31]   His brother worked with him about twelve years, before commencing business with Thomas Appleton.

"The organ now [1902] used in the First Parish Church in Templeton [Massachusetts] is a specimen of his work. This organ was in part donated by him to the society, Mr. Sanger, a native of Templeton, having contributed very generously towards its purchase. It was placed in the church in 1832, and has been in service ever since. The tone of this instrument is still good, although the mechanical part is somewhat worn, and the beauty of the case would do credit to any modern builder. It is to be hoped that if this organ is ever reconstructed or replaced the fine front will be retained." [31] When the church obtained a larger electric organ in 1903 this instrument was given to the Unitarian Church in Gardner, Massachusetts. This caught fire on February 17, 1927 and much of the church and organ were destroyed. One wooden pipe "D#" is in the Narragansett Historical Society Building in Templeton.

[28] Facts Concerning William M. Goodrich, Esq., Organ Builder—Copy from Manuscript in possession of Hook and Hastings Company.
[29] Information supplied by Mr. Francis E. Appleton from family records.
[30] *A Hundred Years of Music in America* p. 326.
[31] Goodrich, Henry A. *Church Organs: Some Early Builders in New England* p. 7 or 8.

"In old-style voicing and tuning instruments William Goodrich has scarcely been surpassed. His reeds in particular were smooth and harmonious and mingled well with the diapasons without over-topping them and destroying their character." [32]

Ebenezer Goodrich was born November 2, 1782 in Templeton and went from there to Boston at an early age and earned his first money there by "drumming for the Ancient and Honorable Artillery, having previously been drummer for his father's company in Temple-ton. He not only had unusual mechanical genius, but was also a great lover of music, played the organ, violin and clarinet. [He also taught organ playing, and met his wife through teaching her.] His music teacher was Francisco Masi, an Italian of celebrity. From correspondence with his son in Brooklyn [1902] it appears that Mr. Goodrich had a most excellent ear for music as was evident in the voicing of his organ pipes. With these qualifications added to this mechanical ability, he made rapid progress in his brother William's factory. He could build every part of an organ from bellows to swell.

"Their shop was located on Milk Street, Boston, where they also engaged in the manufacture of pianos. Timothy Gilbert, one of the veteran piano makers of Boston, worked in their shop. . . . Eben Goodrich at that time introduced the sounding board now [1902] in general use. Before that, the short board of the harpsi-chord was used. But his greatest invention was the musical reed of the reed organ which he then used merely as a stop in his parlor organs." [33] When the brothers had a disagreement Eben set up in business for himself and while William was building an organ in the Orthodox Church in Dover, New Hampshire, Eben was putting up one for the Unitarian Church there.

"Lowell Mason, who was an intimate friend, urged him to make an entire reed organ. Later on, Mason's son, in company with Hamlin, of the well known firm of Mason & Hamlin, com-menced the manufacture of entire reed organs. . . Mr. Goodrich used the reed-stop in his organs 14 years before any other reed was known. After his death numerous letters were found to brass founders, giving directions for forms and dimensions of castings for his plates. An old Chinese instrument [Cheng] made of cane

[32] Parker, Richard G. *A Tribute to the Life and Character of Jonas Chickering,* published 1854, footnote p. 45.
[33] Goodrich, Henry A. *Church Organs: Some of the Early Builders in New England* pp. 8 & 9.

hung over his desk, from which he probably obtained his idea of the famous reed. His shop turned out about 160 organs of different kinds and sizes. Among the large church organs was one each for Dover, New Hampshire; [St. Anne's, Lowell] [34] New Bedford; [the Catholic Church on Franklin St.] [35] Boston; Scituate, Massachusetts; Nashua, New Hampshire; a church in Watertown, Massachusetts, afterwards destroyed by fire; and a Catholic Church in Charlestown, Massachusetts. He was intimately acquainted with Bishop Cheverus, first Catholic Bishop of Boston, and through his influence secured contracts for several organs for Catholic churches largely in the South. His first reed organ was presented to Gilbert Stuart, the most eminent portrait painter of his time. This was the first reed organ ever made [in the United States], and a few years ago [before 1902] was still in existence in Newport, Rhode Island. . . Eben Goodrich died [May 13] 1841." [36] To support the family his widow gave pianoforte lessons and played the organ in the old Second Church of Boston, thus being an early woman organist.

Thomas Appleton was born in Prince Street, Boston, December 26, 1785. He served his time as apprentice with Elisha Larned, cabinet maker, corner of Salem & Cross Sts. When he was twenty years old he became acquainted with William Goodrich and went to work with him building organs in a shop on Chambers St. Mr. Appleton was not a musician, but had a good ear for music. In his later years, when he supposedly was engaged in reading the *Boston Transcript* by the light of a tallow candle, he used to exclaim "Tut, tut, tut," if anyone made mistakes in playing the pianoforte.

In 1810 he joined in Hayts, Babcock & Appleton. After the firm's dissolution in 1820 Mr. Appleton carried on organ building on Hawley Street first with Ebenezer Goodrich and later Corri as voicer and tuner. Later (1848-1851) he manufactured organs in company with Mr. Warren, at 123 Cambridge St., the latter subsequently moving to Montreal where he carried on the business. [37] T. Appleton, who has been called "The Father Smith of New England," and Warren probably built the first organ in Appleton

[34] Information supplied by William B. Goodwin, Lowell organ builder.
[35] Oliver, Henry K. *The Organist's Quarterly Journal and Review* April 1875 p. 5.
[36] Goodrich, Henry A. *Church Organs: Some of the Early Builders in New England* pp. 9-11.
[37] *A Hundred Years of Music in America* p. 326.

Chapel, Harvard University. [38]   His last Boston factory was on Cambridge Street.

Thomas Appleton built good tracker-action organs, many with 3 manuals, "35 for Boston alone and more than 100 for other cities. His first complete instrument was the Church Green organ used for a time in a church on the corner of Summer and Bedford Streets, Boston. This organ was afterwards removed to a Baptist Church in Providence, Rhode Island, where it was used until about the time of the great Boston fire [Nov. 1872]. Then it was brought back to Boston and placed in the new South Church, corner of Tremont and Camden Streets. It was afterward partially rebuilt by George Ryder." [39]   What may be this organ, since it is located in a church at this address now called the People's Baptist Church, is still in use, but it does not appear rebuilt. It is dated 1844 on the name plate which seems too late for his first complete organ. It has 3 manuals and 34 stops, some divided, and a two octave Pedal Organ. Below Tenor "G" on the Swell there is what amounts to a permanent coupler with the Choir Organ. A number of the stops have beautiful tones, particularly the "Flauto Traverso," which is a remarkably fine reproduction of a flute tone.

Another organ built the same year as his first complete church organ was set up in St. Paul's, Boston, and afterward sent to New Orleans. Other organs were sent to Bangor, Portland, New York, Philadelphia, Baltimore, Charleston, Savannah, Columbia, South Carolina, St. Louis, Cincinnati, Buffalo and Rochester, New York.

When in business alone Thomas Appleton built the organ in Barnard Memorial Chapel, Boston. This had 2 manuals, one and a half keyboards, the lower to "40 G" only, Swell to middle "C" and twelve pedal notes.[38] He also built a fine instrument for St. Mary's Church, Lowell, which went thence to Weymouth Roman Catholic Church. [40]   One of his organs built for a Salem, Massachusetts, church was moved to the Avenue Methodist Church, (Railroad Avenue) Beverly, and used there for some years.[41] It probably had 3 manuals, Swell, Great and Choir, originally. The handsome mahogany case was rounded out at the front and flat at the top. When the French Catholics took over this church most of

[38] Statement of James Cole, organ builder.
[39] Goodrich, Henry A. *Church Organs: Some of the Early Builders in New England* pp. 8 & 9.
[40] Statement of William B. Goodwin.
[41] Information supplied by A. C. Foster who played on this organ at one time.

the organ was junked. But the Pedal wood pipes, which were very large scale, are now in the possession of John Hays Hammond, Jr. at Gloucester, Massachusetts.

One of Thomas Appleton's largest organs was built in 1849? for Central Congregational Church, corner of Newbury and Berkeley Sts., Boston. [42] It had 3 banks and 28 speaking stops, and cost $6500. The soft metal of the front pipes, which went to G and were at least 13 ft., caused these pipes to settle several inches at the bottom by the time it was sold in 1879. S. S. Hamill [43] bid $250 for it, as he said, "Just to start the fun." He was startled when nobody raised his bid and he found he had bought the organ. He recovered his outlay, however, as he made three organs out of it and sold them.

One of his most celebrated organs, the second one he built for the Handel and Haydn Society, and used by them before they purchased the German organ, was sent to San Francisco about 1865. Another concert organ of his, built for the Odeon (the old Boston Theatre altered to a concert hall) was taken to a music hall in Philadelphia about the same time. [44]

After a long struggle he failed in Boston, because, in his zeal to make fine instruments, he put in improvements and extras yet charged only the contract price. After finishing up some organs in New York City he moved to Reading in 1851. There his son Edward, an engineer, put up for him in 1852 a two and a half story factory costing $2400, half of it open to the rafters to allow for setting up the organs. [44]

Thomas Appleton's last and biggest organ was built in 1868 for the Baldwin Baptist Church, Canton Street, Boston, when he was eighty-three years old. It had a very ornamental chestnut case and was so large that there was room in the factory for only one-third of it to be set up and tried out. In 1871 he took charge of putting up and altering one for the Unitarian Society (Christian Union Church) now replaced by the Community Church, Reading. He died in Reading July 11, 1872.

An interesting example of an early English organ is one bearing the date of 1805, built by William Gray. It is now on exhibition in the Fogg Art Museum, Cambridge, where it is occasionally

---

[42] Information supplied by William B. Goodwin.
[43] See p. 255.
[44] Information supplied by Mr. Francis Appleton from a family record of Thomas Appleton's statement made to his son in his eighty-seventh year.

played. It was probably used in Holden Chapel at Harvard University, which owns it and had it restored by James Cole. [45]

b. The Advent of the Music Hall Organ, Boston

"Organ playing in this country was given a stimulus when the great organ in Music Hall, Boston was opened November 2, 1863. This large instrument was the first thorough concert organ in the country. A group of organists, B. J. Lang, John K. Paine, Eugene Thayer, S. F. Tuckerman, John H. Willcox and George W. Morgan were the first to play on it." [46] It took five years for E. F. Walcker and Cie. of Ludwigsburg, Germany, to build this great organ, 47 feet wide, 18 feet deep, 70 feet high, with 4 manuals, 89 speaking stops, 58 note keyboards and 5474 pipes, weighing nearly 70 tons. [47-48] This organ had a large-scaled 32 ft. front of tin, certainly the first 32 ft. metal in America. The façade was, and is easily the finest and most imposing in the country. The two largest front pipes, 28 inches in diameter inside and 31 feet 3 inches high, would cost $800 apiece to build now. [49] They were made of tin blocked in and cast in a single sheet. There are none like them in the United States today because though others are as large they are not blocked in. [49]

The influence of the Music Hall organ on American builders, [50] notably Hook and Hastings, the George S. Hutchings Company, and the Roosevelt Company of New York, and on the choice of occupation made by many who became leading organists of the country is so important that its later history is given here. This organ was used in Music Hall for only about twenty years and then removed, because its pitch, nearly a semi-tone above international pitch A 435, made it too high to be used with the Boston Symphony Orchestra, which wanted the platform occupied by the organ, and there was not enough money to have it lowered at that time. Furthermore it had become so badly in need of repair through leakage and defects in the building that not all of it could be used. This organ, the contract price of which had been $55,000 including extras, was sold in 1884 for $5,000 to W. O. Grover. He, as a trustee, had bought

---

[45] Information supplied by James Cole.
[46] Fisher, William Arms. *Notes on Music in Old Boston* pp. 45 & 46.
[47] For further specifications see *The Organist's Quarterly Journal and Review,* April 1874 pp. 4-7.
[48] Lahee, Henry C. "Organs and Organ Building in New England." *New England Magazine,* December 1897 p. 496.
[49] Information supplied by William B. Goodwin, Lowell, Mass., organ builder.
[50] Covell, William King. *The Boston Music Hall Organ* p. 4.

it for a gift to the New England Conservatory of Music. The organ was taken down by the Geo. S. Hutchings Company and stored in a shed back of the Conservatory, which was not then ready for it, until Edward F. Searles of Methuen, Massachusetts, purchased it for $1,500 at an auction held in 1897 to settle the Grover Estate.[51] Mr. Searles had obtained control of the James E. Treat Company and reorganized it as the Methuen Organ Company. This company rebuilt the organ with new chests, reservoirs, and mechanism, but retained the pipes almost as made, except that they were reset to lower the pitch to International and two new pipes were added to each stop to extend the compass to sixty-one note keyboards. [51]

The rebuilt organ was set up in "Serlo Hall," built for the purpose in Methuen, and the reopening recital, December 9, 1909, was given by Everett E. Truette. After Mr. Searles died the organ was purchased in 1931 by Ernest M. Skinner, who has made some further changes in it.

The Walcker firm also built a fine 3 manual organ for the "First Church" Boston, and a lesser instrument for Park Church, Norwich, Connecticut.

What the Boston Music Hall organ did for the development of the modern American pipe organ may be judged from the following. Previous pipe organs of American make had an old English "keyboard hole," sliding doors, no "terraces" for draw knobs, no positive string tones or true "vox humana," no 30 note CCC pedal compass, no notes below Tenor "F" or "G" on the Swell, no 32 ft. stops till within close upon a hundred years, when a single set of stopped wood basses 8 ft. pitch were inserted, usually entitled "Swell Bass," no intermanual pistons, etc., no complete bass for all Swell stops, no balanced swell pedal, no crescendo pedal; and they generally had an 18 or 25 note GGG Pedal keyboard with only 1 or 2 stops, 10 2/3 ft. at the lowest note belonging to it, and very light wind power (2 1/2-3"); noisy action; and poor metal pipes, usually not over 1/3 tin or less.

The need for pneumatic action in large organs is shown by the previous slow response to the organist's efforts which obliged him to play by rule and shut his ears to the result. In some organs the larger bass pipes gave out the tone so slowly that their use was entirely laid aside and they were silent for years. [52] Furthermore a

[51] Covell, William King. *The Boston Music Hall Organ* p. 5.
[52] See *Dwight's Journal of Music*, Vol. 26, October 13, 1866 p. 323, "New Organ in Trinity Church, New Haven, Conn."

great amount of strength was required to play mechanical action instruments.   In 1866 an article in *Dwight's Journal of Music* stated—"in many, indeed in most great organs the pressure required to be brought upon a note is equal to ten pounds, and of course in holding down a chord or series of notes the fatigue is much increased." [52]   "The old organ in Trinity Church, New York, one of the first large organs built in this country, required when the full organ was on a pressure of nine pounds on each key in order to open the valves of the pipes. When the organist was using full chords requiring every finger and both feet, the power exerted was sufficient to lift him bodily from his seat." [53]   William Bradford Goodwin states that he acquired a blister on his thumb from playing one of these old, heavy touch machines for an hour or two, and has seen the gallery floor actually going up and down from the struggles of a muscular performer at the console.

It should also be noted that only too frequently in the past American organ builders have been handicapped by faulty acoustics in building construction.   The average architect seemed to care little for the organ perhaps feeling that it interfered with his plans. [54]

Two organs [55] with some pneumatic action were built by W. B. D. Simmons & Co. in 1859, however, so that in this feature at least one American organ builder was abreast or ahead of the Music Hall Organ.   In 1866 after the Messrs. Hook had secured the services of Mr. Sturm, who came from Germany with the Music Hall Organ, they put into their organ at Trinity Church, New Haven, Connecticut, what appears to have been a complete pneumatic action. [56]   The first use in this country of tubular action to a limited extent was by E. & G. G. Hook in 1866 [57] just after the Music Hall Organ's advent.

---

[53] Lahee, Henry C. "Organs and Organ Building in New England." *New England Magazine,* December 1897 pp. 502 & 503.

[54] Experience of the organ expert from the suburbs of Boston, who repaired in 1910 the oldest (playable) organ in the world, built in 1396? and located in Sion, Switzerland—namely, William Bradford Goodwin of Lowell, Massachusetts.

[55] See organs of St. Joseph's Church, Albany, N. Y. and Appleton Chapel Harvard University p. 159.

[56] *Dwight's Journal of Music,* Vol. 26, October 13, 1866 p. 323, "New Organ in Trinity Church, New Haven, Conn."

[57] Lahee, Henry C. "Organs and Organ Building in New England." *New England Magazine,* December 1897 p. 501, Shawmut Congregational Church organ, Boston, Mass.

4. Some Important Organ Builders Out of Business

The important companies out of business about which a fair amount of information was obtainable, namely—James Cole, George S. Hutchings, Simmons & Willcox (W. B. D. Simmons) and Jesse Woodberry—are discussed here. Whatever information the writer has been able to obtain about other early pipe organ manufacturers is presented in Appendix III.

SIMMONS & WILLCOX (W. B. D. SIMMONS & CO., ALSO SIMMONS & MCINTIRE; AND SIMMONS & FISHER)

In 1845 this company was Simmons & McIntire located on Causeway Street. By 1850 the firm name was changed to W. B. D. Simmons & Co. In 1855 it became Simmons & Fisher, moved May first to 1 Charles St. corner of Cambridge and advertised that it made organs ranging in price from $600 to $12,000. [1] Mr. Willcox was associated with the company then, and for 1858-59 the name was changed to Simmons & Willcox. By 1860 Mr. Willcox had apparently left, for the company, located at 1 Charles St., was again W. B. D. Simmons & Co., which name it retained until it went out of business about 1877. In 1869-70 it was located at 190 Charles cor. Cambridge; after that it was at Charles corner of Cambridge St.

While this company was in existence it built some of the finest organs of that period, notably those located in:

St. John's Church, Troy, New York,
> built in 1853. This was "a first class instrument with 39 registers, arranged, 14 in the Great organ, 8 in the Choir organ, and 12 in the Swell organ, and 5 couplers." [2]

Citadel Square Church, Charleston, South Carolina,
> built in 1856 by Simmons & Fisher. "It was the largest organ yet built in the country." [3]

Dr. Alexander's Church, New York City,
> built in 1856, 3 manuals and 35 stops.

[1] *Dwight's Journal of Music* Vol. 8, November 3, 1855 p. 40.
[2] *Ibid* Vol. 7, May 5, 1855 p. 38.
[3] *Ibid* Vol. 9, September 27, 1856 p. 205.

St. Joseph's Church, Albany, New York,

built in 1859, the largest in the United States at that time. "This had 3 manuals of 58 notes each, a pedal organ of 10 stops, and a total of 50 stops. It was 29 feet wide, 40 feet high and 36 feet deep from the front to the rear row of loud pedal trombone pipes. In addition the pneumatic pressure takes the blow from his fingers, and throws it back upon the bellows blower, so that the touch is never harder than that of a grand piano."[4] This organ was made electric by Jesse Woodberry.

Appleton Chapel, Harvard University, Cambridge,

built in 1859. This had 3 manuals of 56 notes, 40 stops, 27 pedal keys, 56 registers musical and mechanical, and 2300 pipes. "Some of these (imitation stops) were introduced for the first time in an American instrument. Of these we may note the German Viola di Gamba, . . . the kindred tone of the Viola d'Amore. . . . Then there is the Flute Octaviante, that curious much-heard-of-thing, the Vox Humana, . . . the 16 foot Fagott in the swell, which with its kindred Oboe, are here of the richest reediest quality, the Spitzflöte, . . . the 16 foot Posaune, or trombone in the pedal, . . . the Vox Angelica, . . . the Aeolina, . . . the Cornopean and the Corno di Bassetto." These were all spoken of then as "fancy stops." It had "a full swell pneumatic great organ and Tacit pneumatic."[5] The crescendo and diminuendo of a swell arrangement was spoken of as probably to be added.

King's Chapel, Boston.

When this was rebuilt, by Simmons in 1860, it had 3 manuals of 56 notes, C to G, 38 stops and a pedal organ of 27 notes, C¹ to d. Some of the old diapasons, mixtures and other pipes of some 11 stops altogether were retained.[6]

St. Ignatius' Church, Baltimore, Maryland,

built in 1860. This had 3 manuals, a pedal organ and 30 stops. [7]

St. Paul's Cathedral, Louisville, Kentucky,

built in 1860. This also had 3 manuals, of 56 notes, a pedal organ, 35 stops. [8]

Church of the Advent, Boston.

This organ was removed from Williams Hall and placed in this church in 1865. It was "built by W. B. D. Simmons & Co. was always considered one of the best of their many excellent works. It had Great, Swell, Choir and Pedal Organs with Pedal Check and Bellows signal, and 51 draw stops." [9]

[4] *Dwight's Journal of Music* Vol. 15, September 17, 1859 pp. 198 & 199.
[5] *Ibid* Vol. 15, May 14, 1859 pp. 53 & 54.
[6] *Ibid* Vol. 17, April 21, 1860 p. 31.
[7] *Ibid* Vol. 17, May 19, 1860 p. 63.
[8] *Ibid* Vol. 17, July 21, 1860 p. 134.
[9] *Ibid* Vol. 25, October 28, 1865 p. 128.

ORIGINAL MORMON TABERNACLE pipe organ, Salt Lake City, Utah.

> George S. Hutchings is authority [10] for the statement that the firm of Simmons built the action and complicated parts of the interior and did the voicing while the Mormons built the lower bass notes and the case, noted for its Beehives. The action and parts were of fine pipework. This organ has been rebuilt twice.

Organs were also built by this company for Arlington Street Church, Boston; St. John's Church, Jamaica Plain; West Church, Boston; Tremont Street Methodist Church, Boston; the 2 manual Music Hall Organ, Cranston, Rhode Island; and a few others.

GEORGE S. HUTCHINGS COMPANY (HUTCHINGS, PLAISTED & CO. AND ALSO HUTCHINGS-VOTEY ORGAN COMPANY)

This business was started in 1869 by Dr. John H. Willcox, who had associated with him in the J. H. Willcox Co. "three of the most capable organ builders to be found in the country—Messrs. Hutchings, Plaisted and (G. V.) Nordstrom." Dr. Willcox was a noted recitalist and tone worker, who had worked for Hook & Hastings and had been a partner of Simmons & Willcox for a short time. George S. Hutchings and Mark H. Plaisted had also worked for Hook & Hastings. This company had a new factory specially constructed for them at 1758 Washington St. near Eustis, and were located there by 1871.

According to an unlabelled and undated newspaper cutting in the Music Department of the Boston Public Library the J. H. Willcox Company specialized at the start in a "Chapel Organ" for chapels, religious houses and small churches. Dr. Willcox' aim was to produce an instrument of moderate size, which, within its limits as to power and technical resources, was to be a perfectly complete organ, not an isolated section of a larger instrument. By an ingenious and what this article writer considered a novel contrivance, the front of the organ, not occupied with pipes, was made to serve the purpose of the swell, presenting, when the swell was shut, a front beautifully decorated in the religious style, but opening when the swell was opened in a series of reversible folds. This

---

[10] Mr. Hutchings told this personally to William B. Goodwin, organ builder. That Mr. Hutchings and Mr. Simmons were well acquainted is attested by the fact that the latter's widow gave his books on organ building to Mr. Hutchings, who gave one of them to Mr. Goodwin.

allowed the free escape of the sound and thus effected a considerable economy of space.

The first organ of this kind was made for the then new Church of St. Thomas, Jamaica Plain, Massachusetts, and the second for the Chapel of the Theological Seminary of the Jesuit Fathers at Woodstock, Maryland. The article writer stated that the latter instrument, though small, was without the weakness and disagreeable characteristics almost always encountered in instruments of moderate power, and possessed great sweetness and delicacy (the Dulce stop being peculiarly beautiful) with a dignity, solidity and individuality of tone not always found in much larger instruments. In this organ the writer considered that the golden mean between the grand organ and the small rather undecided chapel organ, to which hearers of that period were accustomed, had been happily reached.

At this same time a large, magnificent organ for those days was being constructed for St. Peter's Church, Philadelphia, Pennsylvania.

In the period about 1870 this company probably did the finest work in America. [11] By 1875? they had made nearly sixty organs.

C. H. Preston came into the firm later and the name was changed to Hutchings, Plaisted & Company about 1873 when it was located at North Grove Street corner of Cambridge. Mr. Preston's death caused the company great financial embarrassment for a time about 1881? when the firm became Hutchings & Plaisted Mfg. Co. located at 223 Cambridge St. In 1882 it was Hutchings & Plaisted and back at the previous address. In 1883 it was again Hutchings, Plaisted & Co. Mr. Plaisted also died and George S. Hutchings (1856-1913) became sole owner of the business in 1884. About 1890 the George S. Hutchings Company moved to 23 Irvington Place. In 1901 this business was succeeded by The Hutchings-Votey Organ Company 1901-08. This remained at the same address until it moved about 1905 to Pacific, corner Albany Street, Cambridge, Massachusetts.

The merger with the Votey Company meant the merging of the interests of the Hilbourne L. Roosevelt firm also. The business of Hilbourne L. Roosevelt, a noted pipe organ builder of many innovations, a novel voicer and an inventor of early electric action, which he patented in 1868 and used in 1870, had been carried on

---

[11] Statement of William B. Goodwin, Lowell, Massachusetts, organ builder.

after his death in 1885 by his brother, Frank H. Roosevelt. It was given up in 1893 and the Farrand & Votey Co. of Detroit bought the stock and patents. The Roosevelt Company had built in 1878 the organ in the Cathedral of Garden City, Long Island, of 115 stops, the second largest in the United States at that time. The Chicago Auditorium organ with 109 stops, built by Farrand & Votey, was third in size. [12] The Roosevelt Company used electric action in one of the great 3 manual organs built for the Centennial Exposition in Philadelphia in 1876. This was later sold to the Massachusetts Charitable Mechanic Association in Boston.

About 1909 the company was reorganized, with the Flaherty Brothers, Fred and Charles, supplying some of the financial support, and became the Hutchings Organ Co. The factory was moved to Waltham where it occupied space in E. W. Lane's factory for a few years and then the company built its own plant at Clematis Brook, Waltham. An office was maintained first at 18 Tremont St. and then at 113 State St. till the company failed, about 1917.

Mr. Hutchings while not himself a voicer, gathered a wonderful group of workers who assisted him in building organs of the finest quality. This company built and rebuilt altogether from 1869 to September 1, 1897 433 organs, [13] both church and concert, mainly for New England. The earliest organs had the older tracker mechanical action, but later ones had pneumatic and electrical action.

Among the organs built by this company are the following:

NEW OLD SOUTH CHURCH, Boston,

> before it was rebuilt by Skinner. This was built by Hutchings, Plaisted & Co. and dedicated January 12, 1876. It was described by Eugene Thayer [14] as "one of the largest and best in the country. Its action work and mechanism will bear the closest inspection, and it is a genuine pleasure to examine anything so strongly and beautifully made. The materials used in its construction are of the best quality. . . . The intonation or voicing is, however, the crowning excellence of the work; most of it being of the loveliest character imaginable. The total cost of the work was about $15,000. The framework of the Organ façade is of solid cherry, and the pipes in prospect of pure tin." It had three manuals of 58 notes each and and a Pedal of 30 notes and a total of 3462 pipes, as follows:

---

[12] *American History and Encyclopedia of Music* p. 328.
[13] From a list of their organs.
[14] Thayer, Eugene. *The Organist's Quarterly Journal and Review,* April 1876 pp. 3 & 4.

Manual   I—16 Registers 1276 pipes
Manual   II—14 Registers 1044 pipes
Manual   III—14 Registers 812 pipes
Pedale   —11 Registers 330 pipes

This was rebuilt by Hutchings-Votey to a 4 manual organ, with the "Great" as the bottom manual, French style, and an Echo Organ was added. This has been rebuilt again by the Skinner Organ Company.

St. Bartholomew's Church, New York City.

A new chancel organ was built and the old gallery organ was connected with the console of the chancel organ by Hutchings, Plaisted & Co.

In a table dated 1897 this organ was listed as the ninth of the twenty-two largest organs in the world. It retained the big old gallery organ and had 4 manuals, 98 speaking stops, 26 mechanical stops, 19 pedal movements, 36 piston combinations, 179 tonal stops and 6042 pipes. The average size of the organs of most of the large churches and cathedrals of Europe at this same time (1897) was about 3 manuals, 30-40 stops, and 2000-3000 pipes. [15]

Mission Church, Roxbury, Massachusetts.
3 manuals.

Trinity Church, Boston,

The firm of George S. Hutchings put in a new chancel organ and connected it with the Hilbourne Roosevelt Gallery organ on one console of 4 manuals. This was later rebuilt first by James Cole and then by the Skinner Organ Company which replaced and rebuilt.

Arlington Street Church, Boston,
electric action with old style blind combinations on it.

Jordan Hall, New England Conservatory, Boston,
3 manuals; the gift of Eben D. Jordan, rebuilt by the Skinner Organ Company.

Church of the Advent, Boston,
3 manuals.

Emmanuel Church, Boston.

St. Paul's Episcopal Church, Brookline, Massachusetts,
by Hutchings, Plaisted & Co.

A residence organ for Samuel Carr,
3 manuals; a duplexed house organ with the "Great" as the bottom manual.

[15] Lahee, Henry C. "Organs and Organ Building in New England." *New England Magazine,* December 1897 p. 502.

MEMORIAL CHURCH, Fairhaven, Massachusetts,
3 manuals; a gift of Hugo H. Rogers.

WOOLSEY HALL, YALE COLLEGE, New Haven, Connecticut.

UNIVERSITY OF MICHIGAN, Ann Arbor, Michigan,
since rebuilt.

FIRST BAPTIST CHURCH, Omaha, Nebraska,
3 manuals.

SECOND CONGREGATIONAL CHURCH, Holyoke, Massachusetts,
rebuilt first by this firm and then by Skinner.

BROADWAY TEMPLE, New York City,
by Hutchings-Votey in 1905, 4 manuals, 70 stops and others
borrowed, and electro-pneumatic movable console.

SYMPHONY HALL, Boston,
by George S. Hutchings; of "Fifty-six stops, one of the finest
organs in the United States." [16]   Frederick Dean described it thus
in 1901—"If one wants the newest in organ construction, that in
the new Symphony Hall in Boston is an illustration. It is 50 feet
wide, 36 feet high, 12 feet deep and weighs 30 tons. It contains
25 miles of wire, 6500 pneumatic bellows, and 3492 pipes, ranging
in length from $\frac{3}{4}$ inch to 32 feet. The biggest pipes weigh a
thousand pounds each. When the hall was opened a year ago,
one of the music critics declared that for the first time Boston had
heard a chorus and orchestra fully supported by a thoroughly fine
organ." [17]

The last organization of this concern, The Hutchings Organ
Company, built the organs in:

FREE CHRISTIAN CHURCH, Andover, Massachusetts.

CENTRE METHODIST CHURCH, Malden, Massachusetts.

The Hutchings Company also made under a contract an
"Organette" with one stop of one and a half octaves which played
only from perforated music. [18]

Beside the organs themselves, which are among the finest
American organs ever made, Mr. Hutchings invented, improved
or successfully used for the first time many mechanical features.
This company has contributed the important innovation of applying
to organs the principle of the rotary fan, known as the "Sturtevant
Blower Fan." [18]   Their organ in New York Avenue Methodist
Episcopal Church in Brooklyn and another in a Columbus, Ohio,

[16] *American History and Encyclopedia of Music* p. 328.
[17] Dean, Frederick. "American Organs and Organists." *Junior Munsey.* November 1901
p. 256.
[18] Information supplied by Ernest M. Skinner.

church built at least forty years ago are two of the earliest in which this blower fan was used. [18] It is now well nigh universally employed both in the United States and abroad.

The Skinner replica of the Willis 16' low C Trombone register was first made in this factory after Mr. Skinner's return from a visit to England. [19]

Perhaps the best new tonal features of the Hutchings factory were those acquired from Carlton C. Michell, who exhibited the round, draught-beard, (Schülze?) developing, quick-speaking and extra pungent, almost orchestral string tones, (almost reed tone) and improved harmonic flutes. [20]

In appreciation of Mr. Hutchings' efforts, particularly for his building of the organ in Woolsey Hall, Yale University gave him an honorary M.A., probably the first such degree ever bestowed for organ building prowess.

JAMES COLE [21] (ALSO COLE, & WOODBERRY BROS.; COLE & WOODBERRY; COLE ORGAN CO.)

This company was established in 1886 as Cole, & Woodberry Bros. at 99 Bristol St., Boston. Mr. Cole, an accomplished voicer, and the Woodberry brothers, Jesse and James, had been fellow workers at Hook & Hastings, where the latter had built the special line of small organs. By 1890 Jesse Woodberry had left to form Woodberry & Harris so this firm became Cole & Woodberry. From 1899 Mr. Cole was in business by himself until 1904 as James Cole (after Mr. Woodberry's death?) and then under the firm name of Cole Organ Co. until the World War made continuance of the business difficult. After that time he acted as a sort of consultant, and repaired, rebuilt, voiced and tuned pipe organs until his death, April 8, 1934.

This company built some five hundred church and residence organs located all over the United States.

Among noteworthy organs built by the James Cole company are the following:

SAINT MARTIN'S IN THE FIELDS, Providence, Rhode Island.

[19] Barnes, William H. *The Contemporary American Organ* p. 72.
[20] Statement of William B. Goodwin, organ builder.
[21] This write-up was not verified by Mr. Cole because the revision and checkups were not undertaken until 1935, after his death.

SAINT PATRICK'S, Providence, Rhode Island.

SAINT MICHAEL AND ALL ANGELS, Baltimore, Maryland.
This was the first electric action organ built by this company and one of the earliest electric action organs in the country.

STETSON UNIVERSITY, Deland, Florida,
3 manual tubular action.

HOLY TRINITY, Geneva, New York,
tubular action not changed. Created much interest at the time of its erection.

SAINT LUKE'S, Germantown, Pennsylvania,
built in conjunction with Carlton C. Michell of England and the Hutchings Company. This was a 3 manual tubular organ of 4 sections, and an echo organ built in 1895. It was rebuilt in 1920 and converted into an electric action.

WOODBERRY & HARRIS: ALSO JESSE WOODBERRY & CO. [22]

This firm was started in 1888 as Woodberry & Harris by Jesse Woodberry and Charles T. Harris at 399 Albany St., Boston. Jesse Woodberry came from Vowles' Organ Works, Bristol, England. He was associated with Cole, & Woodberry Bros. in 1886 and 1887 and then withdrew to form this firm. Mr. Harris was a noted flue voicer coming from the Hutchings' factory. He must have left some time later, however, since at the time of his death [23] he was working with E. W. Lane. [24]

They advertised the building of church, chapel and chamber organs, enlarging and rebuilding of old pipe organs, and the furnishing and applying of motors for blowing organs. In 1894 the firm became Jesse Woodberry & Co. and remained that until Mr. Woodberry retired from business in 1910. It was located in 1895 at 414 Albany St. and in 1900 at 520-30 Harrison Ave. This company advertised in 1904 "electric and tubular pneumatic organs a specialty."

This firm built good quality church organs and a few residence organs all over the United States, the largest and latest all electric. Among their notable church organs are the following:

TREMONT TEMPLE, Boston,
pneumatic, 2 manuals and 28 stops, rebuilt and enlarged since.

[22] For this company's successor see Frazee Organ Company p. 181.
[23] Statement of William B. Goodwin, Lowell, Massachusetts, organ builder.
[24] See p. 255.

Saint Mary's Church, Charlestown, Massachusetts.

Church of Redeemer, New Haven, Connecticut.

First Baptist Church, Lowell, Massachusetts.

Saint Paul's Episcopal Church, New Haven, Connecticut.

Christ Church, Rochester, New York.

Saint Dominick's Roman Catholic Church, San Francisco, California,
   3 manuals.

Saint Patrick's Church, Lowell, Massachusetts,
   4 manuals.

St. Jean Baptiste, Lowell, Massachusetts,
   4 manuals, open 32′ front.

St. Mark's Methodist Episcopal Church, Brookline, Massachusetts,
   built about 1896. It has 3 manuals, 36 speaking stops—13 Swell, 11 Great, 7 Choir and 5 Pedal. The Great Organ is particularly well voiced. It may be of interest to note that, due to the architecture of the church, the organ is located as the great French organ builder, A. Cavaillé-Coll, advised, near the centre of the church. That was unusual around Boston when this organ was built.

A fine residence organ was built in the home of Mr. Baxter, a Portland, Maine, lawyer.

5. Present Day Organ Builders

HOOK & HASTINGS CO.

[In March 1936 this company began winding up its long and honorable career, and the Kendall Green factory has been entirely demolished.]

This company established in 1827 is the oldest extant firm of pipe organ builders founded in the United States. Elias and George G. Hook began business in Salem, the former having been an apprentice of William Goodrich. They moved in 1868 to their great Boston factory at 1131 Tremont St., where they earned a high reputation by their work. Francis H. Hastings was engaged by them in 1855 and ten years later became a partner. Later the name was changed to E. & G. G. Hook and Hastings. After the death of George G. Hook in 1880 the company became Hook & Hastings. Elias Hook died in 1881 and in 1893 the company was incorporated as Hook & Hastings Co. Mr. Hastings died in 1916 and the management passed into the hands of Arthur Coburn, President, Norman Jacobsen, Vice-President and Supervising Designer, Alfred R. Pratt, Secretary and Superintendent, all associates of Mr. Hastings for about twenty years. Since Mr. Coburn's death about four and a half years ago Mr. Pratt has been President of the company.

The moving of their main office and manufacturing to the present factory at Kendall Green, Weston, Mass., was gradual as the first wing was put up in 1885 and the second in 1891. Their section of Kendall Green is called "Hastings."

They have had a New York branch for over sixty years, and did have other branches located at Chicago, Philadelphia, and Asheville, North Carolina. At present, however, they are taking care of most of the business from the main office.

This firm has built 3000 church, concert, university and residence organs located in all parts of the United States, "including some of the finest in the country," [1] and some in Canada, one in Mexico, one in Honolulu and a few in Germany. Their first instrument was a parlor organ. This was still in use in a private residence

---

[1] Goodrich, Henry A. *Church Organs: Some of the Early Builders in New England* p. 12.

in Brookline, Massachusetts, up to about three years ago.   Now it is in the Essex Institute, Salem, Massachusetts.   Their second is still in church use having been in constant service from 1827.   They have also built a few theatre organs where the concert type of tone was desired.   Clarence Eddy, the recitalist, says, "The highest pressure I remember to have read of in America was the ten-inch wind which was used for some of the stops in the festival organ that Hook & Hastings made for the Gilmore Jubilee in Boston." [2]

Some of the well known earlier organs built by E. & G. G. Hook or E. & G. G. Hook & Hastings were:

THE FIRST TREMONT TEMPLE organ
> built in 1853.   This was probably the largest and best organ in America at that time.   It had 4 manuals, 70 stops and 3096 pipes. [3]

THE SECOND TREMONT TEMPLE organ
> built in 1880, to replace the first which had been burned.   This also was destroyed by fire in 1893.

THE CHURCH OF THE IMMACULATE CONCEPTION organ
> built in 1863.   It was the largest church organ in the United States at that time, and in 1897 was still considered one of the most effective church organs in Boston.   It had 3 manuals, each of 58 notes, a pedal keyboard of 27 keys, 47 speaking registers, 5 pedal stops, 56 stops altogether, and 3381 pipes.[3-4]

THE MECHANICS' HALL, Worcester, organ
> built in 1864.   This consisted of Great, Swell, Choir, Solo and Pedal organs and was the largest concert organ built in the United States at that time and second only to the Boston Music Hall organ in size.   It had 4 manuals, 73 stops, and 3504 pipes.[5-6]

THE SOUTH CONGREGATIONAL CHURCH (Edward Everett Hale's Church) organ
> built in 1864 according to specifications of the organist, B. J. Lang.   It was the largest in any Protestant Church, and had Great, Swell, and Choir manuals and Pedale, 38 speaking stops, 7 pedal stops, one a Bourdon with 32 foot tone, and 2260 pipes.[7]

NEW ORGAN TRINITY CHURCH, New Haven, Conn.
> This organ was begun in November 1865 and finished in 1866, Messrs. Henry P. Holland and Mark H. Plaisted being the mechan-

[2] *Music.* W. S. B. Mathews, Editor, Vol. XV, April 1889 pp. 615-19.   Clarence Eddy on American Organs.
[3] Lahee, Henry C.   "Organs and Organ Building in New England."   *New England Magazine,* December 1897 pp. 500-2.
[4] *Dwight's Journal of Music,* March 5, 1864, Vol. 23 p. 199.
[5] Lahee, Henry C.   "Organs and Organ Building in New England."   *New England Magazine,* December 1897 pp. 500-2.
[6] *Dwight's Journal of Music,* November 12, 1864 Vol. 24, pp. 339-40 & November 26, Vol. 24, pp. 351-2.
[7] *Ibid* November 26, 1864, Vol. 24, p. 348.

ics who erected it under Mr. Hastings' direction. The *New Haven Palladium* gave credit for much of the success of the instrument to Mr. Sturm. The organ had 3 manuals, a Pedale ranging from C to D and 2000 pipes.

After the opening recital the instrument was described thus— "In the voicing of the reed stops Messrs. Hook have been singularly successful. . . . Several professional organists present at the opening unanimously agreed that the reed pipes could not be surpassed in beauty and purity of tone. The diapasons extending through the whole organ bind the most distant tones together and fill up the intervals so that the ear is perfectly satisfied with the full harmony. Some of the stops are of such singular and rare beauty of tone that they deserve particular mention. The Viol da Gamba and the Violone imitate most exactly the effect of a stringed instrument. One can almost hear the peculiar tone produced by drawing the bow across the strings. The Geigen-Principal, a new stop is much admired. The Clarionet is a perfect imitation of that beautiful instrument, and the Flauto D'Amour is really a flute, only more exquisitely pure than we are often favored with hearing its original. No one who was present will ever forget the beauty of the Döppel Flöte as exhibited by Mr. Willcox in his solo. The execution belonged to the player but the full, sweet, yet delicate tone of this stop belongs to the builder." [8]

The following seems to indicate that this was one of the first successful pneumatic action American instruments built after the arrival of the Music Hall organ. "One of the triumphs of mechanical skill . . . can only be appreciated by a close examination. The Pneumatic Lever is so arranged as to work the whole organ and thus enable the player to bring out its power with perfect ease. . . . Through the whole of the Trinity organ runs a network of valves and pistons like the nerves of the human body, communicating with the player as he sits at the keyboard and enabling him, by the slightest pressure, to convey his will to every part of the great instrument. Nothing is more extraordinary than the promptitude with which every pipe, from the vastest to the smallest responds to the finger." [8]

T HE SHAWMUT CONGREGATIONAL CHURCH organ, Boston, built in 1866. This had 3 manuals, 51 speaking stops, 12 mechanical stops and 3485 pipes. "Tubular action was first used to a limited extent in this country in this organ." [9] This organ was rebuilt by Austin-Treat.

[8] *Dwight's Journal of Music*, Vol. 26, No. 15, October 13, 1866 p. 324, "New Organ in Trinity Church, New Haven," from the *New Haven Palladium*, September 8.
[9] Lahee, Henry C. "Organs and Organ Building in New England." *New England Magazine*, December 1897 p. 501.

THE PLYMOUTH CHURCH, Brooklyn, organ (Henry Ward Beecher's church)

Also built in 1866. This had Great, Swell, Choir and Solo manuals each of 58 notes, a pedal keyboard of 30 notes, 65 stops, 3405 pipes, and a pneumatic lever to lighten the touch for the organist.[10] "The grand crescendo may be pronounced to be without exception the greatest improvement ever introduced into the organ." It had another novelty, "the Tuba Mirabilis, which stop is introduced for the first time in this country." "The pipes are voiced somewhat differently from our English Tubas which too much resemble a roaring mad bull." "The Tuba Clarion is its octave." [11]

Eugene Thayer in January 1875 selected this organ as the first American-built organ to discuss in his *The Organist's Quarterly Journal and Review*. He wrote "We now give the specification of the most noted organ of American manufacture." "The Messrs. Hook [now E. & G. G. Hook & Hastings, Boston] have long been looked upon as representative organ builders in the United States; and not without well deserving the honor. . . .

"We have chosen the Plymouth Church Organ first, simply because it is in reality a Concert Organ; and has been used more probably for concert purposes than any other American-built organ.

"This work has been in constant use for nearly or quite ten years, and is now in as fine condition as when first erected. Its soft registers are many of them very beautiful; and the reed registers are of great power. The chief characteristic of the work is brilliancy. It has much power, although we think it lacks in solidity for a work of this size. We certainly think it is a fine work, and an honor to its makers." [12]

Both this and the Shawmut Congregational Church organ were still in 1897 considered notable instruments.

CENTENARY M. E. CHURCH, Chicago.

Finished in 1868 and described by Der Freyschutz as "By consent and acclamation of all connoisseurs the best organ we have is one just erected in Dr. Hatfield's (Centenary M. E.) Church, by E. & G. G. Hook." "This magnificent instrument is not unlike those in the Swedenborgian and St. James's Churches in Boston, and the beautiful one recently erected in the Westminster Church at Elizabeth, N. J. . . . The Centenary organ has three manuals. The stops are distributed in this wise: Great, eleven stops; Swell, eleven stops; Solo, eight stops; Pedale, four;

---

[10] *The Organist's Quarterly Journal & Review*—January 1875 pp. 7 & 8 has slightly different figures.
[11] *Dwight's Journal of Music*, Vol. 26, April 28, 1866 pp. 227 & 228 and May 12, 1866 p. 244.
[12] *The Organist's Quarterly Journal and Review*, January 1875 pp. 7 & 8.

Mechanical Movements, eleven, two of which are pedals operating stops of the Great Organ. The summary of pipes in this organ is not large, the total being only 2,300. And this is owing to the fact that the organ contains only nine ranks of mixture and one Twelfth. Nor are the reeds numerous. There are: Great, one; Swell, two; Solo, two, one a 'free reed'; Pedale, one. As usual in the Hooks' organs the tone is delightful. The symmetrical adjustment of the power and qualities of tone in the several departments of the instrument is most admirable. The full organ is grand, dignified, sombre enough yet brilliant and clear. Every one of the solo stops is a gem in its way. The Melodia is a well-known 'specialty' of the Hooks. The Clarinet is pronounced perfect. The sweet Dulciana in the solo organ is soft enough to accompany the softest possible solo in the Swell. And then the comfortable and agreeable pneumatic action! And the pneumatic couplers place the instrument under easy control of the player. With combinations prepared the player can place his hands on the keys of the Great organ and control nine distinct degrees of power without removing his hands from the keys or operating the swell pedal." [13]

Henry W. Bowen was superintendent of Hook & Hastings Company when this firm built one of the three organs for the Philadelphia Centennial in 1876 and the Cincinnati Music Hall organ.

THE CINCINNATI MUSIC HALL organ

built in 1880. This was considered in 1897 one of the largest and finest organs on this continent. It had 4 manuals, 98 speaking, and 26 mechanical stops, 19 pedal movements, 36 piston combinations, 110 tonal stops and 6237 pipes, or about 1000 more than the Boston Music Hall organ. The largest pipe was 32 feet and the shortest half an inch in length. It also contained carillons, a feature not frequent although found in several European instruments.[14] It was listed in 1897 as the eighteenth of the 22 largest organs in the world. Dean wrote of it in 1901 "The organ in the Cincinnati Music Hall is one of the largest in the country, and, although it was built twenty years ago, it has no superiors in tonal quality." [15]

Some of their notable modern organs are located as follows:

BOSTON

CATHEDRAL CHURCH OF SAINT PAUL.

[13] *Dwight's Journal of Music,* Vol. 28, No. 2, April 11, 1868 p. 220, "Organs in Chicago" by Der Freyschutz.
[14] Lahee, Henry C. "Organs and Organ Building in New England." *New England Magazine,* December 1897 p. 501.
[15] Dean, Frederick. "American Organs and Organists." *Junior Munsey.* November 1901 p. 256.

FIRST CHURCH OF CHRIST SCIENTIST (The Mother Church)
   4 manuals, 80 feet wide in the interior.

FIRST PARISH (UNITARIAN) CHURCH, West Newton.

HOLY CROSS CATHEDRAL,
   70 stops (speaking) and 5282 pipes.

NEW YORK CITY

THE RIVERSIDE CHURCH.

SAINT AGNES ROMAN CATHOLIC CHURCH.

FIRST CHURCH OF CHRIST SCIENTIST.

THIRD CHURCH OF CHRIST SCIENTIST, Brooklyn
   3 manuals.

OTHER CITIES OF THE UNITED STATES

SAINT HENRY'S ROMAN CATHOLIC CHURCH, Bayonne, New
   Jersey.

BENEFICENT CONGREGATIONAL CHURCH, Providence, Rhode
   Island.

BAPTIST TEMPLE, Rochester, New York
   86 feet wide in the interior.

DRUID HILLS BAPTIST CHURCH, Atlanta, Georgia.

HAMLINE METHODIST EPISCOPAL CHURCH, Saint Paul, Minnesota.

SCOTTISH RITE CATHEDRAL, Dallas, Texas.

JOHNSON C. SMITH UNIVERSITY, Charlotte, North Carolina.

The Riverside Church organ is a good illustration of a modern high grade, large organ. It required over one year to construct this immense instrument at the factory, twenty truckload shipments of the organ parts and about nine months to install. It contains 167 stops, 2900 magnets, 22,000 contacts and the wires, if placed end to end, would extend a distance of over 100 miles.

The main organ has 127 speaking stops and is divided into Great, Swell, Solo, Echo, Percussion, and Pedal organs. With the exception of the Echo organ these are placed in chambers at each side of the chancel. The auxiliary (antiphonal) organ of 40 stops is divided into great, swell and pedal sections which are installed in chambers on the triforium floor and at each side of the rear gallery. The Echo organ is at the rear of the auditorium in a chamber at an elevation close to the main ceiling from which the tones are reflected.

The console is of the latest design, giving the organist complete mastery of registration. The crescendo of the registers is of the selective type. By the use of pistons the organist can control the seven stations at will. The Solo, Echo and Percussion organs are "floating" and can be played from any of the four manuals.

The latest type of swell boxes with their patented sound insulators, together with the working of the opening and closing of all folds in the different sections from one master shoe, make possible fine tonal expression through the flexibility in tempo, power and color of tone.

The company's endeavors for quality of workmanship have been aided by the long periods of service of many of their highly-skilled workmen. Many past and present employees have been with them for twenty-five, thirty-five, forty or even more years. In some instances the second generation is numbered among their employees.

Hook & Hastings Co. make all parts of their organs except sometimes the keys. The scales and gauges used in the gradation of their pipes represent the cumulative experience of over one hundred years. They have special formulae for the composition of the different kinds of metal pipes. For their wooden pipes they use California sugar pine as the best material obtainable.

This company installed their first electric action in an organ in 1895. They were thus among the first firms to do this successfully.

Two features of their electric organs they consider of prime importance. One is their magnets with poles made of softest Norway iron and armatures of the floating type with a special device for regulating. The method of making the magnets has not been changed since they were developed, for their chief repairman never found it necessary to replace one in twenty years' time.

The other is the use of platinum for the main contacts of their key and coupler actions. This metal is a perfect medium for electricity, is wear-resisting and not affected by heat or atmospheric changes. Its noncorroding quality was well proved when the platinum contacts of an organ damaged by the Dayton, Ohio, flood were found by test to be in perfect condition.

Other special features of their organs are:

> The multi-wind chests of the individual vertical valve type with a specially designed dust pocket for each port.

The swell boxes, containing a patented sound insulator.

The couplers are controlled by stop-tablets when few are used, and by toe studs when many are used.

For modern reed tones, including the French horn, English horn, 32 foot Bombarde and others, pocket eschalots and thick weighted tongues are used for better tone quality and for keeping these stops in better tune.

They have an orchestral flute stop patented February 6, 1924 and rights to certain developments of a French horn tone which George Audsley speaks of as follows:

> Very recently our attention has been directed to a lingual stop, labeled FRENCH HORN, which imitates the voice of the orchestral instrument more closely than any other organ stop known to us. This stop is the production of the Hook & Hastings Company, the esteemed organ builders of Kendall Green, Massachusetts. This stop differs in construction from any Horn pipe we have seen. While the Resonator is of the usual Trumpet form, it is surmounted by a pyramidal cap, soldered on, which is a novelty, so far as our knowledge extends, and which, we can readily understand, exerts a considerable mellowing effect on the tone in conjunction with the slot which admits of adjustment both at bottom and top.[16]

The "flute" stop is so constructed that the wind sheet from the tubulator conduit passes across the orifice in the manner employed by the orchestral flute player to reproduce the character of the flute tone.[17]

AEOLIAN-SKINNER ORGAN COMPANY, INC.

The original organization was established in 1901, by Ernest M. Skinner, who had been with the George S. Hutchings Company, and in 1905 was incorporated with the help of Worcester capitalists, as the Ernest M. Skinner Organ Company. In 1919, by the financial help of Arthur Hudson Marks, the Skinner Organ Company was organized, succeeding the Ernest M. Skinner Organ Company.

In 1920 the Steere Organ Company of Westfield, Massachusetts, was purchased by Arthur H. Marks, run independently for about a year and then was merged with the Skinner Organ Company, whose management operated the Steere factory. The Steere Organ

[16] Audsley, George Ashdown. *Organs of the Twentieth Century*, Chapter XVI, "Forms and Construction of Lingual Pipes" p. 466.
[17] Hook and Hastings Company. *Pipe Organs for Municipal Halls, Memorials, Churches, Theatres, Schools, Lodges* p. 23.

Company was formerly Steere & Turner of Springfield, Massachusetts, established in 1867. Mr. Turner died and the firm became J. W. Steere & Son Organ Company. That was succeeded by the Steere Organ Company, which located in Westfield when its Springfield factory was burned. After Henry F. Van Wart became Superintendent in 1911 they built many large fine instruments. These included organs in Woolsey Hall, Yale University, the Municipal Auditorium, Springfield, Massachusetts, Piedmont Church, Worcester, Massachusetts and First Church of Christ Scientist, Kansas City, Missouri.

In 1932 a new company was formed—the Aeolian-Skinner Organ Company—taking over the assets of the Skinner Organ Company and the pipe organ assets and business of the Aeolian Company, the control, however, remaining in the Skinner Organ Company by virtue of its holding 60 per cent of the stock of the Aeolian-Skinner Organ Company.

At that time the pipe organ factory of the Aeolian Company at Garwood, New Jersey, was closed, and since then all of the operations have been carried on at the Skinner factory in Dorchester, Massachusetts. The Skinner Organ Company had studios at its factory, 215 Sidney St., Dorchester, and in New York City, Cleveland, Ohio, and San Francisco and Los Angeles, California. Since the formation of the new company studios are maintained at Dorchester, Massachusetts, and in New York City, one at the Aeolian Company office and another at the Skinner Organ Company office.

This combination of Skinner and Aeolian brought together one of the leaders in each field of work (in the United States)— Skinner, a leading builder of church organs, and Aeolian, the leader in residence organs.

"Aeolian has probably built 80 per cent of all the residence work in this country, and numbers among its clients such well-known people as John D. Rockefeller, Charles M. Schwab, H. C. Frick, W. K. Vanderbilt, Pierre S. duPont and many other distinguished citizens." [18]

The Skinner Organ Company enjoys a prestige in church organs, having built many large instruments for famous cathedrals, churches and universities. It has also built concert, residence and a few theatre organs, none of the last recently, however. A total of about

[18] Statement of George L. Catlin, Vice President and Treasurer of Aeolian-Skinner Organ Company, Inc.

900 of all types of organs have been built by the Skinner Organ Company alone for all parts of the United States, and this even includes instruments for France and Japan.

This company's residence organs generally had a larger proportion of orchestral colors than their church organs, and kettle and snare drums were often used in them to good advantage. The house organs are made both with and without players, in which rolls are used, and their number of stops varies from six or seven to about fifty stops, as in the organ of the Skinner New York studio. At the present time they have a "Program Player," a circular holder by which up to ten records can be played successively.

Some important Skinner installations are the following:

CHURCH ORGANS

NEW YORK CITY
CATHEDRAL OF ST. JOHN THE DIVINE
4 manuals, 98 stops
GRACE CHURCH
4 manuals, 66 stops
FIFTH AVENUE PRESBYTERIAN CHURCH
4 manuals, 78 stops
ST. MARY THE VIRGIN
4 manuals
ST. THOMAS' CHURCH
4 manuals, 81 speaking stops, Great, Swell, Choir, Solo, Echo, and Pedal Organs
ST. BARTHOLOMEW'S CHURCH [19]
5 manuals, 106 speaking stops
KING'S CHAPEL, Boston
3 manuals, 37 stops
SECOND CONGREGATIONAL, Holyoke, Massachusetts
4 manuals, 77 stops
FOURTH PRESBYTERIAN CHURCH, Chicago, Illinois
4 manuals, 60 stops
ST. LUKE'S EPISCOPAL CHURCH, Evanston, Illinois
4 manuals, 64 stops
METHODIST TEMPLE, Chicago, Illinois
4 manuals
TRINITY CATHEDRAL, Cleveland, Ohio
4 manuals, 43 stops

[19] When St. Bartholomew's Church moved uptown about 1917, this new organ was installed.

GRACE CATHEDRAL, San Francisco, California
4 manuals
EAST LIBERTY PRESBYTERIAN CHURCH, Pittsburgh, Pennsylvania
4 manuals

HALL AND THEATRE ORGANS
CAPITOL THEATRE, New York City
CONGRESSIONAL LIBRARY, Washington, D. C.
3 manuals
CARNEGIE INSTITUTE, Pittsburgh, Pennsylvania
4 manuals
SEVERANCE HALL, Cleveland, Ohio
4 manuals, 87 stops, orchestral type of organ to be played with Cleveland Symphony Orchestra
CLEVELAND MUNICIPAL HALL
5 manuals, 140 odd stops, the largest built for a hall by this company

SCHOOL AND UNIVERSITY ORGANS, generally with four manuals and ninety to one hundred stops
COLLEGE OF THE CITY OF NEW YORK, New York City
4 manuals, 70 stops
COLUMBIA UNIVERSITY, New York City
4 manuals
WILLIAMS COLLEGE, Williamstown, Massachusetts
4 manuals, 62 stops
PRINCETON UNIVERSITY, Princeton, New Jersey
4 manuals. This was the beginning of their building of the classical type of organ
UNIVERSITY OF FLORIDA, Gainesville, Florida
UNIVERSITY OF CHICAGO, Chicago, Illinois
4 manuals
CATHEDRAL OF LEARNING, Pittsburgh, Pennsylvania
4 manuals
GROTON SCHOOL, GROTON, Massachusetts
3 manuals
YALE UNIVERSITY (three instruments), New Haven
one 4 manuals, two 3 manuals
UNIVERSITY OF CALIFORNIA, Los Angeles, California
4 manuals
TRINITY COLLEGE, Hartford, Connecticut
4 manuals
HARVARD UNIVERSITY, Cambridge, Massachusetts
4 manuals

Mr. Skinner has, from his beginning in organ work, been an ardent lover of beautiful, especially orchestral tones, and has always bent his energies toward reproducing them in the organ. He is acknowledged by many as the leader of his generation in the invention and development of such organ stops as the French Horn, English Horn, Flute Celeste and other orchestral stops.

Original or improved stops which are peculiarly characteristic of his work and the organs in which the registers [20] were first used are as follows:

> Erzähler—Christ Church, Hartford
> Orchestral oboe (8′ and 16′)—City College, New York City
> Kleine Erzähler—Fourth Presbyterian Church, Chicago
> Tuba Mirabilis—Cathedral of Saint John the Divine
> Orchestral Bassoon (16′)—Skinner Studio
> Bombarde (32′)—City College, New York City
> Violone (32′)—Cathedral of Saint John the Divine
> Contra Bassoon (32′)—Princeton University.

The French Horn (8′) which Mr. Skinner has developed possesses singular beauty and purity.

In 1927 G. Donald Harrison, for many years an associate of Henry Willis of London, came to this country, and joined the Skinner Company as an assistant to Mr. Skinner. He worked with the latter on all of the technical details of the tonal work, quickly absorbing the Skinner methods and voicing practices. Since Mr. Harrison had brought the knowledge and technical training needed to design the "classical" organ and produce the ensemble desired in the present organ world, he became in a few years the master of that organ, a recent development by this company. Hence he was successively called upon by the University of California, Trinity College, Harvard University, Church of St. Mary the Virgin, and Grace Cathedral to design large instruments for them.

As Mr. Skinner is a fine mechanic and inventor, in addition to being a voicer of ability, this company has contributed much to the development of modern organs in the way of improvements and patented inventions.

The Orchestrator invented about 1916 was an interesting development of automatic organ playing. By reducing the size of the holes, the whole organ range of sixty-two notes could be perforated on the player rolls. These "tracker" holes were staggered to form

[20] Registers are all 8 feet unless otherwise noted.

different sets. This permitted division of the tracker board into six sections allowing six solo voices to be played at once. This invention could be used in an organ of two manuals or larger provided it contained a sufficient variety of orchestral stops. It produced beautiful color effects through combinations or different instrumental tone qualities.

As this was a complicated mechanism only a few were made before the World War when production was stopped. One Orchestrator was placed in the home of Mr. Lamborne of Montclair, New Jersey, and another in the home of Mr. Arthur Curtis James of New York City.

The idea, which Mr. Skinner originated, of using in player rolls small holes, which sometimes would play a note and sometimes a stop [21] is used today in this company's player rolls, and a maximum of three voices can be played at once. Three sections play five octaves and the pedal section plays three octaves.

Among the important inventions and improvements of Mr. Skinner are the following:

> The Pitman windchest,[22] invented about thirty-eight years ago. This makes the stop action instantaneous. It is used by most of the principal builders in the United States, England, Germany and France, as it gives precision in changing from one tone color to another, is reliable, less expensive and more comfortable to build. Mr. Skinner wrote as follows to William Harrison Barnes in substantiation of his claim to this invention—"The Pitman windchest is the invention of your humble servant and was published for the first time in Audsley's *Art of Organ Building* p. 347 Vol. 2. I made this drawing for Audsley but he did not give me credit for it." [23]

> The first variable pneumatic swell pedal made in the small organ exhibited in the foreign exhibition on Huntington Avenue in the early 1880's.[24]

> Extremely rapid pneumatic key action.[25]

Some patents of the Skinner Organ Company are:

> Electro-pneumatic crescendo pedal—thirty-five years ago.
> Electro-pneumatic swell engine pedal—twenty-three years ago.[26]

[21] Statement of George M. Catlin, Vice President, Aeolian-Skinner Organ Company, Inc.
[22] For a discussion of this invention see Barnes, William Harrison. *Contemporary American Organ*. 1930 Edition pp. 272 & 273.
[23] Barnes, William Harrison. *Contemporary American Organ*. 1933 Edition p. 283.
[24] Statement of William B. Goodwin, Lowell, Massachusetts, organ builder. Possibly the organ illustrated in the *New England Magazine* 1897 p. 494.
[25] Statement of Ernest M. Skinner.
[26] See Barnes, William Harrison. *Contemporary American Organ*. Whiffletree motor p. 117.

Beginning with January 1, 1936 Mr. Skinner has gone into business with his son at Organ (formerly Serlo) Hall, Methuen, Massachusetts.

FRAZEE ORGAN COMPANY

The founder of the company, Leslie H. Frazee, was born in 1870 in New Brunswick, Canada, where as a lad of fourteen he began working for the Peters Organ Company of Saint John. While there he helped to manufacture the first electric action organ in Canada. In 1894 he entered the employ of the Boston firm of Jesse Woodberry, when he was starting to build his first electric action organ. When Mr. Woodberry retired from business in 1910 Leslie H. Frazee, E. E. Smallman, Mr. Woodberry's foreman, and Henry D. Kimball of the Hutchings Organ Company formed a company under the name of Kimball, Smallman & Frazee located in 1913 at 520 Harrison Ave. Thus this company is a successor to the Jesse Woodberry Company.

Upon Mr. Smallman's retirement in 1915 the firm name was changed to the Kimball-Frazee Organ Company, located in 1917 at 101 Broadway Extension and in 1919 at 101 Bristol St. At the time of Mr. Kimball's death in 1920 Mr. Frazee's son, H. Norman Frazee, joined the business and the firm name was changed to Frazee Organ Company. Since 1924 Harry Upson Camp, an organist and organ architect, has been Sales Manager. Upon the death in December 1934 of Leslie H. Frazee the management of the company was taken over by H. Norman Frazee. The company's present factory, located at 134 Tremont St., Everett, Massachusetts, was acquired and thoroughly equipped in 1925.

This company has built church, school and college, concert and residence organs, about 300 altogether in all parts of the United States, the majority being located in New England. In these extra large scales are used because the company believes that the best tone can be produced only by utilizing large pipe scales and moderate wind pressure.

This firm has been a leader in developing small two manual, inexpensive organs, costing earlier from $4000 to $8500 but, since the depression has reduced the price of materials they now cost only between $2000 and $6000. The company's low overhead enables them to make these organs with an interesting combination of stops.

One of the features of these instruments is the Dulciana selective mixture which is of inestimable value in registration and for delicate coloring as well as in the ensemble. A 16 ft. Dulciana is successfully employed both in the Pedal and Swell divisions of this type of organ. As far as the company knows they have been the first builders to incorporate these tonalities in small organs. They have also a specially scaled and voiced reed stop with a smooth tone, neither Oboe nor Trumpet, which plays an important part in the ensemble and also constitutes a beautiful solo stop.

Because of their development of high grade small instruments the company has naturally built many school organs some of which are as follows:

PHILLIPS ACADEMY, Andover, Massachusetts
    Stone Chapel—3 manuals, Peabody Home—2 manuals
DANA HALL SCHOOL, Wellesley, Massachusetts
    3 manuals
MOUNT HOLYOKE COLLEGE, South Hadley, Massachusetts
    2 manuals
CRANE THEOLOGICAL SCHOOL, Tufts College, Medford, Massachusetts
    2 manuals
SAINT ANSELM'S COLLEGE, Manchester, New Hampshire
    2 manuals
STONY BROOK SCHOOL, Stony Brook, Long Island, New York
    2 manuals
STATE SCHOOL FOR THE BLIND, Talladega, Alabama
    2 manuals
MOUNT BERRY SCHOOL, Mount Berry, Georgia
    3 manuals

Some of their notable organs are as follows:

CHURCH ORGANS
    PARK STREET CHURCH, Boston, Massachusetts
        3 manuals
    TEMPLE MISHKAN TEFILA, Boston, Massachusetts
        4 manuals
    FIRST CONGREGATIONAL CHURCH, Lowell, Massachusetts
        4 manuals
    FIRST METHODIST EPISCOPAL CHURCH, Winthrop, Massachusetts
        3 manuals

TRINITARIAN CONGREGATIONAL CHURCH, Concord, Massachusetts
  2 manuals

CONGREGATIONAL CHURCH, Southington, Connecticut
  3 manuals

ST. MARY'S CHURCH, Lewiston, Maine
  3 manuals

WESTMINSTER UNITARIAN CHURCH, Providence, Rhode Island
  3 manuals

TRINITY EPISCOPAL CHURCH, Potsdam, New York
  3 manuals

CONGREGATIONAL CHURCH, Everett, Massachusetts
  John Herman Loud, who played at the dedication of the new two
  manual Frazee organ, in 1924, wrote of it to the company as
  "an organ which was so satisfactory in every way. The voicing
  of the instrument is exquisite. The strings on the Swell are
  simply beautiful and the same may be truthfully said about the
  Diapasons, Flutes and Reeds: Cornopean, Oboe and Vox
  Humana."[27]

The residence organ of Ernest B. Dane, Brookline, Massachusetts,
  of 4 manuals and 86 stops, is one of the largest private
  organs in the United States today.

HARVARD CLUB
  4 manuals, 67 stops (non-borrowed). This was an outstanding
  concert organ when it was installed, and the only strictly concert
  one about Boston. William King Covell, after playing on this
  instrument described it Oct. 27, 1927 as follows [28] "It is a very
  fine instrument indeed. The voicing of the Diapasons is particularly good, while the Solo Tuba is, without exception, the finest
  I have heard. It would take too long to enumerate the many
  excellencies of the voicing, but I must speak of the excellent quality
  of the Swell and Solo strings and the large flutes of Great and Solo.
  "It is very rare to find a large modern organ possessing the
  advantages of electric action, combination action, etc., together
  with the excellence of tone of the old instruments. This does not
  mean that the instrument is lacking in the more orchestral voices,
  or modern chorus reeds, but simply that, together with these, you
  have preserved the wonderful oldtime Diapason tone to a greater
  degree than has almost any other American builder. I think you
  resemble, in this respect, some of the best of the present day
  English builders; judging not from paper alone but from what I
  heard when visiting England two years ago."

[27] A brochure entitled *Frazee Organs*. Testimonials p. 18.
[28] *Ibid* p. 19.

C. Bells and Bell Chimes Cast by Paul Revere and His Firm's Successors

In the field of bell chimes Boston has had a notable history beginning with the importation in 1745 of the famous first peal of bells brought into the country for Christ Church, Boston. A well known firm of bell chime casters, which carried on an important line of activities started by Paul Revere, was in business in Boston for over one hundred years through its various successors. One of the earliest concerns in the series, the Boston Copper Co., cast the first chimes in America in 1825.

The Boston News Letter described the Christ Church peal thus in its issue of July 25, 1745—"Last week a fine set of 8 bells were brought hither in a vessel from Bristol designed for Dr. Cutler's Church at the North Part of the Town. We hear the largest of them is near 1500 Weight, and the whole set about 7000." These were in the Key of F and cast in 1744 by Rudhall of Gloucester, England. The largest weighed 1545 pounds, the smallest 620 pounds, and the aggregate total was 7272 pounds. They cost £560 in England. The first bells bore the inscription, "This peal of bells is the gift of a number of generous persons to Christ Church in Boston, N. E. A. 1744 A. R." [1] In 1874 Mr. Elbridge Goss, who made a study of "Early Bells of Massachusetts," wrote "It has been the practice for many years to chime these bells for several nights at Christmas time 'ringing the Old Year out and the New Year in.'" [2]

This peal was changed first to a chime action, later by R. A. Cram again made a peal, then finally a chime once more.

The remarkably beautiful tonal quality of these bells doubtless interested Paul Revere, who became an experienced ringer as a member of the guild, "Order of Bell Ringers," which had charge of these bells. He was described by Dr. Waterhouse, the first teacher of the science of mineralogy in the United States, as "the only man in 1794 who appeared to have known anything of the

---

[1] *New England Historical and Genealogical Register.* "Early Bells of Massachusetts," Elbridge H. Goss, Vol. 28, 1874 p. 181.
[2] *Ibid* pp. 181 & 182.

discrimination between the ores of the seven metals." [3] Dr. Waterhouse adds, "We presume not to say how far those things were known and taught in Philadelphia where there was a Medical School. We speak only of Mineralogy, previous to 1783, as it regards New England, and the history of the mineral cabinet at Cambridge which was the first collection of the kind made in North America." [3]

At any rate Paul Revere was appointed first Major, then Lieutenant Colonel, in the artillery regiment raised for the defence of Massachusetts. He was expected to work out the design of anything mechanical needed for the public good. When requested by Washington, he succeeded in rendering useful by means of a newly contrived carriage the cannon at Castle William whose trunnions had been broken by the British when they left Boston.

In 1788 after the Revolution he established an iron foundry at 13 Lynn Street, now Causeway St., where he cast brass cannon and became interested in the development of copper bolts and spikes as substitutes for iron to fasten the copper sheathing which preserved the bottoms of vessels from worms. After repeated trials he succeeded in manufacturing the article to his satisfaction. The new Republic's need for copper sheets and plates was brought to his attention because he had to import from England the copper sheets for sheathing the ship "Constitution" when this was built. The sheets were held in place by handwrought copper nails he made, however. He then set himself to acquiring a complete knowledge of rolling copper into sheets. His son Joseph went into partnership with him in 1801 and they bought an old government powder factory at Canton, Massachusetts, and installed copper rolling machinery in it. The first sale of copper from this first American copper and brass industry was for the dome of the then new Massachusetts State House. [4] The Government gave Revere & Son a loan of ten thousand dollars for the purchase of the copper which was used in recoppering "Old Ironsides," home for repairs in 1803. The event was recorded in the ship's log for June 26, 1803 thus—"The carpenters gave nine cheers, which were answered by the seamen and calkers because they had in fourteen days completed coppering the ship with copper made in the States." [5]

[3] *New England Magazine.* "Early American Artists and Mechanics," by J. T. & E. Buckingham—Original Papers October 1832 No. II Paul Revere p. 307.
[4] Paul Revere's "Waste Book" (day book) with this entry is among the Revere Memorabilia at the Massachusetts Historical Society.
[5] From a *Brief Sketch of the Business Life of Paul Revere* by the Taunton-New Bedford Copper Company.

"The first bell foundry in America was probably that of Col. Aaron Hobart at Abington, Mass. Information relative to the establishment of this foundry is contained in Hobart's History of Abington where it is stated that in 1761 a deserter from the British army, Gillimore, at one time a workman in an English foundry, was employed by Col. Hobart and retained in service for many years. When Col. Hobart gave up business he sent one of his sons with a blacksmith to Boston and taught Paul Revere to mould and cast the first bell which he ever made. This bell was cast in 1792 at the foundry in Lynn Street, now Commercial Street. . . It proved to be a rough, unhomogeneous casting, and its sound was correspondingly harsh, puny, and unmusical. Originally hung in the belfry of the New Brick (Second) Church on Middle now Hanover St., Boston, it is now in use in St. James Church, North Cambridge.

"Revere found that there were many details to be studied in the selection and proportioning of metals, and in heating, casting, and hanging the bell. . . In 1804 he sent his son, Joseph Warren Revere, to visit the principal foundries in England and the continent, and after a few years he was able to turn out superior bells of which his masterpiece is still in use in King's Chapel.[6]

"From the stock book of Paul Revere & Son, it appears that between the years 1792 and 1828 three hundred and ninety-eight bells were cast at this foundry. Of these the heaviest, weighing 2884 lbs., was sent to Providence, R. I. Many of the lighter bells were shipped to Cuba and Porto Rico for use on sugar plantations." [6]

Paul Revere adopted the English method of hanging his bells, but bungling sextons generally bolted a counterweight above the headstock to slow up the rotation. This tended to make the tones harsh, created such friction as to make the bells more or less unmanageable and made the clapper rest upon the sound bow at its impact, thus interrupting the sound waves in such a way as sooner or later to cause a fracture. This has proved the principal mode of destruction of not less than fifty of Paul Revere's bells. [7]

The foundry which cast bells, brass cannon and many iron articles [8] was transferred to the Revere estate in Canton, still owned

[6] From a clipping based on *Essex Institute Historical Collections*, Vol. XLVII October 1911 & XLVIII January 1912 by Dr. Arthur H. Nichols.
[7] *Essex Institute Historical Collections* Vol. XLVII No. 4, October 1911, p. 299-300. The Bells of Paul and Joseph Revere, by Dr. Arthur H. Nichols.
[8] See Bishop, J. Leander. *A History of American Manufactures from 1608 to 1860* p. 497 for a list of these articles.

by his descendants, from Lynn St., after the buildings had been damaged in the October gale of 1804. Bells from this foundry were inscribed in flat Roman letters with no attempt at ornamentation, "Paul Revere," "Paul Revere & Son" or "Revere & Co.," but followed almost without exception by the date of casting. After Colonel Paul Revere's death in 1818 Joseph Warren Revere carried on his father's business till 1828 when it was conveyed to the Revere Copper Company, (since 1930 Revere Copper & Brass, Inc.) which never undertook bell casting. Joseph W. then began his naval career as a midshipman, while his son, John, took charge of the company until his death in 1886. A Boston office has been maintained at various addresses.

An older son Paul was taught the trade of silversmith by his father and continued in that line until his death Jan. 16, 1813. His son Paul, the first to be called Paul Revere, Jr., was one of three grandsons who worked for a while in Colonel Revere's business in Canton.[9] Paul Jr. later went into business for himself casting bells at Bridgewater and later Braintree. His bells were usually inscribed "Revere" and rarely bore a date. Because he was known as Paul Revere, Jr., many people, including apparently Dr. Arthur Nichols, have confused him with his father, and thought he was the elder son of Colonel Paul Revere instead of his grandson.

In 1820 Paul Jr. and William Blake started the business which later became the Blake Bell Co. The Boston Directories of 1821 and 1822 listed this as "Revere (Paul) & Blake (William) brass founders Battery-march" (St.) In the latter year "Revere, Paul house 59 Middle" St. is also listed. In 1823 the firm is given as "Revere, Paul & Co. (William Blake and John W. Sullivan)" at the same business address. Thus began the bell casting business which continued through various successors for over one hundred years and cast many noted bells and chimes.

BOSTON COPPER CO.

formed by William Blake in 1823 and listed in the directory of 1825 as the Boston and Braintree Copper and Brass Company with Henry N. Hooper as agent at 3 Battery March. In 1826 it was given as just the Boston Copper Co. at the same address.

HENRY N. HOOPER & CO.

was listed in 1830 at the same location as successor to the late

[9] Information supplied by a descendant of Colonel Paul Revere. See also copartnership notice, *Boston Gazette*, April 15, 1811, which shows he was also known as Paul Revere 3rd. The third grandson was Frederick W. Lincoln.

Boston Copper Co., and in 1860 at 58 Commercial St. They used as a trade mark a bell with the words "Hooper & Co. Trade Mark" on it. This firm was dissolved December 31, 1868 and succeeded by

Wm. Blake and Wm. S. Blake

under the "style" of Wm. Blake & Co. with the foundry at the corners of Allen, Brighton & Charles Streets, Boston. This firm was succeeded by C. T. Robinson in 1888, which in turn was followed in 1890 by

Blake Bell Co. with Wm. S. Blake as manager.

The Blake Bell Co. was located from about 1890 to 1900 at Allen Street corner of Brighton.

Bay State Brass Foundry & Blake Bell Co.

presently listed as just Bay State Brass Foundry, was located in 1900 at 155 A St., South Boston. This company went out of business sometime around 1913.

Some of the chimes cast by the successors of the firm of Paul Revere & Co. are:

The Boston Copper Co.

cast the first complete chime of bells in America in 1825, consisting of eight bells, the tenor 2000 pounds. [10]

H. N. Hooper & Co.

The second chime made in the country—11 bells, tenor 3000 lbs. E-flat had on exhibition at the Mechanics' Fair, in Boston, in 1850 for which a silver medal was awarded.[11]

1860—Arlington St. Church, Boston—

the "Phillips' Chime" consisting of 16 bells aggregate weight 14,960 pounds.

"This Chime of 15 bells (the 16th was afterwards added by the Rev. Dr. Gannett, the pastor) was a gift from the Hon. Jonathan Phillips to the religious society of which he had long been a member, on the erection of a new Meeting House, 1860." [12]

1860—Tower of Christ Church, Cambridge [13]—

chimed for the first time on Easter Sunday by Henry P. Munroe, who was instrumental in having the number increased from eight to thirteen to represent the thirteen original states. The largest "D" weighed 3108 pounds and the smallest "G" 200, aggregate weight being 12,661. The cost—about $5,000—was raised by subscription.

[10] The place for which they were cast was not stated in the Blake Bell Company's booklet.
[11] *Facts Regarding the Bell Foundry of Blake Bell Co.*—a booklet p. 5.
[12] *New England Historical and Genealogical Register.* "Early Bells of Massachusetts" by Elbridge H. Goss of Melrose, Vol. 28 p. 182.
[13] *Ibid* p. 279.

1861—GRACE EPISCOPAL CHURCH, Providence, R. I.,
>   16 bells, aggregate weight 17,429 pounds.

The pamphlet published by William Blake & Co.
>   in 1876 contained sixty odd testimonials from satisfied customers for whom single bells had been cast by Henry N. Hooper & Co. These included points as far distant as St. Paul's Church, Louisville, Kentucky, 1844; First Baptist Church, Macon, Georgia; and also bells for Manchester, New Hampshire, City Hall, 1845, (3013 pounds); and Lawrence City Hall, 1849, (3446 pounds).

The largest single bell cast by this company for round ringing
>   was for the Androscoggin Mills, Lewiston, Maine, 10,233 lbs. in 1861.

Their largest bell of all
>   was for the Corporation of New York City for a fire bell, the largest at that time in the United States, aggregating some 21,612 lbs.

WM. BLAKE & CO.

1868—FIRST PARISH CHURCH, Harvard Sq., Charlestown [14]—
>   The "Harris Chime," gift of Miss Charlotte Harris, consisting of 16 bells, the largest "D" weighing 3267 pounds, the smallest "A" 129, aggregate weight 14,864, and costing about $7,000.

1869—TOWER OF TRINITY CHURCH, Haverhill [15]—
>   the sixth chime in Massachusetts, consisting of 11 bells, the largest "G" 1393 pounds, the smallest "G" 186 pounds, total weight 5095.

1871—MEMORIAL CHURCH, Amherst [16]—
>   seventh chime in Massachusetts, consisting of 9 bells aggregating 8287 pounds key of E. On one bell is the inscription "1871 These bells are placed here by George Howe of Boston, and are to be made to chime on all suitable occasions in commemoration of the brave patriots connected with Amherst College, who lost their lives in the war against the Great Rebellion of 1861."

1873—GRACE CHURCH, Medford [17]—
>   eighth chime in Massachusetts, consisting of 9 bells, largest 1400 pounds, smallest 200, aggregate weight 5025 pounds, costing $2600 of which $600 was appropriated by the town. "G" was the Town of Medford Bell. The others had interesting names like Rector's Bell, Marriage Bell, Holy Communion, Holy Baptism, Burial, Children's, Christmas and Easter.

[14] *New England Historical and Genealogical Register.* "Early Bells of Massachusetts" by Elbridge H. Goss of Melrose, Vol. 28 p. 178.
[15] *Ibid* p. 284.
[16] *Ibid* p. 288.
[17] *Ibid* p. 184.

1873—GRACE CHURCH PARISH, Newton [18]—
consisting of 9 bells, "E," largest 2150 pounds, smallest
295 pounds, total 8296, costing $4,400 a gift of Mrs. Elizabeth
Trull Eldridge.

1874—ST. MARY'S (Catholic) CHURCH, Lawrence [19]—
the tenth in Massachusetts, consisting of 16 bells, largest "D"
3161 pounds, smallest "A" 132 pounds, aggregate weight
14,635 pounds, cost about $8,000. The article states "These
bells were cast by the well-known bell-founders Wm. Blake &
Co. of this city, are sixteen in number and form one of the
finest peals that have ever,

'Low at times, and loud at times,
And changing like a poet's rhymes
Rang the beautiful wild chimes.' "

William Blake & Co. as bronze bell founders manufactured
church, fire alarm, factory, steamboat, locomotive and plantation
bells. The preface of their business pamphlet stated, "We have
cast some thousands of bells now in use on this continent, and in
other parts of the world, varying in weight from one hundred to
twenty-two thousand pounds each." They also claimed that the
largest and most perfect chimes in the United States (either imported
or made by other bell-founders), consisting of sixteen bells each,
were made by them for Grace Episcopal Church, Providence, Rhode
Island; Arlington Street Church, Boston; and the First Parish
Church, Charlestown. Attention was called to their apparatus for
tolling by using the tongue, so constructed as to make it impossible
to break the bell. The mountings were made to fit each bell to its
hangings. They also pointed out that "Our bells are made of copper
and tin alone; cast in moulding-cases of iron lined with loam (a
method first introduced by ourselves in 1848, [20] but which has since
been copied by other makers, who claim it as their own); and all
bells over five hundred pounds in weight have springs attached to
prevent the tongue from striking a double blow, or resting on the
bell, thereby destroying the vibration of the same. . . . We have
invariably, at all public exhibitions at which we have entered bells,
taken the first premium—either gold or silver medals or diploma—
over all competitors." [21]

[18] *New England Historical and Genealogical Register.* "Early Bells of Massachusetts" by
    Elbridge H. Goss of Melrose Vol. 28 pp. 282 & 283.
[19] *Ibid.* Addenda Vol. 37 pp. 50 & 51.
[20] This would have been by H. N. Hooper & Co.
[21] *Facts Regarding the Bell Foundry of Blake Bell Co.,* a booklet, p. 6.

D. Band, Orchestral, Fretted and Miscellaneous Instruments

1. STANDING OF MASSACHUSETTS MAKERS

In the census of 1860 there were 53 establishments listed as making miscellaneous musical instruments with an annual production value of $315,800. Massachusetts had 6 of these establishments making instruments worth about $60,800 a year. In 1927 [1] some 99 establishments were listed with a total annual production value of $15,311,100. Of these Massachusetts had 8 establishments with products valued at $788,340. These probably did not include many shops of violin makers as only a few hand made instruments are turned out by them in a year, and repair work takes most of the time of the workers in these establishments.

Boston has not been noted for quantity manufacture of band and orchestral instruments, but the quality of some of its products in these lines has made a nation wide reputation for them.

Stringed instruments were made in Greater Boston about the time of the American Revolution or before. With this early start Boston was one of the two first centres of violin and stringed instrument making in the United States. New York was the other. Philadelphia and Chicago became centres later. Even today few cities in the United States have really professional makers, [2] that is—men who have been apprenticed in this highly skilled hand work.

There are now three chief centres for making violins of the art type in this country—New York, Chicago, and Boston. Most of the present Boston firms are known internationally, as is shown by their being listed in one or more dictionaries of violin makers published in Europe. *Die Geigen und Lautenmacher* 1913 edition listed 21 makers in New York, 15 in Chicago, and 14 in Boston. Alberto Bachmann's *Encyclopedia of the Violin* published in 1925 listed 74 American violin makers located in various parts of the United States. Of these New York had 13 establishments, Chicago 10, and Boston 9. If the shops given for Boston are indicative of the

[1] Latest census in which figures are given separately for Massachusetts.
[2] Statement of Erik Gould of John A. Gould & Sons.

general situation the firms listed were those of makers of the handicraft art type of instrument, with generally small shops and only a few highly skilled workers.

Inexpensive stringed instruments for the orchestra can be made in Europe and imported, despite a high duty, for about the cost of the raw materials in the United States. Consequently, Boston violin houses generally do not make instruments retailing for less than $100. [3] These statements seem to be borne out by the fact that the census for 1900 reported only 1503 instruments of the violin family manufactured that year and the census for 1935 reported only 3280 such instruments worth $126,402 for the entire country. This latter total doubtless includes the production of the one firm in the whole United States which makes inexpensive violins on a quantity production basis.

Boston is now the centre of high grade flute making. Dr. Dayton C. Miller wrote that this is due largely to the work of George W. Haynes, who came here from Providence in 1887, and William S. Haynes. "He [the latter] is the most prominent maker in this country at the present time, and I think it is correct to say that he is perhaps the most eminent flute maker in the world. I would make only one possible exception to this statement; that relates to a London maker, but the London makers are apparently losing in standing, while Haynes has been gaining. There are at the present time some other very fine flute makers in Boston also." [4]

In the nineteenth century Boston was a prominent center of brass instrument manufacturing and it still has two manufacturers of the highest grade of brass instruments.

During the Civil War Boston was a centre of drum making for the Union Army Bands. Two present day firms make the finest quality of drums.

Because of the many fine players and teachers of plectrum instruments, which included such men as George C. Dobson, Wm. A. Cole, A. A. Babb, Albert D. Grover, George S. Lansing, Burt E. Shattuck, and later Gad Robinson and Walter Jacobs, Boston became by about 1885 and remains a leading centre for the manufacture of fretted instruments.

[3] Statements of A. J. Oettinger, Musicians' Supply Company and Henry F. Schultz, violin maker.
[4] From a letter of Dr. Dayton C. Miller, Case School of Applied Science, Cleveland, Ohio, owner of the D. C. Miller Collection of Flutes, to the writer.

The contributions of some important former makers and of the present day concerns are discussed in the main text under three headings—"Violin and String Makers"; "Flute, Piccolo and Clarinet Makers"; and "Brass, Percussion, Fretted and Miscellaneous Instrument Manufacturers."

Whatever information the writer could collect, largely from personal knowledge of people interviewed, about other earlier makers of these types of instruments or about makers who have removed to other places is given in the various sections of Appendix IV.

2. Violin and String Makers

a. Some Important Former Makers

Despite the fact that music except hymn singing was disapproved by the Puritans "Massachusetts apart from the Hub may be credited with having produced the first violins made in the country." [1] The earliest violin of New England make known to John A. Gould, who has made a study of early makers, is dated 1776 and was made in Worcester.

One early instrument maker was Samuel Blyth (1744-1795), who made harpsichords and most kinds of stringed instruments. [2] His shop was on Summer Street, Salem, in 1784.

Another maker in colonial days was Benjamin Crehore. He had a shop in his home and as far back as 1791 was well known in New York and Philadelphia as well as in Boston as a maker of violins, violoncellos, Spanish and English guitars, drums, flutes and pianofortes.[3][4][5] In the matter of credit he was helped by Lewis Vose, a relative of the founder of Vose & Sons Piano Company. Whether Crehore made instruments of the viol family before or during the war of the American Revolution is uncertain but an instrument of the 'cello type, dating about 1785, has been examined and possesses the following characteristics:

"The instrument presents very much the appearance of an old Mittenwald 'Cello; that is, it has the 'cut off' effect at the top and bottom that bespeaks the Tyrolean 'Cellos of the period before 1750. Viewed as a whole, this Crehore 'Cello has an old world look and nothing of the crudeness that characterizes much of the early American work in violin making. The workmanship is good and the model is fairly high. There is no purfling, but ink lines to imitate purfling are drawn on the back, and even these are lacking on the top.

"The scroll is surprisingly well done and possesses a good style of its own. The cutting is deep and the 'eyes' are very promin-

---

[1] Spillane, Daniel. *History of the American Pianoforte* p. 47.
[2] Belknap, Henry W. *Artists and Craftsmen of Essex County, Massachusetts.* p. 29.
[3] *American History and Encyclopedia of Music* p. 317.
[4] For information about his pianofortes see pp. 104-5.
[5] Spillane, Daniel. *History of the American Pianoforte* p. 51.

ent. The lower half of the back of the scroll is finished flat. The sound hole slants but little, and although wide is well cut and of good style. The body is 29 inches long: the width of the upper bout is 13¼ inches and of the lower bout 16½ inches. The corners are short.

"The Crehore varnish was of good quality and quite soft in texture. On one bass viol the color was a dark brown. There is a small label, with a garland border as follows:

Base Viols
Made and Sold by
Benjamin Crehore
in Milton." [6]

The first instrument described, which had a new neck, was sold by Ernest A. Anderberg six or seven years ago, supposedly to go to Milton, Massachusetts.

"A large 'cello made by Crehore in Dorchester, in 1788 was played in the Old South Church at Weymouth, Massachusetts." [6]

One of Crehore's violoncellos has been repaired by the firm of Weeman, Beal and Holmberg (possibly the one in the possession of the Preston family?)

William Green, a partner in 1798 of Bent & Green, [7] left about 1800 apparently to make bass viols for church use. A Mr. A. M. Summer owned one of the date of 1800. Other instruments of his were one dated 1801, of high model, and another 1805. Still another bore "the ticket:

Bass Viols Made and Sold by
Green & Allen, Medway, Mass., 1817." [8]

The firm consisted of William Green and Deacon Samuel Allen— earlier a carpenter, draftsman, architect and building contractor at Newburyport, and later inventor of machines—for the years 1815-18.

The first Boston master makers of violins were the White brothers, Asa Warren and Ira Johnson, one of whose violins dated 1835 is now in the possession of Mr. Gould. "The Whites were the first 'family' of American violin makers." [9] Violins made previous to theirs were generally rather amateurish instruments.

[6] Howe, William H. *The Violinist's Guide.* Early American Violin Makers p. 15.
[7] See p. 105.
[8] Howe, William H. *The Violinist's Guide.* Early American Violin Makers p. 17.
[9] *Ibid* p. 18.

Both Whites were fine workmen, having been wood workers before they made violins and some violas. They had no training in violin making other than their studies of instruments by the old makers whom they used as their models. [10]

The elder brother, Ira J. "was borne in Barre, Massachusetts, July 9, 1813." [11]   He was in business from around 1835 to about 1890 probably. [12]   One instrument was made by him in 1844 from wood of the Lexington Street Church Communion Table and from wood of the old Chauncy Street Church.   In 1847-48 he was in partnership with James Henry White [13] under the firm name I. J. & J. H. White at 59 Court St.   Then he and his brother Asa Warren were in business together as I. J. & A. W. White 1849-52 at 52 Court St. and as White Brothers 1853-63 at 86 Tremont St. When they had the Tremont Temple Music Store they advertised "Importers of Musical Instruments, French, German & Italian Strings of the Best Quality, Foreign Instrumental & Vocal Music, Solos, Duos, Trios, Quartuors, Orchestra and CHOIR MUSIC. Instruments Made, Repaired, Tuned, Bought, Sold or Exchanged." [14] After 1863 Ira J. was in business alone first in Malden then in Melrose.

"In the early part of his career he [Ira Johnson] used his own model, but in 1851 he bought a Stradiuarius for $1,000 which he copied.   In 1864 he again made a change of model this time from the Stradiuarius to the Nicholas Amati form; these two models he used the rest of his life.   His long study and fine work placed him at the head of the early American violin makers.   Ira J. White received three medals from the Massachusetts Mechanics' Fair." [11] He used to get $150 apiece for his instruments, while Asa Warren sold his for $75 or $100. [10]   Ira J. White died in December 1895.

"Asa Warren White was born in Barre, Massachusetts in 1826. He worked in his young days for Henry Prentiss [15] [dealer and publisher], with a violin maker named Giradol, a quick workman, who worked on all forms of stringed instruments.   In 1849 Ira J. and A. W. White formed a partnership and worked together repairing and making different instruments.   Asa Warren made his in-

[10] Statement of Edmund F. Bryant, who made his first violin while working for Ira J. White.
[11] Howe, William H. *The Violinist's Guide.* Early American Violin Makers p. 18.
[12] Statement of A. J. Oettinger and Edmund F. Bryant.
[13] See Appendix IV Violin & Bow Makers p. 263.
[14] *Boston Directory 1861,* Advertising Section p. 85.
[15] See p. 11.

struments after the Stradiuarius and Guarnerius models. After Ira J. withdrew from the firm Calvin Baker worked for him [Asa Warren] and made many good violins. After him, Orrin Weeman worked for A. W. White about three years and for a while also a man named Alden." [16]

When Asa W. White was in business alone he continued at 86 Tremont St. until 1870. Later addresses were 50 Bromfield St. from 1876-79 and 147 Tremont St. from 1881-83.

He (A. W. White) turned out several hundred violins "and about ten 'Cellos, several violas, three viol da gambas, and two viol d'Amors. A. W. White received a gold medal from the Massachusetts Mechanics' Fair." [16] He advertised the quality of his instruments thus in 1883:

> "Violins Highest Awards Wherever Exhibited
> Over three hundred now in use
> None have proved inferior
> Endorsed by the best artists in the country
> Every instrument guaranteed
> Only the finest and best old wood used in construction
> Amati, Stradivarius, Guarnerius & Maggini Models
> $75 each" [17]

Asa Warren White apparently followed the lead of Elias Howe in collecting old instruments for sale, as the same advertisement stated, "I keep in stock a line of fine old Violins—Italian, French & German. A list sent upon application." He imported French violins of the celebrated Italian models which he graduated and adjusted and sold for $17 alone, with bow and case for $21. He also graduated and adjusted German violins selling them for $9 alone, with bow and case for $13. He kept in stock for sale violins, violas and 'cellos of different grades, boxes, cases, trimmings of all kinds, and Italian and German strings by the best known makers. [17]

His shop in Boston was a training school for some of the later violin makers. He died in 1893. The following story is related of him:

A short rotund man brought into his shop one day an instrument which he claimed was a Stradivarius. Mr. White, a tall,

[16] Howe, William H. *The Violinist's Guide.* Early American Makers p. 18.
[17] Information from an advertisement of A. W. White in *The Apollo* Vol. 1 Nos. 4 & 5, February & March 1883 inside of front cover.

genteel-looking man, examined it carefully and said he was not interested as it was not a genuine one. The man thereupon swore roundly and vociferously at him reasserting the authenticity. Mr. White simply stamped his foot and exclaimed, "You're an ass!" [18]

Ira J. White was the first Boston maker of wound violin strings. His machine, the first made in Boston for that purpose, [19] is now in the possession of John A. Gould. That Asa Warren White also wound violin strings is shown by the fact that he advertised "G" strings "my own make." [20]

Ira E. White, the oldest son of Ira J. White, was born in Boston April 20, 1830. For about fifty years (1860 to around 1908) he carried on musical instrument work in all its branches, making violins, basses, guitars, harps and drums.[21-22] He repaired these instruments being practically the only repairer of harps in his earlier days, and also repaired concertinas and melodeons. He was located during his business career at such various addresses as 83 Sudbury St. in 1870, 48 Hanover St. in 1890, 144 Friend St. in 1900, 15 Marshall St. in 1905 and 44 Merrimac St. in 1908.

Probably the first really noted violin maker in Boston was George Gemünder,[23] who came here in 1847 from Württemberg, Germany. Violins made during his Boston residence at 357 Washington St. won medals at the London World's Fair held in 1851. He was especially successful in his models, finish and varnishing, and his instruments have often been mistaken for Cremonas. One of the most valuable discoveries made by him was how to acquire results with natural woods not chemically treated. [24] After a few years in Boston he went to New York.

Jerome Bonaparte Squier, called by violin teachers the Stradivarius of America, was another noted Boston violin maker. He was listed in Boston business directories from 1886 to 1906 at 339 Washington St. as J. B. Squier or J. Bonaparte Squier & Co. Later his shop was on Boylston St. for a time and then at his home, Centre Street, Roxbury. He was born in Ohio in 1838, and was originally a shoe pattern designer. Mr. Squier came from Michigan to Lewis-

---

[18] Incident related by Trefflé Gervais, violin maker.
[19] Statement of John A. Gould.
[20] *The Apollo* February-March 1883 inside of front cover.
[21] Howe, William H. *The Violinist's Guide.* Early American Violin Makers p. 18.
[22] For his drum-making locations see Appendix IV Drum Makers p. 273.
[23] See also p. 228.
[24] *American History and Encyclopaedia* p. 334.

ton, Maine, where he became interested in violins and thence to Boston, where he died in 1912.

At first he made violins in his spare time only, reading all he could about the work of the old masters and studying their instruments to obtain his training in this art. At the urging of Signor Leandro Campagnari, first violinist of the Boston Symphony Orchestra, he devoted all his time to making violins. Also at Signor Campagnari's request he made his series of "Apostles violins," which included St. Paul instead of Judas. The "St. Paul" was the first of these instruments. It was made for Signor Campagnari, who played it first in 1884 in Music Hall, Boston, and then took up the "St. Peter" violin and played on it a flute solo producing all the harmonics of the violin. The wood from which the violins "St. Paul" and "St. Peter" were made was an antique English clock case of Italian wood, obtained from Hillsboro Bridge, New Hampshire. "St. Andrew" was the property of Mrs. Campagnari, earlier Miss Bell, also an artist on the violin. The *American Art Journal,* of New York, January 17, 1885 described the "St. Paul" violin thus— "Mr. Campagnari has a new violin, one of a set of twelve beauties made in Boston, and named after the Apostles. Campagnari chose to have the 'St. Paul,' meaning doubtless to make it the great Apostle to the musical gentiles 'born out of due time.' Paul had something to say of trumpets and pipes, though he did not mention the violin; but he *would* if he lived in our day, and Campagnari's will send forth 'no uncertain sound' when time and good playing shall have seasoned its varnish and joints."

Mr. Squier made copies of the following old masters—Antonius Stradivarius, King Joseph Guarnerius, and Paganini patterns; Nicolas Amati, grand pattern; and Gio. Paolo Maggini. His prices ranged from $100 to $500 according to the selection of wood, workmanship and imitation of old appearance. He dealt in violin makers' supplies and made a specialty of his Cremona amber oil varnish which he had in four shades of coloring according to the Italian varnishes, viz: golden red, dark red, orange and golden brown.

This maker "was one of the foremost American makers and repairers and his work was highly esteemed." [25] Among the users who sent testimonials in appreciation of his work were Anton

[25] *The Violinst's Guide.* American Violin Makers p. 39.

Pastorelle who played no. 304 at Crystal Palace, London, in 1904; Henri Appy, Belgian teacher and artist, of the Rochester School of Music, Rochester, New York; August Hagenow of the Nebraska Conservatory of Music, Lincoln, Nebraska; Eugene Greenberg of the New England Conservatory of Music, Boston; and Charles E. White of Lost Springs, Kansas. Mr. Squier made and reconstructed 608 violins, the last three modelled after the Alard Strad and used exclusively his own oil amber varnish. "Included among his most esteemed instruments were the so called 'Apostles' series . . . also the 'George Washington' and 'Abraham Lincoln,' " [25] the latter being no. 499 made in 1893.

His son, Victor Carroll, who worked with him, now has his own business in Battle Creek, Michigan, as stringed instrument maker, repairer and dealer, and manufacturer of wound strings. [25]

Walter Solon Goss was another Boston master violin maker. He was born in 1853 at Danvers, Massachusetts, and worked on violins from 1870 on. He established himself in Lynn, Massachusetts, in 1896. After that he worked for a total of about twelve years as expert and supervisor of repairing for the firms of Elias Howe and Oliver Ditson Company, having his own shop for a while between his employment by these firms. Around 1911 he established himself in Boston at 218 Tremont St., specializing in copies of Cremona instruments and fine repairing. He used to get about $250-$300 apiece for his instruments, [26] for he was one of the finest makers in the country. Later he had charge of the shop for the Musicians' Supply Company, and was with the Brown Music Store in Lynn when he died about 1925.

In a contest held in Chicago, June 1912, an instrument made by Mr. Goss was awarded a diploma [27] as the best in excellence of tone. Eleven modern and eight ancient violins had been entered in this contest by vote of the American Guild of Violinists. This number was first reduced to four, including a genuine Stradivarius, but his violin won over them all. His label reads:

"Model
Walter Solon Goss
Stringed Instrument Maker
Copyist of Famous Italians
Boston, Mass.   A.D. 19—"

[25] *The Violinist's Guide.* American Violin Makers p. 39.
[26] Statement of A. J. Oettinger for whom he worked some years.
[27] See *The Violinist's Guide.* American Violin Makers p. 29.

In addition to master makers there have also been experimenters in Boston who have tried to improve the violin. Such things as filling a glass-backed violin with smoke or sand and playing on it to see the effect of different notes, boring and filling small drilled holes to try to give the effect of an old worm-eaten violin of good tone, have been done.

Emile Berliner [28] patented a contrivance in which the bridge, on which the strings rested, came up through an opening. At the end of this device below the bridge were the holes into which the knotted strings fitted. His idea was to magnetize the strings by some contrivance inside the violin. He was not a violin maker, so he had his models made by Maurice White, an expert maker, according to his designs, which did away with the tail piece and produced peculiar vibrations. He had a wonderful inventive genius, nevertheless, for it was he who invented and sold to the Victor Co. the phonograph disk. He also had the original of the familiar picture, "His Master's Voice," painted in Europe. [29]

In the matter of violin string manufacturing Boston has contributed two notable improvements through the genius of Hugo Schindler. [30] He was the "Father" of the aluminum wound "D" string, used for greater power as early as 1900 by Carl Ondrydzeck of the Boston Symphony Orchestra. This has gradually replaced the gut "D" string on 60 per cent of the violins around Boston. [31] Because of the insistent urging of Charles Martin Loeffler, Mr. Schindler also developed the 14 karat (or better) gold "G" string. This was used first by Mr. Loeffler and later by Fritz Kreisler. Other dealers made cheaper gold strings, using only 10 or even 8 karat gold and the other parts base metal. These did not wind as well because of the stiffer material, nor did they give the quicker vibrations and particularly the purer tone of the 14 karat gold. In fact the tone was not as good as that of the pure silver wound strings generally used now instead. So the idea of the gold "G" string fell into disrepute and was given up generally.

[28] E. Berliner, located at 89 Milk St. in 1879, and at 109 Court St. 1880-84.
[29] Statements of A. J. Oettinger.
[30] For further information about H. Schindler & Co. see pp. 264-5.
[31] Statement of Hugo Schindler.

b. Present Day Makers

WEEMAN, BEAL & HOLMBERG [1]

This firm, established by Orin Weeman in 1872, is the oldest and one of the largest violin houses now in Boston. In April 1910 it became Weeman, Beal & Holmberg [2] and is to be found at 564 Washington St. Mr. Weeman retired in 1919 and has since passed on.

This house is devoted exclusively to the manufacture, import, sale at wholesale and retail of violins, violas and violoncellos, and accessories such as bows, strings, etc., and repair of these instruments. It makes a point of carrying everything required by them. The instruments carried for sale are mainly for artist and professional use and some less expensive ones for school use.

Repairing of all styles of instruments, whether modern, early New England make or old masters, constitutes a large part of this company's business, keeping several men busy all the time. During his lifetime Mr. Weeman was one of the best known violin repairers in New England.

Their own instruments have all been custom made to order, the violins being made mostly by Mr. Weeman from 1880 till his death, and the violoncellos by Mr. Beal, generally with maple back and spruce top. In their instruments the quality of the spruce and proper amount of graduation for resistance is tested by hand. They have experimented with different arches (swells) but have gone back to that used by Stradivarius. One beautiful instrument was made by them in 1901 for Charles W. Allen, formerly one of Boston's most famous violin teachers.

Although it is difficult to obtain instruments made by the noted European masters, this house has imported and sold an Amati violin now in Cambridge, Massachusetts, an Amati violoncello now in Boston, a Joseph Guarnerius violin in Jackson, Michigan, a Petrus Guarnerius in New York City, and many others.

[1] Orin Weeman is listed in the German encyclopaedia, *Die Geigen und Lautenmacher* p. 701.
[2] The other members of the firm are Fenner L. Beal and Bernard Holmberg.

JACOB THOMA & SON [3]

This business was established in 1880 by Jacob Thoma, a German who had had a number of years of experience previously in Leipzig. It was located in the old Music Hall Building in 1898, at 47 Winter St. in 1901, at 100 Boylston St. for some years to about 1934 and is now carried on by Jacob Thoma's son, Alexander, at his residence, 21 Richfield St., Dorchester, Massachusetts.

The business consists of importing and dealing in high grade violins, violas, violoncellos, bows, cases, strings and specialties; repairing violins and bows; violin making; and appraising instruments. While Franz Kneisel was living this firm did work for him and the Kneisel Quartette.

In making their own "Thoma Solo Violins and Violas," which are of selected old tonewood, Stradivarius and Guarnerius are used as models. These instruments are used largely by violin teachers. The firm also winds strings for violins and violas, making a specialty of the silver "G" and aluminum "D" strings.

JOHN A. GOULD & SONS [4]

John A. Gould was born at Windermere, England, in 1860, and was apprenticed to a pianoforte manufacturer at the age of thirteen. He learned his trade, but wanted to make violins which he studied in shop windows, making his first at the age of sixteen. Two years later he worked with F. Archer, starting for himself in 1878 at 119 Oakfield Road, Liverpool, as:

"Pianoforte Tuner and Repairer.
Violins and all stringed instruments
made to order and carefully repaired."

In 1882 he settled with a brother-in-law in Ontario. At the Hamilton Industrial Exposition in 1884 he was granted the first diploma ever awarded in Canada for violin making. This can now be seen hanging on the wall of his shop at 230 Boylston St.

There was not enough business for a violin maker in Hamilton and Toronto, so Mr. Gould came to Boston in 1885 and worked for Orin Weeman for whom his second son is named. Two or three years later he went home to England, returning in 1889 to open

[3] Listed in Bachmann, Alberto A. *An Encyclopedia of the Violin* p. 54.
[4] Listed in Willibald, Leo. *Die Geigen und Lautenmacher* p. 232.

his first shop at the corner of West and Tremont Streets. In 1890 he moved to 43 West St. where he stayed for thirty years until he moved to his present location. His sons, Erik and Orin, are with him in the business.

This firm imports violins from the chief European commercial centres, Markneukirchen and Mittenwald, Germany, Mirecourt, France, and Schonbach, Czechoslovakia, selling at wholesale and retail. They supplied the first fiddles for the Quincy and Winchester schools eighteen years ago when instrumental instruction was started there.

They also make high-grade violins, violas and violoncellos, largely in Rome, Maine, in the summer, following their own patterns since 1905, as Mr. Gould, who has handled violins made by all the old masters, believes just as good violins are made today. Their pattern has points of resemblance to that of Petrus Guarnerius. In his article, *"Facts About Old Violins,"* John A. Gould brings out that instruments by the same great master varied in quality and tone and that the tone of any of these instruments which have been repaired is in reality due to the work of the modern repairer who strengthens thin places, etc. The standing of their instruments is shown by the following statements: "Gould's instruments are well spoken of by those qualified to judge them." [5] "His reputation as a maker and repairer extends through the whole of Northern America." [6]

Bows, strings, polishes, rosin and varnish are also made by them under the name, "Orthotonic Specialties."

At the present time this is the only Boston firm doing a jobbing business in wound strings.

The largest part of their business is restoration. They have had such customers as Bessie Bell Collier, Maud MacCarthy, the Kneisels, Fritz Kreisler and Mischa Elman. Most famous concert violinists known in Boston have had their instruments adjusted at some time by Mr. Gould.

"What is said to have been the largest single repair job in the history of the fiddle" [7] was done by them shortly after the war when the Lindsey Memorial Collection of musical instruments was stored next to the ship's boiler in transit across the Atlantic to the Boston

[5] Bachmann, Alberto. *An Encyclopedia of the Violin* p. 54.
[6] Poidras, Henri. *Critical and Documentary Dictionary of Violin Makers Old and Modern* p. 189.
[7] *Boston Herald*, January 3, 1931 p. 12—"Boston Personalities" column.

Museum of Fine Arts. The stringed instruments, some two hundred violins, violas, violoncellos, harps, were turned over to them for restoration. It took nine months' work by Mr. Gould and his four sons to accomplish this.

This firm also does appraising for banks, United States Appraisers Stores and the Boston Museum of Fine Arts. Not long ago it appraised the stringed instruments of the Searles Estate.

Mr. Gould in his forty odd years of work in Boston has made a study of old New England violin makers. In the course of this he has collected early New England fiddles, hundreds of labels of ancient makers, pictures of famous old violins, business cards of the members of his profession, and has prepared a history of New England's violin makers from this material.

Through Erik Gould, who is a collector of violins, Boston is now the home of the violin which belonged to Robert Burns, the Scotch bard. He bought it from a Mrs. Hill of Enfield, England, whose husband was a direct descendant of the poet. The name of the maker, "A. Hardie, Maxwelton, 1758," is stamped on the inside of the instrument. The top piece is Scotch fir and the strings are attached to boxwood instead of the customary rose or ebony pegs. The tailpiece is fastened to the body of the instrument by means of two catgut strings looped through holes in this part. [8]

HENRY F. SCHULTZ [9]

Mr. Schultz was born in Cambridge, Massachusetts, in 1867 of German parentage. He was apprenticed in 1886 for three years to Clark Powers of Boston, and then worked for Charles Story for two years. He also worked in Chicago and finished learning his trade of violin and double bass making with John A. Gould for whom he worked several years. He was chief maker and repairer for Elias Howe Company for some years until he became a partner in Robinson (Robert) [10] & Schultz in 1902. Later he was in charge of the violin making and repairing department first of the Musicians' Supply Company and then of the Oliver Ditson Company. In 1898 he started his own business in Scollay Square, remaining there until the building burned in 1910. Then he worked at his Randolph

[8] *Boston Traveler*, January 31, 1931 p. 16—"Bostonian Treasures Violin of Bobbie Burns."
[9] Listed in Bachmann, Alberto. *Encyclopedia of the Violin* p. 54.
[10] See Robert Robinson Appendix IV Section A. p. 262.

shop and in 1922 took a place at 775 Washington St. where he is today.

Mr. Schultz has made for himself many violins, violas, violoncellos and double basses, being almost the only maker of the last-named in Massachusetts. He uses spruce and maple wood for the body and ebony for pegs, fingerboard and tail, following Stradivarius and Guarnerius as patterns. Some of his instruments are now used by the New York Philharmonic Orchestra players.

He also imports and sells high-grade new instruments, occasionally some older ones, bows and all kinds of trimmings.

As an appraiser, Mr. Schultz has been called to testify in Boston courts, especially the custom house court in duty cases.

Repairing is one of the most important parts of the business. He has had double basses sent to him from New York for restoration as there are few American workers skilled in this. He has also done the feat of repairing badly broken violins, one of which had been smashed into 96 pieces and another into 427 pieces. [11]

EDMUND F. BRYANT [12]

Mr. Bryant was born at Woodstock, New Hampshire. He made his first violin as a boy and played it at husking bees thereabouts. When he was thirteen years old, he went to Lowell, Massachusetts, to study violin with Oscar Greiner, the concert master of the Germania Orchestra. Later, he studied with Julius Eichberg and Bernhardt Listemann at the old Boston Conservatory of Music of which he is a graduate.

At the age of seventeen, he played in a Lowell theatre orchestra and then went on the road with different companies, such as "Birds of a Feather" and the Swedish "Alle Archestram Drama." After that he settled in Boston as a teacher and player of violin and also had a class in Lowell, Massachusetts.

The art of violin making he learned through working with Ira J. White, the best maker in Boston at that time. His start in business for himself at 165 Tremont St. began with the sale for his friend, Mr. Hathorn, of the latter's collection of sixty old violins. The firm was E. F. & O. H. (his nephew) Bryant around 1905.

[11] Statement of Henry F. Schultz.
[12] Listed in Poidras, Henri. *Critical and Documentary Dictionary of Violin Makers Old and Modern* p. 181 as a contemporary maker.

Mr. Bryant uses Stradivarius, Guarnerius and Amati as patterns for his instruments, all of which have been made to order. In all since 1900 he has made 101 violins, 2 or 3 violas and 2 violoncellos. Anton Gerardi, formerly with the Boston Symphony Orchestra and now with the New York Philharmonic Orchestra, uses one of his instruments.

The larger part of his business is repairing and reconstructing these kinds of stringed instruments.

J. H. EDLER

Mr. Edler comes of a family of violin makers, for his grandfather, Friedrich Christian Edler, started in that business in 1850 in Frankfurt-am-Main, Germany. His father, also Friedrich Christian, continued it and he and his brothers worked there. One of them is still carrying that business on.

To gain wider experience J. H. Edler worked a year in Zürich, Switzerland, and then came to New York in 1898. There he worked for John Friedrich until he came to Boston.

In 1900 he started in business for himself in Boston at 820 Washington St. and moved shortly after to 180 Tremont St. In 1902 Elias Howe Co. persuaded him to take charge of their dealings in old violins and of their repair department. He remained there until 1919 when he again started in business for himself at 228 Tremont St. About two years later he moved to his present address 611 Washington St.

Mr. Edler has made some ten or eleven violins and two violoncellos patterned after Stradivarius and Guarnerius. Of late years his business has consisted mostly of repairing, appraising and dealing in old violins, violas and violoncellos, which he has sold to customers in many parts of the United States. He also imports and sells new instruments and trimmings.

ALBERT LIND [13]

Albert Lind, a violinist, established his own business as a violin maker, repairer, and dealer in 1900 after working in various European shops. He has a high class trade as a dealer in old violins, violas and 'cellos and also handles cases, strings and accessories, at 203 St. Botoph St., Boston.

[13] Listed in *The Violinist's Guide.* American Violin Makers p. 35.

Mr. Lind makes the "Albert Lind" new violins which he finishes with his own varnish. To date he has made 112 violins, using his own model patterned after Stradivarius, some violas and a few violoncellos, all mainly for professional use. His last twelve violins have been made on what he calls "the new scientific principle of perfect vibration." He states that this is attained through a balance of the parts which allows the use of thicker wood for durability, yet is easy to play in correct intonation and does not produce a woody tone. Repairing is a specialty and forms the major part of his business today.

MUSICIANS' SUPPLY COMPANY

Adolph Joseph Oettinger started work as a boy in W. H. Cundy's shop, was in business for himself for a year or two about 1884, and later worked for the Geo. W. Stratton Co., becoming associated with Elias Howe when that firm took over the Stratton Company from Howard C. Barnes.

The Musicians' Supply Company began in 1905 at 164 Tremont St. with the purchase of the stringed instrument and accessories business of Thompson & Odell. The firm consisted of Mr. Oettinger, Carl and Julius Nelson, the latter two being owners of The Vega Co. Mr. Oettinger later bought out the interest of the Nelsons. The company was located in 1920 at 218 Tremont St., in 1925 at 83 Newbury St., and finally at 177 Tremont St. Mr. Oettinger died Dec. 10, 1935. As his sons had their own business interests elsewhere they did not care to carry on this concern, which is now being liquidated.

This company supplies raw materials, bows and tools for all kinds of bow-stringed instruments to makers located all over the United States and in foreign countries, such as Honolulu, South Africa, South America and the Walker Group of Islands. It is the largest dealer in the United States [14] in wood and tools for these instruments.

The business includes also importing, selling and appraising old violins, violas and violoncellos, repairing all kinds of bow-stringed instruments and selling modern violins, bows and trimmings. "Oettinger Products" include their patented specialties such

[14] Statement of A. J. Oettinger.

as a chin rest, a violin tailpiece, a violoncello tailpiece, a banjo tailpiece, a guitar tailpiece, tools, and the products which they sell to jobbers.

From its start the company has had expert violin makers making instruments to order as well as repairing them. For the last eight years Giuseppi (Joseph) Martino, an Italian who previously had his own shop at 181 Tremont St., has been with the company as violin maker and repairer.

O. H. BRYANT & SON

Oliver H. Bryant, born in 1873, has made violins for forty-six years. From 1889-1910 he worked with Elias Howe Company and Oliver Ditson Company but was a member of E. F. & O. H. Bryant around 1905. He started in business independently in 1910 as dealer, appraiser, maker, repairer and expert. His present address is 240 Huntington Ave.

This firm's main business is as dealers and appraisers. As dealers they sold a Stradivarius to a Boston collector for $20,000 and another Stradivarius to a Los Angeles man for $35,000. They deal in violin makers' supplies and tools and carry a full line of accessories.

Oliver H. Bryant is the maker of the "Cremona Art" violin and the principal of the Boston School of Violin Making. [15]

Serge Koussevitsky's Amati Bass has been one of the many instruments repaired by them. Their manufacturing is work done to order. To date they have made 162 violins, 3 violas and 2 violoncellos and many bows. It generally takes two months to make an instrument including the varnishing for which tempered amber oil is used. The woods are maple and spruce. They followed earlier chiefly Guarnerius del Gesu, but now Allard Stradivarius is followed as a pattern, and the height and arching of the plates is varied according as power or quality is desired, depending on whether the instrument is for symphonic or home use. Their instruments have been played mostly by artists and professionals in all parts of the United States. A partial list of users is as follows:

Efrem Zimbalist
Fritz Kreisler, personal use
Ysaye, on short tours

[15] *The Violinist's Guide.* American Violin Makers p. 23.

Felix Winternitz, Boston and New York
Allen Langley, New York and Philadelphia
Valedimar Berlin, Philadelphia
Frederick Fradkin, New York
Morris Hewett, Head of Cleveland Institute of Music
Sylvan Noack, Concert Master, Los Angeles Symphony Orchestra
New England Conservatory teachers
Leo F. Reisman, formerly Hotel Brunswick, Boston

P. BALTZERSON [16]

Peter Baltzerson was born in Tjotta, Norway, came to Boston when thirty years old and was a building trade worker until the World War. He made his first fiddle about thirty-nine years ago and continued fiddle making as a hobby. He worked for O. H. Bryant and started in business for himself in 1920 at 218 Tremont St. after visiting many European shops. He was located around 1930 at 328 Massachusetts Ave., but at present is at 246 Huntington Ave.

He uses the Stradivarius, J. B. Guadagnini, Nicolas Amati and Joseph Guarnerius as patterns for his instruments. In all he has made 198 violins, 6 violas and 2 violoncellos. About ten members of the Boston Symphony Orchestra including the concert master use his violins.

He also makes bows, repairs, and sells old makes of instruments.

C. F. STANLEY

The Stanley family's interest in violins dates back to the time when Carlton F. Stanley's great grandfather in Dixfield, Maine, gave his grandson Isaac a violoncello and a violin. The latter taught himself to play on them. His brother F. O. Stanley, made a three-quarter size violin when ten years old, and learned to play somewhat on it. When he was sixteen years old he made two full size instruments. He used State of Maine pine for the front, obtaining the idea for this from Longfellow's *Tales of a Wayside Inn,* not knowing that the pine referred to there was Swiss pine, the European name for spruce. Ever since then he has made and experimented with violins as a hobby, selling some in the 1870's, when he was a high school teacher.

[16] Listed in Poidras, Henri. *Critical and Documentary Dictionary of Violin Makers, Old and Modern,* p. 178 as a contemporary maker.

In 1924 F. O. Stanley and his nephew, Carlton F. Stanley, who had worked with him, fitted up a shop at 337 Waverley Ave., Newton, Massachusetts. There the latter has made just under four hundred violins, all patterned after one of Stradivarius' best instruments which is in a museum at Florence, Italy, and two violins for one customer patterned after Guadagnini. Recently they added the making of violas also.

Their idea is to make as good an instrument as can be made for the money to sell at a reasonable price. For the fronts they use both American and European spruce and European maple for the rest of the body. Their customers are mostly violin teachers and advanced students located in many different parts of the United States. They made two specially fine violins for Henry Ford who became interested because some players at the Wayside Inn used Stanley instruments.

F. LINCOLN JOHNSON

Frederick Lincoln Johnson has worked for various Boston violin firms for a number of years. He has been a maker of violins for some thirty years. In that time he has made around 100 violins at his home now at 75 Carver St., Boston, and has also bought and sold violins.

He has never had a shop as he was engaged in other work daytimes for many years.

3. FLUTE, PICCOLO AND CLARINET MAKERS

a. *Some Nineteenth Century Makers*

"The first mention of the importation of flageolets, hautboys [oboes] and other instruments" into this country was in 1716.[1] They were imported by Edward Enstone, organist of King's Chapel, Boston.

Probably the first musical instrument maker in Boston proper, aside from an organ builder, was William Callender. He was listed in the Boston Directory for 1789 as an ivory turner. From as early as 1796 at least through 1800 he was given as a musical instrument maker at 59 State Street. He moved his home from Milk Street to Middle Street in 1798 and apparently conducted his business at his house no. 62 Middle from 1803 or earlier through 1818. In 1820 he moved his business to Millpond Street. A wooden fife of his, neatly made with brass bands at the ends, was found in an attic in an old house in East Lexington, Massachusetts, and presented to the Lexington Historical Society.

Possibly the first flutes manufactured in Boston were made by the firm of Walter Crosby, which made the popular Crosby fifes used in the Civil War and flutes. This concern, which was in business from 1836 to 1874, was located at 9 Water St. in 1846, at 15 Hawley St. in 1848, at 19 Hawley St. in 1855 and at 59 Court St. in 1870. F. G. Schauffler & Co. and John Leukhardt in the 1850's and 1860's, and Hüttl & Fischer in the 1870's were other early Boston makers.[2]

The next important name in the manufacturing of flutes and piccolos is that of August Damm.[3] He was born September 20, 1849 at Doelau near Halle, Germany, and served in the Franco-Prussian War, being a member of the band which marched into Paris in 1870. He emigrated to Boston in November 1872 just after the Great Fire.

[1] Lahee, Henry C. *Annals of Music in America* p. 3.
[2] See page 266 for further information about these firms.
[3] Information in the following paragraphs was supplied by August Damm.

Mr. Damm is primarily a musician. As such he has played the flute with Theodore Thomas' Symphony Orchestra, when it was in Boston, has been a member of the Germania Orchestra, was conductor in 1875 of the Dow Opera Company and traveled all over the United States with them, was a member of the Boston Symphony Orchestra under its first three conductors, and was a member and assistant conductor of A. Liberati's band, which played in the United States and Canada. In 1905 he was sent by Mr. Liberati to take charge of the flute making department of C. G. Conn Ltd., while their foreman was in charge of the company's display at the St. Louis Exposition.

Because there were practically no makers of flutes, piccolos, clarinets and oboes when Mr. Damm settled in Boston, he went into instrument making and repairing by the purchase in April 1888 from Emile Bauer of the business started by the latter's father, William Bauer. Mr. Damm continued at the same address, 48 Hanover St., and engaged Mr. Penkert, foreman of Theodore Berteling's factory in New York City, to help him. In 1889 the business was listed in the directory as Damm & Penkert. Sometime that year Eduard H. Wurlitzer came over from Germany to take Mr. Penkert's place. From 1890-96 the firm was known as August Damm & Co. From 1888 till 1897 Mr. Damm allowed first Mr. Penkert and then Mr. Wurlitzer to mark the instruments they made with their names, though they had no partnership in the business.

Mr. Damm had the help of the best players in New York City and Boston who felt the same interest as he in the making of instruments which would produce a good full round tone. His company made flutes (Boehm system), piccolos, clarinets and some oboes and English horns, mostly to order. The customers generally selected their own materials. They used cocuswood (some dealers call it grenadillo)—black Africa being the most favorable kind—also some California rosewood. They made a few metal flutes of silver and built a special English horn (Corno Anglais) for Müller, the first oboe player of the Boston Symphony Orchestra, under Wilhelm Gericke's direction. [4]

When Mr. Damm "gave" the business to E. H. Wurlitzer in 1897, the latter continued at 48 Hanover St. from 1897 until it was bought out by Harry Bettoney in 1900. Mr. Wurlitzer was a

[4] Statement of August Damm.

repairer and maker of woodwind instruments.   These latter included grenadillo-wood flutes and piccolos, solid silver flutes, one flute with a solid gold tube and sterling silver keys for a Boston flute amateur, [4] a few oboes, and clarinets of cocus (grenadillo) wood, all to order. His flutes were Boehm system and had fine tone quality. [5]   Some players of his flutes were Edward Franklin, Charles K. North, and Frank Eaton. [6]

The firms of August Damm and E. H. Wurlitzer made instruments producing a good tone quality, but none of these former firms gave Boston any unusual reputation as a flute making centre.

Other former Boston flute makers are discussed in Appendix IV Section C.

[4] Statement of August Damm.
[5] Statement of William R. Gibbs.
[6] Information supplied by E. U. Wurlitzer, who worked with his uncle.

b. Present Day Manufacturers

WM. S. HAYNES CO.

William S. Haynes and his brother, George W., made their first flutes as boys after study of a flute loaned them by the flutist of the Boston Symphony Orchestra when it came to Providence. It took them about a year to make this instrument which did not work too well at first. After making others they were encouraged to come to Boston to repair flutes as there were few good workmen in this line. In the meantime both of them had received a thorough training in silver manufacturing with the Gorham Silver Manufacturing Company.

George Haynes started a repair shop in Boston about 1888 at 22 Chapman Place and then sent for his brother. The former moved to 40 Sudbury St. by 1893, but became ill and went to California for his health about 1896 while William S. Haynes kept on. He made the flutes for John C. Haynes & Company from around 1897 through 1899 and in 1900 started in business for himself as Wm. S. Haynes & Co. at 453 Washington St.

He succeeded in interesting Carl Wehner of the Metropolitan Opera Company Orchestra in a flute, especially made for him, enough to play it at a performance of the Opera Company in Boston, as his German flute had deteriorated with use. Mr. Wehner afterwards bought this instrument for one hundred dollars and later interested six friends to buy Haynes flutes. Since he was the greatest flutist of that time, the success of the business was then assured. The company was incorporated in 1912. It was located at 34 Columbus Ave. in 1920, but is now situated at 108 Massachusetts Ave.

Mr. Haynes used African blackwood in his instruments and guaranteed them for a year against cracking. Despite the fact that this wood is so hard that it ruins saws and makes it difficult to bore the parabola curve in the head joint, it got out of shape or cracked in this climate after being constantly moistened by condensation of breath. The intonation and scale were thereby rendered incorrect through warping.

So after considerable experimentation to determine the proper size of bore and the correct wall thickness, Mr. Haynes produced about 1912 an all sterling silver flute to eliminate these difficulties. He then had to persuade flute players that an all metal instrument could produce the same woodwind tone as the wooden flute. Charles K. North and Paul Fox of the Boston Symphony Orchestra made the first comparative tests for this purpose. Gradually this new feature was accepted until now almost no wooden flutes are made for professional use by any manufacturers.

The company now makes silver and 14 karat gold Boehm flutes to order, ranging in price from $185 to $1100 for a gold flute. This denser metal produces a more mellow tone.

The Alto flute in G, a comparatively rare instrument, is also made by the company in sterling silver. The French model flute with open holes, used by French players, is becoming an increasingly popular model.

For a time about 1932 a student's flute was brought out for school use. They also were made of sterling silver but were less expensive because special tools were developed so that some parts could be made by machinery instead of by hand as in the case of the regular products.

Boehm piccolos have also been made by Wm. S. Haynes Co. practically from its inception. Since about 1912 the wooden piccolo has been gradually superseded by metal piccolos till about 95 per cent of the piccolos of this concern are made of sterling silver. Until about eight years ago their piccolos were made with cylindrical bore. Since that time they have been making also conical bore C and D-flat piccolos with extremely thick tube, which does not fade out on the lower notes and is freer and easier blowing in the third register, making a more perfect scale and intonation. Both cylindrical and conical bore instruments are made to order in 14 karat gold. Between forty-five and sixty flutes and piccolos are produced monthly in normal times and a total of 14,000 of both, mostly flutes, have been made to date.

For over eight years the Wm. S. Haynes Co. has made a full Boehm system clarinet with drop-forged keys to which a forked B-flat or low E-flat extension is applied when ordered. It is the same size and shape as the best wooden clarinet and is lighter in weight than the average wooden instrument. Two hard-drawn sterling silver tubes are placed one within the other, with an eighth of an inch air space between which provides a thermos. This with the Haynes patented vents make it possible to warm the entire instrument evenly from mouthpiece to bell with a few light breaths. The clarinet then stays warm through an entire performance, which makes a better intonation. The inner tube of the barrel joint telescopes over the inner tube of the clarinet so it may be drawn out to lower the pitch without leaving a gap, and thus acts as a tuning slide. Nearly three hundred of these self-advertised clarinets have been sold, many being in the hands of the finest artists such as:

Two Washington Marine Band solo players.
All the Metropolitan Orchestra clarinet players.
The first clarinet of the San Francisco Symphony Orchestra.
Van Amburgh of the Barrère Little Symphony of New York.

Besides being one of the pioneers in metal flute making William S. Haynes invented a device for making drawn tone holes integral with the tube forming the body of the flute.

Many flute clubs all over the United States use the Wm. S. Haynes flute. Dr. Dayton C. Miller, the first scientist to experiment with platinum, proved that the denser the metal the better the instrument's tone. George Barrère, first great professional player to use a Wm. S. Haynes gold flute exclusively, has just had a platinum flute made to order "90% platinum, 10% iridium, a combination used for the finest jewelry, rating 21.6 in density," [1] costing $3000. Tests made with this new instrument seem to corroborate Dr. Miller's finding.

Some of the other artists using Haynes instruments are:

John Amans	New York Philharmonic Orchestra (solid gold)
John Wummer	Detroit Symphony Orchestra.
Julius Furman	First Flute, Los Angeles Symphony.
Anthony Linden	Solo Flute, Los Angeles.
Domenico Iascone	First Flute, Symphony Orchestra, Washington, D. C.
Clayton Lindsay	Solo Flute, Washington Marine Band.
Walter Whitaker	First Flute, D'Oyly Carte Opera Co., and teacher Conservatory of Music, Toronto, Canada.
Fortunate Covone	Gold Flute user, First Flute, Chicago Opera.
Daniel Maquarre	First Flute, Monte Carlo Casino, Monaco.

[1] *Time*, December 2, 1935, p. 23

Luisa Tetrazzini wrote, "Gentlemen,—Your flute is an inspiration to my voice, and I wish to congratulate you for the production of such a beautiful toned instrument."

THE HAYNES-SCHWELM CO.

This company was started in Boston in 1913 with Wm. S. Haynes, Jr. as manager. It is now located at 4196 Washington St., Roslindale.

They build custom made German silver, sterling silver and gold flutes to order, American models with covered keys, French models with open keys, alto sterling silver flutes with covered keys, and wooden and sterling silver piccolos. Their serial numbers for flutes and piccolos are now in the sixty-four hundreds. They also carry accessories and make repairs.

This firm finds that about three-quarters of its piccolo player customers still prefer the wooden instrument, because it is so difficult to duplicate the same body of tone in an instrument of so small a bore with a thin metal wall in place of a thick wooden wall.

This firm also supervises the making and distribution of a professional wood and metal clarinet, made in Providence, Rhode Island. The metal clarinet is made from spring-hard nickel-silver, as this gives more resonance. These instruments have two walls with the thermos air chamber between and the tone holes are soldered on to the tube, as experiments have shown this to be the best way to retain the hardness and resonant tone. [2] Lead, silver, and gold are used for solder. In the case of the last, hard running solder is used first and then soft running. About 8,000 clarinets have been made in the eight years that the Haynes-Schwelm Company has been interested in their production.

Instruments made by this concern are used by teachers of flute playing and artists like John Fisher, Wm. E. Hullinger and Charles K. North, who was with the Boston Symphony Orchestra, the Boston Band, Boston Opera Company, and was flute soloist with Dame Melba.

VERNE Q. POWELL FLUTES, INC.

Verne Q. Powell was a jeweller at Fort Scott, Kansas, and a flute player on the side. His first flute, made of old scrap silver,

[2] Statements of William S. Haynes, Jr.

which included some old plug coins, old watch cases and silver spoons, assets of a defunct bank, came into the hands of a Boston flute making concern. So he came to Boston in 1913 and became associated with that firm.

He has played the flute and piccolo professionally for many years and was the first professional flutist in the Kansas City Symphony. In Boston he is first flutist for the People's Symphony Orchestra, and teaches flute playing.

Since 1927 he has been in business for himself, his present address being 295 Huntington Ave., and has worked to perfect the scale and bore to meet with his ideas of a flute player's needs. In this time he has built nearly three hundred hand made silver and gold instruments, mostly flutes.

The high standing of his instruments is shown by his users who include:

Boston Symphony Orchestra, all flutists and piccolo players.
Detroit Symphony Orchestra, first flutist—gold flute.
Detroit Symphony Orchestra, second flutist—silver flute.
New York Philharmonic Symphony, 2 flutes and 1 piccolo.
Philadelphia Symphony, 2 flutes.
Cleveland Symphony, 2 flutes and 1 piccolo.

Neither a metal flute nor piccolo has been allowed to play the pastoral symphony of the Messiah at Handel and Haydn Society performances because its tone was considered too sharp with the muted strings. So Mr. Powell made an octave piccolo out of a bamboo fishing pole, which produced a suitable tone quality, and played this instrument at the Society's performance in December 1934.

THE CUNDY-BETTONEY CO.

Harry Bettoney came from England to Boston in 1893 and obtained a job in the orchestra at the old Park Theatre playing the clarinet. In 1897 he also started in business as an employee of W. H. Cundy. [3]

Soon after 1900 Mr. Bettoney bought out E. H. Wurlitzer, [4] a woodwind instrument maker and repairer. One year later he began to make flutes and piccolos, while continuing to import clarinets. His place soon became a service station for New England for re-

[3] For further information about W. H. Cundy and the Cundy Music Publishing Co. see pp. 71-3.
[4] See pp. 213-14 for further information about this business.

pairing all kinds of woodwind instruments. The firm moved from 48 to 30 Hanover St., to 93 Court St., and finally to Jamaica Plain where the factory is now located. About 1907 Mr. Bettoney bought out the Cundy Music Publishing Co. and the firm of E. C. Ramsdell [5] too. The making of clarinets, of which this company is now a leading manufacturer, was begun in 1912.

In 1919 The Cundy-Bettoney Co. bought out the Boston Musical Instrument Company,[6] (Manufactory until 1913). They were well known for their high grade "Boston Three * * * Star Trumpet" and also made good baritones and basses. The Cundy-Bettoney Co. still makes some of these cornets and trumpets, which had no real competitors until 1915.[7] Some noted Boston players who have used these trumpets and cornets are Mathew Arbuckle with his Bayley model cornet [8] and Henry C. Brown, the two best cornet players of that day (1862) in Boston,[9] Walter Emerson, Jack Hammond, John Flockton, Tom Henry, Arthur Wonson and Alexander J. Smith.

This company makes instruments of varying prices to suit all purses, supplying many for school use, the different grades being indicated by trade names. They also carry the necessary accessories and repair each kind of instrument.

In the woodwinds they make the following:

FLUTES
C and D-flat metal, Boehm system, with tone holes made by a patented process, three grades, both American and French models in the highest grade.

PICCOLOS
C and D-flat, three grades, Boehm system, Bettonite and metal.

CLARINETS
Wood and Bettonite materials, Boehm and Albert systems, B-flat, A, C, and E-flat, three grades, but not all in each pitch. Metal—five grades in Boehm and three in Albert systems, B-flat and A and E-flat in the best grade, covered keys on two grades.

As E-flat and bass clarinets, oboes, oboe-saxes, and bassoons, cannot be made to advantage in the United States except in larger

---

[5] See p. 24.
[6] For probable predecessors and further information see Graves & Co. p. 268, E. G. Wright & Co. pp. 226 and 270, and Boston Musical Instrument Manufactory pp. 267.
[7] Statement of Harry Bettoney.
[8] No record is obtainable of when or how the Boston Musical Instrument Company took over the Bayley model cornet from B. F. Richardson, see p. 269.
[9] Statement of Thomas M. Carter, leader of Carter's band.

quantities than the demand warrants, the company made these instruments for a time about 1930 in Germany.

Figures are not available for the total number made to date of each kind of woodwind now manufactured. The largest volume is in clarinets of which 10,000 were made in 1932 as compared with about 600 flutes and 200 piccolos.

Mr. Bettoney, knowing a player's difficulties with the cracking of ebony wood, has created "Bettonite" guaranteed against that for ten years.

Since September 1925 when he brought out a metal clarinet, the "Silva-Bet," patented March 21, 1929, the company has made almost entirely metal clarinets. Since no concern in the world was making metal clarinets when these silver clarinets were introduced, this company may properly be considered the originator of the "first Successful Metal Clarinet." They make different grades of metal clarinets. The popular priced ones are called "Boston Wonder" and "P. X. Laube." Bettoney clarinets have been sold in all parts of the United States and many have been exported to Europe in recent years.

A special hard white metal is used for the body of these. Among the special features are the following:

> It has a single metal tubular body with raised tone holes, F# & F vent holes closed by fingers, and a G vent hole, closed by a cap carried on a lever which is pivoted on bearings. This has been the leader in popularizing the metal clarinet, which is made more accurately and played more easily than the wood clarinet.

"Silva-Bet" clarinets are used by prominent bands such as Herbert Clarke's Band of Long Beach, California, bands in the Government Service,[10] and many others. In fact present United States Government specifications for clarinet are based on the "Silva-Bet" clarinet.

[10] *The Music Trades*, December 17, 1927 p. 131, "The Silver Clarinet is Adopted by the U. S. Army Band."

4. BRASS, PERCUSSION, FRETTED AND MISCELLANEOUS INSTRUMENT MANUFACTURERS

a. *Some Important Nineteenth Century Manufacturers*

Boston was perhaps preeminent about fifty odd years ago in connection with the manufacture of brass instruments. The reason for this was undoubtedly the fact that the first *brass* band formed in this country was organized in Boston in 1835. This subsequently led to Boston's becoming a centre of brass bands. This first band was the Boston Brass Band [1] with Edward Kendall (1808-1861), called "The King of the E-flat Bugle," as leader. He was succeeded by Joseph Green. Later Eben Flagg was leader.

Before the advent of the Boston Brass Band there was a Boston Band. A contributor to the *Boston Musical Gazette* in 1838 wrote of his great thrill as a boy when he first heard the clarinet, French horn and bassoon played by this group at a time when the bass-drum, bugle and octave clarinet were not introduced into the field in this country. [2] There were only four performers for this military muster, the fourth playing the hautboy.

Three notable inventions in Europe of brass instruments preceded the formation of the Boston Brass Band. The first of these was the invention in 1790 by M. Regibo of the bass horn, the first bass instrument made of brass. The bass horn played in the Band in 1835 by James Hill had three finger-holes for each hand and several extra keys. The next notable instrument was the keyed bugle invented by Joseph Halliday, bandmaster of Cavan Militia in 1810. This had five keys and was called the Kent-horn in compliment to Field Marshall, the Duke of Kent. It was used to a great extent as a coach horn. Keyed chromatic instruments then became popular rapidly and greatly changed military music and brass bands. "The principle of the keys was adopted by bass instruments as well. These early bugles were of copper, but the metal was so soft that finally it was discarded for brass, as the instruments were thicker and heavier than practicable. Keyed bugles were produced in A-flat,

[1] For an interesting picture and description of this band in 1851 see *Gleason's Pictorial*, Boston, Vol. 1 No. 12, September 20, 1851, p. 177.
[2] *Boston Musical Gazette*, "The Boston Band," Vol. 1 No. 7, July 25, 1838, p. 52.

F, E-flat, D, C, and B-flat." [3] The third invention was that of the ophicleide in 1817 by Halary, a professor of music and an instrument maker at Paris. It was an enlarged key bugle, the first complete instrument with ten to twelve keys, made as an improvement on the bass horn and serpent and predecessor of the tuba. James K. Kendall was a well known player of this instrument. It is interesting to note that the first maker in London of this instrument was George Astor, elder brother of John Jacob Astor. The double bass or monster ophicleide in F and E-flat, a fifth below the bass ophicleide is another kind of ophicleide. Both an ophicleide alto in F and a second alto in E-flat were used in the Boston Brass Band. Beside these changes pistons were introduced into trombones in 1818. [4]

For James A. Bazin's cornet with a rotary disk made in 1824 and Nathan Adams' invention of the rotary valve before 1825, applied in his "Permutation Trumpet," see page 302. Apparently both devices made possible the playing of a diatonic scale.

By the decade 1860 to 1870 there were other fine bands, namely—Germania, Boston Brigade, [5] Bond's, Hall's Boston Brass and Patrick Sarsfield Gilmore's famous band. Mr. Gilmore's band traveled all over the country giving concerts, and he conducted festivals for years. The climax of his career was the Great National Peace Jubilee held in Boston in 1869, to which President Grant and his cabinet, governors, army and navy officers and citizens from all over the United States came to hear the chorus of 10,000 voices and an orchestra of 1,000 players. A later jubilee held in 1872 was not so successful because a chorus of 20,000 voices and an orchestra of 2,000 were too unwieldy. A little later there were a number of other bands, Boston Cornet, Suffolk, L'Africain's, Carter's, Edmands,' Metropolitan, American, Boston Cadet, and Boardman's. [6]

In such a brass band centre the manufacture of brass instruments naturally developed. Several of these leaders were good players and apparently went into the business of making instruments in order to have the kind of instruments they desired to use in their bands. Brass instrument making in Boston dates back at least to

---

[3] Historical Musical Exhibition Under the Auspices of Chickering & Sons, Horticultural Hall, Boston, January 11th to 26th 1902, Catalogue of, p. 34.
[4] *Ibid* p. 36.
[5] Formed in 1821 as a reed band and converted later into a brass band.
[6] Information supplied by Thomas M. Carter, leader of Carter's Band.

1841 when the name of Elbridge G. Wright, who was also a good cornet player, [6] appears in the city directory as a musical instrument maker. From 1842 to about 1860 he had his own brass band instrument manufacturing business. Then he, like the others in this field, changed his affiliations several times as Section D of Appendix IV shows. Among the instruments made by him was a double bass or monster ophicleide, an octave below the alto ophicleide, for Thomas David of Concord, New Hampshire. According to the catalogue of Chickering & Sons' Exhibition held in 1902 it was the only one made in America. Unfortunately it had been lost track of even then. His firm also made a silver E-flat keyed bugle with eleven keys used by Rudolph Hall, second leader of Hall's Boston Brass Band. He like his brother David was a bugle and cornet player.

Another early maker of brass band instruments was J. Lathrop Allen of Boston. He made in 1845 the silver cornet in the unusual key of A for Harvey Dodworth, whose family obtained the Dodworth patent in 1838, an American invention for cornet, first made in pump valve and later in rotary style. This instrument was a gift from the members of his band and was used by him for over forty years while leader of the Dodworth Band of New York. He played this cornet in the Central Park Concerts for over twenty-five years and at ten inaugurations of Presidents of the United States. It is bell over the shoulder, rotary action, with five valves and is the only one known to have been made. [7]

In 1852 Mr. Allen formed the partnership of Allen & Richardson which seems to have been the start of two firms whose names became well known in brass instrument manufacturing, namely— Allen Mfg., succeeded first by Allen & Hall, then Hall & Quinby and finally Quinby Brothers; and B. F. Richardson, followed by Richardson & Bayley, manufacturers of the Bayley Model Cornet used by a famous player of the day, Mathew Arbuckle, and finally Richardson & Lehnert.

David C. Hall, first leader of Hall's Boston Brass Band and a partner in Allen & Hall, was born at Lyme, New Hampshire, about 1820, and came first to Lowell and then to Boston. He was one of the most noted key bugle players of the day along with Joseph Green, second leader of the Boston Brass Band, later in Providence,

[6] Information supplied by Thomas M. Carter, leader of Carter's Band.
[7] Historical Musical Exhibition Under the Auspices of Chickering & Sons, Horticultural Hall, Boston, January 11th to 26th 1902, Catalogue of, p. 38.

Rhode Island. For nearly fifty years Mr. Hall used a gold plated E-flat keyed bugle, an exact replica of the solid gold one presented to him by the Lowell, Massachusetts, Brass Band. This had twelve keys and one rotary valve to extend the tone. [8]

A silver E-flat cornet, bell over the shoulder with three rotary valves, Boston style of action, and a slide trombone alto in E-flat [9] made by D. C. Hall & Co. were exhibited in 1902. A complete set of instruments with echo attachments, made by Mr. Hall's firm according to his design, was used by Hall's Boston Brass Band in their concert tours. When the echo attachments were used the audience generally supposed that there was an extra band behind the stage. The set of echo instruments loaned from the collection of Mr. D. S. Pillsbury for Chickering & Sons' Exhibition in 1902 was stated by the catalogue to be the only complete set known to be in existence. With the exception of the trombone which had three valves, these instruments were made with four valves, rotary action. They consisted of

> B-flat Tenor made of copper with echo attachment.
> B-flat Baritone Trombone made of copper with echo attachment.
> B-flat Bass Euphonium made of copper with echo attachment.
> B-flat Baritone Euphonium made of copper with echo attachment.
> E-flat Alto made of copper with echo attachment.
> F Ballad or French Horn made of German silver with copper echo attachment. It could be changed to G and C.
> C Trumpet made of brass with copper echo attachment.

A B-flat cornet with piston box valve, by Hall & Quinby, called in the exhibit catalogue a very rare brass instrument, and a B-flat Tenor Trombone, "three valve piston box valve," B. F. Quinby patent of 1872 were also shown.[10] The Quinby Bros. were noted as makers of all kinds of fine brass band instruments.[11]

The firm of B. F. Richardson made fine cornets and trumpets and also trombones, but did not do much business in the larger instruments.[12] From 1866-1878, Richardson & Lehnert made an unusual contribution through their manufacture of Chinese and Turkish cymbals and also gongs, all instruments which previously

[8] Historical Musical Exhibition Under the Auspices of Chickering & Sons, Horticultural Hall, Boston, January 11th to 26th 1902, Catalogue of, p. 46.
[9] Formerly slide trombones were used in different keys, viz: Sop. E-flat, B-flat, alto E-flat, tenor C, B-flat, bass B-flat, and BB-flat. Most of these old slides had handles for extending to the lower notes.
[10] The writer has been unable to learn anything of the whereabouts of the instruments loaned for the Exhibition of Chickering & Sons from the D. S. Pillsbury Collection. It is to be hoped that this Collection is still intact, since the catalogue described it in 1902 as the most valuable collection of brass instruments in the world.
[11] See page 268 for more detailed information.
[12] Statement of Thomas M. Carter.

had had to be imported. Unfortunately at Mr. Lehnert's death the secret of the cymbal specifications passed on also. Mr. Richardson then turned to the making of music stands, thus being possibly the earliest such manufacturer in Boston. He was listed in this business from 1880 to 1895.

About 1852 the firm which may have been the oldest manufacturer of brass instruments in the United States, Graves & Co. (also known as Samuel Graves & Sons) was listed in Boston at 18 Harvard Place. This company had been established at Winchester, New Hampshire, and in 1864 advertised itself as the oldest musical instrument makers in the country, in this business for the past forty years. [13] Since the Winchester factory was burned some time after 1845 (exact year is not obtainable) the business may have been moved to Boston about 1852 or this may have been at first only a branch. The names of the sons were Alpha, Geo. M. and Cyrus. This noted firm made all kinds of brass and reed band instruments. "Its products were made use of in all parts of the country, and many very fine pieces were made on foreign orders." [14] They were the makers of the E-flat copper bugle used in 1837 by Edward (Ned) Kendall with the Boston Brass Band, which bore his name engraved on the bell. A copper keyed Bugle in B-flat used in the band in 1835 and an E-flat Alto made by this company in 1830 with three double slide valves and compensating pistons were also shown in the Chickering & Sons' Exhibition in 1902. Dr. Dayton C. Miller has in his collection a flute and a clarinet made by this firm.

In 1864-65 Patrick S. Gilmore became a partner in this company, which then was called Gilmore, Graves & Co. His duty was to examine and test personally every instrument made by the new combination. In 1866 the firm was listed just as Gilmore & Co. and the following year it was changed to Wright, Gilmore & Co., becoming simply E. G. Wright in 1868. This firm in turn was probably succeeded about 1870 by the Boston Musical Instrument Manufactory, makers of the Three *** Star cornets and trumpets. The firm members in 1874 consisted of Henry Esbach, L. F. Hartman and W. G. Reed.

This company and the Standard Band Instrument Company started in 1884 by Thompson & Odell Company, after the demise of Quinby Brothers, in the factory which had been used by the

---

[13] *Boston Directory 1864*, Advertising Department, p. 109.
[14] Pierce, George W. Winchester. *The Granite Monthly,* November 1896, pp. 280-1.

latter, were the leading manufacturers of brass instruments in Boston for many years.

The chief difference between their instruments and those of today is that the bell of the former was made out of flat stock hammered into shape, and they did not stay in tune quite as well. The workmanship compares favorably with that of any brass instruments of the same kind made today. They were used by the leading bands of that time. [15] The companies which have taken these over, namely The Cundy-Bettoney Company and The Vega Company, are ably maintaining their standing.

The old Boston Brass Band Drum was in use over sixty-five years. So probably no other bass drum has had so important a history in America. It had the Boston coat-of-arms emblazoned on its shell, and also the names of the members on each side of it.

During the Civil War period the name of Elias Howe was particularly prominent in drum making, for his firm made and supplied drums to the Massachusetts Regiments of the Union Army. He also sold them fifes manufactured by the grandson of Jacob Astor. [16] Quite naturally one of his publications was a fife and drum instruction book used in the army.

During the war President Lincoln created the position of Director of Bands [17] for all the Union Army with the rank of Lieutenant-Colonel. This was offered to Elias Howe, Jr. who went to Washington to see about the post, but declined it. Despite hundreds of applications the position was never filled. One reason for this tender may have been that Harriet Howe Wilson, wife of Senator, later Vice President, Henry Wilson, was Mr. Howe's cousin.

Ira E. White, son of Boston's first master violin maker, and Peter Winn also made drums in the Civil War days. A little later the drum makers in Boston included—O. A. Whitmore of Reading, Vermont, who had made drum sticks and probably drums used in the Union Army; William J. Blair, who had been a drummer in the Civil War; and Blair & Baldwin.

Fretted instruments were also made early in Boston. An early master guitar maker was Charles Stumcka. He was listed in business directories in 1842 & 43 at 8 Winter St., 1847 at 13 Winter St. and

[15] Statements of Thomas M. Carter, leader of Carter's Band.
[16] Fact related by A. J. Oettinger.
[17] Facts related by Edward F. Howe.

in 1863 at 289 Washington St. A. J. Oettinger states that one of Stumcka's guitars once owned by himself showed the workmanship of a master maker. He was also a violin maker and repairer, but specialized in guitars. It is possible that Gemünder came to Boston to study guitar making with Mr. Stumcka for Gemünder made his first guitars while in Boston.

Another guitar maker whose shops were a training school for many later good makers was a Swede, Pehr A. Anderberg, who came to Boston about 1880. He later supervised the manufacturing of "Haynes Excelsior," "Tilton," and "Bay State" guitars and "Bay State" mandolins for John C. Haynes & Co.

The "Spanish Students," a strictly professional organization from California, introduced the mandolin to this country through their tours. This led to the formation of the "Boston Ideal Banjo, Mandolin and Guitar Club," trained by Louis T. Romero, who came to Boston from Mexico. This club of noted players and leading teachers of these instruments, George S. Lansing, Albert D. Grover, A. A. Babb and Burt E. Shattuck, made concert tours in every state of the Union for many years and were instrumental in creating a greater interest in the fretted instruments which were then becoming so popular. Their standing is shown by the fact that Wilhelm Gericke had Mr. Lansing and Mr. Babb play with the Boston Symphony Orchestra such parts of a Spanish number as called for their instruments.

About 1890 when the factory of L. B. Gatcomb & Co. was located on Hawkins St. the members of the Boston Ideal Banjo and Guitar Club were associated with Mr. Gatcomb by having their studios in his factory. In 1895 the Gatcomb Company made the "Lansing Banjo" and "Gatcomb Mandolin." Probably it was about this period that L. B. Gatcomb & Co. was the leading manufacturer in Boston in this line.

Information about other important banjo manufacturers like Wm. A. Cole, A. C. Fairbanks & Co. and about other makers of drums, guitars, banjos, zithers, etc. by firms now out of business or moved elsewhere is given in the different sections of Appendix IV.

b. Present Day Manufacturers

THE VEGA CO.

This business was founded in 1881 as a cooperative enterprise by Julius Nelson with five or six other men, among them C. F. Sundberg and a Mr. Swenson, who had worked in Pehr F. Anderberg's guitar shop in Somerville. Julius, a fine cabinet maker, was the foreman of the guitar and mandolin factory. Gradually Julius and his brother Carl, both of whom came from Sweden to the United States at an early age, bought out the interests of the others who continued as workers in the company, [1] which was then called Vega, meaning star. Carl Nelson became the office and sales manager.

In 1904 the Nelsons took over A. C. Fairbanks & Co. [2] which had made only banjos, while The Vega Company had made only guitars and mandolins. After the union of the companies the latter made all three kinds of high grade fretted instruments, under the direction of David L. Day, from the Fairbanks Company, as Sales and General Manager, until 1922 when he went with the Bacon Banjo Co. In 1905 the Nelsons absorbed the plectrum instrument making of Thompson & Odell and added to this about 1909 the brass instrument manufacturing business of the same concern. [3] This was done under the name of Standard Band Instrument Company established in 1884 at 62 Sudbury St.

As the result of the taking over of the business of these companies, [3] this is the only firm in Boston making simply brass and fretted instruments. The present head of The Vega Company, now located at 155 Columbus Ave., is William Nelson, the son of Carl Nelson.

This company's business is primarily manufacturing, of which about 60 per cent is in fretted and plectrum instruments and 40 per cent brass instruments. They make all kinds of brasses except French and Bass horns and more models of trumpets than any other manufacturer in this country, a total of about 1000 a year.

[1] Information about the founding supplied by A. J. Oettinger whose partners the Nelsons were in the formation of the Musicians' Supply Co.
[2] For further information about this company see p. 275.
[3] See also Appendix IV pp. 226-7 and 277.

Their trumpets, trombones and fretted instruments are exported as well as sold all over the United States. To date they have manufactured over 96,000 banjos, 40,000 guitars, 40,000 mandolins, and 30,000 trumpets.

This firm has many patents for improved construction and tone of trumpets and fretted instruments.

"The four most prominent players on national radio broadcasts, Tony Colucci, Earle Roberts, Eddie Connors, and Eddie Peabody all use the Vegaphone Guitar." [4]

Their best trumpets are silver plated and are played by artists like Walter Smith and members of the Metropolitan Opera House Orchestra; Cleveland, Minneapolis and San Francisco Symphony Orchestras; and Roxy and Paramount Theatre Orchestras.

This firm also imports low and medium priced violins and accessories, and jobs these and goods of other manufacturers at wholesale. They also sell at retail some three thousand items, including the steel strings which they manufacture; and appraise, trade in, and repair all kinds of instruments.

A special feature is their band organization and service department for helping to organize and teach school and legion bands, drum corps and orchestras. They arrange for special teachers to do this on any basis desired by a school director or music supervisor.

After taking over the H. F. Odell Company in 1925 they published the "Odell Edition" of fretted music for five years until November 1931, when Walter K. Bauer of Hartford, Connecticut, purchased the plates and stock and still publishes and sells this music.

The "Odell Edition" consisted of original compositions of Mr. Odell and arrangements made by him for banjo, mandolin, guitar and mandolin orchestra. They also published the Odell Company's music journal *Crescendo* till 1930.

GEORGE B. STONE & SON, INC.

This firm was established at Roxbury, Massachusetts, in 1890 by George Burt Stone who had had forty years of experience as band instructor, director, drum major and professional drummer in many musical and military organizations in the Eastern States. Practically

---

[4] Advertisement in *The Guild Reporter*, Official Organ of the American Guild of Banjoists, Mandolinists and Guitarists—March-April 1935 p. 7.

from the start the business has had two major interests, drum manufacturing and a school for teaching the use of percussion instruments. After his son became associated with him George B. Stone devoted most of his time to writing on drum subjects and teaching, as principal of the Stone Drum and Xylophone School, until he retired. George Lawrence Stone, who is an experienced professional player of percussion instruments, is now head of the company's manufacturing and retail business and its school located at 61 Hanover St.

This firm makes all types of drums, except metal shell, mostly single tension. As the shells are solid rock maple steam-bent, not a veneer, they are guaranteed not to warp. The chief styles are:

> Snare drums—street-military and orchestra.
> Tenor drums.
> Scotch pipe band drums.
> Bass drums—big band and orchestra.

The Boston Symphony Orchestra uses a bass and two others of their drums. During the World War period the company's entire output was taken by the government under a contract for military drums.

They also manufacture accessories such as drum heads, covers, cases and bags, and specialize in hand-turned sticks, being one of the few manufacturers to make these.

This concern also sells drums and accessories and all the instruments of a percussionist outfit, singly and in combination at wholesale and retail, and outfits bands, largely school bands and American Legion drum corps at present.

A few years ago they brought out a "Mastercraft Drum" which is a patented innovation. There are two pivots inside the shell to loosen or tighten the rods, which go inside instead of outside, thus eliminating some of the wear on the drum heads. The basis of the patent is the ventilation allowing moisture to come out. The Marlborough, Massachusetts, American Legion band with this kind of drum won the ninth prize offered at the Detroit Convention.

Mail order and retail repairing, rebuilding and replacing of all kinds of percussion instruments, and tuning xylophones constitute an important department of the business.

The Stone Drum and Xylophone School has a staff consisting of George L. Stone and three instructors to give both individual and class instruction in playing drums, bells, xylophones, tympani and accessories. During the winter months they average one hundred students a month. Recently the instructors have been giving outside class instruction in rudimental drumming in schools and legion military drum corps.

CHARLES A. STROMBERG & SON

Charles A. Stromberg, a cabinet maker, came to Boston from Sweden in 1887. He worked for Thompson & Odell eighteen years, and as foreman in their banjo, mandolin and guitar factory, supervised the manufacture of some 3500 of these instruments. He started in business for himself about 1905, producing custom-made guitars, banjos, and snare, bass band and orchestra drums for professional and amateur players. In 1910 he took his son Elmer into the business with him. The manufacturing is done at 40 Hanover St.

To date they have produced about 1000 banjos, 200 mandolins, 100 guitars all custom made and 400 drums which have been shipped all over the United States, and into Canada until a high tariff on musical instruments was put into effect there.

This firm also repairs all kinds of stringed instruments including harps. Since Mr. Stromberg owns pattern molds for casting the ornaments of harps, these instruments are sent to him from Canada and from as far west as California for rebuilding and restoring the ornaments and for repairing.

Mr. Stromberg and his son, being skilled mechanics, make their own tools for manufacturing. They have also developed several innovations and patents.

Their guitars are made of three layers of curly maple wood, a shaded exterior and an inlay bound with ivory. "F" instead of round holes are used in the swell front for better vibration. There is also an adjustable bridge for raising and lowering the strings and an adjustable tailpiece sleeve for tightening the tension. Tenor guitars which have four strings are popular.

Their banjos have a patented feature, the "Stromberg Cupperphone Tone Chamber," consisting of a metal ring placed on a circular series of upright metal tubes or cups on a built-in wooden shelf, next to the rim and directly under the head. This receives and throws out the tone in great volume and makes it sustaining. Over five hundred of these have been sold in eleven years' time.

Various grades of these are made, the prices varying with the amounts of inlay, mother of pearl on the finger board, quadruple gold plated metal ornamentation, and hand engraving.

Some of the professional players using both Stromberg banjos and guitars are, Victor Mondello, Almanac Hotel, New York; Clark Yokeham with Mal Hallet's Orchestra, New York, Columbia Recording Artists; Sam Demar, Princess Hotel, Bermuda; Bernard Addison with Fletcher Henderson's Orchestra, New York; Jimmy Speranza with the Metropolitan Theatre Orchestra, Boston; Don Senna, Boston guitarist and teacher; Ted Zahn, Copley Plaza Hotel, Boston; Julian Anderson, Janssen's Hofbrau Orchestra, New York; and banjo only, Pete Barton, Banjo soloist, Chicago, Illinois.

Their "Stromberg Invincible Orchestra Drum" made with old style wooden hoops and wood shell had a tightening device with special bracket and hooks. Charles A. Stromberg was given for this on March 8, 1904 the first patent issued in the United States for a "separate tension Drum."

The company's modern "Supertone Stromberg Orchestra Drum" has aluminum rings and an independent tightening device. As it has a flush head the tightening hoop does not interfere with the drummer's sticks.

CHARLES W. HOMEYER & CO., INC.

This firm introduced in 1925 and perfected to the present point in 1927 an inexpensive instrument called the "Oboette" intended to help school children learn oboe fingering and production of tone. The *Oboette Method* for playing was written by Francis Findlay of the New England Conservatory. About 500 of these non-profit making instruments have been sold without advertising all over the United States, thus helping to create woodwind players and to develop an interest and knowledge of the oboe, much needed in school bands and orchestras.

During the World War this company performed the service of a clearing house in finding and reconditioning band instruments for army band training corps.

THE CUNDY-BETTONEY CO.

For brass manufacturing see p. 220.

ERNEST A. ANDERBERG

Ernest A. Anderberg, the son of Pehr A. Anderberg [5] one of the early guitar makers in the United States, was born in Mount Vernon, New York.

He worked first for John C. Haynes & Co. while his father had charge of their guitar factory. When his father started his own shop on Cottage Street, Chelsea, he worked there making both guitars and mandolins till about 1893. Then he was with the Snedeker Company of Winchester, Indiana, for about a year after which he went to Philadelphia to start making guitars and mandolins in a small way for George Bauer, who owned a music store there. Presently Mr. Bauer joined S. S. Stewart in the firm of Stewart and Bauer. Ernest Anderberg continued with this firm until his father came to take charge of the plectrum manufacturing department.

After this he worked as a repairer for different Philadelphia concerns until he entered the employ of Elias Howe Co. He remained with this house for about twenty years, first as a repairer and for about ten years as head of their department of old violins and repairing.

Since Elias Howe Co. went out of business he has had his own shop at his home, 145 Bellingham St., Chelsea, Massachusetts, where he deals in stringed instruments and repairs all kinds of them except harps.

Upon the death of William H. Howe Mr. Anderberg acquired a unique collection of twenty-two instruments, rare models, picked up by Elias Howe on his European trips made to find such instruments. So far as is known no one of these has ever been duplicated, because they are "as he explains, the result of efforts to improve on perfection." [6] "One violin, a Württemberg instrument, is flat and is played without the use of a tailpiece, the ends of the fingerboard acting as a bridge. Another, a French model, is twice as large below the bridge as above. Still others have unexpected curves and indentures." [6]

The prize of the whole collection is a model "attributed to Gasparo da Salo of Brescia, who plied his art one hundred years before the great Stradivarius and who is credited with determining the present form of the violin." [6] This is "considered the oldest

---

[5] See Pehr A. Anderberg Appendix IV Section F p. 274.
[6] Ingham, Travis. *Boston Herald,* April 10, 1932 p. 3, "Violin 400 Years Old in Possession of Chelsea Collector."

violin in the United States." [6]   To the layman it appears remarkably like a modern instrument, but it is generally smaller in size of body, neck and fingerboard.   To obtain this instrument "Elias Howe was taxied through the watery lanes of Venice in a gondola to the house of Pietro Benedetti.   The old craftsman lay dying, but he summoned up a smile for his visitor and instructed his wife to bring forth his treasure, carefully wrapped.   When the folds of cloth had been removed there lay one of the rare Gasparo da Salo violins," [6] now almost four hundred years old.

"Probably the most unusual piece in this collection was exhibited at Mechanics Hall thirty odd years ago—a 16 string Moorish instrument, made from one piece of wood with a drumhead stretched over the sound box." [6]

F. PORCELLA [7]

Felice Porcella was born at Genoa, Italy.   He saved up his money as a boy and bought his first accordion, for three lire (60 cents).   He taught himself on this instrument which had just 8 buttons for one scale.   After his family moved to Montoggio he became sexton and bell ringer of the church there for some years. In 1879 he came to Boston and the next year established at 20 Ferry St. his own business of making, tuning and repairing accordions.   As there were practically no players of accordions in Boston at that time he played himself and gave lessons for two years free of charge to help create an interest in that kind of music. Later he also imported accordions.   His later business locations were 473 Hanover St. from 1899 to about 1905, 469 Hanover St. to about 1915, 461 Hanover St. for several years, 457 Hanover St. from about 1920-25, and 441 Hanover St. 1930-32.   Beginning with 1933 the Porcella Accordion Shoppe has been located at 193 Hanover St.

Felice Porcella's sons, Louis F. J. and Peter, have assisted him in the business.   Peter Porcella died soon after the World War and the founder of the business October 27, 1935.   Louis F. J. Porcella and his son, Frederick, now carry on the business which consists mostly of tuning and repairing accordions.   Instruments have been sent to this firm for repair from as far away as California.   Billy Williams, the "memory marvel girl," Frank Aviani,

---

[7] All this information supplied by Louis F. J. Porcella.

Phil Claff, Caesare Mazzioli, Bruno of Bruno's Orchestra, Charles Carrado of Keith's Circuit and The Gallarini Four are among the artists whose instruments he keeps in good condition.

Until about 1890 the largest accordions made had only 16 basses in two rows—consisting of 8 bass buttons and the 8 mate buttons for the major chords. There were no chromatics. Probably 95 per cent of the accordions were double tone with no half steps. This decidedly limited what could be played. As Felice Porcella wanted minor chords and chromatics for his playing he invented and built about 1889 the first bass-coupling mechanism with 42 buttons. This made a 36 bass instrument—12 basses, 12 major chords, 12 minor chords and 6 repeats, three at each end. These accordions sold for $100 each, and were all made to order. This new mechanism enabled the player to shift from a full major chord to a full minor chord by simply pressing one button, and the repeats eliminated the jumping of the player's hand from one end of the row to the other.

One of F. Porcella's instruments with this bass-coupling mechanism was taken on a trip to Italy in 1893 or 94 by Mr. Frank Pettiti. As it got out of order during the traveling Mr. Pettiti sent it to the firm of Soprani at Ancona, Italy, for repair. The mechanism had not been patented. So this firm copied it and the next year shipped instruments with this improvement to the United States. The firm of Soprani extended this principle of the bass-coupling mechanism still further by adding later the dominant seventh and diminished chords and contra-bass tones. These have been generally adopted so that the modern standard accordion averages 120 bass buttons whether it is a piano, chromatic or semitone instrument.

APPENDICES

(Addresses and dates are subject
to minor corrections)

APPENDIX I

A. Firm Names and Addresses of Some Early Pianoforte Makers—Period 1810 to 1850

No Directories issued in 1811, 1812, 1814, 1815, 1817, and 1819.

Year	Name of Firm and Address

THE BABCOCK BROTHERS

1810   Babcock, Lewis & Alpheus, musical warehouse, 49½ Newbury St.

1813   Babcock (Lewis), Appleton (Thomas) & Babcock (Alpheus) 18 Winter St.

1816   Babcock, Alpheus, musical instrument maker, Milk St.
Appleton, Thomas, musical instrument maker, Milk St.

1818-21   Babcock, Alpheus not listed.

1822   Babcock, Alpheus, pianoforte manufacturer, rear 11 Marlboro. Began the period when the Mackays gave the financial support.

1823-9   Babcock, Alpheus, pianoforte manufacturer, Parkman's Market, Cambridge St.

1829-36   Babcock, Alpheus was in Philadelphia and New York.

1837-8   He was back and listed as a pianoforte maker, but apparently working for some other firm as only his house, 2 Jefferson Pl. is given. Teele's *History of Milton* states that he was sent for by Jonas Chickering, but the Company historian doubts this.

1839-41   Alpheus Babcock's house was given as 6 Hayward Place. After this his name disappears from the Directories.

The foregoing pages contain some conflicting information about the dates of the firm Hayt, Babcock & Appleton as the authorities differ about this. The notices and advertisements in the *Boston Gazette* listed below, with the directory addresses above, are given as the most authentic information available.

1811   Jan.   7   Appleton & Hanners, cabinet makers, have removed to a New Furniture Warehouse 49½ Newbury st.

      July   1   Joshua B. Hanners at No. 49½ Newbury st. advertised St. Domingo Mahogany for sale.

1812 Jan. 23   Babcock, Appleton & Babcock advertised that they had just completed six elegant and excellent toned Piano Fortes, which they offer for sale at their Ware House, No. 18 Winter st.

1815 June 5   Notice is given that the copartnership between Charles and Elna Hayt was dissolved by mutual consent May 1, 1815. Until then they had both been at 19 Marlboro st. where Elna was continuing.

    June 5   Notice is given that the copartnership between the subscribers Charles Hayt, Elna Hayt, Alpheus Babcock, and Thomas Appleton was dissolved May 26, 1815. The same establishment will be continued by Charles Hayt and Thomas Appleton at their Organ, Pianoforte Manufactory and Music Store No. 6 Milk st. Advertisements of Hayt & Appleton appear occasionally through Dec. 7, 1815. These also mentioned "other Wind and Stringed Instruments of their own make."

EBENEZER R. CURRIER

1826-9   His name first appears in Currier (Ebenezer) & Gilbert (Timothy) pianoforte makers 393 Washington St. In 1827 they advertised themselves as "Manufacturers of Graved, Cabinet, and Square Piano Fortes, warranted to be equal to any American or imported instruments."

1830-2   Currier, Ebenezer R. & Co. (Philip Brown) pianoforte makers 393 Washington St.

1833   Not listed.

1834   Currier, Ebenezer, pianoforte maker, 393 Washington St. After this his name disappears from the directories.

LEMUEL GILBERT

1831-3   First appearance of name simply as pianoforte maker, house 1 Jefferson Pl.

1834   Gilbert, Timothy & Co. (Henry Safford & Lemuel Gilbert) 402 Washington St.

1835   Company same as before, but address 393 & 406 Washington St.

1836   Firm name and address the same but Increase Gilbert was added to the "Co."

1837   Lemuel Gilbert alone as a pianoforte maker, house 1 Jefferson Pl.

1838   Lord (George), Gilbert (Lemuel) & Cumston (William) pianoforte manufacturers, 352 Washington St.

1839-52   Gilbert, Lemuel, pianoforte manufacturer, 416 Washington St.

1853-8   Same as above except that address was 514 Washington St. Name disappears after this.

TIMOTHY GILBERT

1826-9   Currier & Gilbert as given above.

1830-3   Gilbert, Timothy, pianoforte manufacturer, 402 Washington St.

1834-6   Gilbert, Timothy & Co. address as given above.

1837   Gilbert, Timothy & Co. (Henry Safford & Increase Gilbert) 402 & 406 Washington St.

1838   Same as in 1837 except only 402 Washington St.

1839-44   Gilbert, Timothy & Co. (Henry Safford) 406 Washington St.

1845   Gilbert, Timothy & Co. (H. Safford & Wm. H. Jameson) 406 Washington St.

1846-8   Gilbert, Timothy & Co. (Wm. H. Jameson) pianoforte manufacturers, 406 Washington St.

1849-52   Gilbert, Timothy & Co. 400 Washington St.

1853-60   Firm name the same 484 Washington St.

1861-3   Firm name the same 8 Beach St.

1864-5   Firm name the same 20 Beach St. This name disappears after this.

LORD & CUMSTON

1837   Lord, George, pianoforte maker, house only given 45 Front St.

1838   Lord, (George), Gilbert (Lemuel) & Cumston (William) see Lemuel Gilbert.

1839-42   Lord, (George) & Cumston (William) pianoforte manufacturers, 352 Washington St.

1843-7   Firm the same, 339 Washington St.

1848-50   Lord, George, pianoforte maker, alone 493 Washington St. His name disappears after this.
Cumston was a member of Hallet, Cumston & Allen, 293 & 339 Washington St.

1851-2   Cumston disappears and the firm is Hallet & Allen, 339 Washington St.

1853 to 1900   Hallet & Cumston starting at 339 Washington St. For more information see Hallet, Cumston & Allen.

I. B.   Other Boston Pianoforte Makers—Period 1840-1915

Names of Firms and Information About the Firms

Addresses from Boston Business Directories

HENRY ALLEN; ALLEN & CO.

1862-1872   1873 & 1874

Henry Allen earlier was a member of Hallet, Davis & Co.; Hallet & Allen; Hallet, Cumston & Allen; and Brown & Allen.   See those firms for further information.

1862—344 Washington St.
1868-9—375 Washington St.
1870-4—170 Tremont St.

WM. BOURNE & CO.

Wm. Bourne, an Englishman, began to manufacture pianos in 1837 in Dayton, Ohio, which had a population of 1000, moved to Cincinnati in 1840 and to Boston in 1842. There he became a department foreman for Chickering. In 1846 he started in business for himself, organizing the firm of Wm. Bourne & Company. After his death in 1885 the business was continued by his son, Charles H. Bourne. The firm went out of business about July 1911.

"A piano maker of the old school, Bourne could turn out nothing but thoroughly first-class pianos."[1] He was a good scale drawer. He drew the "51" scale which was used in squares by Chickering & Sons and by W. P. Emerson also.[2] He was an excellent workman and a piano maker of real ability, inventing "an ingenious application of the square action damper,"[3] and several patents of a general character. The firm used English action only. Their squares were among the best made, but the uprights he and his son developed were not a success. By 1870 they also made grands.

1855—324 Washington St.
1858-460 Washington St.
1860—460 Washington St.
1870—490 Washington St.
1890—224 Tremont St. & Lamartine St.
1900—Lamartine St. cor. Wyman

JOHN W. BRACKETT

Started in the 1850's and continued to between 1880-5. He was a good action maker and drew many scales. Chickering's scale drawer, Mr. Bowen, got many points from him for the "123" scales.[2] He also attached organ pedals to pianofortes, the bass pedals being constructed in N. Y. This firm made only overstrung squares. Their "pianoee" was one of the smallest pianos made.

1850—18 Avery St.
1880—581 Washington St.

CHARLES C. BRIGGS & CO.

Mr. Briggs entered W. P. Emerson's shop in 1854 where he immediately rose to foreman. In 1861 he entered into partnership with Geo. M. Guild. After some years this was dissolved and he went into business with his son, C. C. Briggs, Jr., in the firm of Geo. M. Guild & Co. After 1881. As the business grew, they moved into more rooms at 5-7 Appleton St., at 1125 Washington St., erected for them. By 1900, the Briggs Piano Co. was at 621 Albany St. Its last year was 1918.

1881—1125 Washington St.
1890—5 & 7 Appleton St.
1900—621 Albany St.
1910—Briggs Piano Co. 10 Thatcher St.

"Mr. C. C. Briggs, Sr. was an expert scale draughtsman and he made many acoustic discoveries in relation to upright scales." [4]

"This firm was among the first to develop the resources of the upright in America for general use." [5]

S. P. BROOKS

1860—354½ Washington St.
1870—9 Bowker St.
1890—55½ Sudbury St.

This firm was started between 1850-60 and discontinued business between 1890-1900.

Mr. Brooks, who had been an apprentice of C. C. Briggs, made popular priced pianofortes in a small way with a tuning device which was perfected for Mason & Hamlin.

BROWN & HALLET

1833—Washington n. Essex
1834—Cor. Essex & Washington Sts.
1837—370½ Washington St.
1839—323 Washington St.
1841—293 Washington St.
1842-46—Mr. Brown was listed alone at 334 Washington St.

This firm, consisting of Edwin Brown and Russell Hallet, who furnished the capital, started about 1833. "In 1838, Mr. Brown patented a method for damping the strings to produce the effects made possible by a shifting action, which limited the hammer action to striking one string." ...."In 1843, he patented a grand action of a very complicated nature designed to insure more perfect repetition and taking in some principles of the French grand action which was used by Chickering & Sons subsequently. This contained several minor points in which many later action improvements were anticipated." [6]

In 1840 the Franklin Institute Fair Committee on Art Exhibitions bestowed highest honors on a Brown & Hallet among 21 pianofortes shown by important New York and Boston makers because "it is the smallest piano in the collection having only a keyboard of six octaves, but the tone is superior to all others. The patent soft pedal it contains is a very pleasing and effective innovation and entirely avoids the necessity of shifting the action to produce similar results." [6]

Around 1842 their good reasonably priced pianoforte was a real boon to music lovers who could not afford Chickerings and other standard makes. [6]

Mr. Brown about 1847 became a department foreman for Chickering & Sons, who used successfully in their grands the Swiss combined with the Brown action.

JACOB CHICKERING

1850—509½ Washington St.
1860—385 Washington St.

This firm was started comparatively soon after that of Jonas Chickering and went out of business between 1860-1870. It made a spindle leg, six octave, plain phlange-strung square.

[1] Dolge, Alfred. *Pianos and Their Makers* p. 278.
[2] Information supplied by Henry I. Tinkham, formerly with Chickering & Sons.
[3] Spillane, Daniel. *History of the American Pianoforte* p. 171.
[4] *Ibid* p. 174.
[5] Pauer, Ernst. *The Pianist's Dictionary* p. 137.
[6] Spillane, Daniel. *History of the American Pianoforte* p. 165.

I. B.   Other Boston Pianoforte Makers—Period 1840-1915 (Continued)

Addresses from Boston Business Directories	Names of Firms and Information About the Firms

DAVIS (BENJ. B.) & FOBES (EDWIN)

1836—83 Faneuil Hall Market

Sometime before 1836 Davis & Fobes became partners and remained so into 1838. After that Fobes' name was listed only as a tuner.[7] Edwin Fobes is said to have been a pupil of Timothy Gilbert[8] and an apprentice of C. C. Briggs,[9] and began manufacturing in 1843 largely popular priced instruments. "In 1853 he patented an improved vertical or upright piano of a peculiar kind. A full metal plate reached to the extreme top of the case over which the strings stretched. Meanwhile the wrest pins were driven down into the top of the case perpendicularly. The strings rested on rollers and in tuning the angle was therefore avoided." [8]

W. P. EMERSON

1850—393 Washington St.
1870—395 Washington St.
1880—595 Washington St.
1890—174 Tremont St.

This firm was established in 1849 by William P. Emerson who was a good business man and soon developed a large trade.

"The first improvements of distinct value were introduced from this date (1854) forward by Mr. C. C. Briggs, who became in a large measure identified with the musical status of the Emerson Piano during his stay there." [10]

They made squares, plain-strung first, then overstrung, uprights, "cottage" pianofortes, and finally grands. Their squares were among the best made, "scale 13," being a wonderful small square yet inexpensive. Those built from 1875 to 1880 had seven octaves and the last squares seven and a third octaves.

After Mr. Emerson's death, the company went to pieces and Ellenwood & Moore, who ran the company for the estate, sold out about 1890 to a new company consisting of Mr. P. H. Powers, Pres., Orin A. Kimball, and Joseph Grames. This new company failed after Mr. Powers' death and was sold about ten years ago to the United Piano Co. of Norwalk, Ohio.

EVERETT PIANO CO.

1885—383 Federal St.
1890—Albany cor. Wareham
1895—181 Tremont St. (Warerooms)
1900—Albany cor. Wareham
1915—Albany cor. Wareham

This company, headed by Col. Moore, was started between 1883-1885 and discontinued business in 1918 or 1919. It made uprights.

1862—556 Washington St.
1870—881 Washington St.
1880—682 Washington St.
1890—101 Bristol St.

GEORGE M. GUILD & CO. [11]

The George M. Guild piano was first made in 1861, when C. C. Briggs became a partner. By 1870 this firm was succeeded by Guild, Church & Co., consisting of Geo. M. Guild, Cephas Church, who furnished the capital, and Geo. Hews. In 1890 it was Guild Piano Mfg. Co. This went out of business between 1890-1895.

Mr. Guild was a practical pianoforte maker and obtained numerous patents for mechanical improvements some of which were practical. Among these were his stringing and tuning scheme and his sounding board and back arrangement, an adaptation of an old theory, which was used in modified form by other firms. [12] These were well known as good inexpensive instruments.

1844—293 Washington St.
1847—417 Washington St.
1851—409 Washington St.
1862—272 Washington St.
1875—484 Washington St.
1880—436 Washington St.
     and 700 Harrison Ave.
1890—179 Tremont St.

HALLET, DAVIS & CO.; HALLET & DAVIS

This new concern immediately succeeded Brown & Hallet in 1843. It consisted of Russell Hallet, George H. Davis and Henry Allen. Mr. Davis, who came from New Hampshire, acquired his knowledge of the pianoforte business when he first came to Boston. He withdrew about 1847 and formed a partnership with Benjamin Franklin Hallet, as Hallet, Davis & Co. This last firm was a close competitor of Jonas Chickering until its factory burned in the 1860's. After that it was not so successful.

"Their instrument became a standard instrument as early as 1851 when it vied with such well known ones as Nunns & Clark and Hall & Sons, N. Y.; T. Gilbert, Boston; Conrad Meyer, Philadelphia." [8]

At the New York Mechanics' Institute exhibition in 1853, a Hallet, Davis & Co. pianoforte was awarded a gold medal and praise from the committee which included Henry C. Watson and W. Vincent Wallace.

This firm had many patents including "a suspension agraffe bridge" for insuring a more upward bearing and consequently a better quality of resonance and tone production in the extreme treble register." [8] Among their other specialties were their grand action and movable keyboard (from Brown & Hallet?).

Mr. Davis died in 1879. The company was incorporated in 1890 with G. Cook, W. D. Cook and E. N. Kimball, Mr. Davis' factory superintendent, as chief stockholders. The company was continued by the Conways of Chicago, large stockholders, under a finance corporation. In 1931 Jacob Doll & Sons of N. Y. controlled the company.

7 As far as the author could find.
8 Spillane, Daniel. *History of the American Pianoforte* p. 170.
9 *Ibid* p. 172.
10 *Ibid* p. 173.
11 Listed in Pauer, Ernst. *The Pianist's Dictionary* p. 142.
12 Spillane, Daniel. *History of the American Pianoforte* p. 174.

I. B. Other Boston Pianoforte Makers—Period 1840-1915 (Continued)

Addresses from Boston Business Directories

Names of Firms and Information About the Firms

HALLET, CUMSTON & ALLEN; HALLET & CUMSTON; BROWN & ALLEN; AND RUSSELL HALLET & CO.

Hallet & Allen came into being at Mr. Davis' withdrawal from the first Hallet, Davis & Co. William Cumston, a practical pianoforte maker, was taken into the firm about 1847. He had a fine previous record as an inventor having patented in 1839 a damper improvement in squares.

In 1851 Henry Allen withdrew, formed Brown & Allen in 1853 with Edwin Brown of Brown & Hallet, subsequently "10 yrs. foreman in the manufactory of the late Jonas Chickering, Esq., where he perfected and applied his Patent Grand Action." [13] "The Committee on Musical Instruments, at the Rhode Island Society for the Encouragement of Domestic Industry holden Sept. 12-16, 1854 reported about this company's pianoforte thus—'After a careful examination of the workmanship, externally and internally, and after repeated trials and hearings, your Committee feel prepared to say that this (Brown & Allen's) Piano Forte is one of the very best they have ever met with in the course of some seventeen years' observation of the progress of Piano Forte manufacture in this country. In *purity*, combined with *power* and *mellowness of tone*; in *evenness of tone* from the bottom to the top of the scale; in the great excellence of the action; in thoroughness and elegance of workmanship throughout; in all the qualities, in short, which unitedly constitute a first rate Piano Forte, this instrument, in the opinion of your Committee, has not been surpassed by any Seven Octave Square Piano Forte hitherto produced among us, and they consider it eminently worthy of the highest premium in this department.'" [13] Henry F. Miller was trained in the Brown & Allen factory, before Mr. Brown again returned to Chickering & Sons leaving Mr. Allen in business alone 1862-74.

Hallet & Cumston was formed in 1853 and continued to make a popular priced instrument until about 1900. Their earliest squares were plain-strung, later ones overstrung. They were among the first to make uprights. Toward the end they made grands.

Russell Hallet joined Henry Allen during 1851-1852, withdrew from Hallet & Cumston about 1869, and was alone as Russell Hallet & Co. at 143 Tremont St. in 1870, and Russell Hallet 1872-74.

GEORGE HEWS or HEWES

George Hewes was listed as a music teacher in 1833 and 1834 Boston Directories, and appears in 1836 as a manufacturer. "In 1843 the firm consisted of George Hews, Richard C. Marsh, and

---

Hallet, Cumston & Allen
1847-51—293 & 339 Washington St.

Hallet & Cumston
1853-66—339 Washington St.

1880—459 Washington St.

Brown & Allen
1853-7—354 Washington St.

1859—356 Washington St.
Henry Allen; Allen & Co. See page

Russell Hallet & Co.
1870-1—143 Tremont St.

Russell Hallet
1872—147 Tremont St.
1873—32 West St.
1874—339 Washington St.

1847-1854—365 Washington St.

1855—379 Washington St.
1860—324 Washington St.

Nathaniel W. Tileston of Dorchester."[14] In 1855 they advertised their "Patent American Action Pianos."[15] In 1870 they were advertising, pianofortes, organs and melodeons at wholesale and retail, so they may have given up the manufacturing and been simply dealers by that time.[16] They went out of business between 1880-1885.

"Their squares invariably contained a form of the Chickering whole cast plate made so as not to infringe. Their pianos occasionally won awards at the New York Mechanics' Institute Fairs of 1847."[14]

1870—379 Washington St.
1880—595 Washington St.

J. S. HUMBERT

Around 1860. Built a few good squares.

1860—4 Howard St.

A. W. LADD

Mr. Ladd, an apprentice in C. C. Briggs' shop, was in business from about 1846 to between 1875-1880. He built only squares, first plain, then overstrung. The first plain strung were larger than the first Chickering plain strung squares.

1850—296 Washington St.
1875—630 Washington St.

WENDELL P. MARVIN

Between 1840-47 to between 1860-70.

1847—507 Washington St.
1860—324 Washington St.

LORENZO MATT

Between 1850-55 to between 1870-75.
An apprentice of C. C. Briggs and Co. Made a few popular priced squares. The name plate read—"Lorenzo Matt Boston"

He advertised an invention whose value time has apparently disproved, namely—"The greatest invention on the Sounding Board! The best Pianos are now made with the United Double Sounding Board, patented Dec. 31, 1867. These Pianos give a richer, sweeter, and more powerful Tone than any other Piano, and these Sounding Boards never can split or crack. The best and highest references can be given. . . All my instruments are warranted for five years."[17]

1855—575 Washington St.
1860—678 Washington St.
1868—500 Tremont St.
1870—296 Washington St.

JOHN E. McNEIL

Between 1855-1860 to between 1870-1875.

1860—155 Harrison Ave.
1870—313 Washington St.

[13] *Massachusetts Musical Journal*, Vol. 1 No. 3 p. 22.
[14] Spillane, Daniel. *History of the American Pianoforte* p. 171.
[15] *Massachusetts Musical Journal*, Vol. 1 No. 6 p. 48.
[16] *Boston Directory*, Advertising Department p. 934.
[17] *Boston City Directory* 1868, Advertising Department p. 950.

I. B. Other Boston Pianoforte Makers—Period 1840-1915 (Continued)

Addresses from Boston Business Directories	Names of Firms and Information About the Firms

ANDREW M. McPHAIL & CO.

1860—514 Washington St.
1870—385 Washington St.
1883—630 Washington St.
1893—167 Tremont St. A. M. McPhail Piano Co.
1900—784 Washington St.

Andrew M. McPhail was "born at St. Andrews, New Brunswick, [Canada] came to Boston as a boy, and was apprenticed to the renowned piano maker, Gilbert.[18] He learned to make pianos so well that he soon established a high reputation for his own product."[19] Alfred Dolge stated that Mr. McPhail started his own business in 1837, but in an advertisement dated 1900[20] this firm claimed a record of 61 years. It does not appear in the business directories until the decade of 1850.

This firm made three styles of squares, one of which was called "Star" and another "Crown," from their scale names.[21] These and their uprights had a good sale. Their pianofortes had a special action, made by the firm of Severens of Cambridge, Massachusetts, action makers, which was later bought out by Standard Action Co.[21] In March 1883 the company advertised their instruments as "Gold Medal Pianos", and stated that they "Received two silver medals in 1881 and a Gold Medal and Diploma from the Massachusetts Charitable Mechanic Association—Judges Georg Henschel, Louis C. Elson, Chas. J. Capen."[22]

Andrew McPhail "was a piano maker of the old school, who took pride in his work and considered the artistic success more than the commercial, although in his long career, from 1837 to 1891, he met all his obligations with never failing promptness. As a citizen he took a great interest in educational, artistic, and musical affairs, and also served as representative in the Massachusetts Legislature."[19]

Mr. McPhail retired in 1891 and died at Omaha, Nebraska, Oct. 1, 1902. The business was carried on by the A. M. McPhail Piano Co. and later was sold to two salesmen, Mr. Blake and Mr. Owen, who sold it to Lawrence Barry. It has not been officially dissolved, though its assets and name were bought by Mark Campbell. Pianos with this name have been made by Kohler & Brambach of New York for about six years.[23]

GUSTAVUS A. MILLER & CO.

1860—702 Washington St.
1870—798 Washington St.

Mr. Miller was a German. He started making pianofortes between 1850-1860 and his business was auctioned off about 1872. He made overstrung squares only, which were not especially good or popular.

DANIEL MORRIS

1890—Dunlow Court, Roxbury

He was trained as an apprentice of C. C. Briggs & Co. and made mainly a popular priced instrument from between 1885-1890 to between 1890-1900.

NEW ENGLAND PIANO CO.

1885—32 George St., Roxbury
1890—157 Tremont St.
1900—George, Gerard & Howard Sts., Roxbury

T. F. Scanlon was president of this company which started between 1880-1885. They made overstrung squares first, on the lines of the Emerson scale, and then uprights. They were a large concern around 1890, making one of the lowest priced instruments. Between 1900-1910 they went out of business.

This company and McLaughlin of the insolvent Smith American Organ & Piano Co., took over that company between 1900-1910. This latter company had begun to make pianofortes in 1884. In 1889 they exhibited their "Regal Piano" made on novel principles designed by H. W. Smith, which attracted much notice. It consisted of a method of tone qualification and piano case decoration, for the vibratory body of the piano was insulated from the case proper by the covering of the instrument all over with soft velvety material.[24] The New England Piano Co. essayed a reed organ, but without much success.

B. N. PHILLIPS

1890—122 Eliot St.

Mr. Phillips advertised [25] that he had been fourteen years with Woodward & Brown and J. W. Brackett. He made upright pianofortes and attached pedals for organ practice to any make, and apparently was in business only a few years.

ROGERS UPRIGHT PIANO CO.

1880—486 Harrison Ave.

About 1880. Sole manufacturers of the B. F. Baker Upright Piano. Elliot Patent—O. A. Gamage, general agent.[26]

[18] Presumably Timothy rather than Lemuel.
[19] Dolge, Alfred. *Pianos and Their Makers* p. 279.
[20] See *Boston Directory* 1900, Advertising Department p. 2378.
[21] Information supplied by Henry I. Tinkham, formerly of Chickering & Sons.
[22] Advertisement in *The Apollo*, Vol. 1 No. 4 & 5, February & March 1883, inside of back cover.
[23] Information supplied by William E. Merrill, Secretary, New England Music Trades Association.
[24] See Spillane, Daniel. *History of the American Pianoforte* p. 306.
[25] *Boston Directory* 1890, Advertising Department p. 1929.
[26] *Boston City Directory* 1880, Advertising Department p. 1376.

I. B.   Other Boston Pianoforte Makers—Period 1840-1915 *(Continued)*

Addresses from Boston Business Directories	Names of Firms and Information About the Firms
	WILKINS & NEWHALL
1832—23 Temple Place 1835—Boylston near Washington St. 1840-47—355 Washington St. 1850—344 Washington St.	Levi Wilkins was a pianoforte maker at 23 Temple Place from 1832-1834 and a partner from 1835-1837 with Stephen L. Gould who had been alone at 7 Carver St. in 1833 and 1834. In 1835 the firm was Gould, Wilder & Co. (L. Wilkins & D. B. Newhall). Levi Wilkins & Daniel B. Newhall apparently took over the business about 1837 or 1838. They went out of business between 1850-1860. They made overstrung squares and their instrument was known as the Newhall Pianoforte.
	W. P. WINCHESTER & CO.
1847—497 Washington St.	Before 1847—out of business between 1850-1860. Made squares and uprights.
	GEORGE WOODS & CO.
1853—210 Hanover & 323 Washington St. 1870—494 Tremont St. 1875—608 Washington St. Factory at Central Sq., Cambridge	About 1853 to about 1890. He worked earlier at Mason & Hamlin's and made good pianofortes. In 1885 this company was listed under organ builders at 608 Washington St.
	L. P. WOODWARD
1860—364½ Washington St.	Around 1860.
	WOODWARD & BROWN
1842-46—293 Washington St. 1847—352 Washington St. 1855—387 Washington St. 1860—377 Washington St. 1880—592 Washington St. 1885—175A Tremont St. 1895—200 Tremont St.	Isaac Woodward was born and educated at Roxbury, N. H., and learned cabinet making at Keene, N. H. He came to Boston and in the case making department of Brown & Hallet acquired a thorough knowledge of pianoforte making. He started business as "Brown [John P.], Hallet [R.] & Woodward [I.]" in 1842. John Brown was a fellow workman at Brown & Hallet's and a member of Edwin Brown's family. In 1846 it became I. Woodward & Co. and in 1847 Woodward & Brown.

Mr. Woodward and others in the concern patented many improvements "from 1843 to 1890 all of which possessed some utility and value." [27]   They made good full iron plate overstrung squares, but their uprights were unsuccessful.

"Mr. Woodward's most distinguishing personal characteristic was his love of music.   He was one of the oldest members of the Handel & Haydn Society and devoted himself to its art interests." [27] He died in Brookline in 1883.   Sometime between 1885-1890 this firm was out of business though Mr. Spillane speaks of it as a going concern in his book published in 1890.   The Woodward & Brown Piano Co. appears in the business directory around 1895 but was gone before 1900.

[27] Spillane, Daniel.   *History of the American Pianoforte* p. 169.

APPENDIX II. Other Boston Reed Organ Firms - Period 1850-1910

Addresses from Boston Business Directories	Names of Firms and Information About the Firms
1868—6 Avery St. 1872—53 Wareham St.	**BOSTON ORGAN CO.** 1868, became the New England Organ Co. in 1872, till between 1880-90. Made cheap organs.
1869-515 Washington St. 1872—379 Washington St. out by 1878	**BRUCE (J. M.) & CHARD (G.); then GRANVILLE CHARD** 1869-78. Manufacturers of the Mozart Organs & Melodeons for parlors, halls and churches.
1879—101 Border St.	**DAVID CHARD** 1879. Cabinet organs.
1868—179 Washington St. 1880—2130 Washington St.	**WM. H. GERRISH** 1868 to between 1880-90. Earlier a Mason & Hamlin salesman. Small serious maker of good reed organs and organist of one of the largest Masonic lodges of Boston. For publications see p. 26.
1875—101 Bristol St.	**C. B. HUNT & CO.** 1875 to between 1889-90. Manufacturers of Bay State reed organs. Firm C. B. Hunt and P. Kraus.
1880—578 Washington St.	**W. H. JOHNSON & CO.** Around 1880. Orguinettes.
Office Tremont St.; Factory Worcester, Mass.	**MASON & RISCH** The "Vocalion" (Invented by Hamilton of Scotland). A pressure free-reed, reeds much larger, broader, and heavier at tip and thin at butt. Good imitation of pipetone, cost prohibitory.
1879—57 Washington St.	**MASSACHUSETTS ORGAN CO.** 1879 to between 1880-90.
	NEW ENGLAND ORGAN CO. See Boston Organ Co.

NEW ENGLAND PIANO CO.

1900—George, Gerard & Howard Sts., Roxbury

Between 1880-85 to between 1900-10.
Made cheap reed organs after taking over Smith American Organ & Piano Co. after 1900. Not very successful with them. See list of Other Boston Pianoforte Makers for information about their pianos p. 249.

M. O. NICHOLS

1850—293 Washington St.
1853—166 Washington St.

About 1850. Nichols & Woods in 1852.

J. SCHLEICHER & HOCHSTUHL

1881—55 Bristol St.

About 1881. Manufacturer of Reed & Pipe Organs combined.

S. D. & H. W. SMITH

1852—417 Washington St.
1860—511 Washington St.
1870—Tremont St. opp. Waltham
1880—531 Tremont St. opp. Waltham
1900—136 Boylston

Started as S. D. Smith & Co. in 1852. From 1853-74 it was S. D. & H. W. Smith & Co.; 1875-86 and 1998-1900 Smith American Piano Co.; 1887-97 Smith American Organ & Piano Co.

This reed organ company was a close corporation in 1890 with S. D. Smith, Pres., H. W. Vice Pres., E. W., brother of the second, Treas., and Geo. T. McLaughlin, Sec'y., S. D. & H. W. Smith, cousins, were both born at Enfield, Mass. 1830. H. W. Smith, whose father was a noted inventor, learned pianoforte making as an apprentice in the factory of Hill, Ryder & Sons.

In 1868 they advertised themselves in the Boston City Directory on the back colored page as "Also publishers of the two new and popular books 'Organist Parlor Companion' and 'Home Recreations.'"

"This firm has for many years [1890] enjoyed a world-wide reputation as manufacturers of organs." "They have been in business over 37 years as reed organ makers, and during that period have been instrumental in promoting the growth of musical taste in this country in connection with that branch."[1] This house had a great many patents of significance in relation to the organ.[1] They advertised their organs as having "clear sweetness of tone that has passed into a proverb."[2]

Started making pianofortes in 1884.

T. D. WARREN

1852—615 Washington St.

About 1852. Melodeons.

GEORGE WOODS & CO.

1853—210 Hanover & 323 Washington St.
1870—494 Tremont St.
1875—608 Washington St. Factory at Central Sq., Cambridge

Listed 1853 to about 1890.
Earlier with Mason & Hamlin, made fine reed organs and pianofortes.

[1] Spillane, Daniel. *History of the American Pianoforte* p. 305.
[2] *Musical Herald*, January 1880.

APPENDIX III.   Other Boston Pipe Organ Builders - Period 1830-1910

Addresses from Boston Business Directories

Names of Firms and Information About the Firms

1899—415 Dorchester Ave. moved to Hartford, Conn., about 1900

AUSTIN ORGAN CO.

John T. & Basil Austin with C. C. Michell organized in 1899 to make instruments under their patents.

Started their big "Universal Wind Chest" organs in South Boston, but removed to Hartford, Conn., where they became famous. They rebuilt the Mormon Tabernacle Organ, Salt Lake City, and built the great Portland "Kotzschmar Organ," and the 5 manual Medinah Temple Organ, Chicago. Business discontinued in 1935. For Robert Hope Jones see p. 255.

Before 1880

MORITZ BAUMGARTEN

A German who did fine work as voicer for Hook & Hastings. Built some organs himself including one 3 manual one in the Catholic Church on Shawmut Ave., Boston.

1890—Reading, Mass.

WM. HORATIO CLARKE

Born 1840 in Newton, died 1913 in Reading.

He was organist at Dedham and Boston, teacher in the Perkins Institute for the Blind, 1871 music superintendent in Dayton, Ohio, Schools, organist and organ builder (W. H. Clarke & Co. in Indianapolis), and also in Toronto, and Reading, Mass. Was organist in Tremont Temple 1878-87 and after his retirement in 1887 was much sought after as consulting expert in organ building. In 1890 he erected at his estate in Reading a music chapel, "Clarigold Hall," containing a 4 manual organ of 100 stops.

Was also a composer and well known writer. Over 120,000 copies of his *New Method for Reed Organs* were sold. Among other works were *Harmonic School for the Organ, A guide to Improvisation and Musical composition.*

Cambridge, Mass.

GILBERT (J. L.) & BUTLER (GEO. A.) [1]

They worked for George Stevens and succeeded his firm after his death. Built the organ in Leominster Congregational Church, rebuilt by the Frazee Company and now in a Medford Roman Catholic Church; also in M. E. Church, Tapleyville; M. E. Church, West Fitchburg.

SAM'L S. HAMILL [2]

1878—101-103 and 109 Gore St., East Cambridge

About 1878. Had worked with Erben, N. Y. Well known, had good tone, but did rather poor work. Advertised "'Giant Pipe Organs,' a Special Class of Pipe Organs possessing great Power of Tone, at very low prices."[3] His prices gave him a good business mostly in New England. A good specimen of his organs is in the Billerica Unitarian Church.

HOLBROOK (GEO. H., later E[dwin] L., [2,4]

Millis, Mass., formerly East Medway. Main St. & Auburn St. 1830-1904

George H. Holbrook made church bells and organs and may possibly have worked for Thomas Appleton. He built organs for many churches in the Connecticut River valley. One of his largest was in the Baptist Church at South Hadley, Massachusetts. His organ in the First Congregational Church at Ipswich, Massachusetts, had, in 1923, 19 stops, push buttons for the couplers, and tracker action. The Great Organ had a pneumatic coupler to the Swell. He did fine work mechanically, but his tones were not especially colorful. George H. Holbrook took into partnership later J. Holbrook Ware who retired in 1850 and sold his interest to Edwin L. Holbrook who was an organist and made the organs himself.

ROBERT HOPE JONES [2]

He worked in partnership with the Austins when they were in business in South Boston. He was English, the builder of the great organ in Worcester Cathedral, and had made many inventions, including—the 32 ft. Diaphone among other stops, a new electric action, and the first independent console. He went to New York state when the Austin Company moved and died in 1914.

EMORY W. LANE

1890 Waltham, Mass.

After 1890 for about 15 years. Worked in the office of Hook & Hastings, then went in business for himself. Built a few organs, but mostly repaired and rebuilt.

GEORGE H. RYDER [1]

1871—1057 Washington St.
1875—441 Tremont St.
1877—2058 Washington St.
1888—Music Hall Bldg.
1900—Tremont Temple (Off.) Factory in Reading

1871—between 1900-10. Catalogue of 1892 lists 168 organs built or rebuilt. This firm at one time was Geo. H. & T(homas) P(hilander) Ryder and Narramore. Did excellent work. Made 1, 2 & 3 manual good mechanical action church organs, but largely 2 manual organs. His largest, a 3 manual, was in Michigan. He built many Masonic organs. His No. 7 was for St. John's, Lowell, Mass. Others were People's Temple, Boston, Christ Church Episcopal, Plymouth, Mass. and his last a specially fine tubular-pneumatic action one in Exeter, N.H. Ryder was followed in Reading by C. Y. Chadwick, who removed to Springfield, Mass. Then J. D. Brennan formerly with Ryder took the shop.

[1] Information supplied by James Cole and William B. Goodwin, organ builders.
[2] Information supplied by William B. Goodwin.
[3] Boston Directory, 1878, Advertising Department p. 1382.
[4] Information supplied by A. C. Foster.

III. Other Boston Pipe Organ Builders—Period 1830-1910 (*Continued*)

Addresses from Boston Business Directories

Names of Firms and Information About the Firms

Cor. 5th & Otis Sts., Cambridge, Mass.

GEORGE STEVENS [5]

Business started as Stevens & Gayetty and acquired the business of William Goodrich after his death, at least as early as 1838.

When Mr. Stevens was Mayor of Cambridge for 2 years his brother, Wm., took his place in managing the company (about 1855).

Was one of the early organ builders. Built some 800 small church organs, tracker action, including some 27 in Lowell. One organ there lasted 70 years showing its good materials. His voicing, however, was rather poor. He built the organ in the Stoneham, Mass., Congregational church, rebuilt with electrical action. St. Anne's, Lowell, Mass., built in 1855, was noted because this was the first organ built by this company in which zinc was used in the big bass pipes. His largest organ was in a Roman Catholic Church in North Cambridge.

1855-58—120 Leverett St.
1860—130 Leverett St.
1863-64—130 Leverett St.
1865-67—North Grove St.
1868—190 Charles cor. Cambridge
1869-72—No. Grove cor. Cambridge

STEVENS & JEWETT; WM. STEVENS; STEVENS & JEWETT;

1855 became   1856-1858   1860-1862 again

WM. STEVENS

1863-1873.

Wm. Stevens advertised "Manufacturer of Church Organs ranging from $500.—$20,000. Second hand organs for sale. Repairing and tuning promptly done." [9]

1887-90—Reed's Block, 16 Thayer Place

JAMES E. TREAT & CO. [5]

1887-1920. Bought around 1905 by Edward F. Searles and reorganized as Methuen Organ Co.

Mr. Treat was reed voicer for the Hutchings company and C. T. Harris [7] was flue voicer. Mr. Treat was eccentric, for example, the organ he built in Searles' home near Lenox had black naturals and white sharps in the pedal board. He rebuilt the organ in Dr. Webb's Church, Boston, built organs in Grace Episcopal and St. Paul's Methodist in Lawrence, and Great Barrington House, Great Barrington, Mass. One of his largest was in Grace Church, San Francisco, 3 manuals, 50+ stops of such fine workmanship that it took five years to build. It was destroyed by the earthquake and fire. Mr. Searles often gave the difference between the cost and what the churches could pay.

III.a.   Organ Water Motors—Period 1870-1933

Names of Firms and Information About the Firms

Addresses from Boston Business Directories

1871—174 State St.
1872-73—35 Lincoln St.
1874-75—71 Lincoln St.
1875-80—different numbers on Charlestown
1881-88—70 Washington St.
1889-91—32 Oliver St.
1892-1925—65 Sudbury St.

BOSTON HYDRAULIC MOTOR CO.

This organ blower was patented May 10, 1870. The firm was first Hydraulic Motor and Meter Co. and in 1872 became Hydraulic Motor and Meter Asso., H. F. Wheeler being prominently connected with it through 1876. In 1877 it became Hydraulic Motor Company at 23 Charlestown. That same year the Boston Hydraulic Motor Co. is first listed at 33 Charlestown. By 1880 the two seem to have merged and from 1883 only Boston Hydraulic Motor Company is listed. This was succeeded 1889 to 1891 by D. P. Gosline, and that company by F. E. Whitney 1892-1925. Mr. Gosline stated in a business circular that L. R. Stanley was working for him. Mr. Stanley moved to Framingham where he died. When the company was at 71 Lincoln St. the prices of their products ranged from $75 to $250.

Maker of "Boston Water Motor." The first notable reciprocating water motor in general use in America. Rather complicated, but very efficient.[8] It was used for blowing their organs by Cole & Woodberry, Hook & Hastings, Geo. S. Hutchings, George H. Ryder, and Woodberry & Harris. This motor was followed by the water motors "Ross" of Albany, "Jaques" of Brooklyn and "Spencer" of Hartford. (The most elaborate and economical was the "Canning"—not common.) The "Ross" was used considerably by Boston organ builders. Water power was utilized by a variety of "flutter-wheels" and rotary devices such as "The Backus" water wheel, "Amherst," etc. Electricity superseded them all by multiple fans, principally the "Orgoblo" and "Kinetic." The F. E. Whitney Co. followed the trend and developed the "Stanley Organ Blower," not widely used nor especially good. This was bought in January 1925 by C. M. Smith of Pepperell, Mass., who had previously purchased the company's principal business in later years, namely the "Boston" and "Whitney" ice cream freezers.

[5] Information supplied by James Cole and William B. Goodwin.
[6] *Boston Business Directory 1870,* Advertising Department p. 993 and other years too.
[7] See p. 166.
[8] Information about the water motors supplied by William B. Goodwin, Lowell, Massachusetts, organ builder, and by A. C. Foster, Organ Blower Co.

APPENDIX IV

A. Violin and Bow Makers—Period about 1845-1935

Addresses from Boston Business Directories

Names of Firms and Information About the Firms

ALLEN AND GANSHIRT, INC.

1931-32—46 La Grange St.

April 1931—June 1932.

Organized by John M. Allen and William Ganshirt, both of whom had been with Oliver Ditson Company. They sold musical instruments, band and orchestra supplies at wholesale and retail and repaired instruments and radios.

Mr. Ganshirt, born in Roxbury, Mass., was a repairer for the Musicians' Supply Company and other concerns and has had twenty years of experience in the trade.[1] He has made 27 violins and 1 viola, using Stradivarius and Guarnerius as his patterns and has specialized in fine bow repairing. He now repairs violins, cellos and basses for E. U. Wurlitzer Company, 30 La Grange St.

CALVIN BAKER

1880-81—99 Leverett St.

? to about 1915.

Worked for Asa Warren White and later had charge of the repair department of Thompson & Odell. He made many good instruments for both concerns. See p. 197 and p. 262.

PETER N. BORG

A Norwegian, who was a violin player and rather amateur maker of inexpensive fairly good violoncellos.

EDWARD N. CATLIN [2]

1879—Cambridgeport
1880—38 Providence St.
1886—31 Warren Ave.
1904—56 Lorraine St., Roslindale
1908—Moved to Springfield Centre, N. Y.

An amateur maker of good violins, who did this as an avocation at his home.

He was a fine violin player and teacher, but his main occupation was that of musical director. He got his start in this field with Buckley's Negro Minstrels and was successively director at Howard Atheneum, Boston Museum, Park Theatre, and from the 1890's at the Tremont Theatre until it became no longer a regular theatre and he resigned. He also composed orchestra music which was played in the Tremont Theatre.

PETER CYR

Lynn, Mass.

For about 40 years until 1931.
Maker of good violins.[3] Worked for Elias Howe Co. some.

1870—Waltham, Mass.
1877—Hanover St., Boston
1st listing in Directory
1882-86 at 48 Hanover St.

G(EO). W. DANIELS [4]

Around 1870 to about 1922.
Made violins and 'cellos.

1890—10 Tremont Row
1900—73 Hanover St.

ELIJAH EMERSON

1890-1903 had his own shop.

Repairer for Elias Howe before going into business for himself. Made fair violins, his best period as a maker being about 1895.

1916—780 Broadway, Everett, Mass.

CHARLES E. FARLEY [6]

Was an American of pure English descent. His father, Nathan F., had been assistant to Abraham Prescott of Deerfield, N. H., one of the earliest bass and 'cello makers in the country. Charles E. Farley began making violins almost from babyhood. He really started in 1883. Up to 1916 he had made 290 violins. His latest period commenced in 1900 with alteration to a new model considered superior to preceding ones. His violins are of good substantial thickness. He made and used his own amber oil varnish. The color varied. He died toward the close of the World War.

1898—247 Washington St.
1900—48 Winter St.

OSBORNE P. FLATHER

Listed 1898-1900.
Pretty good maker.

? —Boston
1916—206 McCance Block, Pittsburgh

G. M. FRANÇOIS

Came to Boston from France and worked in the Boston City Dispensary as a professional pharmacist. In his free time he repaired and made some violins. He moved to Pittsburgh where he is a maker of violins, on classic models, of forty odd years' experience, and a repairer of old violins.[1]

[1] *The Violinist's Guide*, American Violin Makers p. 27.
[2] Information supplied by William R. Gibbs, a friend of Mr. Catlin.
[3] Statement of A. J. Oettinger, Musicians' Supply Company.
[4] Listed in *Die Geigen und Lautenmacher*, 1904 edition p. 124.
[5] Statement of Edmund F. Bryant, violin maker.
[6] Most of this information from *The Violinist's Guide*. American Violin Makers p. 25.

IV. A. Violin and Bow Makers—Period about 1845-1935 (Continued)

Addresses from Boston Business Directories	Names of Firms and Information About the Firms

TREFFLÉ GERVAIS [7]

1899—171A Tremont St.
1932—170A Tremont St.

Conducted his own shop from about 1899 into 1934.

Mr. Gervais was born Nov. 2, 1863, in Canada of French parents who moved to Boston in 1877. He made his first violin of wood he bought from a lumber yard, because he was fond of music and could not afford to buy one. His fifth instrument interested Elias Howe so that the latter employed him in 1885 and 1886. He also worked for Asa Warren White, making violins and bows, a year for Orin Weeman and two years for J. B. Squier.

Henri Poidras described him in 1928 as "he derives a well earned reputation from his much esteemed works." [8] Up to 1932 he had made thirty-seven violins, two violas and one violoncello all to order. He followed a Guarnerius model almost exclusively because of the beauty of its well rounded lines. The label used in his instruments is reproduced on plate XXII and one of his violins on plate XXV in Bachmann's *An Encyclopedia of the Violin.*[9]

L(EONARD) O. GROVER

1878-1901—27 Union Park
1902-04—12 Greenwich Park

Music teacher first, listed as violin repairer 1878-1904 for himself. Worked for Thompson & Odell as repairer.

Made some fair instruments.

A(LFRED) R. HASKELL [10]

1916—150 Tremont St. (Oliver Ditson Company)

Was born in Mass. in 1875 and learned the trade with O. H. Bryant, beginning as repairer. He started making violins about 1906. He worked somewhat for himself, but was with Oliver Ditson Company in 1916 as expert maker and repairer, and has since died.

ELIAS HOWE CO.

1860—33 Court St.
1870—103 Court St.
1880—88 Court St.
1916—8 Bosworth St.
1924-31—120 Boylston St.

Elias Howe [11] 1860-1931.

This firm was one of the largest houses in the country dealing in fine new and old stringed instruments, bows, strings and all accessories. Ernest A. Anderberg, O. H. Bryant, Peter Cyr, J. H. Edler, Elijah Emerson, Trefflé Gervais, Walter S. Goss, Henry Schultz, Richard Turner, and Joseph A. Young have worked for this firm as repairers and makers to fill orders, some of the above having had charge of the company's department dealing in old instruments and repairing.

At the request of the noted violin maker, Walter E. Colton, the company had made what they called the "Colton Bridge." It was designed by them from three bridges which he selected, one for the shape, one for the "feet," and one for the "heart" (scrolls). The Colton Bridge proved so popular that it was imitated in Europe. It is sold today by Edward F. Howe of the Elias Howe Music Co., 120 Boylston St., dealers, particularly in makers' materials.

For the retail music store and publishing business of this firm see pp. 12-15.

1899-1900—47 Hanover St.

GEO. W. MARQUARDT [12]

Listed—around 1900.

Maker of good violins, violas, violoncellos and basses. He specialized in repairing 'cellos and double basses.

1900—25 Winter St. Rm. 9
1902—608 Columbus Ave.

FREEMAN A. OLIVER

Between 1890-95 to 1905-10.

Had a varied line of violins, his own being made mostly by A. Lind, a violinist.

1895-98—37 Bennet St.
1899—493 Washington St.
1920-26—232A Tremont St.

TERRENCE O'LOUGHLIN

Listed about 1895-99 and about 1920-26.

Came from Connecticut and was originally a shoemaker. Made hundreds of violins.

1900—86 Court St.

CLARK POWERS

Between 1888 to between 1900-05 about 10 years.

Born in Vermont 1856, he worked as a violin helper for 25 years and then spent about two years in England, Germany and Austria. He started for himself in Boston in 1888 as a maker after Cremona patterns according to his own models in which he lays stress upon his "Equipoise." [13]

He used oil varnish and spirits of alcohol.

He was a dealer, good violin repairer and made a few fairly good instruments. [14] Mostly he imported and refinished violins from Markneukirche.

7 The writer has been unable to learn whether he is continuing in business elsewhere.
8 Poidras, Henri. Critical and Documentary Dictionary of Violin Makers Old and Modern pp. 188 & 189.
9 Bachmann, Alberto. An Encyclopedia of the Violin p. 54.
10 Information largely from The Violinist's Guide. American Violin Makers p. 24.
11 Listed in Bachmann, Alberto. An Encyclopedia of the Violin p. 54 as an American violin maker.
12 Ibid. p. 408.
13 See Willibald, Leo, Freiherrn Von Lütgendorff, Die Geigen und Lautenmacher p. 506.
14 Statement of A. J. Oettinger, Musicians' Supply Co.

IV. A. Violin and Bow Makers—Period about 1845-1935 (Continued)

Addresses from Boston Business Directories

Names of Firms and Information About the Firms

RAOUL RETTBERG [15]

Mr. Rettberg is an expert bow maker of many years' standing, and a maker and repairer of violins.

He also knows the ancient stringed instruments as he has made at least one viole d'amour.

1928—309 Huntington Ave.
1930—791 Tremont St.
1932—250 Huntington Ave.
1935—46 La Grange St. [16]

ROBERT ROBINSON

In Boston 1899-1901 alone.

In 1902 he formed the firm Robinson & Schultz. He settled later in Portland, Oregon, where he has his own business.

Born in Sandusky, Ohio, Sept. 12, 1851. Worked in Des Moines, Iowa, 1871-77, Denver, Colo., 1882-84, Des Moines, 1885-91, Salt Lake City, Utah, 1891-92, Chicago, 1893-94, San Francisco, 1897-98. Violin making was a side issue until he came to Boston in 1899. He made violins after Stradivarius and Guarnerius and had his own model which was between the two, using a spirit varnish which he put up himself. Robinson & Schultz were importers, jobbers, makers and repairers of violins, violas, cellos and bows, voiced and adjusted new and old instruments and had strings and fittings. He is also a bow maker. In Portland he is a repairer and dealer and makes only to order. [17]

1902—86 Court St.
1916—15 Russell Bldg., Portland, Ore.

D(AVID) B(AILEY) ROCKWELL

Boston about 1878-1895. Moved to Philadelphia.

Came from Maine. A real artist maker of violins, and bows, and a fine repairer. [18] "He followed old Italian models, using his own varnish." [17] He advertised "We give special attention to fitting up Small Violins for the young class. Bows repaired and straightened. Fine Old and New Violins, Cases and Bows on hand. We make a specialty of Fine Italian Strings, Violin Wood and Trimmings. We furnish teachers on the Violin, Bass and Cello." [19]

1887—88 Court St.
1891—6 Winter St.
1892—88 Court St.
1895—103 Court St.
1916—908 Chestnut St., Philadelphia

THOMPSON & ODELL

1874 to about 1905; 1874 Woods, Odell & Thompson; 1875 on, Thompson & Odell.

Had a retail store, were stringed instrument importers, putting on their name, and repairers. Calvin Baker in charge of their repair department, made good violins, violas, violoncellos and double basses for them and for himself up to about 1915. L. O. Grover also worked in their repair department. For information about their fretted instrument making see The Vega Co. p. 229 and p. 268, for their brass instrument manufacturing p. 229 and for their publishing p. 22.

1874—121 Court St
1878—86 Tremont St.
1880—177 Washington St.
1888—578 Washington St.
1890—523 Washington St.
1905—749 Washington St.

RICHARD H. TURNER

1932-34—2 Park Square

February 1932 into 1934.

Mr. Turner is a violinist who came from Maine to Boston in 1920 and worked as expert violin repairer for the Musicians' Supply Company and Elias Howe before starting in business for himself in 1932.

He had made violins since he was a boy using Amati, Stradivarius and Guarnerius models for patterns, and three or four violas. He is also a violin player and gained his knowledge of the acoustics of the violin from his teachers. Because he never could find a bow which was satisfactory to himself for playing, he began experimenting with them in 1907 with the result that bow making was a specialty of his. He has also made a study of kinds of bridges suitable for different styles of violins.

He is now located elsewhere in a different kind of business.

JAMES H. WHITE

1860—59 Court St.
1880—89 Court St.

Between 1850-1860, by 1880 became James H. & J. Henry White. J. Henry alone 1890-1914. James H. White was a violin and woodwind repairer, maker of violin strings and prompter of the Germania Orchestra.

His son, J. Henry, born in Boston in 1842, acquired a high reputation for his repairing of musical instruments.[20]

MAURICE WHITE

1900—181 Tremont St. Room 32

Between 1895-1900 to between 1905-10.

A German maker of good violins. His name was originally Weiss. He made the instruments for E. Berliner's experiments.[18]

JOSEPH A. YOUNG [21]

Lynn, Mass.
1916—62 LaGrange St. Boston (Musicians' Supply Co.)

Was an American maker, repairer and expert with fifteen years' experience (1916) in the trade. He worked for Elias Howe Co., had a shop for himself in Lynn for a while, and died while in the employ of the Musicians' Supply Co. He made violins and 'cellos.

[15] Listed in Poidras, Henri. *Critical and Documentary Dictionary of Violin Makers Old and Modern* p. 202 as a contemporary bow maker.
[16] This shop has been given up and the writer has been unable to learn whether he is continuing in business elsewhere.
[17] *The Violinist's Guide,* American Violin Makers p. 38.
[18] Statement of A. J. Oettinger, Musicians' Supply Company.
[19] *Boston Directory* 1891, Advertising Department p. 2024,
[20] Howe, William H. *The Violinist's Guide,* Early American Violin Makers p. 18.
[21] *The Violinist's Guide,* American Violin Makers p. 42.

IV. B.   Manufacturers of Musical Strings—Period 1885-1936

Addresses from Boston Business Directories

Names of Firms and Information About the Firms

WM. J. LOCKHART

1891—rear 28 Beach St.
1918—172 Columbus Ave.

Started in 1891 as Hodgdon (Jas. B.) & Lockhart. Became Wm. J. Lockhart from 1894-1918. Established in 1891 by Hodgdon & Lockhart, the latter having been "Late Manager for J. Warren Tuck." Their "ad" featured the firm as "Manufacturers of Covered Strings for Piano-fortes and other musical instruments. Fine steel wire, Gut strings of all kinds." [22] In 1892 they advertised all kinds and sizes of musical strings, the best quality put up in Metal Envelopes, also Brass, German Silver and Silver wire constantly in stock, the best gut expressly prepared and wound with gold or silver-plated or pure silver wire. In 1894 Wm. J. Lockhart advertised himself as, "Sole Manufacturer of Lockhart's improved metal strings." [23]

ALBERT A. McCARTY

1904—36 Beach St.
1920—3 Appleton St.
1925—56 Bristol St.

1904—about 1932.
Worked earlier for Wm. J. Lockhart. Manufactured all kinds of musical strings, especially pianoforte, which he sold to the leading makers in the Eastern part of the United States. [24]

C. SALADINO & SONS

From 1919 on—Chelsea, Mass.

From 1919 on.
Established in 1919 and manufactured musical strings for stringed instruments until about 1935. Now they are making only strings for sport use. Starting with the raw materials they check their strings at each important point and test their finished strings continually. They ship abroad as well as to all parts of the United States.

H. SCHINDLER & CO., INC.

1889—178 Tremont St.
1900—88 Court St.
1911—Lamartine St., Jamaica Plain
Sept. 1933 moved to Canton, Mass.

Started in 1889 as Otto Schindler & Co. Changed by 1900 to Hugo Schindler & Co. This company was started by Messrs. Hugo and Otto Schindler because their nephew, Paul Schindler found it impossible to obtain satisfactory strings for his playing. Hugo Schindler died Oct. 5, 1933, and the company ceased the manufacture of musical strings in the fall of 1934 and now specializes in strings for sporting goods.
Until 1934 this firm was the oldest concern in the United States specializing in strings for bow stringed instruments, though they have made them for banjos, guitars, harps and ukuleles also.

They made the gut from sheep's intestines and wound it. No steel was used only German silver, plated copper, pure silver, aluminum and formerly gold. They shipped their strings all over the United States and to Europe. For strings introduced by Mr. Schindler see p. 201. [25]

1885-1896—19 Harvard Pl.

J. WARREN TUCK
1885-1896 Successor to C. C. Houghton.
"Manufacturer of all kinds of Musical Strings, Wire & Gut—all sizes. Wire for piano strings & fine sizes for other instruments. Brass, German silver and silver wire constantly in stock. The best gut expressly prepared and wound with gold or silver plated or pure silver wire." [25]

1897—19 Harvard Pl.

WATSON WOOD
Listed 1897 only.
Possibly a successor to J. Warren Tuck?

IV. C. Flute and Clarinet Makers—Period 1850-1900

WM. BAUER & SON (EMILE)
1876-77 Wm. Bauer & Son, 1878-82 just Wm. Bauer.
Did chiefly flute and clarinet repairing. The father may have made a few woodwind instruments. He died and the son carried on the repairing with the Envers brothers until August Damm bought the business. Emile Bauer then went with John C. Haynes & Co.

1876—103 Court St.
1882—271 Ruggles St. (his home)
1888—48 Hanover St.

THEODORE BERTELING
About 1850-1858, then in New York.
Good woodwind instruments, typically German. Made flutes and clarinets, mostly to order.

1850—115 Court St.
1851—18 Harvard Pl.
1858—43 Kingston St.

JOHN C. HAYNES & CO.
Started as a music store 1865 and continued to about 1900.
The instrumental manufacturing and repairing of Oliver Ditson & Co. was run separately first under this name, but amalgamated about 1900 with the publishing business. Instruments of all kinds were largely made for them, "Bay State" being their trade name. Imported violins were

1865—33 Court St.
1891—33 Court St. and 453 Washington St.
1900—453 Washington St.
Listed separately for last time in 1904

[22] *Boston Directory* 1891, Advertising Department p. 1754.
[23] *Boston Directory* 1894, Advertising Department p. 2063.
[24] Statement of A. J. Oettinger, Musicians' Supply Company.
[25] *Boston Directory* 1885, Advertising Department p. 1655.

IV. C. Flute and Clarinet Makers—Period 1850-1900 (Continued)

Addresses from Boston Business Directories	Names of Firms and Information About the Firms

JOHN C. HAYNES & CO.—(Continued)

graduated by them to produce proper tone. In the 1890's their flutes were made by Wm. S. Haynes. John C. Haynes & Co. made their own mandolins and guitars in their factory in the rear of the Pope Building. The Vega Co. bought out this factory when they discontinued business. Some of their zithers and autoharps were made for them by Chester B. Holway & Co. They also repaired all kinds of instruments.

1867—13 Hawkins St.
1870-73—20 Court St.

ADOLPH G. HÜTTL

1860-69, became Hüttl & Fischer 1870-73. Mr. Hüttl went to Chicago in 1874. He was a maker of flutes and clarinets.

F. G. SCHAUFFLER & CO.

First listing 1847, became Schauffler & Leukhardt from 1854-57. This company made flutes or dealt in musical instruments. From 1859 to about 1867 it was just John Leukhardt. By 1870 he was in the musical instrument leather business.

1847—555 Washington St.
1849—364 Washington St.
1853—not listed
1854—364 Washington St.
Given under heading musical instruments.
In 1859 again listed as makers.

IV. D. Brass Instrument Manufacturers—Period 1850-1915

ALLEN & RICHARDSON; ALLEN MFG. CO.; ALLEN & HALL

This firm began in 1852 as Allen & Richardson
1853-58 was J. L. Allen
1859-60 was Allen Mfg. Co.
1861 was Allen & Hall who made good rotary valve instruments. Then Allen got out.
1862-65 was D (avid) C. Hall alone
For successors see Hall & Quinby

1852—19 Harvard Pl.
1853-58—17 Harvard Pl.
1859-60—18 Harvard Pl.
1861-65—334 Washington St.

BOSTON MUSICAL INSTRUMENT MANUFACTORY

1870—71 Sudbury St.
1900—51 Chardon St.

Probable successors in 1870 to E. G. Wright & Co. See p. 270 for this. The firm consisted of Henry Esbach, L. F. Hartman and W. G. Reed. Their advertisement of 1874 which bears the subheading "Formerly E. G. Wright & Co." features with a picture their "New pocket E-flat cornet." [26] This firm was incorporated in 1913 and taken over by The Cundy-Bettoney Company in 1919.

Manufacturers of brass instruments. Noted for their Three *** Star Cornets and Trumpets. Made as fine instruments as any of that time, mostly cornets. [27]

GEORGE FREEMANTLE

1862—68 Albany St.
1865—71 Sudbury St.

1862-1865.

An English flute and harp player. Made band instruments for a short time. [27]

GILMORE, GRAVES & CO.; GILMORE & CO.; WRIGHT, GILMORE & CO.

1859-61—61 Court St.
1864-66—18 Harvard Pl.
1867—71 Sudbury St.

Patrick Sarsfield Gilmore was in business as a musical instrument dealer in Gilmore & Russell in 1859. From 1860-61 he apparently was just the leader of Gilmore's Band at the same address. His name did not appear in business directories for 1862 & 1863, but in 1864-65 he was a partner in Gilmore, Graves & Co. which became just Gilmore & Co. in 1866, and Wright, Gilmore & Co. in 1867. By 1868 Mr. Gilmore had apparently given up instrument manufacturing as the firm had become E. G. Wright. See p. 270.

The new combination of Gilmore, Graves & Co. described their business thus in 1864— "Purity of tone, perfection of tune, and elegance of finish, are the qualities in which our instruments excel. Improved tools and machinery for manufacturing have been prepared under the supervision of P. S. GILMORE, leader of Gilmore's celebrated band, who is a partner in our firm, and who personally examines and tests every instrument manufactured in our establishment. SAMUEL GRAVES & SONS, better known as Graves & Co., the oldest and most celebrated Musical Instrument Makers in this country, are also partners in our concern, and it is needless to remark that they are, and have been the acknowledged heads and model manufacturers in this line of business for the past forty years. The best guaranty we can offer, is to say that we warrant every instrument made by us to give PERFECT SATISFACTION." [28]

[26] *Boston Directory, 1874*, Advertising Department p. 1301.
[27] Statement of Thomas M. Carter.
[28] *Boston Directory 1864*, Advertising Department p. 109.

IV. D.   Brass Instrument Manufacturers—Period 1850-1915 (Continued)

Addresses from Boston Business Directories	Names of Firms and Information About the Firms

GRAVES & CO.

1824?—Winchester, N. H.
1852-54—18 Harvard Pl.
1855-61—68 Albany St.
1862-63—18 Harvard Pl.

This company was established by Samuel Graves at Winchester,[29] N. H., about 1824 according to the above advertisement and opened in Boston about 1852. See p. 226. From 1862-63 the business was listed simply as S. Graves. In 1864 Gilmore, Graves & Co. were at the same location, 18 Harvard Pl., while S. Graves was listed at 71 Sudbury St. From 1865 on the name Graves disappeared both in a company and individually.

HALL & QUINBY; AND QUINBY BROS.

For predecessors see Allen Mfg. Co. and Allen & Hall p. 266.

1866—112 Congress St.
1867-83—62 Sudbury St.
        David C. Hall alone
1876-77—126 Court St.
1878—7 Staniford Pl.
1879-80—44 Sudbury St.
1881—59 Bromfield St. &
        17 Montgomery Pl.
1882—292 Washington St.
1883—89 Court St., Rm. 9
1890—178 Washington St.
1895—48 Hanover St.
1899—103 Court St.

1866-75 Hall & Quinby were "manufacturers of rotary valve instruments of every description."[30] They purchased the entire stock and tools of Allen & Hall and introduced new inventions. Beginning in 1872 they had taken over the stock and tools of the late firm of E. G. Wright & Co.[31]

1876-82 Quinby Bros. (B. F. & Geo. W.) stated in 1876 that they had introduced new styles, models and inventions and had rotary valve instruments of every description.[32] In 1880 they described themselves as "Manufacturers of all kinds of band instruments, brass band instruments (round, flat and piston valves)."[33] They made fine instruments, cornets, trumpets, trombones, French horns, E-flat altos, baritones and tubas.[29]

1883 Whipple Music Co. Apparently the sale of stock of this company, a merger of L. E. Whipple and Quinby Bros., was not successful, for in 1884 the Standard Band Instrument Co., which was Thompson & Odell's brass instrument manufacturing business, occupied 62 Sudbury St. They may have started with the stock and equipment of Quinby Bros.

David C. Hall was alone again from 1876 to about 1899 at various addresses. He was listed in 1879-1880 only under Hall's Boston Brass Quadrille Band and Orchestra. Before that and again till 1883 he was listed as an instrument maker. Beginning with 1883 the directory heading includes dealers and manufacturers, so it is uncertain how long he made instruments and how much he was simply a band leader, player and dealer.

B. F. RICHARDSON; RICHARDSON & LEHNERT

1852—19 Harvard Pl.
1855—19 Washington St.
1856-59—26 Washington St.
1860-62—5 Water St.
1863-64—13 Water St.
1865-66—38 Portland St.
1867—46 Portland St.
1873-93—13 Bowker St.
1894—37 Pitts St.

This business started as Allen & Richardson. Allen apparently withdrew in 1853 and B. F. Richardson's name does not appear again till 1855 when he manufactured all kinds of brass instruments. In 1861 the firm was Richardson & Bayley who advertised, "Improved Cornets and all kinds of musical instruments of the most approved styles with all the modern improvements, made to order and warranted.[34] In 1862 Mr. Richardson was alone as an importer, dealer and manufacturer. In 1863 he advertised himself, not bashfully, as "Originator and Sole Manufacturer of the Celebrated 'Bayley Cornet,' Pronounced by all our best Musicians to be 'The Richest Toned Instrument in the World.'"[35] This cornet had a short life.

In 1866 the firm became Richardson & Lehnert. After Mr. Lehnert's death B. F. Richardson was listed from 1880 to 1895 as a music stand manufacturer.

STANDARD BAND INSTRUMENT CO.

1884—62 Sudbury St.

Started in 1884 by Thompson & Odell. Taken over by The Vega Co. around 1905. It was listed last in the 1908 directory.

THOMPSON & ODELL

For their brass instrument manufacturing see Standard Band Instrument Co. above.

L. E. WHIPPLE

1881-82—48 Winter St.

1881 and 1882.

L. E. Whipple's Musicians' Specialties were acme rosin; a brilliant lustre polish; slide trombone oil, compound lubricator for slides and joints of brass and wood instruments; jet black copying ink.

WHIPPLE MUSIC CO.

1883—495 Washington St.

1883 only.

Successor to L. E. Whipple, dealer and publisher and to Quinby Bros. manufacturers of brass band instruments. They continued L. E. Whipple's Musicians' Specialties and advertised themselves as manufacturers and importers of band instruments, who carried violins, banjos, German accordeons, harmonicas, Swiss music boxes, snare drums, violin strings and cases for sale. They featured in *The Apollo* their new cornet, "Whipple's Diamond Cornet" in B-flat and A. For their publishing activities see p. 23.

[29] Information supplied by Thomas M. Carter, leader of Carter's Band.
[30] *Boston Directory 1870*, Advertising Department p. 1043.
[31] See p. 270.
[32] *Boston Directory 1876*, Advertising Department p. 1275.
[33] *Boston Directory 1880*, Advertising Department p. 1261.
[34] *Boston Directory 1861*, Advertising Department p. 62.
[35] *Boston Directory 1863*, Advertising Department p. 29.

IV. D. Brass Instrument Manufacturers—Period 1850-1915 (Continued)

Addresses from Boston Business Directories	Names of Firms and Information About the Firms
1841—house 29 Fayette St. 1842—Bromfield St. 1847—8 Bromfield St. 1851—115 Court St. 1861-64—18 Harvard Pl. 1865-69—71 Sudbury St. 1871—62 Sudbury St.	**E. G. WRIGHT AND VARIOUS AFFILIATIONS**

Elbridge G. Wright, musical instrument maker, was listed first in the 1841 directory at his home. From 1842 to about 1860 E. G. Wright had his own brass band instrument manufacturing business. In 1861 only a dealer, the Wright Musical Instrument Co. is listed. From 1862-64 E. G. Wright's name appears again as a maker and from 1865-66 E. G. Wright & Co. In 1867 he joined Patrick Sarsfield Gilmore forming Wright, Gilmore & Co. In 1868 Mr. Wright apparently absorbed the entire business and continued until 1870. That year his name disappears from the classified list and he may have helped organize the Boston Musical Instrument Manufactory as that company beginning in 1874 advertised themselves as "Formerly E. G. Wright & Co." Yet in 1870 [36] and in 1871 [37] two advertisements are given side by side one by Hall & Quinby and one by E. G. Wright & Co. both with the address 62 Sudbury St. and the same heads of the firms, D. C. Hall, G. W. Quinby and E. G. Wright for the first named, and E. G. Wright's name first in E. G. Wright & Co. Starting with the next year, 1872, Hall & Quinby stated in their advertisement that they were owners and managers of the entire stock and tools of the late firm of E. G. Wright & Co.

The 1870 advertisement read "A First-Prize SILVER MEDAL awarded at the late Fair of Massachusetts Charitable Association for a full set of Brass Instruments. A First-Prize GOLD MEDAL awarded at the late Mechanics' Fair at Lowell, Mass. Messrs. Wright & Co. invite attention to their New Improved Rotary and Piston Cornets, as well as to their large assortment of Brass, Copper, German Silver and Silver Instruments of superior quality and finish. Repairs promptly made by skillful workmen." [38]

Around 1860 he was apparently also a bandmaster, for Wright & McDonald's Quadrille Band in 1860 and Wright & Newcomb's Quadrille Band in 1861 were listed at 27 Portland St., and Wright's Quadrille Band in 1862 at 14 Portland St.

IV. E. Drum Makers—Period 1850-1936

1893-1900—3 Tremont Row

A(LBERT) L. BERRY

About 1893 to 1900-05.

A drummer, played in the First Regiment of Militia in which George Burt Stone was first a drummer and then Drum Major. Made drums and drum shells. Bought the parts and assembled them more than making them entirely.

1893—Abattoir Grounds, Brighton
1894—379 Albany St.
1895-96—not listed
1897-1902—169 Dudley St.

BLAIR & BALDWIN

1893-94 and 1897 W. J. Blair, became Blair & Baldwin in 1898. Purchased about 1905 by F. E. Dodge.

William J. Blair was a drummer in the Civil War and a maker of good drums. Baldwin was a fine workman also. He resigned to manufacture bicycle wood rims and wheels. Later he worked for John C. Haynes & Co. where he was known as "Grandsire Baldwin." [38] When Mr. Baldwin resigned about 1905, F. E. Dodge bought out Mr. Blair who worked first for Mr. Dodge and then for Nokes & Nicolai until his death.

1907—42 La Grange St.

HARRY A. BOWER

Listed around 1907.

Drummer, teacher and drum manufacturer. Played tympani in the Tremont Theatre Orchestra in his early days, and in the Boston Symphony Orchestra. He toured on the vaudeville stage with Mrs. Bower, a pianist. Both are now in Hollywood, Cal., teaching. His manufacturing, done in Massachusetts Chambers, was largely assembling. [39]

1905-11—3 Appleton St.

F. E. DODGE

1905-1911 when he was bought out by Nokes & Nicolai.

Made drums. Bought the patents of Harry A. Bower for snare strainers, drum holders and a tympani device. [39]

[36] *Boston Directory 1870,* Advertising Department p. 1043.
[37] *Boston Directory 1871,* Advertising Department p. 1017.
[38] Information from A. J. Oettinger.
[39] Information supplied by E. J. Nokes of Nokes & Nicolai.

IV. E.　Drum Makers—Period 1850-1936 (*Continued*)

Addresses from Boston Business Directories	*Names of Firms and Information About the Firms*
Factory 1914—17 Chardon St. 1920—62 Sudbury St.	ELIAS HOWE [40] 　Civil War period and 1914-24. 　Manufactured drums and accessories. Made and supplied drums to the Union Army, especially Massachusetts regiments.　See p. 227. Later manufactured drum traps, triangles, metal fittings like violin mutes, bending irons, etc.　Their specialty was drum and music stands.　The latter had a patented top and patented closing device.
Around 1900-36—Main St. Charlestown, Mass.	WM. McINTOSH [41] 　Around 1900 to 1936. 　Drummer, drum maker, radio expert and now mostly a dealer in radios and equipment.
1912—3 Appleton St. 1920—5 Appleton St. 1928—97 Haverhill St. 5th floor	NOKES & NICOLAI [41] 　Started with purchase of F. E. Dodge's business 1912.　Purchased F. E. Cole banjo business about 1919.　Merged with Liberty Rawhide Mfg. Co. of Chicago. This previously had made only drum heads, but started making drums and banjos. Mr. Nokes resigned after about a year and later the Slingerland Co. bought out their equipment. 　E. J. Nokes came from Canada where he had been a drummer from the time he was twelve and one-half years old.　He was in the Tremont Theatre Orchestra under Mr. E. Catlin for eighteen years.　He is now Repair and Drum Corps Expert for C. G. Conn, Ltd. in their Boston Branch at 1517 Columbus Ave., Boston.　Edward F. Nicolai also is a professional drummer, from Lawrence, Mass.　The firm of Nokes & Nicolai shipped to England, France and Germany as well as throughout the United States.
62 Sudbury St.	THOMPSON & ODELL 　See Standard Band Instrument Co. p. 269. 　Manufactured drums in their Sudbury St. factory.

IRA E. WHITE

1864-67—83 Sudbury St.
and
1876-81—83 Sudbury St.

He was listed from 1864-67 and from 1876-81 as a drum maker and from 1868-70 as a repairer. In 1874-75 his cousin, Irving E. White, appeared at this same location, 83 Sudbury St. For his repairing see p. 198.

WHITMORE & BORIS; Also BORIS, WOODS & CO.

P. J. Boris
1874—9 Hamilton Pl., Agt.
1875—608 Washington St.
1877-78—608 Washington St.
1879—608 Washington St.
was listed as a dealer
and a publisher

J. H. Woods & Co.
1877-78—333 Washington St.
1879—433 Washington St.

Osceola Aurelius Whitmore
1876—282 Washington St.
1879—178 Washington St.

Started in 1874 with P. J. Boris as agent. Changed in 1875 to Boris, Woods & Co., Mr. Woods (J. H.) apparently coming from Woods, Odell & Thompson. Boris, Woods & Co. were "General importers and Principal Agents in America for the Celebrated Buffet and Besson Musical Instruments & Dealers in Musical Merchandise." [42]

In 1876 they were also proprietors of the Globe Music School. From 1877-79 they were dealers separately, Mr. Woods' name appearing in J. H. Woods & Co. till 1880.

In 1880 O. A. Whitmore from Reading, Vt., who had made banjos and drums since 1876, joined in forming Whitmore & Boris. Apparently they were in business together only about a year, as the firm was not listed in 1881.

Mr. Whitmore had made drum sticks used in the Civil War. He was a good clarinet player and a member of Carter's Band. He could also play "a good saxophone." [43] Whitmore & Boris made some good drums and drum sticks. Geo. B. Stone & Son bought out their supply of fine rosewood sticks about 25 years ago and turned them into more modern ones.

PETER WINN

1857-61—21 Salem St.

Listed 1857-61.
Drum maker or assembler.

M. WOODMAN

1887-90—Abattoir Grounds, Brighton, Mass.

Listed about 1887-90.
Drum manufacturer.

40 Information supplied by Edward F. Howe.
41 Information supplied by E. J. Nokes of Nokes & Nicolai.
42 *Boston Directory 1875*, Advertising Department p. 1279.
43 Statements of William R. Gibbs and George Lawrence Stone.

IV. F. Banjo, Guitar and Mandolin Makers—Period Around 1850-1915

Addresses from Boston Business Directories

Names of Firms and Information About the Firms

1880—Freemont St., Somerville

1892—128 Cottage St., Chelsea

PEHR A. ANDERBERG [44]

Was born in Sweden and learned his trade at Malmö. He came to this country at the time of the Civil War, worked first for C. F. Bruno in New York City and then started making guitars for himself about 1870 in Mount Vernon, N. Y. He returned to Sweden for a few years after selling this business to his brother and had a retail music store. Then he came to Boston about 1880 and began making guitars exclusively for John C. Haynes & Co. in a shop on Freemont St., Somerville. This shop was the training school for a number of guitar makers, including C. A. Sundberg and Mr. Swenson, two of the founders of the business which has become The Vega Company. When John C. Haynes & Co. bought him out he took charge of their guitar factory, which employed about 25 men, first on Sudbury St., opposite Court St., then at 72 Purchase St. and later on Stanhope St.

Pehr A. Anderberg left John C. Haynes & Co. in 1892 to start making guitars for himself again and also mandolins, this time at 128 Cottage St., Chelsea. Pullmann & Son of New York City absorbed the entire product of this factory employing from 15 to 20 men, and called the guitars "Pullmann." This was burned down in the Chelsea fire, but Mr. Anderberg continued to manufacture for himself in Chelsea until he went to take charge of the guitar making of Stewart & Bauer in Philadelphia. Mr. Stewart died and Mr. Bauer became ill, so the firm was dissolved. Then Mr. Anderberg returned to Boston and became a repairer for John C. Haynes & Co. until his death.

Mr. Anderberg made several grades of instruments ranging in price from about $8 or $10 to $50 apiece. His better instruments were of rosewood and some of the cheaper guitars were made of mahogany. When the popular demand for inexpensive guitars arose he used maple also. All his instruments were plain as he strove for good tone quality in preference to decorations. The guitars he made in his Somerville shop and those whose making he supervised in the John C. Haynes & Co. factory were sold under the names "Haynes Excelsior" and "Bay State" guitars. Mr. Anderberg also made the "Tilton" guitar as the patent on that popular instrument had run out. This was originated by an American maker named William B. Tilton who was in business around 1850. These guitars had two special features. One was that the grain of the wood ran slantwise instead of up and down as is usual. The other was a circular metal disc, attached to the sound bar at the sound hole, which bore the name Tilton.

WM. A. COLE [45]; AND F. E. COLE

Mr. Cole was a partner in Fairbanks & Cole from 1880 until he left about 1888 to go into banjo manufacturing for himself. After his death about 1909 the business was conducted by his brother, Frank, as F. E. Cole. This was continued but a short time after Frank Cole's death, being taken over by Nokes & Nicolai.

Wm. A. Cole was a fine banjo, mandolin and guitar player and a member of the old "Imperial Club." He and George C. Dobson were the most prominent teachers of banjo in Boston before the advent of those connected with the "Boston Ideal Banjo, Mandolin and Guitar Club."

1891-1905—179 Tremont St.
1906-10—286 Washington St.
1911-20—3 Appleton St.

GEORGE C. DOBSON

Listed 1869-1893.

In his time Mr. Dobson was one of the most noted teachers of banjo not only in Boston but in the United States. He made banjos and guitars, mostly assembling them at his home.

1869—687½ Washington St.
1873—59 Essex St.
1876—1107 Washington St.
1877-80—not listed
1881—290 Shawmut Ave.
1890—244 Shawmut Ave.
1893—1521 Washington St.

FAIRBANKS & COLE [45]

A. C. Fairbanks started alone as a banjo manufacturer about 1875. He was a player of the old style five string banjo with long neck and side peg.

Around 1880 he took in Wm. A. Cole as a partner in Fairbanks & Cole. When the latter left about 1888 the company name was changed to A. C. Fairbanks & Company. In 1892 it was simply A. C. Fairbanks. When it was incorporated about 1893 it became A. C. Fairbanks Company, Inc. In March 1904 the company had a disastrous fire. A few months later The Vega Company took over its business and employees. See The Vega Company p. 229 for further information.

1880—121 Court St.
1888—121 Court St.   and
      178 Tremont St.
1890-91—145 Columbus Ave.
      and 178 Tremont St.
1893—179 Tremont St.
1894—27 Beach St.
1904—Washington cor. Hollis St.

ROBERT F. FREEMAN

About 1890.

Made very fair guitars.

1890—691 Washington St.

[44] Information supplied by his son Ernest A. Anderberg.
[45] Dates under "Information about the Firms" supplied by David L. Day, Bacon Banjo Co.

IV. F. Banjo, Guitar and Mandolin Makers—Period Around 1850-1915 (*Continued*)

Addresses from Boston Business Directories	Names of Firms and Information About the Firms
1886—48 Hanover St. 1887—30 Hanover St. 1890—58 Winter St. 1892—58 Winter St. and 15 Chardon St. 1895—171A Tremont St. 1896-99—listed only as a publisher	**L. B. GATCOMB & CO.** 1886-1899. [46] At one time this firm was the most prominent banjo maker in Boston. For the publishing and catalog of this company see Walter Jacobs p. 74. The catalog of this company was first purchased by Mr. Shattuck, then by Mr. Lasalle, manager of Oliver Ditson Company, Inc. and finally by Walter Jacobs. They also published a catalog of "hits" and *Gatcomb's Banjo and Guitar Gazette* later called *Gatcomb's Musical Gazette* see p. 83.
1894—58 Winter St.	**ALBERT D. GROVER** 1894. Banjo player, member "Boston Ideal Banjo, Mandolin and Guitar Club," one of Boston's most noted banjo teachers. He started making banjo bridges and then moved to New York state where the business is being carried on as A. D. Grover & Son, Inc. at Baldwin, Long Island.
	JOHN C. HAYNES & CO. Made "Haynes Excelsior" and "Tilton" guitars and "Bay State" guitars and mandolins. See Pehr Anderberg p. 274. This department gradually ceased as guitars waned in popularity. Amalgamated with Oliver Ditson Company under latter name about 1900.
1887—18 Essex St. 1890—62 Sudbury St. 1896—17 Harvard Pl.	**J. F. LUSCOMB** Listed 1887-93 and 1896-97. Made banjos.
	NOKES & NICOLAI See Drum Makers p. 272.
1897—89 Court St. 1900—24 Tremont Row	**JOHN A. PALM** Listed 1897-1904. He was a Swede, and one of the best mandolin and guitar makers in Boston. [47] He advertised— "Makers of high grade mandolins and guitars—violins, zithers, banjos, strings and findings at lowest prices. Music instruction books. Repairing promptly attended to." [48]

G(AD) ROBINSON
Listed 1883-1903.

Famous teacher of banjo and fine performer, who could play the entire Overture to William Tell on the banjo.[47] Had his instruments made by other firms but sold them under his name.[49]
He is still living at Brockton, Mass.

1883—171½ Tremont St.
1885—171 Tremont St.
1890-95—170 Tremont St.
1900-03—170A Tremont St.

HENRY SCHATZ
Listed from 1845 to 1851 as a guitar and violin maker, with the exception of 1846 when he was given as just a guitar maker.

1845—house 1 Beach St.
1846—327 Washington St.
1847—323 Washington St.
1850—17 Boylston Sq.

E. B. SCHULTZ
Listed only in 1901 as a maker of mandolins and guitars.
"Violins, zithers, strings & findings at lowest prices. Music & instruction books."[50]

1901—24 Tremont Row

BURT E. SHATTUCK & CO.
Listed 1895-97.
One of the leading teachers of banjo, mandolin and guitar and a member of the "Boston Ideal Banjo, Mandolin and Guitar Club." He made banjos for a short time.

1896—88 Court St.

C. F. SUNDBERG
Listed only in 1887. Learned guitar making in the Somerville shop of Pehr A. Anderberg. Made good guitars for himself just a short time. Then he helped to start the company presently called Vega.

1887—10 Hersey Pl.

THOMPSON & ODELL
For their fretted instrument manufacturing see The Vega Company p. 229 and Charles A. Stromberg & Son p. 232.

1900—Factory
62 Sudbury St.

46 Last date for which the company was listed.
47 Statement of A. J. Oettinger.
48 *Boston Directory* 1900, Advertising Department p. 1914.
49 Statement of David L. Day, Bacon Banjo Co.
50 *Boston Directory* 1901, Advertising Department p. 2398.

IV. G. Makers of Miscellaneous Instruments and Accessories—Period 1885-1930

Addresses from Boston Business Directories

1908—41 Bristol St.
1910—33 Broad St.
1916—100 Boylston St., office

Names of Firms and Information About the Firms

THE CHORALCELO CO.

Boston 1908-1916. In 1916 it was listed as the Choralcelo Co. of Mass. Then the office was moved out of town. From 1919—March 1929 it was called the Choralcelo Co. of America, 8946 South May St., Chicago, Ill., with a studio at 630 North Rush St. (The instrument was called "Choir Celestial.") In July 1929 The Aromora Corporation, 310 So. Michigan Ave, Chicago, Ill., were national distributors of the Aromora Choralcelo. Later the agent, W. L. Flint, moved to Hollywood, Cal.

The Choralcelo is an instrument producing a sustained tone with the same general characteristics as that of the tuning fork. The vibrations are produced by electromagnets, whose pulsations are of the same periods as those of the bodies to be set in motion. The sources of sound may be piano strings or ribbons of steel drawn over a soundboard, bars of wood, aluminum or steel, somewhat like a xylophone, used in connection with resonators, or specially constructed diaphragms fastened to the ends of resonant tubes. In the first case each string is set in vibration by the direct action of the magnet behind it giving continuous impulses as long as the note is held. In the other cases soft iron armatures attached to the bars and diaphragms are set in vibration by the magnets, thus moving the air in the resonators. The overtones are provided by sound corresponding generators. Sometimes an instrument with strings is connected by a wire to one of the bars as an echo. The tones produced are clear, vibrant, beautiful and of great carrying quality. "The combinations of such sounds produce unique tonal effects of remarkable musical quality and the possibilities of synthetic tone development are great." [51]

A Choralcelo was installed in the restaurant of Edward A. Filene's store when it was opened and has been in use until the summer of 1935, when it was dropped for lack of new parts and a repairer to put it in good condition.

As yet this instrument has not fulfilled expectations and predictions of its possibilities, perhaps because it is not heard to advantage in such large quarters or possibly because of a constant up and down surge of the tone, and the great cost. Its design was inept. For instance, the "balanced Swell Pedal" worked just the opposite to that common in organs. [52]

CHESTER B. HOLWAY
Listed 1887-95.

Made the "Autoharp" in 3, 5, 8 & 12 bars under their own name and zithers for other firms like John C. Haynes & Co.

1887—103 Meridian St. E. Boston
1890—139 Border St.

W. A. JUDKINS
Listed 1887-93.

Zither manufacturer.

1890—89 Court St.

PHONOHARP CO. OF BOSTON
Listed 1893-1926.

Made the Columbia Zither.

1893—665 Washington St.
1895—630 Washington St.
1905-26—150 Liverpool St., East Boston

GEORGE M. STEVENS & CO.
Est. 1864. Succeeded by G. M. Stevens in 1874, and G. M. Stevens Co., Inc.

Noted for his tower clocks which sounded the pitches 1, 3, 5, 8 of a scale and fire alarms. Built what may have been the first electric Angelus chimes made in Boston, put up in St. Patrick's Church, South Lawrence, Mass. The notes arranged by William B. Goodwin were founded on the Westminster (England) Peal and sounded three times a day.

1864—52 Sudbury St.
1885—15 Chardon St.

U. S. GUITAR-ZITHER CO.
Listed 1900-01.

Dealer or maker of guitars and zithers.

1900—316 Dudley St.
1901—28 Warren St.

EUGENE A. WHITE
Listed 1878-86.

Made portable music stands. One of the earliest Boston manufacturers of music stands.

1878—50 Bromfield St.
1885—352 Atlantic Ave.

51 Miller, Dayton C. *The Science of Musical Sounds* p. 189.
52 Statement of William B. Goodwin, organ builder.

Some Instruments by Greater Boston Makers and Some of Historical Importance by European Makers

With the Places Where They May Be Seen or Heard

NOTE—Instruments marked with a dagger (†) have been seen by the writer but not examined. Instruments marked with an asterisk (*) have been examined by the writer.

Spinets

† SPINNET inscribed "Samuel Blyth Salem, Massachusetts, Fecit." Made in 1784.

In Essex Institute, Essex St., Salem, Mass. Open daily 9-5 p.m. Location 42 M 96 Acc. No. 1575.

Pine case stained, triangular shape with three legs, compass about 4½ octaves.

An illustration of this instrument is given in *Artists and Craftsmen of Essex County* opp. p. 29; also in *Early Keyboard Instruments from Their Beginnings to the Year 1820* by Philip James on the plate opp. p. 112.

Pianofortes

EUROPEAN MAKE

† UPRIGHT CHAMBER PIANOFORTE made in England and believed to be the first upright pianoforte ever made.

At the New England Conservatory of Music, 294 Huntington Ave., Boston, Mass.

Case is of satinwood, inlaid with walnut, amboyna, and other woods. Tuning pins are below the keyboard behind doors opening like a cabinet. "This instrument was at one time the property of Lady Morgan of London. It has been exhibited many times in Great Britain, and is one of the most valuable pianofortes known."

† SQUARE PIANOFORTE made in London by Christopher Ganer for Princess Amelia, youngest daughter of King George III.

At the New England Conservatory of Music, 294 Huntington Ave., Boston, Mass.

This instrument was brought for tuning and repair to John Gould, a cabinet maker, with whom Jonas Chickering was serving his last year of apprenticeship at the age of 19. This work aroused his interest in pianofortes. The 5 octave keyboard took two-thirds of the length of the instrument. At a later date organ pipes and bellows were added to the pianoforte and placed in the body of the instrument under the strings.

An illustration of this is in *"Achievement An Ascending Scale Being A Short History of the House of Chickering & Sons."*

SQUARE VIENNESE pianoforte used by Ludwig van Beethoven in scoring his "Eroica Symphony." Has a wooden frame.

To see apply to M. Steinert & Sons Company, Inc., 162 Boylston St., Boston, Mass.

PIANOFORTES BY BOSTON MAKERS
18TH CENTURY

BENJAMIN CREHORE

† SQUARE inscribed in old script painted on name board "Benjamin Crehore Milton."

In the Music Dept., Boston Public Library, Copley Square, Boston, Mass. Open in winter daily 9 a.m.-10 p.m., Sundays 2-10 p.m.; June 15th-Sept. 15th till 9 p.m. Loaned by Mr. Alexander Steinert.

Oblong mahogany case; natural keys ivory, sharp keys black walnut; has 4 legs. Compass 5 octaves, FFF to f². Hammers covered with buckskin. In a recess and at the left side under the cover is a lever for tightening the strings. The lower bass ones are of brass, the lowest being wound.

† SQUARE made bet. 1800-05. The first pianoforte used in Topsfield, Mass.

In Essex Institute, Essex St., Salem, Mass. Location 61A Acc. No. 2862.

Mahogany veneer case, decorated with painted flowers in colors on name board around signature lettering. Has gilt ornaments at top of the 4 legs.

† SQUARE inscribed "Benjamin Crehore of Milton Musical Instrument Maker." Made about 1800.

In Metropolitan Art Museum, Fifth Ave. at 82nd St., New York, Crosby Brown Collection of Musical Instruments, in a glass case.

Oblong mahogany case with inlaid lines. Compass 5 octaves and a 5th, FFF to c³. Two strings to a note, 8 lower notes wound. Originally furnished with a forte pedal raising the dampers. Length 5 ft. 6½ in., width 1 ft. 11¼ in., height 2 ft. 9½ in.

An illustration of a Crehore pianoforte, formerly in the Boston Art Museum, and also his home and shop are given in *Vose Reminiscences.*

19TH CENTURY

PIANOFORTES MADE BY ALPHEUS BABCOCK IN HIS VARIOUS AFFILIATIONS

SQUARE inscribed "Babcock, Appleton & Babcock." Firm had this name during 1812-13 and possibly in 1814.

In the Taft Museum, Fourth and Pike Sts., Cincinnati, Ohio, the Music Room. Open daily 10-5 p.m., Sundays and holidays 2-6 p.m.

Case of Santo Domingo mahogany with inlays of curly white mahogany, 6 legs with brass casters and trimmed with brass at the top, and three drawers at bottom of case with brass handles. Name in hand painted rectangle surmounted by a motif of musical instruments and sheet music and roses. Compass 5 octaves and a 5th, FFF to c³. Wooden frame.

SQUARE inscribed "Made by Hayt, Babcock and Appleton at No. 6 Market Street, Boston, Massachusetts." This copartnership was ended May 26, 1815.

In the U. S. National Museum, Washington, D. C., the Hugo Worch Collection of Keyboard Instruments. Cat. No. 303520 (Orig. No. 1)

* SQUARE inscribed "Made by A. Babcock for J. A. Dickson Boston No. 34
Market St. Boston." James A. Dickson's music saloon was listed at
this address 1818-28 & may have been there in 1817. (The name
Market St. was changed to Cornhill in 1829.)

In the M. Steinert Collection of Keyed and Stringed Instruments. To see apply
to M. Steinert & Sons Company, Inc., 162 Boylston St., Boston.

Case mahogany with rosewood name board and side panels, brass inlay lines
and brass rings at top of the 6 early-empire style legs, and three drawers underneath
with brass knob handles. Fancy scrolls are painted around the signature lettering.
Compass 5 octaves and a 5th, FFF to c³. Has a half wooden frame with tuning
pins and a harpshaped wooden bridge on it. Hitch pins are on a board attached to
left rear of case. Has 1 pedal. Pianoforte has been restored by the company so the
case is in beautiful condition.

SQUARE made by A. Babcock, Boston, about 1820.

In Woolsey Hall, Yale University, New Haven, Conn., the M. Steinert Collection
of Keyed and Stringed Instruments. Open Sunday afternoons during the college
year, otherwise by appointment with the Curator, Miss Louisa Bellinger. This instrument is Hammerclaviere No. 35 in the Catalogue.

Case in empire style with 6 legs is beautifully inlaid with brass. Compass
6 octaves, FFF to f³. "The pianos of Babcock were of most delicious tone and touch,
and this instrument represents an excellent specimen of his production." From the
Catalogue of the M. Steinert Collection p. 21. A picture of it is given on p. 22.

* SQUARE inscribed "A. Babcock for G.[eo.] D. Mackay, Boston," probably made bet. 1820-29.

Property of Mr. Charles H. Cutting, 357 High St., Newburyport, Mass.

Case mahogany, part veneer and part solid, with rosewood pieces inlaid and
brass inlay lines, three drawers at the bottom of the case with brass handles, and
6 legs. Compass 5 octaves and a 5th, FFF to c³. Has 2 strings to a note, bass
strings wound. Probably had 2 pedals which have been removed. Half wooden
frame at right has hitch pins on it and a harp shaped bridge for the wires. Tuning
pins are on a board attached to rear of case at left. Both case and action are in fine
condition. Pianoforte has a sweet tone.

† SQUARE inscribed "A. Babcock for G. D. Mackay, Boston," on a brass
plate. Probably made bet. 1820-29.

In the Denver Art Museum, City and County Building, Civic Center, Denver, Colo.

Case principally mahogany veneer, though parts like the cover are solid, and
there is a small amount of decorative inlay. The beading appears to be cast iron
gilded except for the brass moulding at top of case. Has a pedal and hammers
graded in size according to size of strings. Has a wooden frame. Case and works
in beautiful condition. Has a sweet tone. This pianoforte was owned for many
years by Dr. Charles A. Powers and was secured from his estate by a friend and
presented to the State Historical Society as a memorial in 1924. Later it came into
the possession of the Art Museum.

† SQUARE inscribed "A. Babcock for G. D. Mackay, Boston," on a brass
plate.

In the House of the Seven Gables, 54 Turner St., Salem, Mass.

Same style as above instrument, but in only fair condition.

SQUARE made by A. Babcock for G. D. Mackay, Boston, prior to 1825.

In the Edison Institute, Dearborn, Mich.

SQUARE inscribed "MADE BY A. Babcock for R. Mackay Boston."

In collection loaned permanently by the Pennsylvania Museum of Art to the Franklin Institute, Philadelphia, Penn.

Case mahogany, legs slightly tapered, round with narrow sunken fluting. Compass 5 octaves and a 5th, FFF to c³. Has two pedals that may be moved out of position, and a wooden frame.

* SQUARE inscribed "MADE BY A. Babcock for R. Mackay Boston," on a brass name plate. Probably made bet. 1820-29.

At the Plymouth Antiquarian Society, Plymouth, Mass.   Open week days 9-5 p.m.

Case mahogany, Empire style? with brass inlay lines and 4 octagonal legs. Compass 5 and a 5th octaves, FFF to c³. Has 1 pedal. Tuning pins in wood bar across left rear, hitch pins and harp shaped bridge on wooden half frame. Gift of Mr. Theodore Steinway June 1, 1921.

SQUARE inscribed "Made by A. Babcock for R. Mackay Boston" on a brass name plate.

In The Belle Skinner Collection of Old Musical Instruments, Wistariahurst, Holyoke, Mass.   Open Fridays 2:30-5:30 p.m. admission by ticket.   Apply to office of the Skinner Company, Holyoke.   Visitors limited to 6 or 8 at one time.

Case branch mahogany with rosewood borders inlaid with brass.   Name-board and side panels are rosewood inlaid with brass lines.   Has 6 legs with brass casters and trimmed with brass at the top.   At bottom of case are three drawers with brass handles.   Has 2 pedals.   Compass 6 octaves, FFF to f³.   "The action is divided into two removable sections.   On the right of the frame of the smaller section is written the name: L. Babcock, and within the case is the number 252.   Width 5 ft. 7½ in., depth 2 ft. 2¾ in., height 2 ft. 9¾ in."   Case and action are in perfect condition, and the tone is well preserved.

This pianoforte is a family heirloom and was first owned by Captain Joseph Allen of Northampton, Mass., the grandfather of Miss Skinner.   Information from *The Belle Skinner Collection of Old Musical Instruments, A Descriptive Catalogue Compiled Under the Direction of William Skinner* p. 178.

An illustration of this instrument is given by Plate No. 88 of the Catalogue.

Other squares made by A. Babcock in the U. S. National Museum, Hugo Worch Collection of Keyboard Instruments, Washington, D. C.

Pianofortes made in Boston all with wooden frames:

Cat. No. 315,719 (Orig. No. 317) in 1824.
Cat. No. 315,720 (Orig. No. 295) in 1828.
Cat. No. 314,526   in 1829.

Pianofortes made in Philadelphia containing his skeleton iron plate patented Dec. 17, 1825 while in Boston with the Mackays.

Cat. No. 291,106 made at Klemm's Piano Factory, Philadelphia, about 1834.
Cat. No. 315,690 made at William Swift's pianoforte factory, Philadelphia, about 1835.   The museum label states—"This is a creditable example of Babcock's superior skill.   It contains the iron frame patented by him in 1825, and well illustrates the advantageous use of iron to resist the tension of the strings, which are all intact, and to prevent the twisting or warping of the woodwork."

PIANOFORTES MADE BY W. & A. BENT

* SQUARE lettered in hand painting "W. & A. Bent [Old English letters] Musical—Instrument—Makers Boston." Made bet. 1800-07.

At the Historical Society of Old Newbury, High St. cor. Winter St., Newburyport, Mass. Open June 1st to Oct. 1st 2-5 p.m.

Small oblong rosewood case inlaid, with spindle legs. No pedal. Strings extremely fine for a pianoforte. Wooden half plate at right has harp shaped wooden bridge and the hitch pins. Iron tuning pins in a wood bar at rear left of frame. Wooden bar with dampers attached near tuning pin bar.

SQUARE made by W. & A. Bent in 1800. One of the first squares made in Boston.

In the U. S. National Museum, Hugo Worch Collection of Keyboard Instruments, Washington, D. C. Cat. No. 299851.

PIANOFORTES MADE BY BROWN & HALLET

* SQUARE inscribed in hand painting "Brown & Hallet, corner of Essex & Washington Sts., Boston." Firm at this address 1834-36. Serial no. 434.

At the Dedham Historical Society, Church St., Dedham, Mass. Open daily 2-5 p.m.

Oblong case veneer except cover solid mahogany. Compass 6 octaves, FFF to f³. Two strings to a note except one for the lowest octave. No pedal now. Contains a half iron plate cast in an ornamental flower and leaves design. Belonged in the Hewins Family of Dedham about 1835.

SQUARE made by Brown & Hallet bet. 1835 & 1843. "Very large and bulky." (Statement of the Institute.)

In the Edison Institute, Dearborn, Michigan.

PIANOFORTES MADE BY JONAS CHICKERING

† SQUARE inscribed on brass name plate "A. Babcock," but was probably made by Jonas Chickering. If so, it would have been before he worked as a journeyman for John Osborn from 1819-23.

In the Metropolitan Art Museum, Fifth Ave. at 82nd St., New York, N. Y. Acc. No. 22,112.

Oblong mahogany case on 4 cylindrical legs with bronze gilt mouldings at top and bottom; stretchers of square section on three sides. Compass 6 octaves, FFF to f³. Has two pedals working in an ornamental lyre, and a wooden frame.

This is considered a Chickering because the donor, Miss Harriet B. Littig wrote in 1922, "[The piano] was made for my grandmother when she was a child. . . It was made by Jonas Chickering himself when he was employed by Babcock of Boston, before he went into business for himself. He was a personal friend of my great grandfather's and so was asked to make this instrument for his daughter." Miss Littig's mother, Mrs. Marion G. Littig, inherited the pianoforte from her mother, Mrs. Samuel Downer of Boston.

SQUARE, the first "Stewart & Chickering" No. 222 as it was not the custom then to begin with No. 1. Sold June 23, 1823, for $275.

In the Edison Institute collection of pianofortes as it was given by Mr. Spain of Chickering & Sons to Mr. Henry Ford for safe keeping.

SQUARE made by Stewart & Chickering in 1824.
In the U. S. National Museum, Hugo Worch Collection of Keyboard Instruments, Washington, D. C. Cat. No. 315718.

* SQUARE inscribed on brass name plate "J. Chickering Boston," the first Chickering pianoforte in Lexington, in 1827. Serial no. 509 cut in wood.
In Buckman Tavern of the Lexington Historical Society, Lexington, Mass. Open daily 10-5 p.m. Sundays 2-5 p.m.
Oblong case, part veneer but cover solid rosewood with decorative brass inlay around name plate and above front legs, and narrow lines of brass inlay around case. Has 4 large 10 sided legs with hand carved tops. Compass 6 octaves, FFF to f³. Has 2 strings to a note, harp scale, all wooden frame, tiny square dampers from an overhead wooden bar at left side near back, & a wreath design hand carved lyre for 2 pedals. In fair condition. Belonged to the Robbins family of Lexington.

* SQUARE inscribed on brass name plate "J. Chickering 20 Common St. Boston." Mr. Chickering was at this address 1826-28, & possibly in 1825 when the number was not listed.
At the Beverly Historical Society, Cabot St. cor. Central St., Beverly, Mass.
Case rosewood with decorative brass trimmings, three drawers with brass handles at bottom of case, and a finely carved lyre for 2 pedals. Compass 6 octaves, FFF to f³. Contains a perfectly plain half iron plate for a harp scale, 2 strings to a note, bass strings wound. Ink stamping on sounding board reads "J. Chickering Harmonic, Cabinet, Grand & Square Piano Forte Maker Boston." Case in wonderful condition. Had a sweet tone but playability has deteriorated in last 3 years. Loaned by Rev. Charles Hastings Brown of Norwood, Mass.

† EARLY SQUARE made by J. Chickering.
In the Essex Institute, Essex St., Salem, Mass. Location 52M Acc. No. 3502.
Plain angular oblong mahogany case. 4 curved legs only ornamental feature. Contains flat perforated half iron plate and a harp scale.

† SQUARE inscribed "J. Chickering Maker 416 [case style no.] Boston."
In the Louisa May Alcott House, Concord, Mass.
Rosewood? case. Compass 6 octaves, FFF to f³. Contains a half iron plate. Belonged to the Alcott Family and was used by them.

* SQUARE hand decorated and lettered on name board "J. Chickering, Maker 416 [case style no.] Boston."
In the Old Colony Historical Society, Historical Hall, Historical Hall, Taunton, Mass. Open Mon.-Fri. 10-12 a.m. & 1-4 p.m., Sat. 9-11:30 a.m.
Oblong mahogany case with some rosewood. No. 1492 cut in edge of keyboard cover serial no.? Compass 6 octaves, FFF to f³. Two strings to a note except one in lowest octave. Two pedals. Contains a half iron plate made in an open flower wheel design. Gift of Mrs. Geo. T. Hartshorne.

FIRST UPRIGHT of Jonas Chickering made in 1830. Cabinet style. Had a silk sunburst.
At the Edison Institute, Dearborn, Mich. Given by Mr. Spain of Chickering & Sons, Inc. to Mr. Henry Ford for safe keeping.

FIRST CHICKERING GRAND, modern style, made about 1840.

At the Edison Institute, Dearborn, Mich.   Also a gift to Mr. Ford by Mr. Spain of Chickering & Sons, Inc.

SQUARE dating from about 1850 used by Jenny Lind at her American debut.

In Woolsey Hall, Yale University, New Haven, Conn., the M. Steinert Collection of Keyed and Stringed Instruments.

Case rosewood with 4 carved legs.   Compass 7 octaves, CCC to c⁴.

* SQUARE inscribed in old English large letters with scrolls "Chickering Boston."   Made in 1852.   Serial No. 12646.

At the Old Colony Historical Society, Historical Hall, Taunton, Mass.   For hours open see before.

Case rosewood with 4 large 12 sided legs and 2 pedals.   Compass 6 octaves, FFF to f³.   Contains decorative wheel design full iron plate.   This pianoforte was shipped originally June 18, 1852 to Colburn & Fields, music dealers, Cincinnati, Ohio, by wagons and canal boats as there were no railroads then.   Purchased second hand by Mr. Lewis W. Young about 1854 or 55, later removed by L. W. Young to Cairo, Ill.   Thence during the flood in 1858 when houses were 12 feet under water, it was taken through the roof, and, covered with blankets, quilts and lumber, was floated on an anchored raft four weeks without injury.   Was returned to Cincinnati in 1859, thence to central Ill.—to Boston—and to Taunton.   It also escaped several fires.   "Its keys have been manipulated by the fingers of many distinguished artists and it has accompanied many singers of note."   Statement of Mr. Young whose son, George M. Young, presented it to the Taunton Historical Society in 1917.

* OVERSTRUNG SQUARE No. 41673, scale "50" also marked "Improved double bearing agraffe."

At the New England Historic Genealogical Society, 9 Ashburton Pl., Boston, in the Atkinson-Lancaster Collection.   Open daily 9-5 p.m. except Sundays & holidays.   May 1st to Labor Day open Sat. 9-1 p.m.

Mahogany case, beautifully carved in India, was sent to Boston in 1872 to be fitted with Chickering works.   All in fine condition.

BABY GRAND.

At the Dartmouth Historical Society and Whaling Museum, New Bedford, Mass.

FIRST CHICKERING SQUARE, upright and grand are illustrated in *Achievement An Ascending Scale Being A Short Story of the House of Chickering & Sons.*

PIANOFORTE MADE BY CURRIER & CO.

† SQUARE.   Ebenezer R. Currier was in business under this name with Philip Brown 1830-32.

At the factory of Vose & Sons Piano Company, 791 Tremont St., Boston.   Property of Mr. George Vose.

Case finely crotched mahogany.   Compass 6 octaves.   Contains a half iron plate and has a perfect harp scale.   In beautiful condition.

Pianofortes Made by W. P. Emerson

* LARGE SQUARE. Metal frame bears in raised letters words "William P. Emerson Piano Forte Manufacturer No. 395 Washington Street, Boston." Serial No. 6914. Firm at this address around 1870.

At the Fitchburg Historical Society, 60 Grove St., Fitchburg, Mass. Open Sept. 15th to June 15th Thursday and Sunday afternoons 2-5 p.m. Otherwise apply to Miss Elizabeth J. Ball, 175 Prichard St., Fitchburg.
Case rosewood? Overstrung, entire metal plate. Compass 7 octaves, AAAA to a³. In use by the Society for its meetings. Easy action, good tone.

SQUARE about 60 years old. "In very good condition." (Statement of the Institute.)

At the Edison Institute, Dearborn, Mich.

Pianofortes Made by Lemuel Gilbert

Mr. Spillane gives his first name as Lemanuel but Directories and his instruments read Lemuel.

* SQUARE. Painted name plate reads "Patent Action Lemuel Gilbert 416 Washington St., Boston." Maker at this address 1839-52.

At the Lynn Historical Society, 125 Green St., Lynn, Mass. Open July and August, Wed., and most Sat. afternoons, 2-5 p.m. Sec'y Miss Ellen M. Burrill, 23 Nahant Place, Lynn, Mass.
Case oblong mahogany. Compass 5 octaves, FFF to f². Wooden frame. Written in pencil on the sounding board is "T.[revett] M. Rhodes 1842 $400.00." This pianoforte was made for Master Henry Moore for his bride and is said to be the second pianoforte brought to Lynn. Mr. Rhodes was a Lynn merchant and some relation to the Moore family. Possibly agent in this purchase? Pianoforte presented by Mrs. Robert Claxton of Schenectady, N. Y.

UPRIGHT made in Boston in 1848. Characterized by the large octagonal legs adopted for squares about this period and used for uprights by a few makers.

In the U. S. National Museum, Washington, D. C., Hugo Worch Collection of Keyboard Instruments Cat. No. 299,839.

UPRIGHT made in 1850. Rather small, in a rosewood case. Had 2 strings to a note.

In the Cincinnati Art Museum, Cincinnati, Ohio.

SQUARE with a patented action. Rosewood case with 4 urn shaped octagonal legs.

In the Edison Institute, Dearborn, Mich.

Pianofortes Made by Timothy Gilbert

SQUARE inscribed "T. Gilbert, Maker, 402 Washington Street, Boston" in hand painting with a scroll around it. Maker at this address only 1837-38.

At the Rowley Historical Society, Rowley, Mass. Open week days 9-5 p.m.
Case mahogany with 4 fluted and tapering legs, brass casters attached. Compass 6 octaves, FFF to f³. Has half iron perforated plate and 2 pedals. Pianoforte was

owned by Deborah Adams Pike, wife of Rev. John Pike, pastor of the Congregational Church in Rowley. They were married in 1841 and she probably owned it before her marriage.

UPRIGHT. "Very ugly looking and very small." (Statement of the Institute.)

At the Edison Institute, Dearborn, Mich.

PIANOFORTE MADE BY EBENEZER GOODRICH

SQUARE. This maker first listed as an organ builder in 1813 & as pianoforte maker in 1822 at 81 Market St. He became known as a pianoforte maker about 1827 according to Mr. Spillane, who confused him with William Goodrich.

In the U. S. National Museum, Washington, D. C., Hugo Worch Collection of Keyboard Instruments. Cat. No. 299,864.

PIANOFORTES BY VARIOUS MAKERS

* SQUARE marked on metal plate "Guild, Church & Co., Boston." Serial No. 18190. Firm bore this name 1870-90.

At the Medway Historical Society, in the Old Parish House, Main St., West Medway. To see apply to Mr. H. N. Hixon, or Mrs. Cole, Main St.

Large square. Case rosewood part ebonized. Nameboard reads only "Guild Boston." Compass 7 octaves and a 3rd, AAAA to c⁴. Overstrung with 1 string to a note bass AAAA-GGG, 2 strings through c², 3 strings c-sharp²-c⁴. Two pedals in attractive lyre. Harp shape scale. This pianoforte was bought from the town music teacher about 20 years ago for the use of the Society. Has a nice tone.

SQUARE made by Hallet, Davis & Co. Contains a patented suspension bridge pat'd Sept. 23, 1851. Has 4 carved legs.

At the Edison Institute, Dearborn, Michigan.

SQUARE made by George Hews, probably about 1840.

At the Manchester Historic Association, 129 Amherst St., Manchester, N. H.

Mahogany case in remarkable state of preservation and has a good tone. Cost $180 when new. Purchased of Clement and Cobb by John Brown and presented by him to his daughter, Julia Eaton Brown, on her 18th birthday, March 20, 1843. The family lived in Chester ? N. H., and this was one of the first if not the very first pianoforte in town. Presented by Mrs. Gertrude Green Wilkins of Milford, N. H., granddaughter of the original owner.

GRAND made by Hill & Owen in Boston, 1850. Firm listed in directories only 2 years 1849-50 as Hill, Ryder & Owen and 1850-51 as Hill & Owen both years at 419 Washington St.

At the U. S. National Museum, Washington, D. C., Hugo Worth Collection of Keyboard Instruments. Cat. No. 303523 (Orig. No. 4)

"This is unique as the stringing is done from the bottom of the instrument, the strings being struck with hammers from underneath. In 1827 Thomas Loud, Jr., of Philadelphia, took out a patent for a downstriking action, the reverse from the patent action used in this grand, but both actions proved fruitless."

SQUARE built by William H. Ivers prior to 1880 when the firm changed to Ivers & Pond. "In fair condition."

At the Edison Institute, Dearborn, Michigan.

SQUARE made by Henry F. Miller. "In fairly good condition." Hand carved legs.

At the Edison Institute, Dearborn, Michigan.

PIANOFORTES MADE BY JOHN OSBORN

UPRIGHT made in 1817. "The first upright made in Boston and one of the earliest of this type made in the U. S." (Statement of the Museum).

At the U. S. National Museum, Washington, D. C., Hugo Worch Collection of Keyboard Instruments. Cat. No. 299858 (Orig. No. 152)

SQUARE made in Boston in 1822.

Same location but Cat. No. 315717 (Orig. No. 307)

UPRIGHT made between 1823-29. It has an iron frame.

At the Edison Institute, Dearborn, Michigan.

FIRST PIANOFORTE MADE BY VOSE & SONS PIANO COMPANY

† SQUARE. First pianoforte made by James Vose at 328 Washington St., Boston.

At the factory of Vose & Sons Piano Company, 791 Tremont St., Boston, Mass.
Rosewood case in beautiful condition. Fine set of ivory keys as he was a key maker first, and contains a highly ornamental flower design full iron plate. Has 4 large legs and a lyre pedal support. Compass 7 octaves, CCC to c⁴.

PIANOFORTES MADE BY WILKINS & NEWHALL

† SQUARE made bet. 1836-46.

At the Essex Institute, Essex St., Salem, Mass. Location 61A Acc. No. 108,534.
Said to be the first pianoforte in Peabody, Mass. Upon it George T. Sanger, born July 2, 1824, in Peabody, took lessons.

† SQUARE marked Wilkins & Newhall, Boylston St., Boston. Firm at this address about 1837-39.

At the Essex Institute, Essex St., Salem, Mass. Location 52M Acc. No. 116,138.

PIANOFORTE MADE BY WOODWARD & BROWN

SQUARE about 40-50 years old. Has very heavy hand carved legs.

At the Edison Institute, Dearborn, Michigan.

Illustrations of Pianoforte Actions and Plates

A. Babcock's skeleton iron plates in Daniel Spillane's *History of the American Pianoforte* plate opp. p. 120, also in Alfred Dolge's *Pianos and Their Makers* p. 50.

J. Chickering's full iron plate in Dolge's book p. 51.

T. Gilbert's action in Spillane's book, plate opp. p. 120.

Astor Pipe Organ Pianoforte

UNIQUE INSTRUMENT. The organ pipes are underneath the square pianoforte case. Has 4 stops.

In the Steinert Collection of Keyed and Stringed Instruments. To see apply to M. Steinert & Sons Company, Inc., 162 Boylston St., Boston, Mass.

Lap Organs, Melodeons, Cabinet Organs

* LAP, ELBOW OR ARM ORGAN. Similar to instruments made by James Bazin of Canton. Possibly made by him around 1800?

At the North Andover Historical Society, North Andover, Mass. Open Mon., Wed. and Sat. 2-5 p.m. No. 217.

Has a piano keyboard with a compass of 4 octaves, top and bottom notes C. Gift of M. T. Stevens Sept. 1920. History unknown.

Instruments by James A. Bazin

* ORGAN, lap organ size enclosed in a box. Unusual number of keys and has couplings.

At the Canton Historical Society, Washington St., Canton, Mass. To see write to Mr. Walter Hall, Curator, 1350 Washington St., Canton.

Case mahogany? Bellows operated by raising and lowering a handle projecting from one end of box. Set lengthwise in an opening in the top are four rows of small flat metal keys, oblong in shape with rounded ends, set on wires. The two center rows consist of lettered natural keys and the corresponding sharp keys marked merely with a design. These keys are set at the ends of wires connecting with the keys of the outer rows. When the outer keys are depressed the inner key on the same wire and, by some coupling device, two octaves of the same note are all depressed at once, except in the case of "D" when three are depressed. Compass 4 octaves, top and bottom notes "D."

* ORGAN PIANOFORTE in an oblong case like an early pianoforte.

At the Canton Historical Society, Washington St., Canton, Mass.

Case light colored mahogany, with 4 slender plain tapering legs. Formerly had 3 stops and 2 treadles for the 2 bellows. Lever under case for swell? Compass 5 octaves and 1 note, bottom note "G" top "A."

* ORGAN PIANOFORTE inscribed "James A. Bazin's Patent Organ Pianoforte Canton, Mass." painted on.

At the Canton Historical Society, Washington St., Canton, Mass.

Case mainly mahogany with rosewood name board. Has 4 large tapering legs turned at top, and 2 bellows formerly worked by 2 treadles. A lever at right under case pulls out, for Crescendo? Compass 6 octaves, FFF to f³. He made his entire instruments including the ivory keys.

REED ORGANS MADE BY MASON & HAMLIN

MELODEON made by Mason & Hamlin in Boston in 1852.
In the Edison Institute, Dearborn, Mich.
　　Bellows and swell pedals are made of metal. Has 4 octagonal legs turned at top and bottom.

† MELODEON inscribed "Mason & Hamlin Organ Co." This was the second organ used in the Mormon Tabernacle, Salt Lake City.
In the Mormon Museum, Salt Lake City, Utah.

† CABINET ORGAN inscribed "Mason & Hamlin Cabinet Organ." This was the first organ used in Salt Lake City Theatre.
In the Mormon Museum, Salt Lake City, Utah.

CABINET ORGANS MADE BY VARIOUS FIRMS

CABINET ORGAN made by the New England Organ Company, Boston.
In Woolsey Hall, Yale University, New Haven, Conn., the M. Steinert Collection of Keyed and Stringed Instruments.
　　Case black walnut, sides enclosed, with music cabinets built in on each side. Has 1 Manual—compass 5 octaves, top and bottom notes "F"—11 stops and 2 pedals.

† MELODEON in a rosewood case made by James S. Parks, Boston about 1855-56. No further information about him.
In Essex Institute, Essex St., Salem, Mass. Open daily 9-5 p.m. Location 61A Acc. No. 104,655.

† MELODEON inscribed "Melodeon No. 1723 Improved Model by Prince & Co."
At the Lynn Historical Society, 125 Green St., Lynn, Mass. Open July & Aug., Wed. & most Sat. afternoons 2-5 p.m. Acc. No. 1762.
　　Has 1 manual. Included because this instrument was used by the Hutchinson Family of Lynn—Judson, Abby, John (W.) & Asa, "AEolian Vocalists"—in hospitals for Northern Soldiers in the South during the Civil War to accompany their singing to the soldiers.

CABINET ORGANS MADE BY S. D. & H. W. SMITH

CABINET ORGAN built in a rosewood case. Has 4 octagonal tapered legs.
In the Edison Institute, Dearborn, Mich.
　　Has 2 manuals, 5 octaves to each, and 2 stops, one being for the octave.

† MELODEON inscribed "S. D. & H. W. Smith 511 Washington St., Boston." Bill for this is dated Sept. 9, 1859, $130. Case mahogany.
In Essex Institute, Essex St., Salem, Mass. Open daily 9-5 p.m. Location 61A Acc. No. 119, 177.

* CABINET ORGAN inscribed on name board "S. D. & H. W. Smith Boston Juvenile Organ."

At the Fitchburg Historical Society, 60 Grove St., Fitchburg, Mass. Open Sept. 15th to June 15th Thursdays and Sundays 2-5 p.m.

Case black walnut encloses the instrument completely like a small cabinet. Compass 5 octaves, FFF to f^2. Has 2 pedals. Width 37 in., depth 18¾ in., height, including top of case when closed, 32¾ in. Used by Cyrus Thurston in his singing school.

* MELODEON labelled in old English letters "S. D. & H. W. Smith Boston."

At the North Andover Historical Society, North Andover, Mass. Open Mon., Wed., & Sat. 2-5 p.m. No. 249.

Case rosewood with lyre supports. Compass 5 octaves FFF to f^2. Two pedals. Gift of the Fisher Estate April 1922 from the Harriet Fisher place on the turnpike.

CABINET ORGAN BY GEORGE WOODS & CO.

CABINET ORGAN by George Woods & Co. of Boston.

In Woolsey Hall, Yale University, New Haven, Conn., the M. Steinert Collection of Keyed and Stringed Instruments.

Case black walnut and mahogany with open side supports. Has 1 manual—5 octaves, top and bottom notes "F"—7 stops, and 2 pedals.

Organs

EUROPEAN MAKE

BRATTLE ORGAN, probably the first pipe organ in New England. Smith, Harris and Jordan of England, makers. For description see pp. 140-1.

In St. John's Church, Portsmouth, N. H. Is still played occasionally.

* OLIVER HOLDEN'S ORGAN. Inscribed in painted old English letters "Astor & Company, 79 Cornhill, London." Probably made about 1798.

In Old State House, 206 Washington St., Boston, Mass., property of The Bostonian Society.

Has 1 manual, 53 note range, CC to f^2, which swings outward when in use, 4 stops—Principle, St. Bass, St. Treble and Op. Diap.—and is blown by foot power. Pipes are hidden by the wire netting and silk of the doors. Owned and used by Oliver Holden when composing, notably "Coronation" in 1830. Organ presented by Mr. Holden's granddaughter, Mrs. Fannie A. Tyler.

* ORGAN inscribed in painted old English letters "William Gray New Road Fitzroy Square, London, 1805."

In Fogg Art Museum of Harvard University, Quincy St., Cambridge, Mass. Played occasionally.

The 1 manual pulls out, compass almost 5 octaves, lowest note "G" top "F." Has 10 stops—on left Sesquialtera, Flute, Principal, Open Diapason, Stop. Dia. Bass; on right Cornet, Fifteenth, St. Dia. Treble, Dulciana and Oboe; and also a Tremolo. Case dull finish mahogany decorated with flower medallions of carved wood. See also pp. 154-5.

BOSTON MUSIC HALL ORGAN made by E. F. Walcker and Cie., Ludwigsburg, Germany. Opening recital 1863.

In Organ Hall (formerly called Serlo Hall), Methuen, Mass., property of Mr. Ernest M. Skinner.

For description of this organ and its influence see pp. 155-7.

ORGANS BY BOSTON BUILDERS

* ORGAN built by Thomas Appleton in 1844. For description see p. 153.

In People's Baptist Church (Colored), cor. Camden and Tremont Sts., Boston. In use regularly.

* CHAMBER ORGAN inscribed on brass name plate "Eben^r Goodrich Boston."

At Narragansett Historical Society, Inc., Templeton, Mass. Open July 1st to Nov. 1st Tues., Fri., & Sat., and the 1st Sun. of each of these months, 2-5 p.m.

Has 1 manual and 5 stops—"Principal, Bass, St. Dia., Op. Dia.", and one the label of which is missing. Blown by foot power. Pipes are concealed behind a sunburst of mahogany colored silk. Case mahogany? Presented by Miss Eleanor Whidden of Marblehead, Mass.

* ORGAN built for The First Parish Church, Templeton, Mass., by William Goodrich in 1832.

One wooden pipe, "D#," is in the Narrangansett Historical Society building, Templeton, Mass.

Bellows and mahogany case, whose finish was blistered when the Gardner Unitarian Church was burned, is stored in the barn of Marcus N. Wright, 249 High St., Gardner, Mass. Could be refinished and used.

Had 2 manuals—the Swell was short, the lowest note being 2nd F below middle C & top G, but the Great had a full range of 56 notes. Probably were about 7 stops for each manual. Information supplied by Mr. G. W. Reed of West Boylston, Mass. For history of this organ see p. 150.

† ORGAN inscribed on name plate "George G. Hook, Maker, Salem." First organ built by this partner of E. & G. G. Hook in 1827 at age of 20.

In Essex Institute, Essex St., Salem, Mass. Open daily 9-5 p.m. Location 24L Acc. No. 121,452.

Has 1 manual, 58 note range, lowest "G" top "F," and 6 stops. Built as a parlor organ, this was in constant use in churches for nearly 50 years, when it came back into Mr. Hook's hands in exchange for a new organ. It was in use in a residence in Brookline, Mass., until about 1933. Given by Mr. Hook's son to the Essex Institute.

SECOND ORGAN built by E. & G. G. Hook in 1827.

In use in the Swedish Congregational Church, Lowell, Mass.

This has one manual and originally had no pedal. It was built for a church in Burlington, Vt., went thence to Billerica and from there to its present location.

† ORGAN PLATE of First Harvard Church organ, Washington St., Brookline, Mass., inscribed "E. & G. G. Hook Co., Boston." Also original draw knob stop plates framed.

In Essex Institute, Essex St., Salem. Location 24L Acc. No. 122,567.

This tracker action organ was dedicated Aug. 26, 1844, its last service was Apr. 27, 1873.

† MEDALS awarded E. & G. G. Hook for organs, framed.

In Essex Institute, Essex St., Salem. Location 24L, side of first organ.

Gold Medal award by the Massachusetts Charitable Mechanic Association for a church organ in the Exhibition of 1853.

Silver Medal award in 1866 by the Worcester Mechanics Association for a Grand Concert Organ.

TALL PARLOR ORGAN built by Mason & Hamlin. Has carved leaves and design on top, and a small mirror above shelf.

In the Edison Institute, Dearborn, Michigan.

ORGAN built by New England Organ Co. Has 9 stops and 5 octaves.

In the Edison Institute, Dearborn, Michigan.

ORGAN (pipe?) of S. D. & H. W. Smith.

At Edison Institute, Dearborn, Michigan.

Has 1 manual of 5 octaves, and 5 stops. A conservatory organ bought by subscription for Miss King's Singing School.

ILLUSTRATIONS OF ORGANS

The BRATTLE ORGAN in Henry C. Lahee's article "Organs and Organ Building in New England," *New England Magazine,* December 1897, p. 485.

Also in *Handbook of Musical Statistics* Published by Boston Musical Bureau, 218 Tremont St., Boston, 1905 p. 14.

KING'S CHAPEL ORGAN in Henry C. Lahee's article "Organs and Organ Building" etc. p. 487.

CHRIST CHURCH, BOSTON, ORGAN showing original case of Thomas Johnston's organ finished about 1758 as part of present organ case, in *Ancestry of Lawrence Williams* by Cornelia Bartow Williams, opposite p. 248.

BOSTON MUSIC HALL ORGAN in William King Covell's brochure reprint from *The Organ,* Vol. XI, Nos. 42 (Oct. 1931) and 43 (Jan. 1932) several illustrations.

Also in Henry C. Lahee's article "Organs and Organ Building" etc. p. 490.

GEORGE G. HOOK's FIRST ORGAN in *Pipe Organs* a brochure of Hook and Hastings Company.

Other organs by E. & G. G. Hook or Hook and Hastings.

> Cincinnati Music Hall Organ in Henry C. Lahee's article "Organs and Organ Building" etc. p. 493.
>
> Holy Cross Cathedral [Roman Catholic] Organ, Boston, *ibid.* p. 496.
>
> "Mother Church," First Church of Christ Scientist, Boston, in *Pipe Organs* a brochure of Hook and Hastings Company.

GEO. S. HUTCHINGS' factory setting-up room, Boston, in Henry C. Lahee's article "Organs and Organ Building" etc. p. 494.

MASON & HAMLIN, a church organ and one of their workrooms, *ibid.* p. 499.

Bells

BY PAUL REVERE OR PAUL REVERE & SON

A few good accessible illustrations of this maker's bells.

A reproduction of this firm's business card may be seen in the Hancock-Clarke House of the Lexington Historical Society, Lexington, Mass., catalog no. 417.

* BELL NO. 1 inscribed "The First Church Bell Cast in Boston, 1792 by P. Revere." Weight 911 lbs.

> In St. James Episcopal Church, 1991 Massachusetts Ave., Cambridge, Mass. Apply to Sexton to see it.
>
> The 500 pound bell used by the Second Church of Boston from 1650 was rescued when the North Meeting House was torn down for firewood by order of Gen. Howe in 1775 and put up in the New Brick Church, of which Paul Revere was a member, in 1780 after the two congregations had joined forces. It became injured in 1792 and was recast by Paul Revere who nearly doubled its weight, at a cost of £74, 7 shillings and 18 pence. An elaborate stone meeting house replaced the New Brick in 1845. This was sold in 1849, including the bell, to the First Methodist Church. When Hanover St. was widened in 1871 the Methodists had to move and went to Temple St. Church, which had no belfry. The bell was put in storage at 30 South St., Boston, until it was sold April 1, 1901 to St. James Episcopal Church where it was set up in the rear of the church and is still used.

* BELL NO. 25 inscribed "Revere, Boston, 1798." Weight 224 lbs.

> In the Dedham Historical Society, Church St., Dedham, Mass. Open daily 2-5 p.m.
>
> This Town of Dedham bell hung in the cupola on the old wooden courthouse until 1827 and was rung just before court sessions. It was deposited in 1894 by the County Commissioners with the Dedham Historical Society. It has a clear musical tone.

BELL NO. 154 inscribed "Paul Revere & Son, Boston, 1815." Weight of bell 907 lbs. and of tongue 22 lbs.

> In the Lucius Beebe Memorial Library, Wakefield, Mass.
>
> Cast Sept. 18, 1815 for the Town of Reading when Wakefield was South Reading. An old bell bought in 1714 and broken was credited for $83.36 toward

the cost of the new bell of $418.05. Bell No. 154 was first hung in the belfry of the Old First Parish Meeting House on Church St. In 1834 it was brought to the bell tower when the Town built its first Town House. That was moved in 1859 to the cor. of Main & Salem Sts. and the bell with it. When this was demolished in 1898 the bell was moved to the High School cor. Common & Lafayette Sts. and connected with the fire alarm apparatus. After 1914 it was moved to its present location. On account of the coincidence in weight it may be a duplicate pattern of the Old Tunnel bell on Lynn Common (No. 171) which was entered in the stock book as 905 lbs.

BELL NO. 161 Weight 2437 lbs., cast 1816. Called by Dr. Arthur Nichols Paul Revere's masterpiece.
In the belfry of King's Chapel, Tremont St., Boston.
A new bell obtained from England in 1772 of 2475 lbs. was recast into this bell by Paul Revere Feb. 16, 1816. It is still in use in perfect condition.

Woodstock, Vermont, has the distinction of having three Paul Revere bells all still in use. They are as follows:

BELL NO. 198 inscribed "Revere & Son, Boston 1818." Weight 711 lbs.
In the belfry of the Congregational Church.
Cast June 2, 1818. Its tonic note is C. At 45 cents a pound it cost $319.95. The weight is written in chalk on the inner waist.

BELL NO. 374 inscribed "Paul Revere & Son." Cast Oct. 1, 1827.
In the bell chamber of the Universalist Church.
Weight is written on its inner waist in blue chalk 1021 pounds.

BELL NO. 392 inscribed "Revere, Boston." Cast June 23, 1828.
In the steeple of the Christian Church.
Weight is marked in blue chalk on the inner waist 849 lbs.

BELL NO. 235 inscribed "Revere, Boston 1821." Recast of a bell recast by Col. Hobart, weight being augmented to 1127 lbs.
In the belfry of the First Parish (Unitarian) Church at Canton Corner, Canton, Mass. Used Sundays and connected with the fire alarm system of Canton.
The Precinct voted Oct. 15, 1764 the sum of £48 to purchase the original bell which was to be "400 pounds or upwards." The bell procured (385 lbs.) proved too light metal. So Col. Hobart recast it and his bill is preserved with the town records. This bell is said to have been broken by Harrison Carroll, sexton, by striking it with a sledge hammer. A committee appointed 1820 ordered it recast.

BELL inscribed "Revere & Son, Boston." Illustration of this bell in the Historical Collections of the Essex Institute, Vol. 48 Jan. 1912, opp. p. 13 of Dr. Nichols' article on "The Bells of Paul and Joseph Revere."
Preserved in the tower of St. Paul's Church, High St., Newburyport, Mass. To see apply to Sexton, John J. McKinney, 35 Oakland St., Newburyport.
This bell was hung Feb. 14, 1811, in the tower of the former edifice of St. Paul's. It became cracked and was taken down in 1899 and replaced by a sweeter toned bell of McNeeley.

Two other illustrations of Paul Revere bells are to be found in Dr. Nichols' article. For one cast in 1819 see opposite p. 5 and for one cast in 1822 see opposite p. 7.

Henry N. Hooper & Co. Bell [1]

BELL inscribed "Henry N. Hooper & Co., Boston, 1859."

In St. Paul's Methodist Church, Lynn, Mass.

This was the third bell of this church, procured and selected for its tone, for use in the building which replaced the one burned in 1859. It was installed for the dedication Aug. 11, 1861, and is noted as the bell which inspired Longfellow's poem *The Bells of Lynn*. It evidently had been intended for a Roman Catholic Church, possibly for a chime, since it bears below the maker's name the Latin stanza in Old English letters:

> "Laudamus te, benedicimus te,
> Adoramus te, glorificamus te,
> Gratias agimus tibi
> Propter magnam gloriam tuam."

Bell Mould Patterns and Bell by Geo. H. Holbrook

* TWO BELL MOULD PATTERNS of the firm of George H. Holbrook, East Medway, now Millis.

At the Medway Historical Society, Old First Parish House, Main St., West Medway, Mass. To see apply to Mr. H. N. Hixon or Mrs. Cole, Main St., W. Medway.

Made of mahogany ebonized. Constructed of small strips of wood glued together. Gift of Mr. James L. Payson whose wife was a granddaughter of Edwin L. Holbrook, grandson of Major Holbrook. Business started in 1816 with the casting of a bell for the East Medway Meeting House, exchanged in 1855 for another, still in Millis, by Major George Holbrook, who had once been an apprentice in a foundry of Paul Revere. Business continued by his son, George Handel, and other descendants till 1882. Firm cast altogether over 11,000 bells.

ONE BELL cast in 1828, sent around Cape Horn to California, was in the Santa Barbara Mission as late as 1925.

Chimes

English Make

FIRST CHIMES in America.

In Christ Church, Salem St., Boston.

Cast in 1744 by Rudhall of Gloucester, England. Consists of 8 bells. Have been rung for every great event from 1744 to the present. Are played every Sunday. See page 184 for more information about them. Illustrated on front cover of booklet *Facts Regarding the Bell Foundry of Blake Bell Company*.

Wm. Blake & Co.

SIXTH CHIME in Mass. Has 9 bells, aggregate weight 5045 lbs., cast in 1869.

In Trinity Church (Episcopal), Haverhill, Mass. Bells rung regularly though they have no regular chime playing.

[1] From The Bells of Lynn, A Paper Given Before The Lynn Historical Society, Dec. 10, 1914, by C. J. H. Woodbury, President, Register of the Society, Volume XVIII, Lynn, Mass., 1915, p. 31.

Range is from the G Major scale inclusive. Lower "G" bell 1393 lbs. is the ordinary service and alarm bell. "A" 987 lbs. is the funeral toll. "B" 715 lbs. is the marriage bell. "C" is 616 lbs. "D" 416 lbs. is the gift of C. B. Caldwell. "E" 299 lbs. is the Sunday School bell. "F" 256 lbs. is the Christening bell. "F#" 257 lbs. and "G" 186 are in Memoriam.

EIGHTH CHIME in Mass. Has 9 bells, aggregate weight 5025 lbs., cast in 1873. See page 189 for more information.

In Grace Church, High Street, Medford, Mass. Used regularly in winter months before Sunday morning service. Also rung at Christmas and other special days and occasionally in the summer.

CHIME OF 9 BELLS key of "E." See page 190 for more information.

In Grace Church (Episcopal), 64 Elbridge St., Newton, Mass. Hymns etc. played regularly on them Sundays.

TENTH CHIME in Mass. Has 16 bells. See page 190 for further information.

In St. Mary's church (Roman Catholic), Lawrence, Mass. Played at least once a week.

Henry N. Hooper & Co.

THE HARVARD CHIME cast in 1859, consists of 13 bells.

In Christ Church, Garden St., Cambridge, Mass. (Near Harvard Square). Rung on church days and Harvard College festivals and special occasions.

Cast at a cost of more than $5000. Is the only set of bells in Cambridge. Each bell bears on it a portion of the Gloria in Excelsis.

No. 1 bears also the inscription

"Let the Name of Mr. Thomas Dowse of Cambridge
BE REMEMBERED,
'THE LIBERAL MAN DEVISETH
LIBERAL THINGS' "

No. 2 is from its inscription in memory of the benefits of the Venerable English Society founded for propagating the Gospel in foreign lands, as a mission of which Christ Church was begun.

No. 3 was cast from the metal of the first bell of the church, weighing over 1500 lbs., the gift in 1760 of Capt. Edward Cahill of London. It states "Recast A. D. 1831 Recast in the Chime A. D. 1859."

The chime is operated from the ringing room in the third story of the tower, where the old-fashioned system of a frame into which the ends of the bell-ropes lead is in use. The five larger bells are provided with pivots and wheels, and can be rung as well as chimed.

Chime procured through the exertions of three Harvard graduates, R. H. Dana, Jr., class of 1837; H. M. Parker, of 1839, and F. L. Batchelder, of 1844, who issued a circular in 1855 proposing the idea and calling for subscriptions from all graduates and undergraduates of the College. A fair held by the women of different religious organizations helped and St. Peter's Roman Catholic Church contributed a considerable sum. It has thus been considered a common object of interest for all of Cambridge.

THE PHILLIPS' CHIMES, cast in 1860, the oldest considerable chime in Boston, (16 bells).

In the tower of Arlington Street Church, Boston.   In regular use.

No. 1 is "D," No. 16 "F."   The bells all have lines or verses on them.   See also page 188.

CHIME OF 16 BELLS cast in 1861, erected in two decks in the tower, first used Easter Sunday, March 31, 1861.

In Grace Episcopal Church, Providence, Rhode Island.   Played by specially trained men before the Sunday morning and evening services and whenever possible at 5 p.m.   A clock mechanism given by a parishoner and installed by the Seth Thomas firm plays the chimes on the hours and quarters.

Funds were raised by popular subscription.   The names of the donors are inscribed on each bell.   Briefly they are as follows:

D	Bishops' Bell	A#	From Providence First Light Infantry Company To be rung on the 19th of Sept. in each Succeeding year forever in memory of Oliver Hazard Perry of R. I. the victor of Lake Erie 1813
E	The Rectors' Bell		
F#	(cut in not cast upon) Brown University Bell Presented by John Carter Brown upon condition that this chime of Bells is to be rung on the Morning and Afternoon of every Commencement Day April 1861 Wardens and Vestry		
		B	From Members of the Rhode Island Bar
		C	From A.D. & J.Y. Smith & Co.
		C#	From the Physicians of Providence
		D	From the Choir of Grace Church
		D#	From three Burgesses
G	From Alexander Duncan	E	From the Sunday School of Grace Church
G#	From Citizens of Providence		
A	From the Providence Marine Company of Artillery	F	From the Personal Staff of William Sprague Governor (sic) of R. I. 1860
		F#	From Walter S. Burgerss (sic) Attorney Gen. of R. I. 1860
		G	(cut in) From the Woonasquatucket Print Works

An illustration of the trade mark of H. N. Hooper & Co. is in the Boston Directory, 1869, Advertising Department, p. 978.

Violin Family Instruments

* VIOLIN made by Lysander O. Makepeace in 1901 when 83 years old.

At Lynn Historical Society, 125 Green St., Lynn, Mass.   Open July & Aug., Wed. & most Sat. afternoons 2-5 p.m. Acc. no. 1793.

Italian pattern.   Had good tone when tried out recently.   Top is spruce taken from first church built in Lynn, 269 years old.   No information whether he was a professional or amateur maker.

BASS VIOL made by Benjamin Crehore of Milton.

Property of William D. Preston at Provincetown, Mass.   Belonged earlier to his father, Mr. John Preston.

* BASS VIOL contained a label reading William Green, Medway, 1803 or 1804.

In the Old Parish House, Main St., West Medway. To see apply to Mr. H. N. Hixon or Mrs. Cole, Main St.

Has a maple head and sides and a possible pine front and back, and a short finger board with some inlaid ivory lines across it. Used in the Old First Parish Church on Bare Hill, East Medway, now Millis. When the parish sold it J. Willard Daniels of Millis bought it. At his death it went to his daughter, Mrs. Marion D. Bullard, who has loaned it to the Medway Historical Society.

An illustration of a Trefflé Gervais violin is given in *An Encyclopedia of the Violin* by Alberto Bachmann, Plate 25 p. 55 and his label, Plate 22 p. 50.

An illustration of a John Alfred Gould violin is given in *An Encyclopedia of the Violin* by Alberto Bachmann, Plate 24 p. 53 and his label, Plate 22 p. 50.

Woodwind Instruments

FIFE, probably English, as it belonged to Edward J. Bestwick who came from England to Dedham.

At the Dedham Historical Society, Church St., Dedham, Mass. Open daily 2-5 p.m.

Made of black grenadillo wood with wide silver-plated brass? bands at ends. Has 6 holes. Played by Mr. Bestwick in the great torchlight parade just previous to the election of Abraham Lincoln in 1860 in escorting the Dedham Wide Awakes on that occasion. Also played by him for many years on Memorial Day. Left in his will to the G. A. R. He was the last member of the Old Dedham Bands 1824-1907.

FIFE inscribed "Callender Middle Street No. 62 Boston," and between mouth hole and end "D."

At the Hancock-Clarke House, Lexington Historical Society, Lexington, Mass. Open daily 9:30-5:00 p.m., Sundays 2-5 p.m.

Light colored wood with brass bands about an inch wide at ends. For further information about this maker and fife see p. 212.

FLUTES by several Boston makers are in the Dayton C. Miller Collection of Flutes. The flutes are not on exhibition but Dr. Miller will be glad to supply information about his specimens as far as he can and has photographs of some. Apply to Dr. Miller, Case School of Applied Science, Cleveland, Ohio. The Boston makers represented are:

Walter Crosby, 4 specimens, Acc. No's. 206, 523, 944 & ? Firm dates 1836-74.

Graves & Co., while at Winchester, N. H., Acc. No. 274. Made of pear wood with ivory rings. Has one brass key.

John C. Haynes & Co. (Instrumental Dept. of Oliver Ditson Company 1861-1900) Acc. No's 182, 1202.

The Wm. S. Haynes Co., 7 specimens. Firm started 1888.

Hüttl & Fischer, Acc. No. 389. Firm dates 1870-73.

Schauffler & Leukhardt, Acc. No. 119. Firm dates 1854-57.

CLARINET made by Graves & Co., Winchester, N. H.

In the Dayton C. Miller Collection of Flutes. Apply to Dr. Miller as stated before.

Boxwood with ivory rings and 5 brass keys. "Is of the ordinary old system and is a comparatively cheap and simple instrument, of the type common about a hundred years ago." (Dr. Miller's statement).

Brass Instruments

* KEY-BUGLE inscribed "Made by N. Adams Lowell, Ms." Made in 1825 and cost $33.

On the U. S. Frigate Constitution (Old Ironsides) Navy Yard, Charlestown, Mass., Berth Deck. Visiting hours daily and Sunday 10-4:30 p.m.

Large bugle, copper except for brass bell rim, mouthpiece, headjoint and fittings. Has 7 brass keys, one double jointed. Made for Paul Heald whose son, Mr. John Heald of Springfield, Mass., donated this instrument in 1927. Nathan Adams was bandmaster on the Constitution in the War of 1812. He was born in Milford, N. H., Aug. 21, 1783 and died there March 17, 1864. According to *The History of Milford* by George A. Ramsdell p. 230 he conceived, while on board the Constitution, the idea of cutting holes in the side of his bugle, thus being enabled to give certain calls in a lower pitch, and later submitted this idea to a noted instrument maker in London who acted upon it in producing the Kent bugle. This last statement seems questionable since Joseph Halliday is considered to have invented the keyed bugle in 1810. Mr. Adams later was a musician and instrument maker at Lowell, Mass., and noted as a repairer of ship chronometers at Nantasket, Mass.

* TRUMPET with inscriptions on several metal plates—"Permutation Trumpet," "Invented & Made by N. Adams, Lowell, Mass.," and "Paul Heald Carlisle Mass. 1825." Made in 1825 and cost $85.

On the U. S. Frigate Constitution, Navy Yard, Charlestown, Mass., Berth Deck. Visiting hours as above.

All brass trumpet with 3 keys, which, when depressed, work the wires of the 3 rotary valves. By three different records Nathan Adams is given the credit of being the first American inventor of the rotary valve for musical instruments. The record of Benevolent Lodge No. 7 A. F. & A. M. of Milford, N. H., March 18, 1864 states "Bro. Adams was the inventor of a valuable improvement in musical instruments new in this country, known as 'The Rotary Valve.' " *The History of Milford* pp. 229-30 reads "He was a noted genius of his time, and some of the greatest improvements in musical instruments, notably the production of the diatonic scale with three touches, the introduction of the valve or piston movement, and other important changes in band instruments were his invention." "Contributions of the Old Residents Historical Association, Lowell, Mass. 1894" states "Nathan Adams, sometimes called Captain Adams, is entitled to recognition as the inventor of the first valve musical instrument and application thereto of the diatonic or natural scale." His "Permutation Trumpet," also donated by Mr. John Heald in 1927, is an excellent example of one of his rotary valve trumpets in working condition.

SAXHORN inscribed "J. Lathrop Allen, No. 17 Harvard Place, Boston." Mr. Allen was at that address 1853-58.

At University of Michigan, Ann Arbor, Michigan, Stearns Collection of Musical Instruments. Coll. No. 938 Case IX Class III Section L., Catalogue p. 133.

Baritone in E flat, German silver, 4 rotary valves. Model length, 72cm. Bell diameter 18.6cm.

* CORNET inscribed "James A. Bazin 1824." A unique early instrument.
At the Canton Historical Society, Washington St., Canton, Mass. To see write to Mr. Walter Hall, Curator, 1350 Washington St., Canton.
Wide bell made of copper with brass trimmings. Different pitches obtained by turning the ebonized round knob in the center of a hollow disk about 5 in. in diameter, revolving within a copper rim. On the disk is marked the letter names for 1 octave, C to B, sharps included. Some brass attachments to the disk possibly keys? This cornet was played by him in the First Parish Church. This with a bass viol provided the church music before there was an organ. It has a pleasant tone.

* CORNET? made by James A. Bazin. It is smaller than the above and also a unique style of construction.
At the Canton Historical Society, Washington St., Canton, Mass.
Has a small brass bell. Different pitches obtained in playing by turning a wooden knob which revolves a narrow cylinder on which are marked the letters including the sharps for 2 octaves "C" to "C."

* CORNET inscribed "Gilmore & Co., a monogram made up of P.S.G., Boston, Mass." This firm name listed in Boston Directories only in 1866.
At Fitchburg Historical Society, 60 Grove St., Fitchburg, Mass. Open from Sept. 15th to June 15th, Sunday and Thursday afternoons 2-4 p.m.
Key of E flat? German silver? This cornet was used by Joseph C. Brown, inventor of the Brown-Bag-Filling Machine, up to the time when he lost his arm. Presented by his Estate in 1933.

† KEYED BUGLE SOPRANO IN C, inscribed "Graves and Co., Winchester, N. H." Made about 1840 before the company moved to Boston.
At the Metropolitan Art Museum, Fifth Ave., New York, Crosby Brown Collection of Musical Instruments. Acc. No. 2326 Case 108.

FLUEGEL HORN, inscribed "Graves & Co., Boston."
At University of Michigan, Ann Arbor, Michigan, Stearns Collection of Musical Instruments. Coll. No. 855 Case VIII Class III Section J. Catalogue p. 122.
Soprano in B flat, German Silver, 3 rotary valves. Length 35.5cm. Bell diameter 11.8cm.

BOX VALVE, 2 pistons, made in 1830 by Graves & Co. Firm then located in Winchester, N. H.
At University of Michigan, Ann Arbor, Michigan, Stearns Collection of Musical Instruments. Coll. No. 1438 Construction Case XVI. Catalogue p. 218.
"This valve consists of a tube sliding within another. A hole in the inner tube allows free passage of the air, which when the piston is pressed down, is directed to a crook which lengthens the vibrating length." Mechanism introduced by this firm.

CORNET inscribed "Hall and Quinby, Boston."
At University of Michigan, Ann Arbor, Michigan, Stearns Collection of Musical Instruments. Coll. No. 856 Case VIII Class III Section J. Catalogue p. 122.
In B flat, German silver, 3 rotary valves. Length of model 40cm. Bell diameter 12.2cm.

For illustration of Hall & Quinby rotary valve musical instruments see Boston Directory 1870, Advtg. Dept., p. 1043.

BOX VALVE, 3 pistons made by B. F. Quinby, Boston, 1875.
At University of Michigan, Ann Arbor, Michigan, Stearns Collection of Musical Instruments. Coll. No. 1439 Construction Case XVI. Catalogue p. 218.
An application in a mechanism introduced by B. F. Quinby of the same principle used by Graves & Co. in the 2 pistons listed before.

† SILVER BUGLE inscribed "Quinby Brothers, Boston."
In the First Corps Cadets' Museum, First Corps Cadets' Armory, cor. Arlington St. & Columbus Ave., Boston, Mass. Open Mon. to Fri. 9-5 except during lunch hour, Sat. 9-12n.

CORNET made by Quinby Bros. Has 3 rotary valves.
At The Edison Institute, Dearborn, Michigan.

† CORNET inscribed "B. F. Richardson, Maker." Used in Civil War.
In the First Corps Cadets' Museum, First Corps Cadets' Armory, cor. Arlington St. & Columbus Ave., Boston. Open as stated above.
Silver, 3 rotary valves. Additional inscription "Presented to J.[ohn] Spofford by the Officers of the 45th Cadet Regiment M.[ass.] V.[olunteer] M.[ilitia] October 1862." Mr. Spofford's bandmaster's warrant and discharge are also preserved.

For illustration of the "Bayley Cornet" made by Richardson & Bayley see Boston Directory 1863 Advtg. Dept. p. 29.

† BRASS BUGLE inscribed "Made by Standard Band Instrument Company 62 Sudbury St., Boston."
In the First Corps Cadets' Museum, First Corps Cadets' Armory, cor. Arlington St. & Columbus Ave., Boston. Open as stated above.
Presented to the First Corps Cadets July 10, 1893 and used by them.

† BRASS BUGLE inscribed "Whitmore & Mansfield, Makers, Boston, Mass."
In the First Corps Cadets' Museum, First Corps Cadets' Armory, cor. Arlington St. & Columbus Ave., Boston.
& Columbus Ave., Boston.
Presented to the First Corps Cadets July 10, 1893, and used by them. No information obtained by writer about this firm.

KENT BUGLE made by E. G. Wright & Co. of Boston. This horn has 10 keys.
At the Edison Institute, Dearborn, Michigan.

* BUGLE inscribed on a bronze medallion "Made by E. G. Wright Boston," also on bell "Sergeant McKendry—b. Ponkapog, Nov. 8, 1834. 22nd Mass. Vols."
At the Canton Historical Society, Washington St., Canton, Mass. To see write Mr. Walter Hall, Curator, 1350 Washington St., Canton.
This bugle made of German silver with a brass edge to the bell was sent him by his family. He enlisted from Canton, in Co. D, 22nd Regiment M. V. M. and served as sergeant in the Peninsular Campaign of the Civil War. He died Aug. 28, 1874. Presented by his nephew, Elliot A. Curtis, of Stoughton, Mass., Oct. 12, 1927.

For illustration of rotary and piston cornets made by E. G. Wright & Co. see Boston Directory 1870, Advtg. Dept., p. 1043.

Percussion

† DRUM, maker unknown, lettered "Battle of Lexington April 19, 1775" with painting of a row of soldiers and officer on horseback ready for action.

At the Hancock-Clarke House, Lexington Historical Society, Lexington, Mass. Open daily 9:30-5:00 p.m.   Sundays 2-5 p.m.

A snare, of wood, rope and leather, no metal.   The long roll beat on this drum by the drummer boy, William Dimond, announcing to the Minute Men the coming of the British was the first overt act of the American Revolution.

† DRUMS, 2 snare and 1 bass, purchased or made 1784, and used by the Ancient and Honorable Artillery Company of Massachusetts, organized 1638.   Makers unknown.

In the Armory of the Ancient and Honorable Artillery, Fanueil Hall, Boston, Mass.

† DRUMS, 2 snare, one big bass and 1 tenor, procured in 1786 by the First Corps Cadets and used by them.   Makers unknown.

In the First Corps Cadets' Museum, First Corps Cadets' Armory, cor. Arlington St. & Columbus Ave., Boston, Mass.

First three in fine condition, including hand painting of the Cadets' motto "Monstrat Viam" surrounded by elaborate design of flags, trumpets.   Tenor drum not in so good condition.

† OLD HOOKER DRUM made by Ditson (John C. Haynes & Co. its Instrumental Dept.)   Boston about 1863.   Had a notable military career. Present head used since June 9, 1863.

In the Museum of the Loyal Legion of the U. S., the Commandery of the State of Mass., First Corps Cadets' Armory, cor. Arlington St. & Columbus Ave., Boston, Mass.

Snare has a metal shell, wood rims with hand painted design around tightening rope holes.   Played by George A. Cole, member of H Co., 11th Mass. Infantry, Gen. Hooker's Old Brigade, 2nd Div., 3rd Army Corps, assigned to band.   Drum reached the Regiment May 28, 1863 and two days later started on the march to Gettysburg and service with the Army of the Potomac.   Used at Gettysburg, Mine Run, Brandy Station, Wilderness, Spottsylvania, & Cold Harbor; at serenades to Lincoln, McClellan, Burnside, Hooker, Meade and Grant; and the dedication of the Hooker Statue.   It also sounded the death note of five deserters.   Silver band on one drumstick reads "Geo. A. Cole Band 11th Regt. Mass. Vols."   Drum and sticks are the gift of Mrs. Ada B. Cole as Mr. Cole requested that the drum be deposited after his death with the Loyal Legion.

* A SNARE.   Label inside reads in old English letters "White Brothers 86 Tremont St. Boston."   Firm at this address 1853-63.

At the Old Colony Historical Society, Historical Hall, Taunton, Mass.   Open daily 10-12 a.m. 2-4 p.m. Sat. 9-11:30 a.m.

Drum made of wood, rope and leather, no metal.   Label inside bore a sketch of a drum and flags above the lettering.   This firm of violin makers was evidently one of the firms which helped to make Boston a centre of drum making during the Civil War period.   This was Allen K. Bassett's Drum, Co. K, 4th Mass. Militia, 1863-64.

Fretted Instruments

* BANJO, maker unknown.

At Lynn Historical Society, 125 Green St., Lynn, Mass. Open July & Aug., Wed. & some Sat. afternoons 2-5 p.m. Acc. no. 1763.

Has 4 strings and shield flag design metal bracket eyes. This was used by the Hutchinson Family of Lynn with their melodeon to accompany their singing in the Northern Hospitals in the South during the Civil War. Not in good condition.

GUITAR made by Henry Ant Schatz, listed in Boston Directories 1845-1850. Has 6 strings.

At the Edison Institute, Dearborn, Michigan.

TILTON GUITAR made by Pehr Anderberg about 50 years ago. Rosewood.

Property of Mr. S. V. Swenson, 60 Willard St., Maplewood, Malden, Mass.

Miscellaneous Instruments and Accessories

* SMALL HARP made by James A. Bazin of Canton.

At the Canton Historical Society, Washington St., Canton, Mass.

Has 27 strings and a wooden frame, metal tuning pins for strings. The high long base has 9 holes at one end arranged symmetrically as if they might have been for pedals or mechanical devices.

ZITHER made by E. Link. 31 string American concert zither. No further information obtained about this maker.

At the Edison Institute, Dearborn, Mich.

FIRST STRING WINDING MACHINE made in Boston. Made and used by Ira J. White.

Property of John A. Gould, John A. Gould & Sons, 230 Boylston St., Boston.

* MUSIC STAND made by B. F. Richardson. Words "Worlds Peace Jubilee" are cast in the iron base which has 3 legs and is very heavy. Rack is of wood.

Property of Edward F. Tracy, Director of the Commonwealth Band and Orchestra, 47 Hanover St., Boston, Mass.

BIBLIOGRAPHY

General

American History and Encyclopedia of Music. History of American Music with Introductions by Chadwick, George W. and Damrosch, Frank. W. L. Hubbard, Editor. Irving Square, Toledo, 1909
Instrumental Music, Bands and Orchestras, pp. 255-87.
The Music Trades, pp. 313-45.

Belknap, Henry Wyckoff. Artists and Craftsmen of Essex County, Massachusetts. Salem, The Essex Institute, 1927. viii,127 pp.

Bishop, John Leander. A History of American Manufacture from 1608-1860. Added notes on the principal manufacturing centres. Philadelphia, E. Young, 3 vols. 1861-1868. portraits in vol. III

Boston Directories, 1789-1934. illus. in Advertising Dept. pages

Boston Music Directory. Civic Music Association, Inc. First Edition, 1929

Dwight, John Sullivan. The Memorial History of Boston. Justin Winsor, Editor, Boston, 1881
The History of Music in Boston, Vol. 4, pp. 415-65.

Fisher, William Arms. Notes on Music in Old Boston. Boston, Oliver Ditson Company, 1918. xvi,100 pp. illus. & portraits

Grove's Dictionary of Music and Musicians. Waldo Selden Pratt and Charles N. Boyd, Editors, New York, The Macmillan Company, 1935, 3d edition—American Supplement. 438 pp.

Hipkins, A. J., F. S. A. Musical Instruments Historic, Rare and Unique. London, A. and C. Black, Ltd. 1921. 123 pp. illus.

Historical Musical Exhibition Under the Auspices of Chickering & Sons Horticultural Hall, Boston, January 11th to 26th 1902—Catalogue of. 78 pp. illus.

Hood, George. A History of Music in New England, with Biographical Sketches of Reformers and Psalmists. Boston, Wilkins, Carter & Co. 1846. 252 pp.

Howard, John Tasker. Our American Music. New York, Thomas Y. Crowell Company, 1930 and 1931. xxiii and 713 pp. illus. & portraits

A Hundred Years of Music in America. W. S. B. Mathews, Associate Editor. Chicago, G. L. Howe, 1889
Chapter XV, Musical Instruments and the Music Trade, pp. 325-58. portraits.

Lahee, Henry C. Annals of Music in America. Boston, Marshall Jones Company, 1922. vii and 298 pp.

Williams, Cornelia Bartow, compiler. Ancestry of Lawrence Williams. Chicago, privately printed, 1915. Thomas Johnston pp. 177-9. illus.

Music Printing and Publishing

Biennial Census of Manufactures U. S. Department of Commerce, Washington, D. C.
    1927 Music Printing and Publishing, pp. 598-602.
    1931 Music Printing and Publishing, pp. 519-20.

Birchard Broadsheet
    September 1929, Vol. II, No. 1, pp. 1 & 7.
    September 1931, Vol. IV, No. 1, pp. 1 & 5.

Birge, Edward Bailey. History of Public School Music in the United States. Boston, Oliver Ditson Company, 1928. 296 pp. portraits

Boston Musical Gazette, May 2, 1838—April 3, 1839, pp. 64, 66, 72, 80, 152, 176, 184, 200

Damrosch, Frank. The American History and Encyclopedia of Music. History of American Music
    Music in the Public Schools, pp. 17-37.

Fisher, William Arms. One Hundred and Fifty Years of Music Publishing in the United States, 1783-1933. Boston, Oliver Ditson Company, Inc. 1933. 146 pp. illus.

Fisher, William Arms. Ye Olde New England Psalm Tunes (1620-1820) with historical sketch. Boston, Oliver Ditson Company, 1930. music

Hale, Philip. Tribute to Arthur P. Schmidt. Boston Herald, May 6, 1921

Hundred Years of Music in America. W. S. B. Mathews, Associate Editor. Chicago, G. L. Howe, 1889
    Chapter XVI, Literary Factors in Musical Progress, pp. 359-409. portraits.

Mathews, W. S. B. Music, Vol. XV. John S. Dwight, Editor
    Critic and Man, pp. 525-40.

Music Book Printing. Boston, Stanhope Press, F. H. Gilson Company, 1915. 32 pp. illus.

Newton, Elbridge W. Ginn & Company, Copyright Letter of January 1932

Publishers of "Edition Wood." Music Trade News, September 1930, pp. 11 & 12. portraits

Schmidt, Arthur P., Articles on, Musical America, May 14, 1921. p. 55, portrait. Tributes by Arthur Foote and Mrs. Edward A. MacDowell. May 28, 1921, p. 22. Editorial

Stratton, George W. A Sketch of the Life of G. W. Stratton, Written especially for the Cheshire County Gazetteer, a book published by subscription in the county, 1885, printed as pp. 97-123 of the "Catalogue— Stratton Free Library and Art Gallery," West Swanzey, New Hampshire. Second Edition printed in 1900. portrait

Pianofortes

Achievement—An Ascending Scale—Being a Short History of the House of Chickering & Sons. 1920. illus.

American Cyclopaedia. George Ripley and Charles A. Dana, Editors. New York, D. Appleton & Company, 1889
    Pianoforte, pp. 487-93.

American Musician—In the Early Days—Seventh Paper—The Early Boston Piano Makers, July 2, 1887

Biennial Census of Manufactures. U. S. Department of Commerce, Washington, D. C.
1927 The Musical Instruments Industries, Pianos, pp. 1209-11.
1931 The Musical Instruments Industries, Pianos, pp. 1121-28.

Boston Gazette—Advertisements and Copartnership Notices—Babcock, Appleton & Babcock Jan. 23, 1812; Hayts, Appleton & Babcock and also Charles and Elna Hayt issues of May 29, 1815, June 5, 1815, June 15, 1815; Hayt & Appleton same ad repeated Oct. 5, 1815; Nov. 2, Nov. 9, Advtg. Supple.; Nov. 20, Extra Edition; Dec. 7, 1815

Commemoration of the Founding of the House of Chickering & Sons, 1823-1903. Boston, Privately Printed, 1904 (Arranged and printed by The Wayside Department of the University Press, Cambridge, Massachusetts) illus. & portraits

Connell, Margaret E., Historian, Chickering & Sons. Tercentenary Letter of January 29, 1930

Dolge, Alfred. Pianos and Their Makers. Covina, California, Covina Publishing Company, 1911. 478 pp. illus., portraits, diagrams

Dwight, John Sullivan. Journal of Music. Vol. XXVI, No. 17, Nov. 10, 1866, p. 339, American Pianos

Encyclopaedia Britannica, Supplement to Edition XIII—Vol. II. Musical Instruments, Mechanical, Some Reproducing Pianos, p. 1007 and Ampico, pp. 1007-8. diagram

Hipkins, A. J. A Description and History of the Pianoforte. London, Novello, Ewer & Company, 1896. 130 pp. illus.

Ivers & Pond Policy Past and Present (1880-1926)—Behind the Footlights in Piano Building. illus.

James, Philip. Early Keyboard Instruments from Their Beginnings to the Year 1820. London, Peter Davies Ltd. 1930. 153 pp. illus.

Luxton, Denning D. Vose Reminiscences. Vose & Sons Piano Company, Watertown, Greater Boston. illus.

Manufactures of the United States in 1860—compiled from the Original Returns of the Eighth Census Under Direction of Secretary of the Interior, Washington, D. C. 1865
Massachusetts Totals, pp. 254-5, United States Totals, p. 738.

Mason, Henry Lowell. How Has The Pianoforte As an Instrument Developed Since 1876? Reprint from Music Teachers National Association, Volume of Proceedings for 1928, 15 pp.

Massachusetts Musical Journal. Vol. 1, No. 1 May 1, 1855 p. 6; No. 3 June 1, 1855 p. 22; No. 4 June 15, 1855 p. 31; No. 6 Aug. 1, 1855 pp. 44 & 48. Advertisements

Parker, Richard G. A Tribute to the Life and Character of Jonas Chickering. Boston, William P. Tewksbury, 1854. 162 pp.

Pauer, Ernst. Dictionary of Pianists and Composers for the Piano with Appendix of Manufacturers. London, Novello, Ewer & Company, 1895. pp. 135-56

The Belle Skinner Collection of Old Musical Instruments, A Descriptive Catalogue Compiled Under the Direction of William Skinner, p. 178 and Illustration on Plate No. 88

Spillane, Daniel. History of the American Pianoforte; Its Technical Development and the Trade. New York, D. Spillane, 1890. 396 pp. illus., diagrams & portraits

Steinert, Morris. The M. Steinert Collection of Keyed and Stringed Instruments, with various treatises on the history of these instruments, the method of playing them, and their influence on musical art. New York, Charles F. Tretbar, 1893. 170 pp. illus.

Teele, A. K., Editor—The History of Milton, Massachusetts, 1640 to 1887, Rockwell & Churchill, Boston, p. 378 (It is a question how accurate the dates given in this are.)

Organs

Audsley, George Ashdown. The Art of Organ Building. New York, Dodd, Mead & Company, 1905. Vol. I 600 pp. Vol. II 760 pp. illus. & diagrams

Audsley, George Ashdown. The Organ of the Twentieth Century. New York, Dodd, Mead & Company, 1919. 519 pp. illus. & diagrams

Barnes, William Harrison. The Contemporary American Organ. New York, J. Fischer & Bros. 1930. 341 pp. illus. & diagrams. Second Edition 1933. 361 pp. illus. & diagrams

Batchelder, S. F. Christ Church, Cambridge, Some Account of Its History and Present Condition, Especially Prepared for Visitors. Cambridge, 1893. pp. 17, 39, 46, 48-9, 51, 54, & 60

Biennial Census of Manufactures U. S. Department of Commerce, Washington, D. C.
   1927 The Musical Instruments Industries, Organs, pp. 1212-13.
   1931 The Musical Instruments Industries, Organs, pp. 1121-28.

Boston Gazette—Advertisements of Thomas Appleton's early business connection—issue of Jan. 7, 1811, and his partner separately Aug. 26, 1811; Showing of the Panharmonicon July 1, 1811, and Sept. 2, 1811.

Clarke, William Horatio. An Outline of the Structure of the Pipe Organ. Boston, Oliver Ditson & Co. 1877. 128 pp. illus. & diagrams

Covell, William King. The Boston Music Hall Organ. London, Musical Opinion, 1931. Reprint from The Organ, Vol. XI, Nos. 42 (October 1931) and 43 (January 1932) 16 pp. illus.

Dean, Frederic. Americans Organs and Organists. Junior Munsey, November 1901, pp. 255-63, illus.

Dwight, John Sullivan. Dwight's Journal of Music
   Vol. VII, May 5, 1855, p. 38, New Organ—Cathedral Music—Psalm Tunes, St. John's Church, Troy, New York
   Vol. IX, Sept. 27, 1856, p. 205, A New Organ (Citadel Square Church, Charleston, South Carolina)
   Vol. XV, May 14, 1859, pp. 53-5, Organs—Appleton Chapel

Vol. XV, Sept. 3, 1859, p. 182 and Sept. 10, 1859, p. 189, A Superb Organ, and Sept. 17, 1859, p. 198, The Great Organ for Albany

Vol. XVII, April 21, 1860, p. 31, Opening of a New Organ (King's Chapel)

Vol. XVII, May 19, 1860, p. 63, Organ for St. Ignatius' Church, Baltimore

Vol. XVII, July 21, 1860, p. 134, Organ for St. Paul's Cathedral Church, Louisville, Kentucky

Vol. XXIII, Aug. 22, 1863, p. 87, New Organ in Worcester (Influence of German Organ)

Vol. XXIII, March 5, 1864, p. 199, The New Organ at the Church of the Immaculate Conception

Vol. XXIV, Nov. 12, 1864, p. 339, The Worcester Organ (Its Trial and Acceptance)

Vol. XXIV, Nov. 26, 1864, pp. 351 & 352, The Worcester Organ (Inaugural Concert)

Vol. XXIV, Nov. 26, 1864, p. 348, Another Large Organ (South Congregational Church, Boston)

Vol. XXV, Oct. 28, 1865, p. 128, The Church of the Advent Organ

Vol. XXVI, April 28, 1866, p. 227 and May 12, 1866, p. 244, The Plymouth Church Organ, and Aug. 18, 1866, p. 291, The New Organ at Plymouth Church

Vol. XXVI, No. 15, Oct. 13, 1866, p. 323, New Organ in Trinity Church, New Haven, from The New Haven Palladium, Sept. 8

Vol. XXVII, No. 6, June 8, 1867, p. 48, Great Reed Organ by Mason & Hamlin from the N. Y. Musical Gazette

Vol. XXVIII, No. 2, April 11, 1868, p. 220, Organs in Chicago by Der Freyschutz

Family Records of Thomas Appleton and William and Ebenezer Goodrich—supplied by Francis E. Appleton

Foote, Henry Wilder. Annals of King's Chapel From the Puritan Age of New England to the Present Day. Boston, Little, Brown and Company, 1882, Vol. I, the Brattle Organ, pp. 209-11 & 214

Frazee Organs—a brochure. Testimonials, pp. 18 & 19. illus.

Goodrich, Henry A. Church Organs: Some of the Early Builders in New England. Fitchburg Historical Society, Sentinel Printing Company, 1902. 16 pp.

Goodrich, William, Esq., Organ Builder, Facts Concerning. Copy from a manuscript in the possession of Hook and Hastings Company

Hook & Hastings Company. Pipe Organs for Municipal Halls, Memorials, Churches, Theatres, Schools, Lodges. 32 pp. illus.

Jacobsen, Norman. Organ Building Views—With Hook & Hastings. The American Organist, Vol. 1, Sept. 1928, pp. 456-64, illus.

Jameson, Ephraim Orcutt. The History of Medway, Mass. 1713 to 1885. Published by the Town, Millis, 1886. The Manufacture of Church Organs and Organ Pipes, (Holbrook and Holbrook & Ware) pp. 201-2

Lahee, Henry C. Organs and Organ Building in New England. New England Magazine, December 1897, pp. 485-505, illus.

Lovewell, Harrison. Boston's Oldest Organ. The Diapason, Sept. 1, 1925, p. 35

Manufactures of the United States in 1860—compiled from the Original Returns of the Eighth Census Under Direction of the Secretary of the Interior, Washington, D. C. 1865
Massachusetts Totals, pp. 254-5, United States Totals, p. 738.

Mason, Henry Lowell.   The History and Development of the American Cabinet Organ, a booklet

Mason, Orion Thomas.   The Handbook of Medway History; A Condensed History of the Town of Medway, Massachusetts, 1713-1913. Medway, Billings, 1913, p. 35

Oliver, Henry K.   An Account of the First Organs in America.   The Organist's Quarterly Journal and Review, Vol. II Part 1, April 1875, pp. 4-6

Skinner, Ernest M.   The Modern Organ.   New York, The H. W. Gray Company, 1917. 48 pp. illus. & diagrams

Thayer, Eugene.   The Organist's Quarterly Journal and Review
    Vol. I Part 1, April 1874, pp. 4-7, Music Hall Organ, Boston. Specifications
    Vol. I Part 4, January 1875, pp. 7 & 8, The Plymouth Church Organ, Brooklyn, N. Y. Specifications
    Vol. III Part 1, April 1876, pp. 3 & 4, The Great Organ of the Old South Church, Boston. Specifications

Bells and Bell Chimes

Abbott, Edward.   St. James's Parish, Cambridge, Massachusetts, The Bell's Own Story As Told at the Public Reception of the Paul Revere Bell in the Church Friday Evening April Nineteenth A. D. 1901 By the Rector Edward Abbott.   Cambridge, Press of Powell & Co., 1901, a booklet

Batchelder, S. F.   Christ Church, Cambridge, Some Account of Its History and Present Condition, Especially Prepared for Visitors. Cambridge, 1893

Bell Foundry of Blake Bell Co., Facts Regarding the—a booklet. Boston, Massachusetts, 1876. 28 pp. cover illus.

Boston Gazette—Copartnership Notices of Paul Revere & Son—in issues of April 15 and May 6, 1811

Brief Sketch of the Business Life of Paul Revere—a folder of the Taunton-New Bedford Copper Company. illus. & portraits

A Description of the Chime of Bells in Christ Church, Cambridge.   Cast by Ourselves in 1860.   Article in the booklet—Facts Regarding the Foundry of Blake Bell Co.

Essex Institute Historical Collections, Vol. 47, No. 4, October 1911, pp. 293-316 and Vol. 48, No. 1, January 1912, pp. 1-16—The Bells of Paul and Joseph Revere, Dr. Arthur H. Nichols. illus. in Vol. 48

Goss, Elbridge H.   Early Bells of Massachusetts.   New England Historical and Genealogical Register, Vol. 13, 1859, p. 77; Vol. 28, 1874, pp. 176-84 and pp. 279-88; and Addenda Vol. 37, 1883, pp. 46-52

Huntington, Henry B.   History of Grace Church (Episcopal, Providence, R. I.) published in 1929, information about the Chimes.

Jameson, Ephraim Orcutt.   The History of Medway, Mass. 1713 to 1885. Millis, 1886.   The Holbrook Bell Foundry 1816-1880, pp. 197-9

Munroe, Henry P.   Chime Bells in Boston, Cambridge and Portland.   For William Blake & Company, Boston, Massachusetts, 1876. 18 pp.

New England Magazine.   J. T. and E. Buckingham, Editors, October 1832—Original Papers—Early American Artists and Mechanics, No. II, Paul Revere, pp. 305-14

Robbins, Chandler, Minister. A History of the Second Church, Or Old North, in Boston, to Which Is Added, A History of the New Brick Church. Published by a Committee of the Society, Boston: Printed by John Wilson & Son, 22, School Street, 1852, p. 316

Woodbury, C. J. H., President. The Bells of Lynn, A Paper Given Before The Lynn Historical Society December 10, 1914. Reprinted from the Register of the Society, Volume XVII, Lynn, Mass., 1915

Band, Orchestral, Fretted and Miscellaneous Instruments

1. VIOLINS

Bachman, Alberto. An Encyclopedia of the Violin. New York, D. Appleton & Company, 1925. Translated by Frederick H. Martens, edited by Albert E. Wier. Alphabetical List of Violin Makers in America, pp. 49-54. illus. & labels

Biennial Census of Manufactures. U. S. Department of Commerce, Washington, D. C. 1927. p. 1121-28

Gould, Erik. Bostonian Treasures Violin of Bobbie Burns. Boston Traveler Article, Jan. 31, 1931, p. 16. illus.

Gould, John A. Boston Personalities Column, Boston Herald, by Mason Ham, Jan. 2, p. 4 & Jan. 3, 1931, p. 12

Gould, John A. Facts About Old Violins. Jacobs' Orchestra Monthly, April 1930

Ingham, Travis. Violin 400 Years Old in Possession of Chelsea Collector— One of Gasparo da Salo's Rare Products Among Anderberg's 22 Unique Instruments. Boston Herald, April 10, 1932, p. 3, illus.

Manufactures of the United States in 1860—compiled from the Original Returns of the Eighth Census Under the Direction of the Secretary of the Interior, Washington, D. C. 1865
Massachusetts Totals, pp. 254-5; United States Totals, p. 738.

Mason, Orion Thomas. The Handbook of Medway History; A Condensed History of the Town of Medway, Massachusetts, 1713-1913. Medway, Billings, 1913. Deacon Samuel Allen and William Green p. 31

Poidras, Henri. Critical and Documentary Dictionary of Violin Makers Old and Modern. Translated by Arnold Sewell, Rouen, 1928, Imprimerie de La Vicomte
Miscellaneous Schools, pp. 177-209.

The Violinist's Guide, 1916, Written for the use of the Violin Buying Public—Containing Information Pertaining to the Violin Making Industry—The Blue Book of the Violin Making Profession. Chicago, The Violinist Publishing Company, for A. E. Taylor, 1916
Howe, William H. Early American Violin Makers, pp. 15-18.
American Violin Makers, pp. 19-42.

Willibald, Leo, Freiherrn Von Lütgendorff. Die Geigen und Lautenmacher, vom Mittelalter Bis Zur Gegenwart. Frankfurt-a-M., Verlag von Heinrich Keller, 1904 Edition; also 1913 Edition, Erster Band 407 pp., Zweiter Band 937 pp.

2. FLUTES AND CLARINETS

Bettoney, Harry. Boston Personalities Column, Boston Herald, by Mason Ham, May 13, 1931

Bettoney, Harry. The Temperament of the Clarinet. Jacobs' Band and Orchestra Monthly, October 1926

Boehm, von, Theobald. Die Flöte und Das Flötenspiel. München, Verlag von Joseph Aibl, 1871. Original German edition. The Flute and Flute Playing in Acoustical, Technical and Artistic Aspects. Translated and Annotated by Dayton C. Miller. Cleveland, Miller, 1922. Second English edition revised and enlarged, xxvii and 197 pp. illus. & diagrams

How Wm. S. Haynes Improved the Clarinet—a brochure

Music Trades. Dec. 17, 1927, p. 131, The Silver Clarinet Is Adopted by the U. S. Army Band

Powell, Verne Q. Boston Personalities Column, Boston Herald, by Mason Ham, March 28, 1931

Time, Dec. 2, 1935, p. 23—Music

3. MISCELLANEOUS INSTRUMENTS

Boston Musical Gazette. The Boston Band, Vol. I No. 7, July 25, 1838, pp. 51-2

Gleason's Pictorial. Boston, Vol. I No. 12, Sept. 20, 1851, p. 177, illus. Boston Brass Band, article on & picture of, in new uniforms.

Guild Reporter. Official Organ of the American Guild of Banjoists, Mandolinists and Guitarists, Mar.-Apr. 1935, p. 7, Advertisement

Miller, Dayton Clarence. The Science of Musical Sounds. New York, The Macmillan Company, 1916. Lecture VI, Tone Qualities of Musical Instruments, pp. 175-214

Ramsdell, George Allen. The History of Milford (N. H.) Family Registers by William P. Colburn. Concord, N. H., The Rumford Press, 1901. Nathan Adams pp. 229-30

Stanley, Albert A. Catalogue of the Stearns Collection of Musical Instruments. Ann Arbor, Michigan, University of Michigan, 1918, 260 pp.

Stone, George Burt and George Lawrence. Editorial. Jacobs' Orchestra Monthly, Vol. VIII, No. 3, March 1917

General Index

Adams, Nathan, brass instrument maker, 223, 302 ; rotary valve inventor, 223, 302
Aeolian American Corporation, 117, 127
Aeolian Company, 117, 119, 127, 129, 176
Aeolian-pianos of Timothy Gilbert & Company, 109
Aeolian-Skinner Organ Company, Inc. 175-81. *See also* Aeolian Company ; Skinner ; Steere
Allen, Henry, 242 ; member of Brown & Allen, 246 ; of Hallet & Allen, 246 ; of Hallet, Cumston & Allen, 246 ; of Hallet, Davis & Co. 245
Allen, J. Lathrop, brass instrument maker, 224, 266, 302
Allen & Co. pianoforte dealers or makers (?) 242
Allen and Ganshirt, Inc. musical instrument dealers and repairers, 258
Allen & Hall, brass instrument manufacturers, 224, 266, 268
Allen & Richardson, brass instrument manufacturers, 224, 266, 269
Aluminum wound "D" string, invention of, 201
American Book Company, educational music publishers, 66-8 ; Summer School, 68
American Institute of Normal Methods, the Summer School of Silver, Burdett and Company, 63-5
American Piano Co. 117, 119, 127
Ampico reproducing mechanism, 118-19
Anderberg, Ernest A. guitar maker, and violin repairer and dealer, 195, 234-5
Anderberg, Pehr A. guitar and mandolin maker, 234, 274, 306
Apostles violins, 199, 200
Appleton, Thomas, 104
    cabinet maker, 105, 152, 239
    organ builder, 105, 152-4 ; celebrated organ for Handel and Haydn Society, 154 ; first complete church organ, 153 ; with Corri and Ebenezer Goodrich as voicers, 152 ; with William Goodrich, 147-8
    member of Appleton & Hanners, 239 ; of Appleton & Warren, 152-3 ; of Babcock, Appleton & Babcock, 239, 240, 282 ; of Hayt & Appleton, 240 ; of Hayts, Babcock & Appleton, 104, 105, 152, 239, 240, 282
Appleton & Hanners, cabinet makers, 239
Appleton & Warren, organ builders, 152-3
Ashmall, William E. publisher of organ and anthem music and *The Organist Journal,* 71
Ashton, John Jr. 11
Ashton, John & Co. music and umbrella dealers, 11
Astor pipe organ-piano in The M. Steinert Collection, 131, 291
Austin Organ Co. 254

Babcock, Alpheus, pianoforte maker, 105, 106-7, 117, 239, 240, 291 ; instruments of his, 106-7, 282-4 ; member of Babcock, Appleton, & Babcock, 239, 240, 282 ; of Hayts, Appleton & Babcock, 105, 152, 239, 240, 282
Babcock, Lewis, pianoforte maker, 105, 106, 239

Babcock, Appleton & Babcock, pianoforte and organ manufacturers, 239, 240, 282
Baker, B. F. upright pianoforte, 249
Baker, Calvin, violin maker and repairer, 197, 258, 262
Balch, Edward L. printer, 94
Baldwin, "Grandsire," drummer and drum maker, 271 ; member of Blair & Baldwin, 227, 271
Baltzerson, Peter, violin maker and repairer, 210
Barnes, Howard, manager of Geo. W. Stratton & Co. 21-2, 208
Bates & Bendix, music publishers, 24-5, 74
Battelle's Boston Book Store, 5, 28
Bauer, Emile, flute repairer, 213, 265
Bauer, William, woodwind instrument repairer, 213, 265
Bauer, Wm. & Son, 265
Baumgarten, Moritz, organ builder and voicer, 254
Bay State, trade name for instruments sold by John C. Haynes & Co. 265, 274, 276
Bay State Brass Foundry & Blake Bell Co. 188
Bay State reed organs, product of C. B. Hunt & Co. 252
Bayley model cornet, 220, 224, 269
Bazin, James A. brass instrument maker, 223, 303 ; harp maker, 306 ; reed organ maker, 136, 291-2
Beal, Fenner L. 'cello maker and violin repairer, 202 ; member of Weeman, Beal & Holmberg, 202
Beethoven's Piano Forte Sonatas, possible earliest complete American edition, 29
Bell foundry, probably the first in America, 186, 297
Bendix, Theodore, composer and publisher, 24-5, 74
Bent, Adam, pianoforte maker, 105, 285
Bent, William, pianoforte maker, 105, 195, 285 ; member of Bent & Green, 105, 195
Bent & Green, musical instrument makers, 105, 195
Berkeley (Dean) organ, second (?) organ imported into New England, 141
Berkshire pianofortes, 130
Berliner, Emile, inventor of phonograph records, 201
Berry, Albert L. drummer and drum maker, 271
Berteling, Theodore, woodwind instrument maker, 213, 265
Bettoney, Harry, musician, 219 ; publisher, 73 ; woodwind instrument maker as member of The Cundy-Bettoney Co. 213, 219, 221
Bettonite material, 220, 221
Billings, William, first real American composer, 4-5 ; Stoughton Musical Society director, 5
Birchard, Clarence C. 45, 68
Birchard, C. C. & Co. general music publishers, 45-8, 97
Blair, Samuel W. printer and publisher, 95
Blair, Wm. J. drummer and drum maker, 227, 271

Blair & Baldwin, drum makers, 227, 271
Blake, William, bell caster, 187, 188
Blake, William S. bell caster, 188
Blake, Wm. & Co. bell casters, 188, 189-90, 298-9
Blake, Wm. & Wm. S. bell casters, 188
Blake Bell Co. bell casters, 187, 188
Blanchard, L. A. music dealer, 18; publisher, 18
Blyth, Samuel, early spinet, harpsichord and stringed instrument maker, 104, 194, 281
Borg, Peter N. violin maker, 258
Boris, Woods & Co. introducer to U. S. of Buffet Clarinet, 72 footnote 5, 273; proprietors of Globe Music School, 273
Boston and Braintree Copper and Brass Company, immediate successor to Paul Revere & Co. (business of grandson of Lt. Col. Paul Revere) 187
Boston Copper Co. successor to above company, 184, 187
Boston Group of Composers, their compositions, 31, 39-40, 93
Boston Hydraulic Motor Co. maker of water motors, 257
Boston Ideal Banjo, Mandolin & Guitar Club, 228, 275, 276, 277
Boston Music Company, general music publishers, 41-3
Boston Musical Instrument Company (earlier Manufactory) 220, 226, 267
Boston Organ Co. reed organ maker, 252
Boston Symphony Orchestra, 115, 116, 122, 128, 155, 164, 199, 207, 210, 213, 215, 216, 218, 228, 231
Boston Three *** Star instruments (brass) 220, 226, 267
Boston Water Motor, first notable reciprocating water motor in general use in organs, 257
Bourne, William, pianoforte maker, 242
Bourne, Wm. & Company, pianoforte makers, 242
Bowen, Henry W. Superintendent of E. & G. G. Hook & Hastings, 172
Bower, Harry A. drum making and patents, 271
Brackett, John W. pianoforte maker, 242
Bradlee, Charles, music publisher, 10
Brass instrument manufacturers, earliest company in U. S. (?) 226, 268
Brattle, Thomas, 140
Brattle organ, first (?) imported into New England, 140-1, 143, 293, 295
Brennan, John D. organ builder, 255
Briggs, C. C. Jr. 242
Briggs, Charles C. pianoforte maker, 242, 243, 244, 247
Briggs, Charles C. & Co. pianoforte makers, 242, 247
Briggs Piano Co. 242
Bromfield, Edward Jr. first New England organ builder (?) 143
Brooks, S. P. pianoforte maker, 243
Brown, Edwin, pianoforte maker, 246; member of Brown & Allen, 246; of Brown & Hallet, 243, 246
Brown, John P. member of Brown, Hallet & Woodward, 250; of Woodward & Brown, 250
Brown & Allen, pianoforte makers, 246
Brown & Hallet (R.) pianoforte makers, 243, 250, 285
Brown (John P.), Hallet (R.) & Woodward (I.) pianoforte makers, 250
Bruce & Chard, makers of Mozart reed organs, 252
Bryant, Edmund F. musician and violin dealer, maker, and repairer, 206-7; member of E. F. & O. H. Bryant, 206, 209

Bryant, E. F. & O. H. violin makers and repairers, 206, 209
Bryant, Oliver H. violin maker, 209; head of Boston School of Violin Making, 209; member of E. F. & O. H. Bryant, 206, 209; of O. H. Bryant & Son, 209
Bryant, O. H. & Son, violin dealers, makers and repairers, 209-10
Buffet Clarinet, introducers of to the U. S. 72 footnote 5, 273
Burns, Robert, violin of, 205

Callender, William, musical instrument maker, 212, 301
Catholic Music Publishing Co. 71
Catlin, Edward N. musical director and violin maker, 258
Chard, David, reed organs, 252
Chard, Granville, 252
Chickering, Charles Francis (C. Francis) member of Chickering & Sons, 112, 113, 114, 117
Chickering, George H. member of Chickering & Sons, 113, 117
Chickering, Jacob, pianoforte maker, 243
Chickering, Jonas, 107, 108, 111, 112, 113, 117, 118, 119-20; instruments of his, 285-7
Chickering, Thomas E. member of Chickering & Sons, 113, 117
Chickering & Mackay, 107, 112
Chickering & Sons, pianoforte makers, 108, 111-23, 242, 243, 246, 247, 287
    Ampico Hall, New York City, 122
    artists using and endorsing Chickering pianofortes, 122-3
    celebrations of the Company's service, 116-17
    Chevalier of the Legion of Honor Decoration, 114
    Chickering Halls, 113, 120-2
    concerts under management of, 122
    early keyboard and stringed instruments revival under Arnold Dolmetsch, 115-16
    inventions, 117-19
    list of awards and medals for Chickering pianofortes, 114-15
    Liszt testimonial, 114
    See also Chickering & Mackay; Stewart & Chickering; also personal names beginning with Chickering
Chimes, first cast in America, by Boston Copper Co. founders, 184, 188; first imported into America, for Christ Church, Boston, 184, 298
Choralcelo, The, 278; companies making, 278
Christ Church, Boston, organ, 141-2, 143, 148, 295
Christ Church, Cambridge, Mass. chimes, 188, 299; Snetzler organ's part in the Battle of Bunker Hill, 144-6
Church, Cephas, member of Guild, Church & Co. 245
Church, John, and establishment of John Church Co. publishers, 30
Clarigold Hall of Wm. Horatio Clarke, 254
Clarke, Wm. Horatio, organ builder and writer, 254
Cole, Frank E. banjo manufacturers, 272, 275
Cole, James, organ builder, 155, 165-6
Cole, William A. banjo player, teacher, 192, 275; banjo manufacturer, 228, 275
Cole & Woodberry (James) organ builders, 165
Cole, & Woodberry Bros. (James and Jesse) organ builders, 165, 166
Cole Organ Co. organ builders, 165
Colton Bridge for violins, 261

Crehore, Benjamin, early pianoforte maker, 8, 104-5, 147; instruments of his, 282; early bow-stringed instrument maker, 8, 194-5; instrument of his, 300; member of P. A. von Hagen, Jun. & Co. 8, 105

Cremona Art Violins, 209

Crosby, Walter, early fife and flute maker, 212

Crown pianoforte, 248

Cummings, J. A. & Co. printers, 95

Cumston, William, pianoforte maker, 246; member of Hallet & Cumston, 241, 246; of Hallet, Cumston & Allen, 241, 242, 246; of Lord & Cumston, 241; of Lord, Gilbert & Cumston, 241

Cundy, W. H. musician, dealer and publisher, 71-2, 92, 208, 219

Cundy & Whitcomb, music publishers, 71

Cundy-Bettoney Co. The, inventions of, 221 publishers of instrumental music, 71-3 woodwind and brass instrument manufacturers, 219-21, 227

Cundy Music Publishing Co. 73, 220

Currier, Ebenezer R. pianoforte maker, 109, 240

Currier, Ebenezer R. & Co. pianoforte makers, 109, 240; instrument of, 109, 287

Currier & Gilbert (Timothy) pianoforte makers, 109, 240

Curtis pianofortes, 130

Cyr, Peter, violin maker, 258, 260

Damm, August, composer, 23; musician, 212-13; head of August Damm & Co. 213; member of Damm & Gay, 23

Damm, August & Co. woodwind instrument makers, 213-14

Damm & Gay, music publishers, 23

Daniels, George W. violin maker, 259

Davis, George H. member of the two firms Hallet, Davis & Co. 245, 246

Davis, (Benj. B.) & Fobes (Edwin) pianoforte makers, 244

Dellmuth, William, engraver, 93; member of Manicke & Dellmuth, 93

Ditson, Charles H. 30

Ditson, James Edward, 30

Ditson, Oliver, music publisher, 7, 11, 13, 28, 29, 30, 137

Ditson, Oliver, Company, Inc. (earlier Oliver Ditson & Co.) general music publishers, 17, 18, 22, 23, 26, 28-35, 91, 92 first American editions, 29, 31 instrumental department, 30, 205, 209, 265-6, 276; instruments of, 301, 305. See also Haynes & Co., John C. major publications, 32-4 music journals, 79, 81-2, 85 music store, 30, 136 See also personal names beginning with Ditson

Dodge, F. E. drum manufacturer, 271, 272

Dolmetsch, Arnold, maker of and performer on earlier stringed instruments, 115

Dwight, John, pianoforte maker, 107, 108

Dwight, John Sullivan, journal contributor, 78; editor, 79 and footnote 3; translator, 31, 32

Dwight's Journal of Music, 15, 16, 79, 137, 157

Echo attachment brass band instruments, 225

Edes & Gill, early music printers, 4, 88

Edition Wood, second largest edition in U. S. 44

Edler, J. H. violin dealer and maker, 207, 260

Eichberg, Julius, editor and school music director, 54, 55, 56, 66; musician, 206

Electrotyping process, 90

Emerson, Elijah, violin maker and repairer, 259, 260

Emerson, William P. pianoforte maker, 242, 244; instruments of, 288

Enstone, Edward, organist and instrument importer, 140, 212

Equipoise for violins, 261

Everett Piano Co. 244

Exporter, first in U. S. (?) of pianofortes, 108

Fairbanks, A. C. banjo player, 275; manufacturer, 275

Fairbanks, A. C. & Co. banjo manufacturers, 228, 229, 275

Fairbanks, A. C. Company, Inc. banjo manufacturers, 275

Farley, Charles E. violin maker, 259

Farrand & Votey Co. organ builders, 162

Farwell, Arthur, founder of Wa Wan Press, 27

Fischer, Carl, music publisher, 7, 49

Fischer, Carl, Inc. 18, 22, 26, 49-50

Fisher, William Arms, of Oliver Ditson Company, Inc. 31, 41, 42

Flagg, Josiah, pioneer musician and publisher, 4, 9, 87

Flather, Osborne P. violin maker, 259

Fobes, Edwin, pianoforte maker, 244; member of Davis & Fobes, 244

François, G. M. violin dealer and maker, 259

Frazee, H. Norman, organ builder, 181

Frazee, Leslie H. organ builder, 181

Frazee Organ Company, organ builders, 181-3, 254

Freeman, Robert F. guitar maker, 275

Freemantle, George, musician and band instrument maker, 267

Ganshirt, William, violin maker and repairer, 258; member of Allen and Ganshirt, Inc. 258

Gatcomb, L. B. & Co. banjo and mandolin makers, 228, 276; fretted instrument music publishers, 74; music journal publisher, 83

Gay, Mace, music publisher, 74; member of Damm & Gay, 23

Geib, Adam and John, early organ builders, 146

Gemünder, George (Georg) violin maker, 198; guitar maker, 228

Gerrish, Wm. H. publisher, especially Masonic music, 26; reed organ maker, 26, 252

Gerrish Collection, The, 26

Gervais, Trefflé, violin maker and repairer, 260, 301

Gilbert, Lemuel (called Lemanuel by Daniel Spillane) early pianoforte maker, 108-9; 240-1; instrument of, 288; member of Timothy Gilbert & Co. 108, 240; of Lord, Gilbert & Cumston, 240, 241

Gilbert, Timothy, pianoforte maker, 107, 108, 109, 151, 241, 244; instruments of, 109, 245, 288-9; inventions of, 109; member of Currier & Gilbert, 109, 241; of Timothy Gilbert & Co. 109, 241

Gilbert, Timothy & Co. pianoforte makers, 109, 241

Gilbert (J. L.) & Butler (Geo. A.) organ builders, 254

Giles, John F. (J. Frank) music printer, 95; member of Giles & Gould, 95

Gilmore, Patrick Sarsfield, band leader, 223, 267; Great National Peace Jubilee, 223; member of Gilmore & Co. 226, 267; of Gilmore & Russell, 17, 267; of Gilmore, Graves & Co. 226, 267

Gilmore & Co. brass instrument makers, 226, 267, 303

Gilmore & Russell (J. M.) music publishers and music and musical instrument dealers, 17, 267

Gilmore, Graves & Co. brass instrument makers, 226, 267, 268

Gilson, A. P. music book printer, 97

Gilson, F. H. music book printer, 97

Gilson, F. H. Company (Stanhope Press) music book printers, 97

Ginn & Co. educational music publishers, 55-8, 65, 92 ; National Summer School of Music, 58

Ginn & Heath, educational music publishers, 65

Gold "G" string, invention of, 201

Goodrich, Ebenezer, early organ builder, 151-2, 294 ; pianoforte maker, 151, 289 ; reed stop inventor, 135, 151

Goodrich (Goodridge first), William M. early organ builder, 142, 144, 146-51, 294

Gosline, D. P. Boston Water Motor, 257

Goss, Walter Solon, violin maker and repairer, 200

Gould, Erik, violin dealer and repairer, 204, 205 ; member of John A. Gould & Sons, 204, 205

Gould, George, music printer, 95

Gould, John A. violin dealer, maker, and repairer, 194, 195, 198, 203, 204, 205, 301, 306

Gould, John A. & Sons, violin dealers, makers and repairers, 203-5

Gould, Stephen L. pianoforte maker, 250 ; member of Gould, Wilder & Co. 250

Gould, Wilder & Co. 250

Goullaud, Louis P. music publisher, 22 ; member of White & Goullaud, 22

Grace Church, Providence, R. I. chimes, 189, 300

Graupner, Johann Christian Gottlieb, musician and pioneer music publisher, 8, 9-10, 29 ; member of Graupner & Mallet, 9

Graupner, John Henry Howard, engraving and printing, 29

Graupner & Mallet, music publishers, 9

Graves, Samuel, reed and brass band instrument maker, 268

Graves, Samuel & Sons, reed and brass band instrument makers, 226, 267

Graves & Co. reed and brass band instrument makers, 226, 267, 268 ; instruments of, 301, 302, 303

Green, William, early bass viol maker, 105, 195, 301 ; member of Bent & Green, 105, 195 ; of Green & Allen, 195

Grover, Albert D. banjo bridge maker, 276 ; fretted instrument player and teacher, member of Boston Ideal Banjo, Mandolin & Guitar Club, 192, 228, 276

Grover, A. D. & Son, Inc. banjo bridge makers, 276

Grover, Leonard O. violin maker and repairer, 260, 262

Guild, George M. pianoforte maker, 242, 245

Guild, Church & Co. pianoforte makers, 245, 289

Guild Piano Mfg. Co. 245

Hale, Philip, music critic and editor, 81, 83

Hall, David C. band leader and player, 223, 224-5, 268, 270 ; brass instrument maker, 266, 268 ; member of Allen & Hall, 224, 266, 268 ; of D. C. Hall & Co. 225 ; of Hall & Quinby, 224, 225, 266, 268, 270

Hall, D. C. & Co. brass instrument makers, 225

Hall & Quinby, brass instrument makers, 224, 225, 266, 268, 270 ; instruments of, 225, 303

Hallet, Benjamin Franklin, pianoforte maker, 245 ; member of 2nd Hallet, Davis & Co. 245

Hallet & Allen, pianoforte makers or dealers, 242, 246

Hallet, Davis & Co. pianoforte makers, 1st company, Russell Hallet, George H. Davis and Henry Allen, 242, 245, 246

Hallet, Davis & Co. pianoforte makers, 2nd company, Benjamin Franklin Hallet and George H. Davis, 245 ; instrument of, 289

Hallet, Russell, member of pianoforte making firms Brown & Hallet, 242, 243, 246 ; Hallet & Allen, 242, 246 ; Hallet & Cumston, 246 ; Hallet, Cumston & Allen, 242, 246 ; Hallet, Davis & Co. 245, 246 ; Russell Hallet & Co. 246

Hamill, Sam'l S. organ builder, 154, 255

Hamlin, Emmons, discoverer of voicing reeds, 136 ; member of Mason & Hamlin, 136

Handel and Haydn Society, 9, 11, 12, 119-20, 154, 219, 251

Handel selected (?) organ of King's Chapel, Boston, 143-4, 147, 295

Harris, Charles T. organ builder, 166 ; flue voicer, 166, 256

Harris, John, pioneer spinet maker, 104

Harrison, G. Donald, organ builder of Aeolian-Skinner Organ Company, Inc. 179

Harts, Harry L. music editor and composer of White-Smith Music Publishing Company, 37

Harvard Chime, The, (Christ Church) 188, 299

Haskell, Alfred H. violin maker and repairer, 260

Hatch Music Company catalog, 42

Hathorn Collection of Violins, disposal of, 206

Haynes, George W. flute maker and repairer, 215

Haynes, John C. president of Oliver Ditson & Co. 29

Haynes, John C. & Co. instrumental dept. of Oliver Ditson Company, 30, 215, 234, 265-6, 271, 274, 276, 279, 301, 305

Haynes, William S. flute, clarinet and piccolo maker, 215, 216, 217, 266 ; inventions of, 217 ; founder of Wm. S. Haynes Co. 215

Haynes, William S. Jr. flute, clarinet and piccolo maker, 218 ; member of The Haynes-Schwelm Co. 218

Haynes, Wm. S. Co. flute, clarinet and piccolo makers, 215-18, 301

Haynes Excelsior Guitars, 274, 276

Haynes-Schwelm Co., The, flute, clarinet and piccolo makers, 215

Hayt, Charles and Elna, music dealers, 105, 240 ; members of Hayts, Babcock & Appleton, 105, 148, 152, 239, 240, 282

Hayt & Appleton, pianoforte makers and organ builders, 240

Hayts, (Hayt) Babcock & Appleton, organ builders and pianoforte makers, 105-6, 148, 152, 239, 240 ; instrument of, 282

Healy, P. J. of Lyon & Healy, start as a publisher, 15, 30

Heath, D. C. & Co. educational music publishers, 65

Henning, M. O. engraver, 91

Henning. M. O. & Son, engravers, 91-3

Hews (Hewes), Geo. pianoforte maker, 245, 246-7 ; member of Guild, Church & Co. 245 ; of Geo. Hews, 245

Hill & Owen, pianoforte of, 289

Hill, Ryder & Owen, pianoforte makers, 289

Hobart, Col. Aaron, owner of first (?) bell foundry in America, 186 ; bell of his, 297

Holbrook, Edwin L. organist and organ builder, 255

Holbrook, George Handel, bell caster, 298; organ builder, 255

Holbrook, Major George, bell caster, 298

Holmberg, Bernard, member of Weeman, Beal & Holmberg, 202

Holt, H. E. editor and music supervisor, 59, 61; founder of first publisher's summer school, 63, 64

Holway, Chester B. autoharp and zither manufacturer, 279

Homeyer, Charles W. 60; founder of Charles W. Homeyer & Co., Inc. 69

Homeyer, Charles W. & Co., Inc. music dealers and publishers, 69; musical instrument dealers, 233

Hook, Elias, 168

Hook, E. & G. G. organ builders, 142, 157, 168, 169-72, 294-5, 296

Hook, E. & G. G. & Hastings, organ builders, 168, 169-72

Hook, George G. 168, 294, 296

Hook and Hastings Company, organ builders, 141, 143, 144, 155, 160, 165, 168-75, 296; features of their organs, 174-5; inventions, 175

Hooper, Henry N. agent of the Boston and Braintree Copper and Brass Company, 187

Hooper, H. N. & Co. bell casters, successors to the Boston Copper Co. 187-8; bells of, 189, 298; chimes of, 188-9, 299-300

Horn, Charles Edward, musician and pioneer music publisher, 12

House Organs (journals) 85

Howe, Elias, Jr.
    collector of rare old instruments, 14-15, 197, 234-5
    drum manufacturing, 227, 272
    music publisher, 7, 12-14
    music store, 14, 260
    violin dealer and repairing, 260

Howe, Elias Co. violin dealers and repairers, 15, 22, 205, 207, 208, 209, 234, 258, 259, 260, 263; accessories manufacturing, 272; Colton bridge, 261; music publishers, 15

Howe, William H. President of Elias Howe Co. 15, 234

Humbert, J. S. pianoforte maker, 247

Hume pianoforte, 130

Hunt, C. B. & Co. reed organs, 252

Hutchings, George S. organ builder, 160, 161, 162, 164; M. A. degree for organ building, 165

Hutchings, Geo. S. Company, organ builders, 142, 155, 158, 160-5, 166, 175, 296
    inventions of, 164-5
    notable organs of, 162-4
    start of company as J. H. Willcox & Co. 160-1

Hutchings & Plaisted, organ builders, 148, 161

Hutchings & Plaisted Mfg. Co. organ builders, 161

Hutchings Organ Company, The, 162, 164, 181

Hutchings, Plaisted & Co. organ builders, 142, 161, 162-3

Hutchings-Votey Organ Company, 161, 163

Hutchins, Rev. Charles, founder of the Parish Choir, 69, 70

Hüttl, Adolph G. flute maker, 266

Hüttl & Fischer, flute makers, 212, 266, 301

Hydraulic Motor and Meter Asso. (later Co.) maker of Boston Water Motor, 257

Ivers, William H. pianoforte maker, 125, 126, 290

Ivers & Pond Piano Company, pianoforte makers, 125-6

Ivers & Son, 125

Jacobs, Walter, musician, teacher and publisher, 73-4, 83

Jacobs, Walter, Inc. instrumental music publishers, 24, 27, 73-6, 97; journals of, 83, 84-5

Jewett pianoforte, 129-30

Jigs, reels and songs, first collection in U. S. arranged for violin, 7, 12

Johnson, A. N. music journal publisher, 79

Johnson, F. Lincoln, violin maker, 211

Johnson, W. H. & Co. reed organs, 252

Johnston, Thomas, engraver, 87; pioneer organ builder, 141, 142, 143, 148, 295

Jones, Robert Hope, organ builder, 254, 255

Journals, music, 78-85

Judkins, W. A. zither manufacturer, 279

Keith, Charles H. music dealer and publisher, 11-12, 31

Keith & Moore, publishers, 12

Kidder, Andrew B. printer, 94

Kidder, A. B. & Son, printers, 94

Kidder & Wright, stereotypers and printers, 78, 94

Kimball, Henry D. organ builder, 181

Kimball-Frazee Organ Company, 181

Kimball, Smallman & Frazee, organ builders, 181

Klemm, J. G. connection with Alpheus Babcock, 107, 284

Koppitz & Pruefer (also Prüfer) music publishers, 18

Ladd, A. W. pianoforte maker, 247

Lane, Emory W. organ builder, 166, 255

Leavitt, Dr. Josiah, pioneer organ builder, 143, 146

Lenfest, T. H. printer, 95

Lenfest & Anderson, music printers, 95

Leukhardt, John, member of Schauffler & Leukhardt, 212, 266

Lincoln, Abraham, violin, 200

Lind, Albert, violin dealer, maker and repairer, 207-8, 261

Lindsey Memorial Collection of musical instruments, repairer of, 204-5

Link, E. zither of, 306

Liszt organ (reed), 138

Lithographic process, 88, 89

Liturgical Music Co. church music publishers, 70-1

Lockhart, Wm. J. musical string manufacturer, 264

Lord & Cumston, pianoforte makers, 241

Lord, Gilbert & Cumston, pianoforte makers, 240, 241

Luscomb, J. F. banjo manufacturer, 276

Lyon & Healy, music publishers, start of, 30

(M', Mc alphabetized in this index as Mac)

M'Alpine, William, pioneer music publisher, printer and binder, 88

McCarty, Albert A. musical string manufacturer, 264

MacDowell, Edward, introduction of as a composer, 39, 40

McIntosh, Wm. drummer, drum maker, radio expert, 272

Mackay, Captain John, partner of Alpheus Babcock, 106, 107, 239; of Jonas Chickering, 107, 111-2

Mackay, G.(eo) D. financial backer of Alpheus Babcock, 106, 239; instruments made for him, 106-7, 283

McLaughlin, James M. music supervisor and church music publisher, 56, 70, 71; founder of Catholic Music Publishing Co. 71

McLaughlin & Reilly, church music publishers and musical instrument dealers, 70-1

McNeil, John E. pianoforte maker, 247
McPhail, Andrew M. pianoforte maker, 248
McPhail, Andrew M. & Co. pianoforte makers, 248
McPhail, A. M. Piano Co. 248
Maelzel, An early, 5
Maelzel's Panharmonicon, 148, 150, 310
Makepeace, Lysander O. violin maker, 300
Mallet, Francis, musician and pioneer publisher, 8, 9, 147; his Repository—music store, 107; member of Graupner & Mallet, 9; of Mallet & Shaw, 105, 107
Mallet & Shaw, pianoforte makers, 105, 107
Manicke, Ernst, engraver, 93
Manicke & Dellmuth, engravers, 93
Mann, H. printers and publishers, 10
Mann & Co. pioneer printers and publishers, 10
Marquardt, George W. violin maker, 261
Martino, Giuseppi (Joseph) violin maker and repairer, 209
Marvin, Wendell P. pianoforte makers, 247
Mason, Henry L. of Mason & Hamlin, 128, 135
Mason & Hamlin Company,
  pianoforte manufacturers, 126-8, 243, 250
  artists using their pianofortes, 128
  inventions, 127-8
  pianists introduced by them, 128
  pipe organ manufacturing, 138, 295
  reed organ manufacturing, 136-9, 252, 253
    Cabinet Organ, 137, 138
    concert hall, 138
    instruments of, 137-8, 292
    inventions, 137, 138
    Liszt organ, 138
    Organ-Harmonium, 137
    Pedal organ, 138
Mason, Lowell, musician and teacher, 33, 54, 78, 110, 120, 135, 136, 151
Mason, Luther Whiting, music supervisor and editor, 54, 55, 56, 59
Mason & Risch, manufacturer of "The Vocalion," 252
Massachusetts Organ Co. reed organs, 252
Matt, Lorenzo, pianoforte maker, 247
Metcalf, P. B. head of Tracy Music Library, Inc. 77
Methuen Organ Company, 156, 256
Michell, Carlton C. organ builder, 165, 166, 254
Miles & Thompson, music publishers, 26
Miller, Gustavus A. pianoforte maker, 248
Miller, Gustavus A. & Co. 248
Miller, Henry F. musician and pianoforte maker, 124, 290
Miller, Henry F. Piano Company, 124-5; concert halls, 125
Millet, J. B. Co. publishers, 25, 92
Missud, Jean, bandmaster and publisher, 74
Mitchell, Dr. Albert G. music supervisor and editor, 33, 37
Morris, Daniel, pianoforte maker, 249
Motion picture pianists and organists, catalog for, 75
Mozart organs (reed) and melodeons, 252
Munroe, Francis & Parker, music store, 10
Music appreciation records, only educational music publisher making, 57-8
Music Hall Organ, Boston, and influence on American builders, 155-7, 294, 295
Musical Herald Company, publishers, 82
Musicians' Supply Company specialties, 208-9; stringed instrument dealers, 208; violin makers and repairers, 208-9

National Summer School of Music of Ginn & Co. 58
Nelson, Carl, of The Vega Co. 208, 229
Nelson, Julius, of The Vega Co. 208, 229
Nelson, William, of The Vega Co. 229
Nevin, Ethelbert, first recognition of as a composer, 42-3
New England Organ Co. reed organs, 252, 292
New England Piano Co. 249, 253
Newhall, Daniel B. pianoforte maker, 250; member of Wilkins & Newhall, 250
Newton, Elbridge, of Ginn & Co. music editor, 56, 57, 58
Nichols, M. O. reed organs, 253
Nichols & Woods, reed organs, 253
Nicolai, Edward F. drummer, 272; member of Nokes & Nicolai, 272
Nokes, E. J. drummer and drum manufacturer, 272
Nokes & Nicolai, drum and banjo manufacturers, 272, 275
Nordstrom, G. V. organ builder in J. H. Willcox & Co. 160

Oakes, W. H. printers and publishers, 12
Oboette, 233
Octavo catalog of sacred and secular songs, largest in U. S. 32
Odell, Herbert F. musician and composer, 26, 230
Odell, H. F. & Company, publishers, 26, 230; journal of—Crescendo—26, 84, 230
Odell, Ira H. musician, music dealer and publisher, 22, 26; member of Thompson & Odell, 22
Odell Edition, 230
Oettinger, Adolph Joseph, musical instrument dealer, 208, 228; President of Musicians' Supply Company, 208
Oettinger products, 208-9
Offset process, 89
Oliver, Freeman A. violin dealer, 261
Orchestrator, invention of Ernest M. Skinner, 179-80
Ordway, A. & J. P. music publishers, 12, 31
Organ, first constructed in New England, 143
Organ builder, first in New England, 141, 143
Organette (Hutchings organ company product) 164
Organist Journal, The, (Wm. Ashmall, publisher) 71
Organs, earliest imported into New England, first (Brattle organ) 140-1, 293, 295
  first in a Congregational Church in Boston, 141
  second (?) the Berkeley organ, 141
  third (?) Christ Church, Boston, 141-2
Organs, other noted early, in New England—
  Christ Church, Cambridge, John Snetzler, builder, 144-6
  King's Chapel, Handel selected (?) organ, 143-4
  St. Peter's Church, Salem, John Clark builder or importer (?) 142
Orguinettes (W. H. Johnson & Co.) reed organs, 252
Orthotonic specialties, (John A. Gould & Sons) 204
Osborn (Osborne), John, pianoforte maker, 107-8, 109, 111; instruments of, 290; partner of James Stewart, 108

Palm, John A. guitar and mandolin maker, 276
PanHarmonicon of Maelzel, 148, 150, 310
Parish Choir, The, publications of Episcopal Church music, 69-70

Parker, Colonel Samuel H. publisher, 10, 11, 28, 29
Parker & Ditson, music publishers, 11, 29
Parks, James S. melodeon maker, 292
Patent, first for a musical instrument issued to a Mass. resident, 107; second to a Boston resident, 108
Perkins Institute and Massachusetts School for the Blind, training pianoforte tuners, 110
Perry, John F. member of White, Smith & Perry, 22, 35
Perry, John F. & Co. music dealers and publishers, 22, 35
Philharmonic Society (Philharmonio and Philo Harmonic) 9
Phillips, B. N. pianoforte maker, 249
Phillips' Chime, The, 188, 300
Phonoharp Co. of Boston, 279
Photolithography, 89
Pianoee of John W. Brackett, 242
Pianoforte on which Beethoven scored the "Eroica Symphony," 131, 281
Plaisted, Mark H. organ builder, 160, 161, 169; member of Hutchings & Plaisted, Hutchings & Plaisted Mfg. Co. and Hutchings, Plaisted & Co. 161; of J. H. Willcox Co. 160
Pond, Clarence H. President of Ivers & Pond Piano Company, 126
Pond, Handel, musician and partner in Ivers & Pond Piano Company, 125-6
Pond, Shephard, member of Ivers & Pond Piano Company, 126; of Poole Piano Company, 128
Poole, William H. maker of pianofortes and parts, 128; founder of Poole Piano Company, 128
Poole Piano Company, 128
Porcella, Felice, accordion maker and repairer, 235-6
Porcella, Louis F. J. 235
Porcella, Peter, 235
Porcella Accordion Shoppe, 235
Powell, Verne Q. flute player and maker, 218-19; founder of Verne Q. Powell Flutes, Inc. 219
Powell, Verne Q. Flutes, Inc. flute makers, 218-19
Powers, Clark, violin dealer, repairer and maker, 205, 261
Prentiss, Henry, umbrella and music dealer and publisher, 11
Prentiss & Clark, music dealers and publishers, 11
Presser, Theodore, Company, 24; connection with Oliver Ditson Company, Inc. 30-1
Preston, John Aiken, pianoforte teacher and early editor of The B. F. Wood Music Company, 44
Protection of the Retail Dealer policy, early promoter of, 44
Pruefer (Prüfer), Carl, music dealer and publisher, 7, 18, 31, 91; member of Koppitz & Pruefer, 18

Quinby, B. F. brass band instrument maker, 225, 268, 304
Quinby, Geo. W. brass instrument maker, 268; member of E. G. Wright & Co. 270
Quinby Bros. (B. F. & Geo. W.) brass band instrument manufacturers, 23, 225, 269, 304; members of Hall & Quinby, 268

Ramsdell, E. C. band and orchestra music publisher, 7, 24, 220
Reed, George P. music store and publisher, 15, 17

Reed, G. P. & Co. music dealers and publishers, 7, 15, 17
Reilly, Dr. James A. musician, 70; member of Liturgical Music Co. 70, 71; of McLaughlin & Reilly, 71
Reproducing pianoforte, first American make, 118-19
Rettberg, Raoul, bow and violin maker, 262
Revere, Joseph Warren, bell founder, 186, 187
Revere, Lt. Col. Paul, bell caster, 186-7; bell ringer, 184; copper and brass founder, 185; music engraver, 4, 87
Revere, Paul (son of above) 187
Revere, Paul, Jr. also called 3rd, (grandson of Lt. Col. Paul) 187
Revere, Paul & Co. bell founders, 187, 188 (company of the grandson)
Revere, Paul (Lt. Col.) & Son (Joseph), brass, copper and iron founders and bell casters, 185, 186; some bells of, 296-7
Revere (Paul Jr.) & Blake (William) brass founders, 187
Richardson, B. F. brass instrument manufacturer, 224, 225, 269, 304; music stand manufacturer, 226, 306; member of Allen & Richardson, 224, 266; of Richardson & Bayley, 224, 269, 304; of Richardson & Lehnert, 225, 269
Richardson, Nathan, pianist, 16; music publisher, 7, 16-17
Richardson & Bayley, brass instrument manufacturers, 224, 269, 304
Richardson & Lehnert, cymbal and gong manufacturers, 225, 269
Riker, Brown & Wellington, music publishers, 27
Ripley, Frederic H. editor, 37, 66; publisher's summer school organizer, 68
Riverside Church organ, 173-4
Robinson, C. T. bell casters, 188
Robinson, Gad, banjo player, teacher and maker, 192, 277
Rockwell, David Bailey, violin maker, 262
Rogers Upright Piano Co. 249; makers of the B. F. Baker Upright piano, 249
Roosevelt, Frank H. later head of Hilbourne L. Roosevelt Co. 162
Roosevelt, Hilbourne L. organ builder, inventor of early electric action, 161
Roosevelt, Hilbourne L. Company, 121, 155, 161-2
Ross, Louis H. music publisher, 23-4
Ross, Louis H. & Co. music publishers, 23-4
Ross, Louis H. Music Publishing Co. 24
Rowe, John, early organ builder, 146
Russell, Geo. D. music publisher and dealer, 15, 17; member of G. D. Russell & Co. 7, 17, 31; of Russell & Fuller, 17; of Russell & Richardson, 17; of Russell & Tolman, 17
Russell, G. D. & Co. music publishers, 7, 17, 31
Russell, Joseph M. music dealer and publisher and musical instrument dealer, 17, 26, 38; member of Russell & Pattee, 17
Russell & Fuller, music dealers and publishers, 17
Russell & Pattee, music dealers and publishers, 17
Russell & Richardson, music dealers and publishers, 17
Russell & Tolman, music dealers and publishers, 13, 17
Russell Bros. music publishers and retailers, 17, 31
Ryder, George H. organ builder, 153, 255
Ryder, Geo. H. & T. P. and Narramore, 255

St. Peter's Church, Salem, Mass. organ, 142
Saladino, C. & Sons, musical string makers,
    264
Samuels, E. A. band and orchestra music pub-
    lisher, 7, 22
Schatz, Henry, guitar and violin maker, 277,
    306
Schauffler, F. G. & Co. flute makers, 212, 266
Schauffler & Leukhardt, flute makers and prob-
    ably dealers, 266, 301
Schindler, Hugo, musical string maker and in-
    ventor, 201
Schindler, H. & Co., Inc. musical string
    makers, 264-5
Schindler, Otto, founder of Otto Schindler &
    Co. 264
Schindler, Otto & Co. musical string manufac-
    turers, 264
Schirmer, Ernest C. founder of E. C. Schirmer
    Music Co. 50
Schirmer, E. C. Music Co. general music pub-
    lishers, 50-3, 92, 97
Schirmer, Gustave, Jr. publisher, founder of
    the Boston Music Company, 41, 42
Schirmer, G., Inc. general music publishers, 41,
    42
Schleicher, J. & Hochstuhl, organs, 253
Schlimper, Charles F. W. engraver, 91
Schlimper, Frederick W. flute player and
    teacher and engraver, 91
Schlimper, Henry, engraver, 91
Schmidt, Arthur P. music dealer, 17, 26, 38,
    69; music publisher, 38, 43, 84
Schmidt, The Arthur P. Co. 24, 38-41, 93, 97
Schultz, E. B. mandolin and guitar maker, 277
Schultz, Henry F. violin and double bass
    maker and repairer, 205-6, 260; member of
    Robinson & Schultz, 205, 262
Searles, Edward F. of Methuen Organ Com-
    pany, 116, 156, 256
Searles, Estate of, 205
Serlo Hall for the Music Hall Organ, now
    Organ Hall, 156, 181, 294
Shattuck, Burt E. player, member of Boston
    Ideal Banjo, Mandolin and Guitar Club, and
    teacher, 192, 228; head of Burt E. Shattuck
    & Co. 277; editor, 83
Shattuck, Burt E. & Co. banjo makers, 277
Shaw, Francis, pianoforte maker, 107; member
    of Mallet & Shaw, 105, 107
Silva-Bet clarinet, 221
Silver, Burdett and Company, educational
    music publishers, 59-65, 92; first publisher's
    summer school for training music super-
    visors, 63-5
Silver, Edgar O. founder of above company, 59
Simmons, W. B. D. & Co. organ builders, 158,
    159-60
Simmons & Fisher, organ builders, 158
Simmons & McIntire, organ builders, 158
Simmons & Willcox, organ builders, 144, 158-
    60
Singenberger, Johannes B. composer and pub-
    lisher of The Caecilia, 81
Skinner, Ernest M. organ builder, 156, 165,
    175, 179, 180, 181, 294; inventions of, 179,
    180
Skinner, Ernest M. Organ Company, 144, 175
Skinner Organ Company, 163, 175, 176
Small, William T. head of The John Worley
    Company, 97
Smallman, E. E. member of Kimball, Small-
    man & Frazee, 181
Smith, Dexter, music journal editor, publisher
    and owner, 80-1
Smith, S. D. & Co. reed organ makers, 253
Smith, S. D. & H. W. & Co. reed organ
    makers, 253, 292, 295

Smith, W. Frank, member of White, Smith &
    Co. 35; of White, Smith & Perry, 35; of
    White-Smith Music Publishing Company, 35
Smith American Organ & Piano Co. reed organ
    and pianoforte makers, 249, 253
Smith American Piano Co. 253
Squier, J. Bonaparte, violin maker, 198-200,
    260
Standard Band Instrument Company, brass in-
    strument manufacturing dept. of Thompson &
    Odell, 226-7, 229, 268, 269, 304
Stanhope Press—F. H. Gilson Company, music
    book printers, 97
Stanley, Carlton F. violin maker, 210, 211
Stanley, F. C. violin maker, 210, 211
Stanley, L. R. connected with D. P. Gosline
    and then F. E. Whitney Co. successive con-
    cerns making the Boston Water Motor, 257
Stanley Organ Blower, 257
Star pianoforte, 248
Steere, J. W. & Son, Organ Company, 176
Steere & Turner, organ builders, 176
Steere Organ Company, 175-6
Steinert, Alexander, head of M. Steinert & Sons
    Company, Inc. 129, 282
Steinert, Morris, founder of M. Steinert &
    Sons Company, 129, 130, 131; M. Steinert
    Collection of Keyed and Stringed Instru-
    ments, 131, 281, 283, 287, 291, 292, 293
Steinert, Robert S. 129
Steinert, Rudolph, 129, 130
Steinert, M. & Sons Company, musical instru-
    ment dealers and pianoforte manufacturers,
    129-31
    Murphy, Jerome F. manager, 129
    pianofortes of, 129, 130
    Steinert Hall, 130
    Steinway & Sons, first American dealer of,
        with exclusive franchise, 129
    stores, 130
    See also personal names beginning with
        Steinert
Stereotyping process, 90
Stevens, George, organ builder, 142, 146, 254,
    256
Stevens, George M. maker of tower clocks and
    Angelus chimes, 279
Stevens, George M. & Co. 279
Stevens, G. M. Co., Inc. 279
Stevens, H. B. & Co. music publishers, 24
Stevens, William, organ builder, 256; member
    of Stevens & Jewett, 256
Stevens & Gayetty, organ builders, 142, 256
Stevens & Jewett, 256
Stewart, James, pianoforte maker, 108, 111;
    partner of Jonas Chickering, 108, 111; of
    John Osborn, 108
Stoddard, Charles Fuller, inventor of first
    American reproducing pianoforte, 118, 119
Stone, George Burt, drummer, drum maker,
    230, 271; teacher and author, 76, 231;
    founder of George B. Stone & Son, Inc. 230
Stone, George B. & Son, Inc. drum, drum
    sticks and accessories manufacturers and re-
    pairers, 230-1
    Drum & Xylophone School, 231-2
    patent of, 231
    publishing, 76
    See also personal names beginning with
        Stone
Stone, George Lawrence, percussion player, 231
Stoughton Musical Society, early director of, 5
Stratton, George W. composer, musician,
    teacher, music dealer and publisher, 7, 19-21
    music journal, 20, 80
    operettas, 19, 20, 21
    Stratton Free Public Library and Art Gal-
        lery, 20-1
    wholesale house, 19, 21-2, 208

Stromberg, Charles A. guitar, banjo and drum maker and stringed instrument repairer, 232, 233, 277
    founder of Charles A. Stromberg & Son, 232
    inventor of first separate tension drum, 233
    other patents of, 232-3
Stromberg, Charles A. & Son, banjo, guitar and drum makers, and stringed instrument repairers, 232-3
Stromberg, Elmer, 232
Stumcka, Charles, early guitar maker, 227-8
Sundberg, C. F. guitar maker, 229, 277
Surette Summer School, 50

Tension resonator of Mason & Hamlin, 127
Thayer, Eugene, music journal editor, 81, 162
Thoma, Alexander, violin maker, 203
Thoma, Jacob, violin maker and repairer, 203
Thoma, Jacob & Son, 203
Thomas, Isaiah, pioneer music publisher, 5
Thompson, C. W. musician, 22; member of Thompson & Odell, 22
Thompson, Charles W. music publisher, 26; founder of C. W. & Co. 26; member of Miles & Thompson, 26
Thompson, C. W. & Co. music publishers, 26, 42
Thompson & Odell
    brass instrument manufacturers, 22, 226-7, 229, 268, 269
    fretted instrument manufacturers, 22, 229, 232, 277
    music publishers, 7, 22, 50
    percussion instrument makers, 272
    retail store, 22, 262
    stringed instrument business, 208, 262
Tolman, Henry, music dealer and publisher, 17; publisher of Boston Musical Times, 80; member of Henry Tolman & Co. 17; of Russell & Tolman, 17, 80
Tolman, Henry & Co. publishers and musical instrument and umbrella dealers, 17
Tourjée, Eben, music journal editor, 79, 82
Tracy, George Lowell, musician, founder of Tracy Music Library, 76
Tracy Music Library, 76-7
Treat, James E. voicer and organ builder, 256
Treat, James E. & Co. organ builders, 156, 256
Tremont Temple Music Store of White Brothers, violin makers, dealers and repairers, 196
Trifet, F. publisher of Trifet's Monthly Galaxy of Music, 82
Tuck, J. Warren, musical string maker and dealer, 265
Tufts, John W. editor and composer, 55, 59, 60, 61; teacher, 63
Tufts, Rev. John W. pioneer hymn book publisher, 3
Turner, Richard H. bow and violin maker and repairer, 260, 263
Turner Centre, Maine, Summer School, 56
Typographic method, 88, 90, 97

U. S. Guitar-Zither Co. 279

Vega, Company, The, 208, 229-30
    brass instrument manufacturers, 22, 227, 229, 230, 269
    fretted instrument manufacturers, 229, 230, 266, 275, 277
    fretted music publishers, 26, 230
    jobbers and retailers, 230
Violin of "Bobbie" Burns, 205

Virtuoso Music School publications, 74
Vocalion, The, 252
von Hagen, Peter Albrecht, Jr. musician and publisher, 8-9; member of P. A. von Hagen Jun. & Co. 8; partner of Benjamin Crehore, 105
von Hagen, Peter Albrecht, Sr. musician and publisher, 8, 10; head of P. A. von Hagen & Co. 8; Musical Academy, 8
von Hagen, P. A. & Co. first established music publishers in Boston, 8
von Hagen, P. A. Jun. & Co. music publishers and pianoforte dealers, 8, 105
Vose, George Atherton, President of Vose & Sons Piano Company, 109, 124
Vose, James Whiting, key and pianoforte maker, 123; founder of Vose & Sons Piano Company, 123
Vose, Willard Atherton, 124
Vose & Sons Piano Company, pianoforte makers, 123-4
Votey Company, organ builders, 161

Wa Wan Press, music publishers, 27
Wade, Eben H. music publishers, 11, 12, 31
Walter, Rev. Thomas, compiler of "first practical American instruction book" in singing by note, 3
Ware, J. Holbrook, organ builder with Geo. H. Holbrook company, 255
Warren, T. D. melodeon manufacturer, 253
Washington, George, violin, 200
Webb, George James, music journal editor, 78
Weeman, Orin, violin maker and repairer, 197, 202, 203, 260
Weeman, Beal & Holmberg, violin dealers, makers and repairers, 195, 202
Whipple, L. E. musicians' accessories dealer, 23, 269; instrument importer, 23
Whipple Music Co. successor to above, and Quinby Bros. 23, 269; publisher of music and The Apollo 23, 82, 269
Whipple's Diamond Cornet, 269
White, Asa Warren, violin maker and dealer, 195, 196-8, 260; member of White & Goullaud, 22
White, Charles A. composer and founder of White-Smith Music Publishing Company, 35
White, Charles A. grandson of above, President of White-Smith Music Publishing Company, 35
White, Daniel L. 35
White, Eugene A. music stand manufacturer, 279
White, Ira E. son of Ira J. drum maker, 276; instrument repairer, 198, 276
White, Ira Johnson, first Boston maker of really fine violins, 195, 196; first Boston maker of wound violin strings, 198, 306
White, James H. prompter of the Germania Orchestra, 263; violin and woodwind repairer, 263; member of I. J. & J. H. White, 263; of James H. & J. Henry White, 263
White, J. Henry, son of above, musical instrument repairer, 263; member of James H. & J. Henry White, 263
White, Jean, musician, 18; band and orchestra music publisher, 7, 17-18, 92
White, Jean, Publishing Company, 8, 50
White, (Weiss) Maurice, violin maker and repairer, 201, 263
White, Smith & Co. music publishers, 35
White, Smith & Perry, music publishers, 22, 35; their music journal, 80

White-Smith Music Publishing Company,
  engravers, 35, 91
  general music publishers, 23, 35-8
  house organ, 85
  printers, 96
White & Goullaud, music publishers and dealers, 22
White Brothers, music dealers and publishers,
  and instrument dealers and makers, 22, 196,
  305
White family, early violin makers and stringed
  instrument repairers, 195-8, 273
White, I. J. & A. W. violin makers and
  dealers, 196, 197
White, I. J. & J. H. 196
Whitmore, Osceola Aurelius, drummer and
  drum maker, 227, 273; member of Whitmore
  & Boris, 273
Whitmore & Boris, musical instrument dealers,
  273
Whitmore & Mansfield, instrument of, 304
Whitney, F. E. & Co. organ motor makers, 257
Wilkins, Levi, pianoforte maker, 250; member
  of Wilkins & Newhall, 250, 290
Wilkins & Newhall, pianoforte makers, 250;
  instruments of, 290
Willcox, Dr. John H. organist, 155; organ
  builder, 158, 160; founder of J. H. Willcox
  Co. start of Geo. S. Hutchings Company,
  160; member of Simmons & Willcox, 158
Williams, Ernest S. musician and publisher of
  band and orchestra music, 26-7, 74
Willis Music Company, music publishers, 42
Winchester, W. P. & Co. pianoforte makers,
  250
Winn, Peter, drums, 273
Wood, Benjamin Frank, musician and teacher,
  43; founder of The B. F. Wood Music
  Company, 43
Wood, The B. F. Company, general music
  publishers, 43-5, 92, 97
Wood, Watson, musical strings, 265
Woodberry, James, organ builder, 165; member
  of Cole & Woodberry, 165; of Cole, &
  Woodberry Bros. 165, 166

Woodberry, Jesse, organ builder, 159, 165, 166,
  181; member of Cole, & Woodberry Bros.
  165; of Woodberry & Harris, 166; of Jesse
  Woodberry & Company, 166-7
Woodbury pianoforte, 130
Woodman, M. drum maker, 273
Woods, George, pianoforte and reed organ
  maker, 250, 253
Woods, George, & Co. pianoforte and reed
  organ makers, 250, 253; instrument of, 293
Woods, J. H. musical instrument dealer, 273;
  member of J. H. Woods & Co. 273; of
  Woods, Odell & Thompson, 262, 273
Woods, Odell & Thompson, music and mu-
  sical instrument dealers, 262, 273
Woodward, Isaac, pianoforte maker and music
  lover, 250, 251; member of Brown, Hallet &
  Woodward, 250; of I. Woodward & Co.
  250; of Woodward & Brown, 250
Woodward, I. & Co. pianoforte makers, 250
Woodward & Brown Piano Co. 251
Woodward, L. P. pianoforte maker, 250
Worley, John, music printer, 96; founder of
  John Worley Company, 96, 97; member of
  Zabel-Worley Company, 96
Worley, John, Company, music printers and
  binders, 96-7
Wright, Elbridge G. bandmaster and cornet
  player, 224, 270; brass instrument maker,
  224, 226, 267, 270; member of Hall &
  Quinby, 270; of E. G. Wright & Co. 268,
  270; of Wright, Gilmore & Co. 246, 267,
  270; of Wright Musical Instrument Com-
  pany, 270
Wright, E. G. & Co. brass instrument manufacturers, 268, 270; instrument of, 304
Wright, Gilmore & Co. brass instrument
  makers, 226, 267, 270
Wright Musical Instrument Company, dealers,
  270
Wurlitzer, Eduard H. woodwind instrument
  maker, 213-14, 219

Young, Joseph A. violin maker and repairer,
  260, 263

Index of Publications
Major Series, Music Journals and Works Widely Used

A Cappella Series (E. C. Schirmer), 51
Adams and Liberty! 7, 9
Analytic Symphony Series, The, 34
Apollo, The, 23, 82, 269

Bay Psalm Book, 3, 87
Birchard Broadsheet News of School Music, 85
Birchard Cantatas and Choral Specialties, 47;
Catalog of Instrumental Music, 48; Ope-
rettas and Operas, 47
Blanchard's Brass Band Journal, 80
Boston Group of Composers' compositions, 31,
39-40, 93
Boston Music Company Edition, 43
Boston Music Company's Popular Concert Li-
brary, 43
Boston Musical Gazette, 78
Boston Musical Herald, 82
Boston Musical Journal, 79
Boston Musical Times, 80
Boston Patriotic Song, 7

Cadenza, 83
Caecilia, The, 71, 81
Cecilian Series of Study and Song, 60
Columbia Collection of Patriotic and Favorite
Home Songs, The, 74
Commonwealth Series, 51
Concord Series, 51
Course of Study in Music Understanding, The,
34
Creation (Haydn), first American reprint, 29
Crescendo, 84, 230
Criterion Band Book, 45
Cundy's Edition of Popular Music, 73
Cundy's Five Cent Series of Popular Music,
72-3, 95

Dexter Smith's Musical, Literary, Dramatic,
and Art Paper, 80-1
Diamond Series, The, 14
Ditson, Oliver, Series, 34
Ditson Edition, The, 34
Dwight's Journal of Music, 15, 16, 79, 137

Eby Scientific Methods, 74
Eclectic Series (instruction books), 14
Edition White-Smith, 36-7
Edition Wood, second largest edition in U.S.
44
Eleanor Smith Progressive Music Course, 66
Ethiopian Glee Book, The, 13
Euterpeiad or Musical Intelligencer, 78

Faelten System publications, 40, 93
Famous Composers and Their Music, 25
Famous Singers Series, 33
First American book of sacred music, 3
First practical American instruction book in
singing by note, 3-4
Folio, The, 80
Foresman's Books of Songs, 67
Franklin Square Song Collection, 67
Fretted Instruments and Mandolin Orchestra
Catalog (Walter Jacobs), 74

Gatcomb's Banjo and Guitar Gazette, 83
Gatcomb's Musical Gazette, 83
Gateway to Music, A, 65
Genevieve, 20, 21

Half Hours with the Best Composers, 25
Hall's, R. B., Bandbook of His Most Famous
Marches, 75
Hollis Dann Music Course, The, 67
Howe's School—instruction books, 12-13

Jacobs, Walter, Ensemble, 76; Evergreen Col-
lection of Fifty Famous Old Songs, 75; Folio
for School Orchestras, 76; Folio of Classics,
76; Loose Leaf Collection of Standard
Marches, 76; Piano Folios, 75; School
Choruses and Octavo Miscellany, 76; Stand-
ard Marches and Galops, 75
Jacobs' Album of Master Classics, 76; Band
Book of Classics, 76; Concert Album, 76
Jacobs' Band Monthly, 84-5
Jacobs' Orchestra Monthly, 84-5

Laila, 19, 20
Laurel Library Books, 47
Laurel Music Text Books, 46
Laurel Octavo Choruses, 46-7
Laurel Series, The, 46
Laurel Song Book, The, 45
Laus Deo—The Worcester Collection of Sacred
Harmony, 5
Loomis's Progressive Music Lessons, 66

Manual of School Music (Carl Fischer, Inc.)
49
Marches, Famous—Bay State Commandery, 74,
75; Boston Commandery, 24; The Com-
mander, 74; De Molay Commandery, 74, 75;
Father of Victory, 75; National Em-
blem, 74, 75; Our Director, 74, 75; Up the
Street, 75
Marguerite, 35
Mason Music Course, The, 56
Massachusetts Musical Journal, 79-80; and
Keynote, 79; and Literary Gazette, 79-80
Master School of Modern Pianoforte Players
and Virtuosi, The, 49
Melody, 85
Mitchell's Class Methods for the Violin, 33
Modern Music Series, 60
Modern School for the Piano, 16
Monthly Musical Record, 81
Music Appreciation Course, 61
Music Cabinet, The, 78
Music Education Series, 57
Music Hour Series, The, 61-2
Music Review, 81, 85
Music Students Library, The, 32
Music Students Piano Course, The, 33
Musical Art Series, The, 57
Musical Herald, The, 82; of the United
States, 82
Musical Library, The, 78
Musical Magazine, (P. A. von Hagen & Co.),
8

Musical Record, 81, 82 ; & Review, 81, 82
Musical World, The, 83
Musician's Companion, The, 12, 13
Musicians Library, The, 32-3
Musicians' Omnibus, 14

National Music Course, 55-6, 59
Natural Music Course, 66
New Educational Music Course, 56-7
New England Psalm Singer, 4-5, 88
New Method for the Piano-Forte, 16
New National Music Course, 56
New Normal Music Course, 61
New Public School Music Course, 65
Normal Music Course, The, 59

Odell Edition, 230
Organist's Quarterly Journal and Review, The, 81, 95, 171
Overtures, Suites and Selections Catalog (Walter Jacobs), 75

Parish Choir, The, 70
Passion Music according to St. Matthew (J. S. Bach), first American edition, 31
Percussion instrument instruction books (Geo. B. Stone & Son, Inc.) 76
Philharmonic Orchestra Series, 33-4
Physician, The Frantic (Le Médecin Malgré Lui), 62-3
Pocket Music Student Series, The, 34
Progressive Music Series, 61
Public School Music Course, The, 65

Rosary, The, 42-3
Rudiments of the Art of Playing the Pianoforte, 10

St. Dunstan Edition of Sacred Music, 52
Scherzo, 85
Schmidt's Educational Series, 39
School Song Book, The, 45
Seraph, The, 78-9
Sheet music, first publications of, in America, 6
Stanhope Edition of School Music, 36, 37
Symphonic Band Series, The, 34
Symphony Series of Programs for School and Community Orchestras, 63

Teacher's Library, 36
10 World Famous Band Marches, 75
Trifet's Monthly Galaxy of Music, 82-3
Tuneful Yankee, The, 85
Twice 55 Series, 46

Universal Library of Music, The, 25
Universal Series, 36

Watermelon Vine (Lindy Lou), 75
Wellesley College Appreciation Album, 52
Well-Tempered Clavichord (J. S. Bach), first American edition, 29
Western Series, The, 14
Williams, John M. Piano Books and Educational Series Music, 43
Without a Master Series, 13
Wood Octavo Series, 45